SHECHEM IV

THE PERSIAN–HELLENISTIC POTTERY OF SHECHEM / TELL BALÂṬAH

By

Nancy L. Lapp

shechem

Archaeological Excavations

Edited for the Expedition by Edward F. Campbell

American Schools of Oriental Research • Boston, MA

Shechem IV

The Persian–Hellenistic Pottery of Shechem/Tell Balâṭah

By

Nancy L. Lapp

The American Schools of Oriental Research © 2008

ISBN 978-0-89757-079-4

Library of Congress Cataloging-in-Publication Data

Lapp, Nancy L., 1930-
   Shechem IV : the Persian-Hellenistic pottery of Shechem/Tell Balatah / by Nancy L. Lapp ;
       edited for the expedition by Edward F. Campbell.
     p. cm. -- (American Schools of Oriental Research archaeological reports ; no. 11)
   Includes bibliographical references and index.
   ISBN 978-0-89757-079-4 (alk. paper)
  1. Shechem (Extinct city) 2. Excavations (Archaeology)--West Bank. 3. Pottery, Ancient--West
       Bank--Shechem (Extinct city) 4. Bronze age--West Bank--Shechem (Extinct city) 5.
       West Bank--Antiquities. I. Campbell, Edward Fay. II. Title. III. Title: Shechem four.

DS110.S543L37 2009

933--dc22   2008051711

Printed in the United States of America on acid-free paper.

To Paul

Husband, Colleague, and Inspiration

Contents

List of Illustrations

TEXT FIGURES

POTTERY PLATES

List of Tables

Preface

The study of this pottery was first a joint project with my late husband, Paul W. Lapp. Since his death in 1970, I have intermittently carried on with these studies. Through the years there have been numerous people who have assisted us. At the risk of omitting some, a few from whose help I have benefited must be mentioned. The study of the Attic ware in 1985 was aided by Dorothy K. Hill of the Walters Art Gallery, Baltimore, and J. D. Beazley. More recently, William J. Fulco contributed to the section on the Rhodian jar handles. The mortarium studies of Jeffrey Blakely, W. J. Bennett, and William Glanzman included some Shechem sherds, and some of their conclusions are in this publication; we hope they will continue with further work on this pottery. Howard Kee did some preliminary work on the Hellenistic pottery back in 1957. Paul first published some of the Hellenistic pottery in *Pottery Ceramic Chronology, 200 B.C.—A.D. 70*, and he published a few of the significant Persian sherds from Stratum V in 1970; these publications have been basic to the studies here. Thanks are due to those whose field reports have been consulted and have aided in the determination of the Persian and Hellenistic stratigraphy: Larry Toombs, H. Neil Richardson, Lawrence Sinclair, Edward Campbell, Siegfried Horn, Joseph Callaway, Paul Lapp, and James Ross. Ovid Sellers' study of the Balâṭah coins has provided significant information, and our participation in his 1957 excavation at Beth-zur and his subsequent permission for us to publish the Hellenistic pottery from that site became a foundation for the study of the Shechem pottery. It was our mentor, George Ernest Wright, who first suggested that we undertake the study of this pottery; he provided many notes and records and was available through the remaining years of his life with suggestions and encouragement.

Three close friends and colleagues, R. Thomas Schaub, Marilyn Schaub, and Walter Rast, have provided continual help and encouragement through the years. Unfortunately, too many of those recognized in this preface are deceased, but future Palestinian archaeological scholarship remains dependent upon their work.

In the technical production for this volume we have to go back to the many students who did on-site pottery drawings as we first learned the many procedures of archaeology. The initials of Edward Campbell, Robert Boling, Mary Lou Huffmon, Art Talbot, Paul and Nancy Lapp, Lawrence Sinclair, Jack Irwin, and Jerry Vardeman appear frequently on some of these drawings, which are finally reaching publication. Through the years, other students and volunteers at the Bible Lands Museum at Pittsburgh Theological Seminary have contributed drawings, including most notably Robert Laos, Ellen Campbell, and, recently, Mary Cooper. Work-study students have learned to record ware descriptions, and Brian Cumer finished the job last year by describing hundreds of sherds. In the near final stages, thanks are due to Mary Cooper and Kate Lockard for aid in setting up figure plates and for their patience with my ever-changing demands for consistency. Work-study student Suzanne Vitale did some final checking of references. For photographs, it is necessary to recognize the many years that the late Lee Ellenberger devoted to the Shechem publications. During the final process for some photography and scanning, David Brennan, Electronic Services Librarian at Pittsburgh Seminary, came to our aid. Among the several readers acknowledged elsewhere, a near-final editing by Prescott Williams, long-time Balâṭah staff member, helped pick up many loose ends. The readers and editor in the publishing stage should also be thanked for their suggestions. I wish to acknowledge a Harris grant through the American Schools of Oriental Research, which made possible some of this work. Generous donations to help on printing costs have come from Mary Louise Ellenberger in memory of Lee C. Ellenberger, Shechem photographer, and from ASOR's great friend P. E. MacAllister. Our deepest appreciation!

My retirement from Seminary obligations was one condition that allowed my sustained effort to complete this project, but it would not have been possible without the cooperation of the administration at Pittsburgh Theological Seminary in providing laboratory space and facilities. The help and encouragement from the present Curator of the Bible Lands Museum, Karen Bowden Cooper, has been of great consequence. Through her efforts, I have continued to receive student help. I must express my overwhelming thanks.

Finally, it is to Edward Campbell, editor of the Shechem publication series and successor to George Ernest Wright as Director of the Balâṭah excavations, that I owe the most and deepest thanks. Through the years he has been faced with my questions and requests. His exemplary publication of Shechem III, *The Stratigraphy and Architecture of Shechem/Tell Balâṭah*, made it possible for me to take up the publication of the Persian and Hellenistic materials once more. Through the past two years, he has continually responded to my requests and inquiries. He has never waivered in his support and patience. Often the difficulties have been immense: we have been working with records a half-century old, and these come from a time at the beginning of recording in field archaeology, as it was developing toward the accepted norm in the Near East today. Ted's wife, Phyllis, has often come to the rescue when demands like my own became overwhelming. Through their efforts there are surprisingly few places where we falter because the evidence is not available. As colleagues and friends, I am most grateful to them, for without their help this work would have been impossible.

Abbreviations

CVA	F. Villard, *Corpus Vasorum Antiquorum*. France, fasc. 19, Musée du Louvre, fasc. 12. Paris: Champion, 1958.
PCC	P. W. Lapp, *Palestinian Ceramic Chronology, 200 B.C–A.D. 70*. New Haven, CT: American Schools of Oriental Research, 1961.
Shechem III.1	E. F. Campbell, *Shechem III: The Stratigraphy and Architecture of Shechem/Tell Balâṭah* (Vol. 1: Text). Boston, MA: American Schools of Oriental Research, 2002.
Shechem III.2	G. R. H. Wright, *Shechem III: The Stratigraphy and Architecture of Shechem/Tell Balâṭah* (Vol. 2: Illustrations). Boston, MA: American Schools of Oriental Research, 2002.

Chapter 1

Introduction

This publication represents the Balâṭah pottery corpora of the Persian-Hellenistic period, Strata V–I, in accordance with the publication plans of the Joint Expedition to Shechem (*Shechem III.1*: 1). As noted there, this report is very late in coming, but it has been an effort that has covered over forty years of study by my late husband and myself. Strong impetus to this final study was given by the publication in 2002 of *Shechem III.1* and *III.2* by Edward F. Campbell and G. R. H. Wright. With their detailed presentation of the stratification and history of the site, clear reference points were provided for the pottery typologies based upon the stratigraphy.

It should be mentioned here that ceramic studies forty years ago, when this pottery was excavated and selected for study, were almost wholly considered for chronological purposes.[1] Recent pottery studies, and even some in the decades to follow the Balâṭah excavations, have been concerned with the utilization of pottery by the ancients, its manufacture, its trade, and how the vessels served them.[2] Our purpose has been primarily to present pottery typologies based on stratified deposits, in order that we might date the occupations, structures, and material remains at Balâṭah, and develop our typologies so that they may aid in dating archaeological remains at other sites, thus contributing to the typologies for all of Palestine and the ancient Near East. When the Balâṭah Strata V–I pottery was excavated and

the selection of pottery was made for study it was for chronological purposes, and it thus precluded some types of the later studies.[3]

THE STRATA

The absolute dates for Strata V–I at Balâṭah are as follows:

Stratum V	—	ca. 525–475 BC[4]
Stratum IV	—	ca. 325–250 BC
Stratum III B	—	ca. 250–225 BC
Stratum III A	—	ca. 225–190 BC
Stratum II	—	ca. 190–150 BC
Stratum I	—	ca. 150–110 BC

These dates were generally established by the early campaigns at Shechem, because these layers were the surface and first levels to be reached in excavation. Coinage and pottery have been correlated with the stratigraphy of the mound. Coin identifications and their stratification are presented in Appendix III.

The use of the designations Early Hellenistic and Late Hellenistic should be noted. Early Hellenistic usually refers to the Ptolemaic occupation of Palestine, 330–198 BC and Late Hellenistic to the Seleucid, 198–63 BC (P. Lapp 1961: 4; Sauer 1973: 3). At Balâṭah this would place the division of Early and Late Hellenistic between Strata IIIA and II. As the pottery is discussed, however, it will be seen that in Stratum IIIA many forms were in-

FIG. 1.1   *An impression of an archer from the Persian period on a lump of clay that was used to seal a document. The other side shows the imprint of the papyrus.*

FIG. 1.2   *Electrum coin (B56 #6) minted on Thasos, dated to Stratum V. Obverse and reverse.*

FIG. 1.3   *Bronze coins of Ptolemy I (B56 #21, #22, and #23) from the hoard found on the ledge of the Hellenistic tower foundation. Obverse on the top, reverse on the bottom.*

troduced that became common in Strata II and I, with a more definitive break between the IIIB and IIIA pottery.[5] This sometimes results in assigning a particular occupation and its pottery to late in Stratum IIIA, as in the discussion of the construction of the Hellenistic House in Field II. Yet some development in pottery occurs early in Stratum IIIA. Thus, on occasion the pottery of IIIA may be referred to as Late Hellenistic. This does not require a change in the historical designations or the stratum dates, as it is very possible that Late Hellenistic pottery characteristics began late in Early Hellenistic times and the last quarter of the third century BC.

Stratum V

As pointed out by G. E. Wright (1965: 166–69), there were a number of factors that indicated a stratum with limited occupation between the Iron Age and Hellenistic levels. In addition to the pottery that belonged to neither period, particularly the imported wares, there were characteristic bricks, at least one rough structure, and some surfaces

(*Shechem III.1*: 299). Some small finds point to a Persian occupation: a seal impression on a jar handle with a roaring lion that fits the Persian period (see fig. 2.3, pl. 2.2:13, and V jar handles in pottery discussion Chap. 2), an impression of Persian type on a lump of clay that was used to seal a papyrus document (fig. 1.1), and one of the oldest coins found in Palestine, a Thasos coin dating to the late sixth century BC (B56 #6, fig. 1.2).[6]

It was the imported black- and red-figured ware that provided the authoritative evidence and defined the period. The Attic ware was published in detail by the author in 1985 (N. Lapp 1985: 25–42) and is republished here in Chapter 2 to make this final report comprehensive. In addition to the imported wares, the local wares lend support to the dates for the Stratum V occupation, 525–475

BC.[7] As pointed out below in the discussion of the local pottery, since the Stratum VI pottery has not yet been presented in detail, there is the possibility that some of the types assigned here to Stratum V may go back to that period.

Stratum IV

Suggested dates for Stratum IV came as early as the 1956 campaign at Balâṭah. The hoard of Ptolemaic coins found on the ledge of the Hellenistic tower foundation pointed to a fourth- to third-century occupation (B56 ## 18–25, fig. 1.3; Wright 1956: 13). In the next campaign in 1957, an Alexander the Great coin (#93, fig. 1.4) on a lower floor behind the fortifications in Field I helped date the strata there (Toombs and Wright 1961: 41 and n. 32, and see locus discussion below). A number of Ptolemy I and II coins came from Field VII in 1960 (Toombs and Wright 1961: 44), though none were in clear Stratum IV loci.

When Field VII was excavated, it was clear that there were two phases for Stratum IV: IVA and IVB. Absolute dates of 325–300 BC have been suggested for IVB, 300–250 BC for IVA. The pottery typologies support these as possible dates. Two phases for Stratum IV were also distinguished in Field IX.

Stratum III

Stratum III was defined in Field VII by structures along totally different lines (*Shechem III.1*: 323), and again there were two phases. Stratum IIIB is dated about the third quarter of the third century BC (250–225 BC), IIIA, about 225–190 BC. In 1960, coins of Ptolemy II (285–246 BC) were generally below the IIIA levels, whereas Seleucid coins appeared above the floors (Toombs and Wright 1961: 44). A juglet with a collection of Ptolemaic silver tetradrachmas (B60 ## 532–555, 557–567, fig. 1.5) dated from Ptolemy I (285 BC) through Ptolemy V (two dated 198 and 193 BC). The jug was related to a Stratum III context (Toombs and Wright 1961: 44), so the coins determine the end date of Stratum III, about 190 BC.

The two phases could not be distinguished in Fields I and III where there was some Stratum III occupation.

FIG. 1.4 *An Alexander the Great coin (B57 #93), found on the lower floor in Field I in 1957. Obverse and reverse.*

FIG. 1.5 *Juglet (B60 #531) with the Ptolemaic silver tetradrachmas related to a Stratum III context in Field VII.*

Stratum II

This stratum was first determined by the black earth fill in Field II by comparison with other stratified pottery (P. Lapp 1961: 42–44), but some sub-surface constructions and much debris in Field VII confirmed the existence of this occupation. Coins of Antiochus IV (175–164 BC) and other Seleucid sovereigns found above the Stratum IIIA floors support the date for Stratum II in the first

Chapter 2

The Early Persian Pottery
Stratum V

The Persian pottery, that assigned to Stratum V, is presented by types and significance of loci. There are discussions of each type and the various sub-types. Plates that present the sherds in profile and section and accompanying charts with ware descriptions of the illustrated sherds, as well as ware descriptions for other similar sherds, can be found in the plate section of this volume. The pottery is illustrated and listed by stratum, with that from identifiable Stratum V contexts first, Stratum V pottery in later strata next, and significant unstratified sherds last.[1]

As has been noted, pottery from Stratum VI, the last Iron II stratum, has not been fully studied, nor is it available for comparison with the Stratum V material. It is thus possible that some of the forms assigned to Stratum V, particularly when there is no comparative material from other Persian sites, will be found to date back into the late Iron Age. This will be noted in the case of some pottery types.

The difficulty in distinguishing Stratum V should perhaps be mentioned once more. Although little architecture was found that could be assigned to this stratum, early in the excavations some pottery was recognized as later than that of the Iron II strata but not Hellenistic in form or ware. Persian pottery was little known at the time, and still today the Early Persian pottery of Palestine is becoming distinguished and classified. Notable also are the regional differences in pottery that appear in the Persian period. Some of the well-known forms

typical on the Coast and even in the Shephelah are not present at Shechem. In Transjordan, the repertory suggests some unique regional developments (see Chap. 1, n. 38). On the other hand, the differences are chronological as well as regional and these must be distinguished. The importance of having stratified groups cannot be overestimated, and although the Shechem excavations did not produce much architectural evidence, the material is often well stratified and even fills present important termini. As parallels to the Shechem material are cited below, some of the material is dated to the sixth and early fifth centuries BC on typological grounds from cisterns and tombs (Tell en-Naṣbeh, Bethshemesh, Lachish), but other sites have an Early Persian occupation (Gezer, Tell el-Fûl, Tell el-Hesi, Tel Michal).[2]

JARS

Variant Profile-Rimmed Jars

The most typical Stratum V jar at Balâṭah is one with a rim that is a variant of the late Iron II profile rim (pl. 2.1:1–15). The jar form is undoubtedly that indicated by the large jar fragments, pl. 2.1:20. This elongated, bag-shaped form is variously described as a cylindrical/ovoid shape (Gitin 1990: 73, Type 121), or as from rounded and sacked to narrow and cylindrical (Stern 1982: 104, his type F). The whole jar can probably best be compared to one from Tell en- Naṣbeh (Wampler 1947: pl. 19:313), which cannot be closely dated, but the sixth and fifth centuries BC are suggested as its main period (p. 10).

This is probably a degenerate form of a common late Iron II type that continued into the early Persian period apparently at inland sites. The Iron II profile rim was sharply cut (cf. P. Lapp 1970a: 181, n. 13), but in Stratum V the profile is less sharp and more rounded. It was well represented in Stratum V layers (pl. 2.1:1–2, and other sherds listed) and plentiful in the IVB fills that contained much Stratum V pottery (pl. 2.1:3–13 and others).

Some of these profile-rimmed jar rims come from Stratum VIII at Samaria, dating to the sixth century (Kenyon 1957: 129, 132; fig. 12:22, 27, 29). Another from a sixth-century context comes from Bethel (Kelso 1968: pl. 67:10, and cf. P. Lapp 1970a: 181, n. 14). It appears in mid- and late-fifth century contexts at Taanach (Rast 1978: fig. 80:1, Stratum VIA, and fig. 87:1, Stratum VIIB), but does not appear later (cf. P. Lapp 1970a: 181–82).

Many of these rims have a slight groove or furrow in the top. This is thought to be a later development, since it did not appear in mid-sixth-century groups at Tell el-Fûl and Bethel (P. Lapp 1970a: 182) or in sixth-century groups at Samaria. At Balâṭah they occurred principally in IVB loci (which may indicate that they belong late in Stratum V), where sometimes there is little or no ridge on the neck (pl. 2.1:8–14). The grooved rim without the neck ridge appeared in Stratum VIA at Taanach (mid-fifth century; Rast 1978: fig. 80:2, 3). P. Lapp thought this developed into the fully rounded rim by late Persian times and the type with the undercut popular in early Hellenistic times (P. Lapp 1970a: 182 and cf. fig. 9:1, 2; see Hellenistic jar types in Chap. 3).

Other Jars

Jars without necks from Stratum V, but with rims attached at the top of the shoulders (pl. 2.1:16–18), are perhaps smaller versions of the large "neckless" jars of Iron II (cf. for example those from Tell el-Fûl, N. Lapp 1981: pl. 49:18–28). These rims are usually compared to the Iron II "sausage" jars (see below) with pointed bases. The pointed bases do not ap-

pear in the later Shechem strata, so the jar form may be more like the usual Balâṭah rounded jars. The rims, however, are paralleled in fifth-century Persian loci at Taanach and Tell Abu-Hawam (the rounded-top, Rast 1978: figs. 81:3; flat-topped, Rast 1978: 48, fig. 81:1, Hamilton 1935: 4, fig. 3).

A unique rim from a Stratum IVA drain may possibly be an Early Persian fragment from a cylindrical jar with a sharp shoulder (pl. 2.1:19). It may, however, belong with Stratum IV, although it differs from other Shechem Early Hellenistic forms.

The largest fragment of a Stratum V jar came from an unstratified context (pl. 2.1:20). The fragments illustrate the bag-shaped jar, but the rim, drawn to a point at the top, is a new form that is more commonly associated with sausage jars, according to P. Lapp (1970: 182–83). The rim type is that found on a common Persian period jar with a flat shoulder and pointed or stub base, the "sausage" jar type of Iron II (Gitin's "exaggerated cyma-shaped" jar, type 122, 1990: 229; Stern's type H6 and H7, 1982: 109–10). This type jar dates from the late sixth to the fourth centuries and is limited mainly to coastal areas and the Shephelah (Stern 1982: 109; Gitin 1990: 231). Jars with similar rims come from Taanach (Rast 1968: fig. 81:2, Stratum VIA; 83:1, 2, Stratum VIB), Tel Mevorakh (Stern 1978: fig. 6:1, 2), and Gezer (Gitin 1990: pl. 28:12–15, 17).

Jar Handles

Jar handles from deep fill below IVB surfaces are shown in pl. 2.2:1–4. These have at least an incipient ridge and could date to Iron II. Missing completely are any of the twisted handles that look as though they were attached in a careless manner, which are found on the typical Persian jar of the coastal region. Artzy has studied the construction of these twisted handles and concluded that the distorted appearance was intentional in order to aid handling and shipping (1980: 69–73).

Ṭêt Handles

Handles with a unique stamp were first published along with Ptolemaic handles (P. Lapp 1963), but are now generally thought to date with the Stratum V material (fig. 2.1). The stamp has an oval form

FIG. 2.1 *Ṭêt handles from the 1960 and 1962 excavations. Top row: B62 536, B60 1081, B60 3897, B60 5124A; bottom row: B62 530, B62 768, B60 3847.*

with a crossbar, the Hebrew or Aramaic *ṭêt;* a line like an antenna goes away from the top of each side of the oval, and beneath the oval is a bent mark followed by six vertical strokes (pl. 2.2:5–12). Four of these stamped handles were found in the 1960 excavations, three in 1962, two in the 1964 season (one shown in fig. 2.2), and one from the later Balâṭah excavations from an unknown context. Seven can be identified from the Austro-German expedition (cf. *Shechem III.1*: 309; P. Lapp 1963: 27, n. 24).[3] Unfortunately, none of these seventeen stamps are from Stratum V contexts; all are associated with later fills or constructions, or are otherwise unstratified.

Although first published with some Ptolemaic stamped handles, Lapp realized at the time that the handles could be assigned to "an earlier post-Iron II horizon also represented in Stratum IV fills" (P. Lapp 1963: 27, no. 24). This became the Stratum V horizon. Further study has shown that the one

FIG. 2.2 *Ṭêt handle no. 38,900 from the 1964 excavations.*

considered from Stratum IV (5124A, # 620) is not from a sealed locus. Lapp also thought that the ware pointed to an earlier date. Thereafter Wright placed these handles in Stratum V, and he related them to the Gibeon wine jar handles, which he dated not before the second half of the sixth century BC (Wright 1965: 167, n. 33).

There is general agreement that the symbols represent the number twenty-six and designate the capacity of the jar (*Shechem III.1:* 309; Cross 1969: 21–22). Cross has compared the symbols to a fourth-century Phoenician stamp from Shiqmona, where there is also an indication of capacity, an indication of the royal standard, and the *ṭêt* symbol. Campbell concludes that when comparative seals found in Palestine are taken into consideration, the Shechem handles are from wine jars with the *ṭêt* as the official marker of the standard size (*Shechem III.1:* 309).

Other Stamped Handles

Another handle with a stamp (fig. 2.3; pl. 2.2.13) has been dated to the Persian period by Wright (1965: 167–68) and Campbell (*Shechem III.1:* 309). It was not from a stratified context, but its depiction of a crude lion is a common motif of this time. Wright points to the parallels at Ramat Raḥel (Aharoni 1962: fig. 9:9–12), and Stern finds numerous animal depictions on seals from sites near Jerusalem and the area of Benjamin (Stern 1982: 210–13). All have been dated to, or can be assumed to come from, the Persian period.

Other stamped handles listed in the pl. 2.2 chart have oval stamps without further markings, or they have varied stamps. The varied markings or the ware indicate that they do not belong with the *ṭêt* stamped handles.

JUGS AND JUGLETS

Wide-Mouth Jugs

A typical Stratum V wide-mouthed jug had an out-turned rim and a ridge on the neck (pl. 2.3:1–10). This jug appeared in late Iron II strata at Tell Beit Mirsim (Stratum A, cf. Albright 1932: pl. 58:4–5, 7–9; 1943: pl.14:1, 4) and other Judean sites (Lachish

FIG. 2.3   *Lion seal impression on handle typical of the Persian period, B62 #349.*

III, Tufnell, 1953: pl. 86:248–50; En-Gedi V, Mazar, Dothan, and Dunayevsky 1966: fig. 20:7; and Ramat Raḥel V, Aharoni 1962: 11:25), as well as Meṣad Ḥashavyahu on the coast (Naveh 1962: fig. 5:7). At Tell el-Fûl it appeared in late Iron II period IIIA (N. Lapp 1981: 90, pl. 57:1–5), but many fragments were found imbedded in the lowest silt layer of the large, plastered cistern in the homogeneous IIIB deposit (587–538 BC, N. Lapp 1981: pls. 53–56). The Balâṭah rims are generally more thickened than the Tell el-Fûl rims and sometimes out-turned with an undercut, and as far as can be determined, the Balâṭah jugs did not have the pinched lip opposite the handle that was represented in the Tell el-Fûl cistern jugs (and some of the Iron II jugs).

Other Early Persian jugs with the ridge on the neck come from Ain Shems Tomb 14 (sixth century BC, Grant and Wright 1938: pl. 68:11), Lachish (Tufnell 1953: Tomb 109, 188–89, pl. 86:246), and Tell en-Naṣbeh (Wampler 1947: pl. 33: 584–88, dated 700–500 BC, p. 17).[4] At Hesi in Substratum Vd, 500–450 BC, a "jar" is perhaps a jug of this type (Bennett and Blakely 1989: fig. 147:1), and a jug (fig. 142:4) should probably be shown with only one handle. The Taanach jug fragment from period VIB (425–400 BC) is related to this type by P. Lapp (1970a: 183), but except for the meager Hesi evidence there are as yet no other jugs of this type that need to be dated into the fifth century (cf. N. Lapp 1981: 90 and Stern 1982: 116, type C).

FIG. 2.4   *Partially reconstructed juglet B60 503.*

Narrow-Necked Jugs, Decanters, or Flasks

Belonging to Stratum V are four fragments of narrow-necked vessels with ridged necks from jugs, decanters, or flasks (pl. 2.3:11–14). The sherds are so fragmentary that the shape of the whole vessel cannot be determined. Three of them (pl. 2.3:12–14) may actually be from a vessel that has been called the "Gibeon jar," after the site where its discovery was "re-established" (Amiran 1975: 132). Though not found in stratigraphic contexts, these inscribed handles from Gibeon jugs (Pritchard 1959: fig. 6:1–4) are dated to the mid-sixth century BC by most scholars on typological and paleographical grounds (Wright 1963: 211, n. 1; Cross 1962: 23; P. Lapp 1968b: 392). Amiran traces the "jar" back to a two-handled type from Iron I that becomes amalgamated with the water-decanter form at the end of Iron II (Amiran 1975: 129–32).

From Tell el-Fûl, two fragmentary rims (N. Lapp 1981: pl. 57:16, 17) from period IIIB (587–538 BC) could be of this narrow-necked type. At Tell el-Fûl they were compared to decanters (p. 90). If the Balâṭah rims represent decanters, early Persian parallels can be pointed out from Tel Michal Stratum XI (525–490 BC; Singer-Avitz 1989: fig. 9.1:5), and Ain Shems, Tomb 14 (sixth century BC; Grant and Wright 1938: pls. 68:6, 13, 14).

Similar rims to Balâṭah pl. 2.3:12–14 appear on flasks or narrow-necked jugs that appear later in the Persian period: from Tel Michal Stratum VIII (450–400 BC; Singer-Avitz 1989: fig. 9.5:15), Gezer Stratum IV (500–300 BC; Gitin 1990: pl. 29:22), Tell en-Naṣbeh (Wampler 1947: pl. 76:1742–45), and Hesi Stratum Vc (about 450 BC; Bennett and Blakely 1989: figs. 150:45, 153:2 [probably only one handle]). In Tel Mevorakh Stratum IV (late Persian period) a similar rim appeared on what is said to be the "most common jug in the Persian period in Palestine" (Stern 1978: 27–28, 37; fig. 9:4, 5).

Balâṭah pl. 2.3:11 differs from the other rim fragments and seems to have its best parallel in a "decanter" from Tell en-Naṣbeh (Wampler 1947: pl. 40:750), dated there to the end of the Iron Age. A rim from Hesi Stratum Vd (500–450 BC; Bennett and Blakely 1989: fig. 140: 36) may be from a similar vessel.

Juglets or Bottles

The juglet pl. 2.3:15 (fig. 2.4) is unique to Balâṭah and is not a common form in the Palestinian literature. It seems to be similar to an East Greek amphoriskos published from Hesi (Stratum; Vd, 500–450 BC; Bennett and Blakely 1989: 93, fig. 87:2). Parallels are suggested from Rhodes, as well as vases found in Palestine from Atlit (Johns 1932: 86, pl. 29, no. 704) and Gil'am (Stern 1970: fig. 10:1). The Balâṭah vessel is incomplete, without rim or handles, and it is perhaps a local imitation rather than an actual import, although the ware is an unusual consistent dark reddish brown. The dating of the Greek vases to the end of the sixth century (Bennett and Blakely 1989: 93) and those found in Palestinian contexts places the Balâṭah vessel with the Stratum V material.

The juglet top with a handle indicated from its neck, pl. 2.3:16, has parallels from Hesi Stratum Vd, 500–450 BC, and their descriptions may indicate a similar whitish ware (Bennett and Blakely 1989: figs. 144:17, 147:3, 4, 7). The whole form of this juglet is probably best shown by the juglet from a Persian level at Shiqmona (Eligavish 1968: pl. 40: 57). Other juglets from the Persian period with a handle from their neck to the body are published from Shiqmona (pls. 40:52–56, 41:62), En-Gedi (Mazar and Dunayevsky 1967: pl. 33:1, 3), and the Beit Lei cave (Naveh 1963: fig. 2:4).

Juglet rim pl. 2.3:17 could belong to an elongated juglet, such as those from Tell el-Fûl (N. Lapp 1981: pl. 60:8–10; the Shechem fragment is a small fragment only of the rim and could well have a handle) assigned to period IIIB (587–538 BC), Tell en-Naṣbeh, Type 788 (Wampler 1947: 24, pl. 41:788), dated sixth and fifth century BC, and Ain Shems (Grant and Wright 1938: pl. 68:3) from sixth-century Tomb 14. Numerous similar rims come from Hesi Stratum Vd (500–450 BC; Bennett and Blakely 1989: figs. 141:18, 144:15, 16), and it is probable that they belong to the type of elongated juglet with rounded base that tends to occur early in the Persian period.

The body of an elongated bottle, pl. 2.3:18, is similar to those from the Tell el-Fûl IIIB period, 587–538 BC (N. Lapp 1981: pl. 61:10–14). Other early Persian bottles of this type have come from the Ramat Raḥel refuse pit 484 (Aharoni 1964: fig. 14:40, 41), Ain Shems sixth-century Tomb 14 (Grant and Wright 1938: pl. 68:10), and Hazor Stratum II (Yadin et al. 1958: pl. 80:22). The earlier form, which belongs in Late Iron II, was usually painted and considered to be of Assyrian origin (Henschel-Simon 1945: 75–77; Yadin et al. 1958: 58–59; Stern 1982: 125–27). Whether the unpainted, cruder form

continued into the Hellenistic period may still be disputed, but its occurrence in the Early Persian period cannot be doubted.

BOWLS

That the variety of Persian bowls, small, medium, and large, does not fall into any easy classification has often been noted by excavators (cf. N. Lapp 1985:22). At Keisan, the large variety of forms observed throughout the Persian epoch defied the establishment of a clear typological evolution (Nodet 1980: 122). At Tel Mevorakh "scores of bowls were uncovered in the Persian period strata," but only a few types could be distinguished and "it was impossible to trace their development during the successive phases of this period" (Stern 1978: 30). When types are distinguished, reports almost always qualify that they appear in many variations of body and rim sizes and shapes.

At Balâṭah, the forms here are assigned to Stratum V because of either their findspot or their ware. They do not belong with the usual Iron II bowls that are often burnished on the interior, although some of the shapes may continue into the exilic and Persian periods (N. Lapp 1981: 93); neither are they of the usual Hellenistic wares. Although these forms are not familiar from other periods, it is always possible that they have been wrongly assigned to Stratum V. There are no whole forms or profiles, so any classification is on the basis of the fragmentary rims.

The most common Persian bowl seems to be one with a simple rim, in many sizes, and varying shapes. They may be small or medium in size, shallow or deep, with rounded or slanting sides, and the rim plain upright or slightly inverted. Balâṭah pl. 2.4:3 would fit this category. At Hesi (where bowls were not singled out for study), most of the bowls were of this type and many variations can be seen. They appeared in Stratum Vd (500–450 BC; Bennett and Blakely 1989: figs. 139:9, 30, 140:3–5, 25, and especially in pits, figs. 141, 142, 147, 148), and continued throughout the Persian sub-phases (through Va, to 380 BC). At Gezer in Stratum IV, fifth–fourth centuries, Gitin distinguishes several types with simple rims (1990: 76–77, types 138, 141, 142). Stern identifies simple rims, inverted and upright, in medium, small, and larger bowls (1982: 94–96, types A1, A2, A4, B1).

The other type rim usually singled out is an everted ledge rim (Stern 1982: 94 –96, types A3, B2; Gitin 1990: pl. 31:2–4).[5] None of the Balâṭah rims falls into this category, though pl. 2.4:2 and 7 are thickened on the exterior. Others are flat-topped (pl. 2.4:1 and 6), profiled (pl. 2.4:4), or turned out and rounded off (pl. 2.4:8 and 10). The bases, pl. 2.4:5 and 9, could belong with any of the small or medium bowls. Other bowls listed but not shown are thought to belong with the Stratum V assembly, some similar to those represented and others with variations.

KRATERS

A fair number of krater rims can be assigned to Stratum V. Some were in stratified contexts; those in later deposits are assigned to Stratum V by ware or type. Rims and sherds with particular characteristics were varied, but they can be grouped.

High-Necked Kraters

There were a number of rims from high-necked kraters, most of them with thickened out-turned rims (pl. 2.5:1–10). Stern (1982: 98–99) has high-necked kraters in both his "Hole-mouth Kraters" class (type C), which seem to be distinguished by their rounded sides, and his "Kraters" (type D), of which the complete specimens illustrated are carinated and have ring bases. He has subtypes without handles, with two or four handles, or with horizontal handles. At Balâṭah, the bases, handles, and possible carinations cannot be determined, since we have no complete profiles. High-necked kraters of the Persian period with complete profiles and usually with thickened out-turned rims, like those from Balâṭah, are illustrated from Megiddo Stratum I, with rounded sides (Lamon and Shipton 1939: pl. 13:66); from Tell en-Naṣbeh, assigned about 700–500 BC, with carinated sides but plain, rather short vertical rim (Wampler 1947: 41, pl. 68:1531); from Samaria, cistern 7, strip 1, with carinated sides and ring base (Reisner, Fisher, and Lyon 1924: fig. 168:11a); from Mevorakh Stratum IV, carinated sides with base missing (Stern 1978: fig.

5:7); and the Beit Lei pottery cave, rounded sides and ring base (Naveh 1963: fig. 2:5). High-necked krater rims similar to those from Balâṭah are also published from Samaria (probably kraters, not jars) period VIII (Kenyon 1957: fig. 12:30–32) and phase F (Hennessy 1970: fig. 13:1, 21, 25); Taanach period VIA (Rast 1978: fig. 77:6), period VIB (fig. 86:2); Gezer Stratum IV (Gitin 1990: 77; pl. 31:21, 23); Tell en- Naṣbeh, dated subsequent to 600 BC (Wampler 1947: 40, pls. 66–67:1508–25); Tell el-Fûl period IIIB (N. Lapp 1981: pl. 65:5–8, 10–12); Ramat Raḥel pit 484 (short necks; Aharoni 1964: fig. 12:25, 30); Jerusalem "Early Jewish Fills" (Tushingham 1985: fig. 15: 2–5, 7–9, 11, 12, assigned to second half of the sixth century BC, p. 35); Hesi Substratum Vd (Bennett and Blakely 1989: fig. 139:19); Dor Stratum VI (Stern et al. 1995b: fig. 2.3.1–2); Tel Michal Stratum IX (Singer-Avitz 1989: fig. 9.2.3); and 'Umayri, Integrated Phase 7 (Herr et al. 2002: figs. 3.6.17, 5.13.3).

Sloping-Shoulder Kraters

The Balâṭah krater sherds pl. 2.5:11–14 have shoulders sloping from the rims. A Taanach rim from Stratum IVA is similar (Rast 1978: fig. 79:4). There are a number of kraters from Ramat Raḥel pit 484 that have sloping shoulders, but most of them have out-turned rims, not as evident in the Balâṭah rims (Aharoni 1964: figs. 12:23, 24, 26, 29, 13:3, 4, 6, 7, 9). However, one rim (fig. 12:28) may be similar to Balâṭah pl. 2.5:13.

Ledged and Lug-Handled Bowls and Kraters

Two distinctive attributes, ledged rims and lug handles, characterize quite a number of fragments (fig. 2.5). Interestingly, the rough ware and rather poor workmanship of fragments with these characteristics seem to belong to two vessel categories, bowls (pl. 2.6:1, 5–6) and kraters (pl. 2.6:3–4, 7–8). Small crude handles appear on both types, either at the rim or on the shoulder. Unfortunately, none have been found in Stratum V loci, but quite a number of fragments come from fills for Stratum IV constructions, as well as later and unstratified debris.[6]

Comparative material is rare. A krater with ledged rim but four typical vertical handles was

FIG. 2.5 *Bowls and kraters with ledge for a lid and crude handles from the 1960 campaign. Top row: nos. 5015, 3177; bottom row: nos. 5142, 7371.*

published from Tell el-Fûl and probably dates to the time of our vessels (Sinclair 1960: pl. 23:17; cf. N. Lapp 1981: 95 and 1985:23). The bowl form with ledged rim is found at a number of sites, as pointed out by Stern (1982: 96, type B4). He states, "This bowl is the continuation of a common Iron Age bowl and dates only to the first part of the Persian period: sixth to fifth centuries BC." This fits with the Balâṭah evidence, but the basis for his dating is not clear. The parallels he cites are Megiddo strata III–I (Megiddo I, p. 168, pl. 23:8–9 [not 7–8]); Samaria cistern 7, strip 1 (Reisner, Fisher, and Lyon 1924: fig. 169:19A) and period VIII (Kenyon 1957: fig. 12:1 [probably a seventh century type, p. 132]); and Lachish (Tufnell 1953: pl. 101:646 [not closely comparable and not well-stratified]). Stern publishes several sherds from Dor with ledged rims as kraters (Stern et al. 1995b: fig. 2.3.4–6), but they are fragmentary and could belong to bowls. One has indications of a vertical handle. These are listed from Stratum VI. A fragment of a lug handle also came from Dor (Stern et al. 1995b: fig. 2.37.26). Published right above it is a ledged rim on what is designated a jar from a different locus. Both con-

texts, though, are from Stratum IVB, late Persian.[7] A fragment with what could be a lug handle on a small krater with a ledge (?) rim is published from the Persian fortress north of Ashdod (Porath 1974: fig. 4: 12). Zertal publishes a "bowl" (more likely a krater) found on his Manasseh hill country survey at el-Qitneh with a deep grooved rim and "yellow" ware – the fragment did not have a handle – which he dates to the Persian period (Zertal 2004: 137, fig. 77.5).[8] From Samaria period VIII also comes a krater rim similar to the Balâṭah krater rims (Kenyon 1957: fig. 12:5). However, this vessel fragment and the one cited above from Samaria period VIII are probably from the seventh century make-up of that period (Kenyon 1957: 132). It is possible that this is a late Iron II form, and as the earlier Balâṭah material is studied this must be considered.

Kraters with Wedged and/or Circle Impressions

Unfortunately, none of the wedged or circle impressed kraters came from firm Stratum V loci. However, these impressions have been dated to the late sixth century and early fifth century in the most

FIG. 2.6 *Kraters with wedge and circle impressions. Top row: B62 722, B62 477; bottom row: B60 532, B60 4161.*

recent detailed studies (Zorn 2001: 692 and Stern 1982: 133–36).[9] Zorn gives a particularly detailed study of this ware, suggesting a possible origin in Arabia and brought to Palestine by Babylonia with its control over the spice trade (Zorn 2001: 693–95), although the usual assumption is that Mesopotamian cuneiform was the inspiration for the wedge impressions (Stern 1982: 136; Wampler 1940: 15). Zorn points to some sherds with this design from Qaṣr al-Ḥamrā' at Taymā' and al-Hirj in northwestern Arabia, unfortunately all without clear stratigraphical contexts (Zorn 2001: 690–92, figs. 34.1–34.5). The sparse evidence at this time cannot lead to sure conclusions (pp. 694–95).

The wedged and circle sherds from Balâṭah fit the late sixth–early fifth century date; in fact, the Balâṭah evidence helps determine the date because of the Stratum V occupation at this time (Stern 1982: 135). The Balâṭah forms are mainly those of Stratum V kraters. Twelve of the twenty-eight listed are shown in pl. 2.7 (and see fig. 2.6). High-necked kraters are probably represented by pl. 2.7:2, 5–8, 10, kraters with sloping shoulders by pl. 2.7:1, 3–4. (Fragmentary sherds do not easily indicate their vessel form.) Circles with wedges are shown on pl. 2.7:3, 5–6, and one other unstratified body sherd (no. 76). Three handles not shown had impressed circles only (nos. 5267, 3739, 5261, the last being a double handle with a line of impressed circles on each). When circles appear alone it is most often on handles (Zorn 2001: 690, n. 3). The remaining sherds not shown had varied wedge designs. As noted, the wedges are usually on the rims; the decoration seems to continue below the rim on pl. 2.7:3–6.[10] Note pl. 2.7:6 with wedges on the rim but impressed circles on its body. Four fragments not illustrated have a wedge design on their bodies (nos. 5209, 144, 3884, 146).

In addition to the many chevron-designed vessels cited in the studies above, additional fragments from 'Umayri in Transjordan should be noted (Herr et al. 1991: 241, figs. 3.12:34, 12.121:11). The large part of a vessel shown in the second illustration indicates another form for these kraters. In an unusual use of this design, in the 1989 excavation season at 'Umayri the incised chevron motif was found on the rim of a juglet (Herr et al. 1997: 245, fig.3.22.12).[11]

FIG. 2.7   *Typical Persian mortarium fragments. B62 465/366, 499, and 452.*

MORTARIA

Persian mortaria have been studied in detail by Blakely and Bennett (1989) and Bennett and Blakely (1989). They conclude that what are often called Persian bowls or mortaria are of two kinds: the flat-based variety has been found in Palestine from the end of the seventh to the early fifth century BC, while the ring-based form was popular from the end of the sixth century to the end of the fifth (Blakely and Bennett 1989: 61). What Bennett and Blakely call the Levantine mortarium of the Persian period is described as a mold-made ceramic form whose rim is 30 ± 3 cm in diameter and is turned over and joined on the exterior. Its height is 8 ± 2 cm and its thickness is about 1.5 cm to 2 cm. Its ware contains coarse, sharp inclusions. Typically, this vessel will be white to yellowish white to greenish white to pinkish white on the surfaces, and the ware will be a bit pinker in color than the surface. Used vessels will exhibit heavy abrasion on the lower interior surfaces and often the vessel will be broken in the center (Bennett and Blakely 1989: 196). Their technical studies indicate the vessels were imported, most probably from a manufacturing center in northern Syria and/or southwestern Anatolia,[12] where they were mass-produced, mold-made, well-levigated and well-tempered, constructed to serve as grinding vessels (Blakely and Bennett 1989: 59). From their earliest appearance until the mid-fifth century BC, the association of the mortarium with various imported transport jars and amphorae indicates Persian governmental or military contexts. The ring-based variety appears first with the Persian conquest of Egypt, ca. 525 BC, and disappears with the Persian turmoil and the Egyptian revolt about 400 BC. Blakely and Bennett thus equate the ring-based mortaria with the Persian occupation and its system of roads and military stores for grain throughout the empire. The mortaria were government-issued for grinding; the standard form was easily imported into Palestine (Blakely and Bennett 1969: 61).[13]

The Shechem evidence generally fits this hypothesis. The one whole mortarium profile (pl. 2.8:1, fig 2.7) has a flat base, and one fragment of the bowl came from Stratum VI (ca. 714–600 BC), the period from which the type with the flat base is known.[14] Most of the rims, however, in all probability belong with Stratum V (pl. 2.8:2–28) along with the high ring bases (pl. 2.9:1–9). Besides the complete form (pl. 2.8:1), there are a few other flat bases which probably belong with the Stratum V mortaria (pl. 2.9:10 and those listed). The rims are remarkably standard. The rim is best described as triangular, thickened toward the exterior, with a rounded top and variably defined lower rim lip (Glanzman 1993: 24).

In the publication of the stratigraphical and architectural volume of Shechem, Campbell points out that, though there is little architectural evidence for Stratum V, the finds, including a substantial amount of Greek imports (see below), hint that Shechem had official standing in the Persian administration, perhaps as the district capital of the Province of Samaria (*Shechem III.1*: 309b; cf. Stern 1982: 244–45; Avi-Yonah 1966: 24–25). As noted above, Blakely and Bennett associated these vessels with a government or military presence.

A student of Bennett's, L. Wakefield, undertook a study of mortarium contexts and associated finds, and he concluded that mortaria are usually associated with domestic buildings, and most often with other kitchen ware (Blakely and Bennett 1989: 54). Blakely and Bennett then examined the contexts of mortaria at Hesi, and later those published from Tel Michal, and could state they were often recovered in contexts and with implements compatible with grinding and food preparation (pp. 54–55). Unfortunately, at Balâṭah no grinding implements are recorded in loci with the Persian mortarium fragments.

In 1992, W. D. Glanzman undertook a study of some of the Shechem mortaria to elucidate manufacturing methods and reconstruction of the potters' craft (Glanzman 1993: 1–2).[15] Seventeen sherds that are believed to belong to the Stratum V occupation were analyzed as to fabric group, morphotypes, and evidence of manufacture and use wear.[16] The potter's wheel was used in the production of all vessels, evident from the wheel marks and ridges left on the clay from the potters' hands and the wet smoothing marks from the later stages of production. However, visual inspection could not determine whether the form was jiggered over a convex mould, as the earlier Blakely and Bennett replication of the process suggested (1989: 46), or whether it was wheel-thrown in an upright mode without the aid of a mould (Glanzman 1993: 37). The rim was formed by rolling to the exterior or was folded, creating the thickened triangular shape. Wet-smoothing marks, tightly-spaced and horizontal, are evident on both surfaces of the rims, except when abrasion or roughened surface have erased some of the marks. Trimming, evident on a few sherds, is also significant in determining the

mode of production. There is evidence of abrasion on many of the sherds, which indicates their use (Glanzman 1993: 25–26).[17]

The number of fabric groups Glanzman distinguishes (seven for the Stratum V sherds), representing variations in raw materials, permits him to hypothesize that products reflect several geologically different regions. These regions would supply mortaria for distribution in Palestine. Given the consistency in manufacturing methods of the Persian mortaria, it can be hypothesized that they were "made using a common, regionally widespread pottery tradition" (Glanzman 1993: 42).[18]

With the comprehensive studies that have been carried out on the Persian mortaria it is not necessary to cite parallels (see Bennett and Blakely 1989: 196 and Gitin 1990: 235–36, as well as Singer-Avitz 1989: 119–20, 124; Stern et al. 1995b: 53; and Berlin 1997: 123–27, not included in the former studies).[19] It should be noted that at Hesi the round-sided mortaria with folded rim (Gitin's type 149, 1990: 235) are divided into a smooth-rounded type [rim], an undercut-rounded type [rim], and a thin type (Bennett and Blakely 1989: 196). The thin type is closer to the Hellenistic mortarium (p. 198). At Shechem, the undercut type would include pl. 2.8:2–3, 5–6, 8, 11, 15, 20, 22, 27. However, no chronological distinction is made between the two types, even though their construction may have differed (Blakely and Bennett 1989: 57). About half of the Hesi mortaria examples belonged to Substratum Vd (500–450 BC). No new forms appeared in later substrata Vc and Vb, and the limited number recovered from these substrata makes it likely that few if any of these vessels were imported into Hesi during these periods (Bennett and Blakely 1989: 198).

It should be noted that few of these Persian mortaria are known from Transjordan: one is published from Saidiyeh (Pritchard 1985: fig. 17:1) and another from 'Umayri (Herr et al. 1991: fig. 3.29:4), where it is noted that they are "rare in Transjordan" (p. 241).

COOKING POTS

In discussing the Stratum V cooking pots (as with some other ceramic categories) it is necessary to

FIG. 2.8   *Grooved cooking pot rims: heavy type in back row: B60 4664, B60 6925, B62 224; and the lighter grooved rims in front: B62 382, B62 1033.*

take into consideration only those forms that we can be fairly certain belong with that stratum. The Iron II high-necked cooking pot, which probably continued in some form through the Persian period and into the Hellenistic, will not be discussed, because in mixed debris it is difficult to distinguish earlier from later forms all in cooking pot ware. The high-necked cooking pot is the standard Persian period cooking pot at Hesi (forty-nine cooking-pot fragments of sixty-four in this group) and is discussed there in depth (Bennett and Blakely 1989: 203). One rim of this type from a Stratum V locus is published here (pl. 2.10:1).

The cooking-pot form that is typical of Stratum V at Balâṭah is the globular pot with two handles and an everted grooved rim, forming a rounded or pointed interior angle (perhaps for a lid), usually of thin ware (pl. 2.10:2–20; fig. 2.8). It is a late Iron II form, but it continued through most of the sixth century. This cooking pot was common in IIIB (587–538 BC) loci at Tell el-Fûl, and the form with parallels is discussed there (N. Lapp 1981: 96). Gitin did not think this form appeared in the Persian period (1990: 221), but the Persian period at Gezer is dated fifth–fourth centuries, and this form probably disappeared by 500 BC.[20] It does appear at Hesi in Substratum Vd, dated to the first half of the fifth century, and could have been

in use then (Bennett and Blakely 1989: 203, 205). The form appears with the seventh–sixth-century pottery at Heshbon in Transjordan (Lugenbeal and Sauer 1972: pl. 5: 312–13), and in Stratum IV (which may extend into the Persian period) at Saidiyeh (Pritchard 1985: fig. 17: 10, 13). An everted cooking pot rim, but without a ridge, which would probably receive a lid and seems to have a wide mouth, is published with Persian pottery from Tell Nimrin in Jordan (Flanagan, McCreery, and Yassine 1994: fig. 19:5.)

Another unusual form, perhaps related, is common in later fills and could belong to Stratum V (pl. 2.10: 21–33 and fig. 2.8). It is a heavier pot, without a neck and probably generally shallow or squat rather than globular, with a thick rim that has an inner flange, again perhaps for a lid. The rim is often almost square-shaped, as the top may be slightly everted. It is easily distinguished from common Iron Age cooking pots, particularly because of the very heavy appearance of its rim. Yet, it is possibly a late adaptation of the Iron Age shallow cooking pot, a variant of Gitin's type 105. It should also be noted that some of the preceding cooking pot types are of heavier ware (such as pl. 2.10:6, 9) and perhaps transitional to this type. The closest parallel from Gezer is attributed to the eighth–seventh centuries (Gitin 1990: 217, pl. 24:14). It is noted that a similar

FIG. 2.9 *Persian lamp fragments. In back: B57 317, B60 451, and in front two-spouted lamp B60 5911A.*

rim from Bethshemesh "cannot be dated within Stratum II" (Stratum II is Iron Ic–II; Grant and Wright 1938: pl. 63:41 and description on opposing page). Among the varied "holemouth" cooking pots at 'Umayri a pot possibly of similar form and rim is published (Herr 1989: 309, fig. 19.17:4).

As the Iron Age material, particularly that of Stratum VI, is studied, it will have to be seen whether this or a similar form appears in late Iron II.

LAMPS

A group of Persian-period lamps are shown in pl. 2.11 and fig. 2.9, representative of the lamps that belong with Stratum V. Most of the lamp fragments are from fills, but the occupational history of Balâṭah places them without doubt in the Stratum V period.

This lamp is an open flat lamp with a flat base and a wide rim, which is sometimes burnished.[21] It is thought to be the last in a series of saucer lamps that goes back to the third millennium BC. It is considered to be one of the important diagnostic types of the Persian period (Stern 1982: 127).

These lamps have been assigned to the entire Persian period (Stern 1982: 128). They appear at Hesi in sub-phases Vd through Va (500–380 BC; Bennett and Blakely 1989: figs. 144:22, 23, 161:27, 29, 162:8, 163:7, 24); at Keisan in phase 3 (580–380 BC; Nodet 1980: pl. 21:1–5); at Mevorakh in strata VI–IV (450–333 BC; Stern 1978: fig. 10:1–5); and

at Tel Michal in strata VIII and VII (430–350 BC; Singer-Avitz 1989: figs. 9.7:7, 9.9:3), However, none have been published from earlier sixth-century deposits at el-Jib, Ain Shems, Beth-zur, or Tell el-Fûl (the only one uncovered at Tell el-Fûl is from a late context; N. Lapp 1981: 99, pl. 21:14). With the possible exception of a lamp from Ain Shems Tomb 14 (Grant and Wright 1939: 144–45), the Balâṭah collection seems to represent the earliest date that can be given to these lamps[22] – the latter part of the sixth century BC.[23]

The Balâṭah lamps are typical of the many of this type that have been published since early excavations (for example, Tell Abu Hawam; Hamilton 1934: 4, fig. 5). The only unusual variation is the lamp that seems to have two spouts (pl. 2.11:2; fig. 2.9; cf. N. Lapp 1985: 23). William Anderson has called attention to a similar lamp from Sarepta (Pritchard 1975: figs. 27:2, 60:3). He believed it to be "...the frontal fragment from a two-spouted (6th–5th cent. BC) 'Punic' lamp."[24] In the publication of the objects, this lamp is attributed to Group 8 (Pritchard 1988: 154, no. 16, figs. 57–58), "Shallow Saucer with Broad Flange and Rounded Base" (Anderson 1988: 231), whereas his Group 9 is the "Shallow Saucer with Broad, Everted Flange and Flattened Base," which "...although it has its antecedents in the later phases of Iron II, ...is most characteristic of the Persian period" (p. 232). The Balâṭah example would definitely be placed in his Group 9. Anderson continued in his personal let-

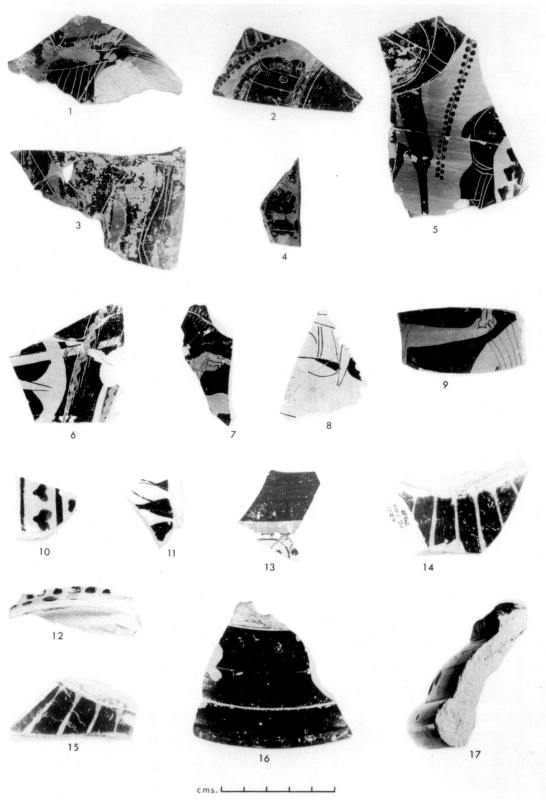

Fig. 2.10 *Black- and red-figured krater fragments: (1) B62 1267, (2) B62 86/87, (3) B60 5330A/928A, (4) B62 800, (5) B60 5310A, (6) B62 VII, (7) B62 1266, (8) B62 807, (9) B62 83, (10) B60 5285, (11) B60 3848, (12) BB62 159, (13) B60 6249, (14) B62 1123, (15) B60 5291A, (16) B60 5309, (17) B62 1536.*

ter, "if the fragment from Balâṭah is indeed from a two-spouted lamp, it would be the only example that far inland that I know." No other Palestinian parallels have appeared.[25]

There are two other lamp types that appear in the Persian period. The high-based late Iron II lamp continues for at least a while into the exilic period (N. Lapp 1981: 98, pl. 71:4–13), but whether it continued into the fifth century has been questioned (Stern 1982: 128).[26] High-based lamp fragments from Balâṭah are not considered here, as they may belong with Stratum VI. The locally-made small, closed lamp appears in the Persian period in imitation of imported Greek lamps. Stern dates their appearance in Palestine as early as the fifth century, but principally to the fourth century (1982: 129; cf. Gitin 1990: 237, type 126). From the 1984 excavations at Madaba in Transjordan, a locally-made closed lamp spout appeared in a late Iron II context (Herr 1989: 309, fig. 19.17:4). It was thought that this might push back the earliest appearance of this type lamp in Palestine by 250 years. However, the seventh–sixth century dates for this period at Heshbon have steadily been pushed forward, and differences between the Persian pottery of western and eastern Palestine have been emphasized (see Chap. 1, n. 41), so that the verdict on the appearance of locally-made closed lamps is still out. At Balâṭah, none of the delphiniform lamps in imitation of Attic forms appear before Stratum IIIB (the middle of the third century BC).

ATTIC / IMPORTED WARE

The Attic ware from Balâṭah was published in 1985 (N. Lapp 1985: 25–42), where its importance for Stratum V was stressed (pp. 19, 25). The descriptions and discussion here will be principally an adaptation of what was published then. The stratification has been further studied and can be defined with more certainty. The fragments listed in the charts should be noted for the changes and additions. It should be emphasized, however, that the context of none of the fragments is significant for dating. All Attic fragments are from fills or constructions of the Hellenistic occupants. On the other hand, the comparative study of the imported Attic vessels and one of the oldest coins found in

Palestine provided the chronological framework for Stratum V (Wright 1965: 167–68, and see Chap. 1, above).[27]

Black- and Red-Figured Kraters

Fragments of several black- and red-figured kraters have been recovered (pl. 2:12–13, fig. 2.10, and see the charts).[28] The fragments pl. 2.12:1–5 are probably parts of one Attic black-figured krater, to be dated about 500 BC. A chariot scene is portrayed; this is a very common subject on large black-figured vessels. The driver's arm holding the reins is shown in pl. 2.12:1. A fragment from the rounded upper body of the vase (pl. 2.12:2) depicts parts of two horses' heads, one behind the other. The incised lines of pl. 2.12:3–4 are probably parts of garments, but the fragments are very worn and hard to interpret. A male figure in front of the forelegs of a horse is depicted in pl. 12:5 (cf. Toombs and Wright 1961: 53, fig. 20).

These fragments represent a vessel of late black-figured technique. The incisions are particularly poor, and the schematic branch-and-vine are typical of late vessels. The clay is typically Attic red. The figures and designs are in black paint with some use of purple.

Similar Attic black-figured column kraters are dated between 550 and 490 BC (see CVA III H e, pls. 164–89). Chariot scenes occur frequently (pls. 169:1–2, 170:5–6, 171:2–3, et passim). The schematic branch-and-vine filling ornaments are common particularly in the later vases dated about 500–490 BC (cf. especially pls. 182:8, 183:3, 185:2, 187:1, and 188:1).

An early red-figured piece, pl. 2.13:1, dates a little before the black-figured krater in pl. 2.12, and is probably from the latter part of the sixth century BC. Part of a chariot wheel is shown behind the tails of horses. The relief lines are good. The tails as well as the chariot wheel are partly reserved (left unpainted) as in red-figured style, but purple paint and incised lines are added in characteristic black-figured technique. The piece represents the transition from black-figured to red-figured technique on these large vessels. The fragment with two hands of a chariot driver (pl. 2.13:2) is undoubtedly part of the same vessel.[29] There is similar paint and

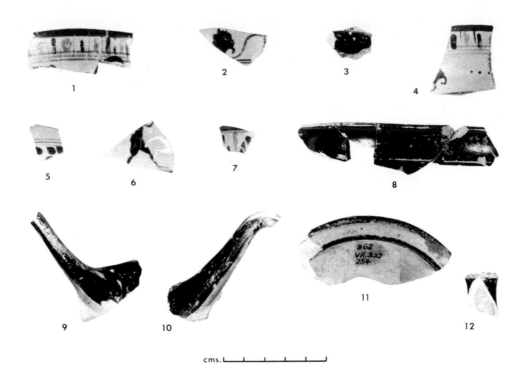

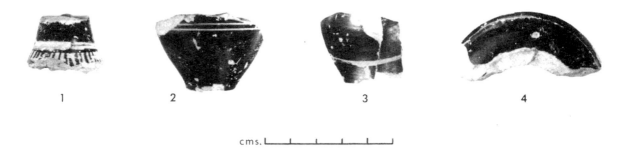

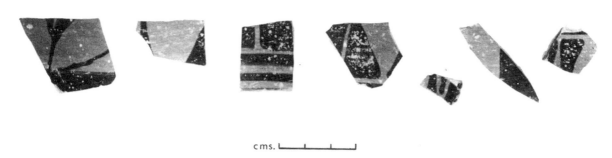

FIG. 2.11 *Attic cup fragments: (1) B60 4625, (2) B60 5874, (3) B60 6894, (4) B62 303, (5) B60 4626, (6) B60 5125, (7) B60 4955, (8) B62 215, (9) B60 1283, (10) B62 593, (11) B62 254, (12) lid handle B60 6270.*

FIG. 2.12 *Attic lekythos fragments: (1) B60 3873, (2) B60 2764, (3) B60 2759/4673, (4) B60 5105.*

FIG. 2.13 *Black-on-brown fragments: left to right, B62 686, B60 5878, B60 6168, B62 686b, B62 1954, B62 1955, B60 6167.*

ware and comparable carefully incised lines and use of purple paint. Another small fragment (B62 VII.4.136 found on IVB floor 1521) with black-relief lines and purple paint was probably part of the same scene.

An outline drawing with relief lines, pl. 2.13:3, probably portrays a soldier's cuirass. Since it is drawn in outline on red ground, with the lower part of the body in black, it should be classed with the black-figured pottery. In the red-figured period this type of cuirass is replaced by the leather cuirass. Another example of the cuirass rendered like gleaming metal is presented by Graef (1909–1933: pl. 36, no. 611a).

The latest fragment in red-figure technique portrays an arm of a dancing figure with castanets (pl. 2.13:4). The edges of the figure are not sharp as in the other examples. The piece dates to about 480 BC, possibly even as late as the second quarter of the fifth century.

The remaining fragments in plate 2.13 are parts of black- or red-figured kraters, possibly from the same vessels as those described above. A small piece of the lower rim (pl. 2.13:5) is from a black-figured krater with the common ivy pattern. Plate 2.13:6 probably represents the horizontal part of the same rim. (See some of the references above, which illustrate whole kraters, for the form of this rim.) On the side of this fragment – not shown – is a part of the ivy leaf pattern of the exterior lower rim, like in pl. 2.13:5. A similar combination of patterns is shown in CVA: pl. 173:1.

Another rim fragment, pl. 2.13:7, depicts carelessly made circles (deteriorated ivy leaves) on the lower exterior side and poorly made lotus buds on the upper side. An exact parallel is found in the "petit cratère à colonnettes," CVA: pl. 187:2, which dates to 490–480 BC. A rim fragment, pl. 2.13:8, with good relief lines and a band of purple paint is perhaps part of the same red-figured vessel, pl. 2.13:1–2, above.

There are a number of fragments of the lower part of a large Attic krater. Two fragments of the heavy foot were recorded (pl. 2.13:10, nos. 5309 and 1536); they have a band of purple paint about 2 cm wide at the very bottom. From just above the foot on the lower body of the same vessel are the fragments pl. 2.13:9, nos. 1123 and 5291A.

Remains of a narrow purple band at the top of the foot, separating it from the lower body, is visible on all four fragments. A third base fragment, no. VII.6.185 5065, is also from the same krater. The black-figured column kraters noted above similar to pl. 2.12 also have heavy feet and lower bodies with rays in reserve (especially CVA: pls. 166:5, 169:1, 171:3, and 178:1–2), although the reserved rays in the Balâṭah vessel are narrower and less carefully made.

Other fragments of black- or red-figured kraters include a heavy base from a different vessel, pl. 2.13:11, and a different style base, pl. 2.13:12. A fragment picked out of the dump, pl. 13:2.13, is similar to pl. 2.13:6 but less definite in outline. A purple and black fragment, B60 VII.5.86 3982, is similar in style to krater decorations described above; fragments with incised lines include B60 VII.3.152 6271 and B62 VII.1.73 998. Fragment pl. 2.13:14 is from a krater handle, and there is another similar fragment (no. B62 IX.4.14 7). Finally, pl.2.13:15 may be the rim of an amphora.

Cups

Assorted cup fragments are illustrated in pl. 2.14 and fig. 2.11:1–11. Connecting fragments of a Cassel cup and other fragments certainly from the same vessel were recovered from Strata IV and IIIB fills (pl. 2.14:1–4). Cassel cups are a variant type of band-cups in the "Little Master Cup" classification according to Beazley (1932: 191–92).[30] In lip-cups, the lips are clearly marked off from the bowl, but in band-cups the lip passes gradually into the bowl. Both have handles, feet, and lower parts of the bowls that are glazed black.[31] The outside lip of the lip-cup is reserved (left red), whereas the band-cup is black, and the space between the handles in the lip-cup is either figured or left plain; sometimes it has only the artist's signature. In the band-cups, figured decoration reaches from handle to handle. Cassel cups have the shape of the band-cup but different decoration. Bands of patterns or floral and other designs cover the lip and the bowl, without the black glaze over the lower part of the body or below the rim. (For examples of lip-cups, a band-cup, and a Cassel cup, see Folsom 1975: pls. 8a–d; and the listings of Cassel cups in Beazley and Payne

1929: 271 and Beazley 1932:192.) As in the Balâṭah vessel, occasionally the handle zone has a pattern of little animals or people in silhouette (pl. 2.14:2, 3). In a letter to the writer, J. D. Beazley wrote:

> The silhouette palmettes are frequent in this class of cup. The decoration is usually of patterns only, but some of the Cassel cups have a few figures of animals or people; a cup in Taranto has a cock in silhouette between mock inscriptions, and another in Taranto has [a] sphinx between mere dot inscriptions like yours, below a row of tongues.[32]

An ordinary band-cup or lip-cup, which shows part of a naked male and the forelegs of a white horse, is represented in pl. 2.14:5. Plate 2.14:6 is from a "pattern band-cup," and pl. 14:7 has the typical reserved exterior lip of a lip-cup.

Fragments of a black-glazed kylix are represented in pl. 2.14:8. This is an early type of cup dating to the sixth and early fifth centuries BC (Sparkes and Talcott 1970: 109, pl. 25 and fig. 6:562–79). The concave lip is usually set off sharply from the body. Other rim fragments of the same or similar kylikes are listed in the chart.

Kylix handle fragments could be from either "Little Master cups" or black-glazed kylikes (pl. 2.14:9–10). These are black-glazed on the outside and edges, but reserved underneath. Plate 2.14:11 could be a base from one of these types of cups.

An Attic-type fragment of the Corinthian skyphos is a deep cup with no foot or a low foot and two handles (pl. 2.14:12). The Attic skyphos differs from the Corinthian by its thicker wall and completely black glaze; Corinthian skyphoi have areas of brown glaze. The Attic type begins about the middle of the sixth century BC, displaying a single curve from rim to foot (Sparkes and Talcott 1970:

84, pls. 16–17 and fig. 4:334–54). Plate 2.14:13–14 may represent the heavy feet of skyphoi.

A small fragment of a lid knob for a pylix (toilet box) or a perfume container is shown in pl. 15:1 and fig. 2.11:12. It is black-glazed with a black-on-red design on its top.

Lekythoi

A number of fragments of black-figured lekythoi were found (pl. 2.15:2–6; fig. 2.12). They include the neck of one (pl. 2.15:2), part of the rounded body of another (pl. 2.15:3), fragments from just above the base, and base fragments (pl. 2.15:4–6). These and other lekythos pieces (see chart) were very fragmentary and mainly from unstratified contexts. They probably can be dated with the black-figured lekythoi, which appear about 500–480 BC (cf. Folsom 1975: pls. 12c, 13b, 13c, 14a, 14b).

Other Fragments

Small sherds of black-on-red patterns (cf. pl. 2.15:7–8 and see chart) may have traces of decoration from kraters, amphorae, cups or lekythoi. Plate 2.15:7, as well as other listed black-and-red fragments and some of the handle fragments, could belong to the banded cups as illustrated from Dor (Stern et al. 1995b: fig. 3.6–7); many of these date from the late sixth century and into the fifth century (pp. 93–95). One or more vessels of black-on-brown ware or black-tan fragments may be earlier and East Greek (pl. 2.15:9–12 and fig. 2.13), but they were not well enough represented to be certain. The many small black-glazed fragments that were recovered throughout the fills could be background parts of red- and black-figured kraters, amphorae, and cups, or parts of black-glazed kylikes and skyphoi.

NOTES

1   See Chap. 1, final section, concerning the publication of the pottery and the pottery charts for full discussion of the way the pottery is presented and the listings in the charts. For convenience, it is summarized here:

Representations of the various pottery forms (types and subtypes) are illustrated in the plates.

Usually, a number of examples are illustrated representing the stratum in which they appear. They are listed in an accompanying chart by stratum; included are some sherds that are not in closed loci but are important for comparative purposes (indicated by "cf." in the lists). Some unstratified examples are shown or listed; this is because they are fairly complete examples that help define the type, or because they are from Fields I, II, or III and indicate the chronological occupation in these Fields. Note that the charts also list sherds of the types or subtypes that are not illustrated in the plates, these also listed by stratum. The lists for each type present most of the stratified pottery available for study; if not all the pottery excavated is listed, what is listed does suggest the proportional representation for the sherd type.

As mentioned in Chapter 1, in the charts, unless otherwise noted, Area and Basket are from 1960 for Field VII, except for areas 21–23, which were not excavated until 1962; 1957 for Field II and III (unless 1968 is indicated for Field II); 1962 for Field IX. For Field I the year is noted: "56" = 1956, "57" = 1957, "64 = 1964. Sometimes the charts note the year for a group of listed sherds.

2   Note also that some wares from the excavations of Jerusalem are dated to the early part of the Persian period (Tushingham 1985: 33).

3   After study of all the Balâṭah material, the total of seventeen is the most probable count for these handles. Campbell and P. Lapp suggest there was one in 1957 from a Middle Bronze context (P. Lapp 1963: n. 24), but a closer examination places this handle in the Middle Bronze Age. It is doubtful that a fourth handle from 1962 has this stamp (IX.3.71 197).

4   See also Zorn 2003: fig. 13: x32. In Zorn's reexamination of the Tell en-Naṣbeh excavations, he has distinguished specifically two four-room houses, dating from 586 BC to near the end of the fifth century (p. 428), and two important cisterns (p. 429). Zorn's dating for this Babylonian–Early Persian period is in general agreement with Wampler's earlier publication (pp. 429, 444).

5   These types should not be confused with Stern's type B4, discussed below with the consideration of ledged and lug-handled bowls and kraters.

6   Numerous unstratified sherds of this form, as well as the next (wedged kraters), are listed because they are unique types probably dating to the Stratum V period.

7   For stratum dates at Dor, see Stern et al. 1995a: 275, as well as the collation of absolute dates, chap. 6.

8   Zertal's first volume of *The Manasseh Hill Country Survey, The Shechem Syncline* (to the north and north west of Shechem) "covers 11 landscape units of the syncline's interior, whose overall area is about 400 square km" (Zertal 2004: 34). His results seem to indicate that "during this period settlement in the Shechem syncline flourished in an unprecedented way" (p. 59). The reading of the Persian pottery seems to be based mainly on the Persian mortaria found throughout the area, a common bowl with a thick straight-walled bowl and flat base, and jars "easily recognized by their thickened ring rim" (p. 44). Below, we note parallels to the Persian mortaria, but it is difficult to classify his straight-walled bowls and jars with "ring rims." In any case, these are survey finds, and although they speak to the history and economy of the region (p. 60), since it is not stratified material they cannot contribute to our typology. If some of these many settlements are excavated in the future, the contributions may be significant.

9   Zorn continues to query the sherds Aharoni first published from the floor of the courtyard of the Stratum VA citadel at Ramat Raḥel (1956b: 142–43, pl. 13B). As pointed out in N. Lapp 1981: 94, Aharoni later dated material on these floors the same as mixed debris, particularly in reference to the royal jar handles found there (Aharoni 1964: 34). The impressed ware found with these does not particularly point to an early sixth-century date, as Zorn thinks they might (2001: 692).

When the Tell el-Fûl pottery was published, it was thought that some of the chevron- or wedge-designed sherds might belong to Iron II, particularly those with burnishing (N. Lapp 1981: 94). However, all of the fragments cited are from find spots that could extend at least slightly beyond the end of Iron II. The fine burnishing was considered to be a reason to date to Iron II, and the fine quality even suggested importation. Stern notes this distinction in burnishing, which appears on other vessels early in the Persian period, a wide light-colored burnish that "apparently continued the Iron Age tradition of burnish though it is clearly distinguished from it in its colour" (Stern 1982: 133).

10   To be particularly noted is the holemouth krater from a disturbed cistern at Qadum in Samaria (Stern and Magen 1984). In addition to the wedged design on the rim and below, there are painted pictures and an inscription. (There is at least one other sherd from this site with the wedged design, fig. 9:1.) Since the agreed date for the use of this decoration is the late sixth–fifth century BC, and there are close parallels of the cistern material to the pottery of Wadi ed-Daliyeh (see jars, jugs, and cooking pots) dated to the very end of the Persian period, this can hardly be considered a "homogeneous assemblage belonging to the Persian period" with a date in the fifth century BC, particularly the second half (p. 24). With the early Persian wedged ware, Attic ware of the fifth century (p. 24), and the later Wadi ed-Daliyeh types, the group can hardly be that homogeneous. It should also be noted that the grooved rims and handles on several vessels from the Qadum site (fig. 6:1–5) are an Early Hellenistic type at Shechem (see Chap. 3, below); the Qadum examples probably belong late in the fourth century.

11   Note also the bowl bases with wedged marks on the interior (Herr et al. 1991: 242, fig. 8.22:22–23). The numerous examples of wedged bases at Balâṭah were assigned to Stratum VI, perhaps contemporary with those from ʿUmayri. One is also published from Stratum IV at Saidiyeh (Pritchard 1985: fig. 16:14). Zertal assigned those found in his Manasseh survey to Iron III, the late Iron Age (Zertal 2004: 44).

12   Stern, without the benefit of Blakely and Bennett's studies, considered them East Greek imports; others consider them Cypriot (1995b: 53). Petrographic examination of the mortaria from Meṣad Ḥashavyahu, which were of the early flat-based type, showed that they were probably produced in Cyprus (Fantalkin 2001: 80).

13   Alternate suggestions are mentioned by Fantalkin 2001: 80 n. 44.

14   When the Stratum VI pottery corpus is studied, it will be interesting to know if more of these appear.

15   Unfortunately, this study has not been completed. It is still hoped that the visibly discerned fabric groups may be examined by non-destructive radiography. The remarks here are from an unpublished paper by Glanzman after the initial phase of his study.

16   Pls. 2.8:1, 4–6, 8–9, 13–14, 16, 18–19, 21–22; 2.9:2, 9, and listed nos. 269 and 499. For the other sherds analyzed see the Hellenistic mortaria in the next chapter.

17   In determining methods of manufacture, the reconstructed or whole profile forms were very important. In addition to pl. 2.8:1, Glanzman considers Hellenistic fragments with rim and base (Chap. 3, Hellenistic mortaria, pls. 3.1:22 and 3.2:8). See discussions: Glanzman 1993: 23–26, lab. nos. B–21, B–23, and B–26.

18   Glanzman assigned all the Balâṭah Persian mortaria to his morphotypes 1–5 and 17, which were considered related (1993: 24).

19   Mention should be made of the abundance of Persian mortarium fragments Zertal found in his Manasseh hill country survey, probably his main identifying feature for Persian occupation (Zertal 2004: 44). From many examples, typical mortarium rims include figs 34.7, 143.1, 172.5, 201.11, 260.1, 3; high ring bases, 32.7, 88.3, 181.2, 352.4; flat bases, 198.7, 214.6, 222.11, 352.5.

20   P. Lapp thought the form might have persisted through most of the Persian period because of a form found at Taanach, but note remarks N. Lapp: 1981: 96 and other parallels discussed there. It should also be noted that this is not just a southern form (Gitin 1990: 229), as it is well attested at Balâṭah.

21   Balâṭah lamps pl. 2.11:4 and listed sherd 5555 have remains of burnishing on their slips. Slips as well as the burnishings were worn and spotty, and it is very possible that slips on other lamps were burnished. This is in contradiction to Stern's claim that burnished lamps are known only from coastal sites (Stern et al. 1995b: 67).

22   Wright (1965: 171) mentions that the Balâṭah lamp pl. 2.11:5 (object #141) was found with a silver coin of Alexander the Great (# 43) on the lowest Hellenistic floor. This does not necessarily date the lamp to this time, as it could be earlier (*contra* Stern 1982: 128).

23   In Transjordan, Herr notes that the thinned-walled lamps which come from ʿUmayri are similar to the Persian lamps of western Palestine, suggesting they may begin somewhat earlier in the east (1989: 309, fig. 19.17:15–16; also Herr et al. 1991: fig. 8.22:15–17; 1997: fig. 3.18:4); Saidiyeh (Pritchard 1985: fig. 16:18); and Heshbon (Lugenbeal and Sauer 1972: 59; no. 543 [?]). Most of these are fragmentary and their flatness is hard to determine. None have the wide rim common in western Palestine.

24   Personal letter from William P. Anderson, The University Museum, Philadelphia, PA, dated March 26, 1985.

25   Joseph Greene (personal correspondence of April 4, 2007) has called my attention to a two-spouted metal lamp in the Cyprus exhibit in the Semitic Museum

(No. 1995) at Harvard University and a number of similar lamps from Cyprus, both bronze and ceramic, as well as an unpublished example from the Carthage tophet excavated in 1979 used as a lid to an urn (reg. no. 6029). They have been dated from 750 BC to the fourth century (the Carthage example).

26 It is possible that the high-based lamp from Taanach (P. Lapp 1970: fig. 5:17), along with a cooking pot fragment (fig. 5:15), should be dated with earlier material in the cistern (cf. Rast 1978: 50, fig. 82:5, 3; cooking pot fig 84:4 also seems to be of a type that may have ended about 500 BC [see cooking pots, above]).

27 Note that at Dor, although they have late sixth-century imported forms, a date for the beginning of Stratum VI at the beginning of the fifth century seems to be preferred (Stern et al. 1995b: 272, 275). See also the study by Stewart and Martin (2005). The difference between this site and Balâṭah should be emphasized. Dor is a coastal site and numerous imports can be expected from trade and its seaport activity. Its Persian period occupation was lengthy. On the other hand, Balâṭah's inland location, the short duration of its Persian occupation, and the relatively small amount of Attic pottery limit the dates that can be assigned to Stratum V.

28 These fragments were first published by the writer in Wright 1965: 238–41, fig. 113. As I did there, I express my appreciation to the late Dorothy Hill, formerly of the Walters Art Gallery, Baltimore, Maryland, for her study and suggestions concerning these fragments. The drawings of the figured ware indicate what was probably represented, not just the paint or glaze remaining on the fragments.

29 Pl. 2.13:2 was from IVB fill, excavated in 1962 in Field VII. No information was recorded about pl. 2.13:1, except that it came from Field VII in 1962.

30 For examples of lip-cups, a band-cup, and a Cassel cup, see Folsom 1975: pls. 8a–d; see also the listings of Cassel cups in Beazley and Payne 1929: 271 and Beazley 1932: 192.

31 The term "glaze" for these wares is not strictly correct, but is retained here as the traditional term used for this bright glossy slip. As Rotroff writes, "The conventional term 'glaze' has been retained for black and red wares, despite the fact that the glossy slip in question is not, properly speaking, a glaze. Its color, degree of shine, and preservation are mentioned for both Attic and imported pieces. The term 'slip' is used for the duller surface application on light-ground wares" (1997: 241).

32 Personal letter to the author, September 1963.

Chapter 3

The Hellenistic Pottery
Strata IV–I

The Hellenistic pottery, that assigned to Strata IV–I, is presented by type in a manner similar to the Persian pottery from Stratum V. The Hellenistic occupation was much longer and more widespread; consequently, there is a greater quantity of pottery to present. As in Chapter 2, there is a discussion of each type and the various subtypes. Plates that present the sherds in profile and section, accompanied by a chart that has descriptions for the illustrated sherds and those of other similar sherds, are found in the plates section of this volume. The pottery is illustrated and listed by stratum, with that from Stratum IV first and significant unstratified sherds last.[1]

JARS

The stratified and unstratified Hellenistic jars and jar fragments that could be reconstructed indicate that Hellenistic storage jars at Balâṭah were cylindrical or bag-shaped (fig. 3:1). Totally missing were conical jars with a sharp angle from the side walls to the flat shoulder found in the early Hellenistic stratum at Keisan (Briend 1980: pl. 7:1–5), with parallels at Shiqmona and the end of the Persian period (p. 105). This latter form is a coastal and northern form, and does not appear in central and southern Palestine. Tell Keisan also has the common cylindrical jar, contemporary with the conical jars.

The only certain base type is the common Hellenistic rounded base (see pl. 3:13) with the interior spiral ending or smudge where the clay was cut (P. Lapp 1961: 14; Corpus 11.9). There were no late type ring or footed bases that could be assigned to jars of the Hellenistic period (cf. P. Lapp 1961: Corpus 13, 14). Many jar rims, however, are strong chronological indicators. The great number of jars present in the Hellenistic occupation at Balâṭah should be noted, as jar rims, handles, and body sherds constitute a large proportion of the Hellenistic sherds recovered.

Type A. Rims with exterior lower Point

Jar rim type A represents the earliest Hellenistic type, and it was the most common form that appeared in Strata IVB , IVA and IV fill (pls. 3.1, 3.2). The characteristic feature is a rim that curves or turns to an exterior lower point which then returns to meet the neck at another point. This is sometimes in the form of an undercut or crescent, a characteristic of early Hellenistic jars that has previously been noted (N. Lapp 1964: 17). The form had its beginning late in the Persian period as found in the Wâdī ed-Dâliyeh cave clearance (N. Lapp 1974: 31, pl. 19:1–4), and it is basically a Stratum IV form. Many rim type A forms are from Stratum III fills (note the many examples of subtypes A-2 and A-3 beneath IIIB structures in Loci

1216, 1217, 1220–1224, 1226), or they may belong to IV occupation (note particularly Locus 3 on the pavement in the Field I 1956 excavations, subtype A-1 and A-3). Others found beneath IIIB and IIIA surfaces and structures could belong to Stratum IV or Stratum III, but probably their production had ceased and been replaced by other types soon after the middle of the third century BC.

In the first sub-group (A-1, pl. 3.1:1–8) the jar shoulder slopes up to an interior rounded point or turn, and then the rim rounds out and down to a lower exterior point and back to the shoulder. Sub-group A-2 (pl. 3.1:9–23) usually has a short neck that turns out to an upper point and then rounds down to the lower point and into the neck. The almost completely reconstructed jar pl. 3.1:12 has a variant grooved neck, and it can be determined from the preserved fragments that it did not have handles. A third sub-type, A-3 (pl. 3.2) has a more rounded rim with no upper points before turning down to the exterior lower point and then into the neck.

Type B. Short Neck to rounded Point at Rim, then rounded out and down and into Neck

As the Hellenistic period progressed, in the most common Hellenistic jar type the shoulder slopes in or up forming a short neck, then the rim rounds out and down to meet the neck at a point or angle. The exterior lower point has disappeared. Some have an upper point, often rounded itself (type B, pl. 3.3). If the rounded point is at the top of the neck or shoulder, it is perhaps related to the first sub-group, A-1, of type A above. Most of the rounded rims that appear in Stratum IV, particularly IVB and IVB fill, have this inner rounded point (pl. 3.3:1–7). Later, when the rim turns out (pl. 3.3: 9–11, 13–14, 18–19) and sometimes has a rounded top point (cf. N.

FIG. 3.1   Reconstructed storage jar B57 2117.

FIG. 3.2   Reconstructed storage jar B57 2123, with potter's mark.

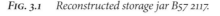

Lapp 1964: 17), it is transitional to the characteristic Hellenistic collar rim (see below).

Type C. Rim curves out, down, and into Neck at lower Point or Angle

A rounded rim that curves out and then down and in to meet the usually short neck at a point or angle is the most popular Hellenistic jar rim in the third century BC (type C, pls. 3.4–3.6, figs. 3.1, 3.2). It may form from a shoulder slope (pl. 3.4:1, 10), but there is usually a relatively short neck. Some rims have begun to lengthen (pl. 3.4:4, 8), which may be another development toward the collar rim. Plate 3.4:6 shows the rim folded over, probably the way all these rims were formed (cf. type B rims, pl. 3.3:11, 19). This rounded rim occurs first in Stratum IVA at Balâṭah, although it appears in the Wâdī ed-Dâliyeh cave material dated closely to the end of the Persian period and transitional to the Hellenistic period (N. Lapp 1974: pl. 18:5). At Balâṭah it is very popular through the third century (Strata IIIB and IIIA). A number of these rounded rims were found

FIG. 3.4   *Jar sherds* in situ *on Stratum II Floor 7099 in the Hellenistic House.*

FIG. 3.3   *Reconstructed storage jar B56 #15, which held delphiniform lamp, B56 #16*

on IIIA floors or surfaces (L. 1203, 1802–1508, 1227, and 1703, listed under Stratum II) and, although they were not sealed by Stratum III constructions, they probably belong to the IIIA occupation.

Note the potter's mark on the handle of pl. 3.4:15 and that on the side of the jar pl. 3.5:1 and fig. 3.2.

A variant of type C (labeled Cv) is rounded and meets the shoulder or neck smoothly without a point or angle (pl. 3.7). An early form appears in Stratum IV with an inner upper point (pl. 3.7:1–7), and these may be related to subtype A-1.

Type D. Collar Rim

An everted rim leading to a point, then lengthened to a lower point or angle has become known as the Hellenistic collar rim (type D). Those that are slightly rounded or curved (type D-1, pl. 3.8) may be related to the rounded rims above and transitional to the usual collar type, which is flattened (D–2, pl. 3.9 and fig. 3.3) or depressed (D–3, pl. 3.10). A variant of the collar rim has inner and outer up-

per points, becoming almost a squared rim (type Dv, pl. 3.11). Although there may be occasional earlier collar forms, they have become common by the last quarter of the third century BC (Stratum IIIA). By the second quarter of the second century BC they had replaced the popular third century rounded rim (cf. N. Lapp 1964: 21). Jar types D–2 and D–3 were in the assembly of jar sherds in the destruction layer over Stratum II Floor 7099 in Field II (fig. 3.4).

Jar Handles and Bases

Jar handles (pl. 3.12 and fig. 3.5) are vertically placed from the shoulder to the side wall of the storage jar (see reconstructed jars in pls. 3.1–3.13), usually curved in what has sometimes been called an "ear shape" (Gitin 1990: 83, type 170 P, Q). In early Hellenistic times, they are usually well made and round or oval in cross section, and their attachments are fairly neat (pl. 3.12:1–8). Sometimes one side is somewhat pointed (pl. 3.12:9–11), probably reflecting how the handle was constructed. Handles with a central ridge are fairly common (pl. 3.12:12–17), particularly in Stratum III, although the ridge is not a typical Hellenistic characteristic as it is in Iron II. More flattened handles that are carelessly constructed and some with very poor

FIG. 3.5 *Jar handles from the 1957 campaign with rounded to oval sections (above 82 and 815) and carelessly made handles (below 293 and 294).*

attachment appear as early as Stratum IIIB (pl. 3.12:18–21). The sloppy handle attachments are characteristic of later Hellenistic times, although some handles are still neatly formed.

The typical storage jar of Hellenistic times had a rounded base, and the interior spiral is an indication of its formation (pl. 3.13). These are found throughout the Hellenistic period.

Comparative Material for Jar Types A–D

Many Balâṭah storage jars are similar to the closely dated Wâdī ed-Dâliyeh large cylindrical jars belonging to the end of the Persian period (N. Lapp 1974: 31). The earliest Balâṭah group, type A, is represented by the majority of the Wâdī ed-Dâliyeh jars that have the undercut back to the neck (N. Lapp 1974: pls. 18:1–4; 19:3; 20:2, 3). The rounded rim with a rounded upper point, Balâṭah type B, is represented by one jar (N. Lapp 1974: pl. 20:6), but

type C, the fully rounded rim, is well represented (N. Lapp 1974: pls. 18:5, 19:1, 2, 20:1, 5, 7). Type C is not found at Balâṭah until Stratum IVA, but the tradition obviously goes back to the late Persian period if not earlier.

At Keisan there is early Hellenistic material (Period 2b, 380–312 BC, and 2a, 312–250 BC; Briend and Humbert 1980:27), but the trench (mainly F. 2003) from which most of the material came is not phased. Rounded rims, Balâṭah types B and C, are represented at Keisan (pl. 8:1, 1a, 1b, 1d, 3, 7). Balâṭah type A is also represented (pl. 8:1c, 1e, 1f). The everted, more elongated rim may be represented (pl. 8:1h and 4) and belongs with the phase 2a material.[2]

At Samaria, rims from the Hellenistic Fort Wall deposit (pre-150 BC; Kenyon 1957: 220) represent both Balâṭah type A (Kenyon 1957: fig. 42:8–11), some with undercut reminiscent of Early Hellenistic forms, and type C (fig. 42:12–14), more representative of the third and second centuries. From the theater excavations, dated early in the Hellenistic period (Zayadin 1966: 53–54), come some of the early Hellenistic rims, Balâṭah type A (Zayadin 1966: pl. 27:2, 6, 7, 9, 10), and others with rounded rims, Balâṭah types B and C (Zayadin 1966: pl. 27:1, 3–5, 8).

At Gezer the rounded or "bulbous" jar rim appears in the first Hellenistic stratum, Stratum III, dated to the mid-third century BC, and "continues as a dominant jar form through the mid-second century horizon" (Gitin 1990: 238). The mid–third-century forms, type 159, pl. 32:1–4, are related to Balâṭah types B and C, but the forms illustrated after the third century appear everted and lead to an upper exterior point (pl. 36:3–5), similar to Balâṭah types B and D-1. The other common Early Hellenistic form is everted, with an oblong rim section (Gitin 1990: Type 160A, pl. 33:3, 4, of Balâṭah D-1 type) and a "triangular" rim curved outward (Type 160D, pl. 33:5). The latter, with its "collar" rim (Balâṭah type D-2), is the dominant form through the first half of the second century (Gitin 1990: 238, pls. 34:14–16; 36:6, 7, 9). The Gezer rounded and oblong rims (Gitin's Types 160A and 160B) have been replaced by the "triangular" rims by the beginning of the second century. Gitin then distinguishes a "flanged" rim (Type 161, pls.

34:17–22; 36:8, 12–18), appearing in the mid-second century, Stratum IIC, and continuing to the mid-first century (p. 239), which is similar to the Balâṭah type D–3. He separates out less prominent flanges that continue into the first century BC (Pls. 39: 8, 9; 41: 7, 8; 43:19), all of which would be considered collar rims at Balâṭah and type D-3.

At Beth-zur in the Hellenistic Stratum II (175–165 BC) and Stratum I (140–100 BC), the jar rims are everted and lead to an upper point, Balâṭah type D. The "rounded" rims of Stratum II (P. and N. Lapp 1968: 71, fig. 22: 1, 3) are close to Balâṭah D-1, while the squared rims (fig. 22:2, 6) can be compared to D–2, and the elongated rims (fig. 22: 4, 5), which also appear in Beth-zur Stratum I (140–100 BC), are of the Balâṭah D–3 type. At Bethel, where the first Hellenistic phase was dated ca. 200–160 BC, the rounded rim was already lacking (P. Lapp 1968a: 77–78). From Bethel phase one, rims pl. 68:1–17 are of the Balâṭah D–2 type, pl. 68:18–25 are of the Balâṭah D–3 type, and pl. 69:1 can be compared to type D-1. At Tell el-Fûl, where the main Hellenistic period is IVB (135–100 BC), most of the rims are of Balâṭah type D. Some of the rounded rims can still be classed best with Balâṭah type C, although they are all out-turned and tend to lengthen (N. Lapp 1981: pl. 73:24–35) and "are either already related to the square rims or are a varied assortment of dying forms" (N. Lapp 1981: 102). The heavier third-century-BC rims and forms with an undercut are missing (p. 102). The "narrow-profiled collared" rims are the most popular in Period IVB at Tell el-Fûl (N. Lapp 1981: 102, pl. 72; cf. Balâṭah type D–3). There are also "squared" rims (pl. 73:1–22), which can be compared to Balâṭah type D–2, and some of the rounded rims (pl. 73:27–34) are similar to Balâṭah type D-1.[3]

Jar rims of all Balâṭah types, A–D, come from the Jerusalem Early Jewish fills, where there is no distinction in date (Tushingham 1985: figs. 17:23–39, 41; 18:1–17).

Jar rims from Transjordan are published from ʿAraq el-ʿEmir (N. Lapp 1983: 66, 68): type A with slight undercut (fig. 30:1), type C, out-turned rounded rims (figs. 30:2–3; 31:19–22, 32:35–39), and type D, those flattened or depressed (figs 30:5; 31:23–24; 32:40–49). At Heshbon, an out-turned rounded rim (type C) is published (Sauer 1973: 12,

fig. 1:2) and there are lengthened rims of type D from the Roman Forum on the Amman citadel (Hadidi 1970: pl. 3:6–7). These are all part of Late Hellenistic occupations. In the Pella excavation of various Late Hellenistic areas, jar rim fragments principally of type D are published (along with some rim types that belong to the first century BC and Early Roman times): the fortress on Jebel Sartaba (McNicoll, Smith, and Hennessy 1982: 67, pl. 127), the West Cut (McNicoll, Smith, and Hennessy 1982: 73, fig. 131:5), and Plot XXIII A (Edwards et al. 1990: fig. 10:6, 7; McNicoll et al. 1992: pl. 76:6–10).

Rhodian Jars

Two fragments of Rhodian handles appear in Stratum IIIB (pl. 3.14:1–2), and although these are not inscribed, the type is easily recognized by its shape and fine ware; Rhodian handles are present in the third century throughout the Middle East. The other fragments were generally from fills or unstratified contexts, except for one from the Field II Hellenistic House Room 1 Stratum I occupation (pl. 3.14:6). The end of the second century is not too late for its presence, although it may well be a relic from earlier times. The three inscribed handles (pl. 3.14:5, 9; fig. 3.6) are from unstratified contexts or contexts which are not clear. Professor William Fulco has provided us with descriptions of these handles.[4]

Handle B57 #167

This Rhodian-type handle (pl. 3.14:5; fig. 3.6a) is inscribed with the eponym of Theudōros, thus:

$$\text{ΕΠΙ ΘΕΥ}$$
$$\text{ΔΩΡΟΥ}$$

This type is usually dated 300–100 BC. This name is known from other sources, and is listed in Grace 1953: 123, no. 95, Hiller von Gaertringen 1931, no. 160, and Nilsson 1909: no. 238.

Handle B68 #1

The eponym on this Rhodian-type jar handle (pl. 3.14:9; fig. 3.6b) is ΚΛΕΩΝΥΜ[ΟΣ]. After ΕΠΙ, the

FIG. 3.6 *Rhodian fragments. Base B57 1222 and inscribed handle #167 (a); inscribed handles (b) B68 #1 and (c) B64 #513.*

abbreviated form would have been in the genitive: ΚΛΕΩΝΥΜ[ΟΥ].

The second word is surely ΔΕΥΤΕΡΟΥ, "second." What is here taken as Υ at first glance looks like a Χ, but if it were the latter, the lower left stroke would be angled out more and reach the bottom. This stroke is apparently just an elongation of the upper-left stroke of the Υ. The awkward spacing is not unusual on Rhodian-type handles, an effort to fill the line.

The final word is ΠΑΝΑΜΟΥ. ΠΑΝΑΜΟΥ designates a month of the year attested in many inscriptions.[5] The relationship of ΔΕΥΤΕΡΟΥ to the preceding or following word is not clear. The entire stamp reads:

ΕΠΙ ΚΛΕΩΝΥΜ

ΔΕΥΤΕΡΟΥ

ΠΑΝΑΜΟΥ

This type of handle usually dates c. 300–100 BC. There is no exact parallel to this particular inscription in the literature.

Handle B68 #513 (fig. 3:6c) is broken and unclear and could not be interpreted.

JUGS

No complete jugs were recovered. From the few large reconstructed fragments and the rims, handles, and bases from stratified contexts, it seems that the common jug throughout the Hellenistic period had a relatively wide mouth and neck, a piriform body, and often a concave base. Late Hellenistic jugs of this form are known from Beth-zur (cf. P. Lapp 1961: 15), and these were apparently of an established Hellenistic tradition. Note the late Persian jugs from Wâdī ed-Dâliyeh (N. Lapp 1974: pl. 21). The larger reconstructed Balâṭah jug fragments were from unstratified contexts, but the stratified rims particularly and the handles and bases to some extent do indicate typological development through the third and second centuries BC. There is sound stratigraphic evidence for several types, and the larger unstratified fragments are presented with the corresponding forms.

As noted above, most rims indicate wide-mouthed jugs. Heavier jug sherds are difficult to distinguish from jars, and confusion in classification is very possible (see also Gitin 1990: 242);[6] but usually a jug rim may be recognized by its lighter ware and smaller diameter, even if there is no handle attachment preserved. Earlier jugs tend to be heavier (note the heavier Wâdī ed-Dâliyeh jugs [N. Lapp 1974: pl. 21]), and the tendency for them to be made of thinner ware increases during the course of the second century (cf. P. Lapp 1961: 15, 157, Observation 2).

Type a. Plain Rim, narrow-necked

A rather plain rim with an inside upper point before rounding down smoothly to the neck appeared only in the early Hellenistic strata and mainly in fills (pl. 3.15:1–4). They seem to have smaller mouths and narrower necks than the usual jug rim and may represent an earlier type jug. Most typical in form, pl. 3.15:1 was recovered with the removal of IVB Wall 1117. Other sherds were from various fills for Stratum IV constructions or under floors that may have included fill.

Type b. Rounded Rim with Undercut

More typical of the early Hellenistic strata was a rounded rim, usually slightly out-turned to a lower outer point, sometimes with remnants of an undercut to meet the neck (pl. 3.15:5–17). Note the early jar rim type A with an undercut. Some of the earlier jug rims also had an inner upper point at the turn. Note that some fragments represented very short necks, and thus may be from more squat jugs (pl. 3.15:6, 8). This rounded rim with undercut probably continued through most of the third century and was found beneath Strata IVA, IIIB and IIIA floors. The rim pl. 3.15:17 comes from above IIIA Floor 1227 and may represent IIIA occupation. A rim from ʿAraq el-ʿEmir believed to come from the early second century BC also has this typical crescent shape (N. Lapp 1983: 66, fig. 30:11). From Gezer Stratum III, dated late third–early second century BC, one jug type is of this form (Gitin 1990: pl. 33:8).

Type c. Rounded Rim

The rim rounding to a lower outer point or undercut was probably transitional to the very typical rounded rim, type c, generally out-turned and rounded to meet the neck (pl. 3.16:1–15). The rounded rim jug should of course be compared to jar type C with a rounded rim. A few of the rounded rims came from IV fill, and they become numerous in Stratum III. The Balâṭah rounded rim is probably best related to Gezer type 177 (globular shaped, high wide neck, rim thickened with bulbous profile [Gitin 1990: 84]), particularly those where the rim is rounded. It is first attested at Gezer in the early mid-second century and may have continued until the late second century BC (Gitin 1990: 242, pl. 34: 4, 23, 24). The rounded rims were found at ʿAraq el-ʿEmir in the first part of the second century BC (N. Lapp 1983: 66, figs. 30:13–14, 32:53–55). The flared rounded rim at Tell el-Fûl, popular near the end of the second century, tends to be lengthened like type d, below (N. Lapp 1981: 102, pl. 75:1–7). A rounded rim occurs in Beth-zur II (175–165 BC; P. and N. Lapp 1968: fig. 22:16, 17), but well-rounded rims do not occur in Beth-zur I (165–135 BC)

Type d. Out-turned Rim, usually to outer Point

By the middle of the third century (Stratum IIIB), sometimes the rounded rims were out-turned, usually to an outer point (pl. 3.17:1–13). Characteristic rims are pl. 3.17:1 (IIIB), 3.17:5 (IIIA) and 3.17:9 (from a II pit). Many are still slightly rounded as the rim turns down (cf. N. Lapp 1964: fig. 2:9 [= pl. 3.17:2 here] and p. 20), but in Stratum IIIA and especially Stratum II (225–150 BC), they are beginning to flatten and appear to lengthen (pl. 3.17:6 and 7, Stratum III; 3.17:10, 11, Stratum II). Unstratified fragment pl. 3.17:13 is of this rim form, but the vessel has quite heavy ware. It is quite similar to a Tell el-Fûl reconstructed jug that came from Period IVA, dated 175–135 BC (N. Lapp 1981: pl. 75:21). From ʿAraq el-ʿEmir come two flattened round rims dated to the early second century BC (N. Lapp 1983: figs. 30:12; 32:56). At Tell el-Fûl, most "rounded" jug rims from Period IVB, late second century, were lengthened and/or flattened (N. Lapp 1981: pl. 75:

FIG. 3.7   *Hellenistic jug rims with ridged necks. B60 7377/7381, B60 5521, and B57 157 (below).*

1–13; p. 102). The rounded out-turned rim occurred in Beth-zur II (P. and N. Lapp 1968: fig. 22:16), and flattened rims were typical of the cistern jugs of Beth-zur I, mid-second century (fig: 25:2, 4, 5). At Gezer, the everted rim (type 178) from the late third through the late second century developed into a first-century splayed rim (Gitin 1990: 242, 84–85). An earlier jug from Wâdī ed-Dâliyeh (second half fourth century BC) is rounded, out-turned, and lengthened, and another rounded rim is flattened (N. Lapp 1974: 31, pl. 21:1, 3). The Wâdī ed-Dâliyeh jugs are probably modeled more on jar rims rather than on this later jug type; note the rounded bottom on the first vessel, but the typical Hellenistic concave base on the second.

Type e. Ridged Neck

A particular Shechem characteristic that emerged in Stratum IIIB was a jug with a rippled neck (pl. 3.17:14–23 and fig. 3.7). The rim was usually rounded, but some had an upper point and had begun to flatten (pl. 3.17:14–18; cf. N. Lapp 1964: fig. 1b:24, 25, although the rippling is not indicated in fig.1b: 24 = pl. 3.17:15 here). Whether it continued to be made after the IIIB occupation cannot be determined, because those found in later strata could have been from the earlier occupation, although a reconstructed jug with the Late Hellenistic characteristic of a rim ledge for a lid (see Type g, below)

had a ridged neck (pl. 3.19.3). A large fragment was from an unstratified context (pl. 3.17:23).

A rim and neck sherd from Samaria, designated a jar (Kenyon 1957: 232, fig. 42:7), has the ridged neck, and the rim shape, ware, and ware thickness are very similar to the Balâṭah type. The sherd belongs to the Hellenistic Fort Wall deposit, which is pre-150 BC, and thus fits well with the Balâṭah material. With the jars and jugs published from the Jerusalem excavations is a ridged neck fragment that is compared to pl. 3.17:14 here (Tushingham 1985: fig. 17:37; p. 39 mentions its publication, N. Lapp 1964: fig. 1:36). At Paphos in Cyprus a number of rilled-necked jugs occur in second-century contexts (Hayes 1991: 28, fig. 16:1–2). The rims at Paphos seem closer to that on our completely reconstructed jug, pl. 3.19:3, and the base resembles the Shechem ring bases, pl. 3.20:15–16. It is unusual to find a parallel as far as Cyprus for ordinary kitchen ware vessels.[7]

Type f. Squared Rim

The squared rim, a typical late Hellenistic form, becomes quite common in Strata IIIA and II (pl. 3.18; cf. N. Lapp 1964: fig. 2:10). As time goes on, the ware tends to get thinner (pl. 3.18:4–7, 9). Note that pl. 3.18:8 is unusually heavy (cf. pl. 3.17:13). The squared type was common in Tell el-Fûl Period IVB, late second century BC (N. Lapp 1981: 102, pl.

FIG. 3.8   Jug with ledge for lid, B62 883 (see pl. 3.19:3), found in pit near Stratum IV Column Base.

75:14–21). It occurs in second-century Beth-zur II and I (P. and N. Lapp 1968: figs. 22:18; 25:6). At Gezer, squared rims occur in Stratum IIC, early/mid-second century BC (pl. 34:5), and Stratum IIB, mid-second century (pls. 36:25; 37:1) and late second century BC (pl. 39:16). The square or "triangular" rim appeared at Herodian Jericho by the beginning of the first century BC, but with an internal groove, characteristic of the Jericho jugs (Bar-Nathan 2002: 39–40).

Type g. Rim Ledge for Lid

A few sherds seem to be shaped to receive a lid and may have a groove (pl. 3.19). This becomes a common form in the first centuries BC and AD (P. Lapp 1961: 159, Corpus 21.1.M, Q, R). A sherd of late ware registered from Stratum IVA is probably intrusive (no. 5846). Otherwise this form does not appear until Strata IIIA and II, or the last quarter of the third century BC. Note the thin ware in the Strata

II and I examples, pl. 3.19:4–6. The nearly complete jug pl. 3.19:3 (fig. 3:8), also has the ridged neck (see jug type e, pl. 3.17:14–23). The unstratified jug top from the surface in Field III was very warped (pl. 3.19:7). With two handles and a disfigured mouth, it probably was used more as a vessel for storage than for pouring, if it was used at all. The jug rim that probably could receive a lid appears at Gezer in Stratum IIC (early/mid-second century; Gitin 1990: pl. 34:25) and in IIB (late second century; pl. 39:12); by the early first century BC (Stratum IIA, pl. 41:20, 21; type 181, see pp. 142–43), it appears with a narrow neck as in examples cited in the corpus above. At Tell el-Fûl, rims of this form in Period IVC (first quarter of the first century BC) were smaller and of thinner ware (N. Lapp 1981: 102, pl. 75:22–25). Those with an "internal groove" from Herodian Jericho may be from the same tradition (Bar-Nathan 2002: 40, pl. 8).

The jug handle was generally oval in shape, usually extending from the rim to the shoulder of the vessel. Workmanship was better through the third century than later.

Concave Bases

The Hellenistic concave jug base, pl. 3.20 and fig. 3.9, appeared in the third century BC at Shechem. The earlier examples tend to be heavier and less concave (pl. 3.20:1–3; cf. N. Lapp 1964: 17). By the second century, it had become thinner (pl. 3.20:4–7) and an angular form (pl. 3.20:10–12) was beginning to develop. (See also the unstratified unique vessel, pl. 22:8.) However, the sharpness of the first century BC has not yet appeared (cf. P. Lapp 1961: Corpus 21.1.M). The earliest example of this concave base comes from the Wâdī ed-Dâliyeh cave clearances, dated 350–335 BC (N. Lapp 1974: 31, pl. 21:3). At Gezer, an angular form appears in Stratum IIC, early to mid-second century BC (pl. 34:30). The whole cistern vessels from Beth-zur I (165–135 BC) had concave bases, and numerous base fragments were found at that site (P. and N. Lapp 1968: fig. 25).

Ring Bases

Throughout the fills were found a few ring base fragments (pl. 3.20:15, 16), which must be from jugs

interior base B60 844

B60 961   B60 110

FIG. 3.9   *Typical concave bases of Hellenistic jugs from the 1960 excavations.*

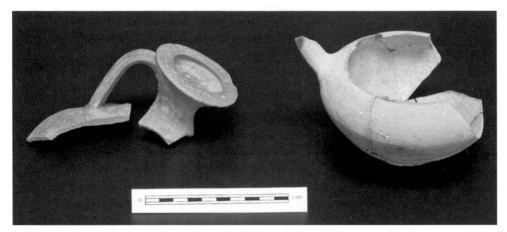

FIG. 3.10   *Parts of two jugs, B60 779 and 1189, which may be imported.*

FIG. 3.11   *Hellenistic vessel, B60 3914, with jug and cooking pot features.*

766   3   952

FIG. 3.12 *Fragments of Hellenistic flasks from the 1957 excavations.*

or jars because of their roughly finished interiors and high walls. A particular type of jug with a ring base cannot be distinguished. Although ring base fragments, which are probably from jugs, occur at other Hellenistic sites (Tell el-Fûl: N. Lapp 1981: pl. 75:23; Beth-zur: P. and N. Lapp 1968: figs. 22:19; 26:2), a whole form is not yet known. It is of course possible that these are from small jars. The ring base may be the common form on later vessels (cf. Herodian Jericho jugs: Bar-Nathan 2002: pl. 8).

Other jugs may have had round bases. Note the rounded base on the reconstructed jug from Wâdī ed-Dâliyeh and the parallels cited for that vessel (N. Lapp: 1974: 31, pl. 21:1). Unfortunately, the base was missing from the largest jug that could be reconstructed from Balâṭah (pl. 3.19:3), although a rounded base seems to be indicated.

Unique Jugs

There are a number of vessels that seem unique (pl. 3.21), and parallels in the Hellenistic period are difficult to find. It is possible that some are pre-Hellenistic in date. Several have bands of red paint around the vessel or on the rim (pl.3.21:1, 2, 7, 8). Plate 3.21:1 could possibly be the side of an amphora such as one from Yoqne'am (Avissar 1996: fig. X.7.1); also note the red decoration on another vessel (fig. X.7.9). At Dor, a lagynos painted sherd shows part of a vessel that could be similar to Balâṭah pl. 3.21:1 (Guz-Zilberstein 1995: 310, photo 6.35 and fig. 6.33.2). The rim profile of pl. 3.21:2 is similar to an amphora or jug from Yoqne'am (Avissar 1996: fig. X.7.5, 7), but the Balâṭah jug does not indicate a handle at or near the rim. What

may be imported vessels, pl. 3.21:3 and 4 (fig. 3.10), have parallels from Samaria, but the contexts are not helpful for their dating (cf. P. Lapp 1961: 48, 125, Corpus 128: B, C). The upper portion of the jug pl. 3.21:3, with a dark red glaze or heavy slip, is similar to the rim and neck of a smaller jug from Samaria (Crowfoot, Crowfoot, and Kenyon 1957: fig. 58:4). A jug from Yoqne'am is related to this vessel by Avissar (1996: 53, fig. X.7.3). The lower part of the *bibelot*, pl. 3.21:4, has an unstratified parallel from Samaria (Reisner, Fisher, and Lyon 1924: fig. 182:22a). These two Balâṭah vessels, pl. 3.21:3 and 4, are from Strata II and I in Field II, but they could belong with earlier material in the fills. The complete profile and form could be reconstructed for one jug (pl. 3.21:8; fig. 3.11), but this came from an unstratified context. It had some atypical features: the ware and base were those of a Hellenistic jug, but the form of rim and the two handles were typical of a Hellenistic cooking pot. It had a band of paint around the jug beneath the handles.

FLASKS

Several flasks could be partially reconstructed, and there are stratified flask sherds, but they are not easily typed. Banded rims of varied width are most common. The longer or wider rims, 1–1.5 cm, are generally from the earlier Hellenistic strata (pl. 3.22:1–6) and perhaps represent a developmental feature.

Somewhat narrower rims are represented in Stratum IV (pl. 3.22:7) and Stratum III (pl. 3.22: 8–10), and there are several from late or unstratified contexts (pl. 3.22:11–13; fig. 3.12). Plate 3.22:11, though not from a firm context, with its wide rim and short neck suggested an earlier date to P. Lapp (cf. P. Lapp 1961: 16).

The flask pl. 3.23:1 was partially reconstructed from sherds removed from IVA Oven 1024 and nearby IIIA Wall 1010. The narrow rim therefore also appeared in Stratum IV but probably became the usual form later. Several were found in Stratum III (pl. 3.23:2–4) and another is shown from Stratum II (pl. 3.23:5).

A similar flask fragment to pl. 3.23: 3 with its narrow band rim and slightly thinner ware came from Beth-zur Stratum II (175–165 BC), but the latter has a slightly twisted handle and poor attachments (P. and N. Lapp 1968: 72, fig. 23:1). Rims with varied bands come from Tell el-Fûl IVA and IVB, 175–100 BC (N. Lapp 1981: fig. 76:1–7), Beth-zur Stratum II, 175–165 BC (Lapp 1968: fig 23:2), and Gezer, where the banded rim flasks are dated to the late second and first century BC (Gitin 1990: 243; pls. 39:18; 41:24, 25). At Dor, where the flasks are said to be mainly early Hellenistic (Guz-Zilberstein 1995: 310), fig. 6.34.1 (phase questionable) and 2 (second-century-BC phase) are amazingly parallel to Balâṭah pl. 3.23:1–5.

A few rims are plain and without bands (pl. 3.23:6, 7). A parallel plain rim came from the Hellenistic Fort Wall deposit at Samaria, which is dated pre-150 BC (Kenyon 1957: fig 42:3).

Several neck and handle flask fragments should not be placed late in the Hellenistic period because the handles do not yet tend to twist (note that handles pl. 3.23:1 and 8 are from Stratum IVA; pl. 3.23:3 from IIIB). Other fragments with handles attached near the rims and relatively thick ware from later fills or surface debris (pl. 3.22:9–13) may indicate that they actually date earlier in the Hellenistic period. The most complete reconstructed flask (pl. 3.23:10) was from an unstratified context; its handles were poorly attached and the side view may illustrate the beginning of the twisted handle. It can be dated in the second century BC. At Tell el-Fûl there seemed to be a trend toward smaller flasks around the turn of the second–first centuries BC (Period IVC, 100–75 BC; N. Lapp 1981: 103). The two partially reconstructed Balâṭah flasks (pl. 3.23:1, 10) were very large and may point to earlier dates. The Balâṭah flask assemblage belongs

to a time before the distinctive late-second- and first-century characteristics appear: smaller size, longer and thinner necks, and twisted and poorly attached handles (cf. Gitin 1990: 243). It should be noted that only undistinguishable flask fragments appeared in Field II, where most of the latest Hellenistic material was found.

JUGLETS

Bottle Form

Two types of juglets could be distinguished in the Balâṭah Hellenistic strata. One is what is often identified as a bottle form (pl. 3.24:1–5). Only identifiable base fragments of this type appeared. These are probably Hellenistic bottle or amphoriskos forms that developed from Persian types, typically of heavy ware and Assyrian origin (Amiran 1969: 296). At Tell el-Fûl, pointed bottles dated to Period III B, the exilic or early Persian period (N. Lapp 1981: 92). Note the heavy thick Tell el-Fûl bottoms (fig. 61:11–14), which are all pointed. The Balâṭah forms indicate flat or small disc bases. Gitin relates his juglet type 137B, Stratum IV (Persian: fifth and fourth centuries), to bottle-juglet types, and thinks the Gezer example with a flat thickened base may be the beginning of the unguentarium tradition of the Hellenistic period. This development could also be deduced from the Balâṭah examples; the bottle bases may well lead to some of the heavier unguentaria noted below.[8] The Balâṭah bases pl. 3.24.3–4 could possibly be compared to the "small plain" unguentaria at Dor (Guz-Zilberstein 1995: 304, fig. 6.26.22). The five fragments (pl. 3.24:1–5) could all date with the earlier Hellenistic material. One base and lower body fragment came from IVB fill (pl. 3.24:1) and two were from IIIB pits (pl. 3.24:2, 3).

Globular

The other recognizable juglet is the globular type (pl. 3.24:6–11), a very characteristic form of the Late Hellenistic and Roman period (P. Lapp 1961: Corpus type 31). Two reconstructible pots with neck and rims missing were from unstratified contexts, but probably pre-date 200 BC. One, pl. 3.24:8

FIG. 3.13 *Juglet B60 #531, which contained a cache of coins (see fig. 1.5).*

FIG. 3.14 *One of the heavy juglets (B60 5894) found with its top missing.*

(fig. 3.14), was associated with Hellenistic material that predated 200 BC. The other, pl. 3.24:7 (fig. 3.13), contained a cache of Ptolemaic silver coins, the latest dating to 193 BC (cf. fig. 1.5). The workmanship of these two pots was cruder and heavier than the more carefully made later pots. Another globular juglet (pl. 3.24:6), also with the top missing, came from spotty Floor 1602–1604, dating to Stratum IIIA (though it could easily have predated this stratum). These heavy globular juglets appeared in the Wâdī ed-Dâliyeh cave at the end of the Persian period (N. Lapp 1974: pl. 22:4, 5, 7). Some of these earlier juglets had small flat bases, but all the Balâṭah bases are rounded (cf. N. Lapp 1974: 32, and the parallels noted there).

A reconstructed globular juglet, pl. 3.24:9 (fig. 3.15), is of the late Hellenistic type. This and two other fragments, pl. 3.24:10–11, are from unsealed loci with Stratum II material. The rim form is cup-shaped, similar to vessels from Beth-zur II–I, 175–100 BC (P. and N. Lapp 1968: 72, fig. 26:4), and Tell el-Fûl Period IVB, ca. 135–100 BC (N. Lapp 1981: 103, pl. 76:13–18; for similar Late Hellenistic and Early Roman globular juglets, cf. P. Lapp 1961: 16–17, Corpus type 31). In Transjordan, some fragments of this type juglet are published from Hellenistic Stratum II at Saidiyeh (Pritchard 1985:

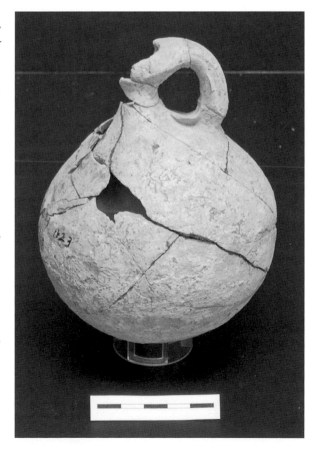

FIG. 3.15 *Typical late Hellenistic globular juglet, B57 1123.*

fig. 19:31, 34–36). Bar-Nathan (2002: 55) claims that this juglet with the well-formed "cup-mouth" and finer ware is most characteristic of the first century BC to first century AD.

Miscellaneous

Some miscellaneous fragments from stratified contexts are shown. Only additional stratified material can tell us more about their types. Wide-mouthed juglet pl. 3.24:12 may have a parallel at Gezer, Stratum III, late third-early second centuries (Gitin 1990: 244, pl. 33:11). A whole wide-mouth juglet came from Ashdod, Stratum II (Hellenistic; Dothan 1971: fig. 79:12, pl. 71:5). From Stratum IIIB, a rim fragment, pl. 3.24:13, may be from a small bowl similar to the squat globular pyxis from Herodian Jericho (cf. Bar-Nathan 2002: 63, ill. 51). Plate 3.24:14 and 15 may be juglets of the Gezer "ovoid-shaped" type (Stratum IIB, mid-second century BC; Gitin 1990: pl. 37:6) or of the Dor "squat dipper juglets" (Guz-Zilberstein 1995: 307). The last fragment (pl. 3.24:15) from late fill has poor remains of paint or slip.

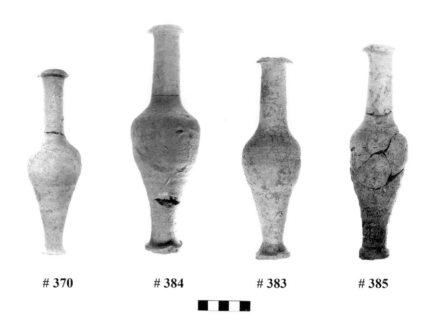

#370   #384   #383   #385

FIG. 3.16 *Typical Hellenistic unguentaria from the 1960 excavations.*

UNGUENTARIA

This vessel, characterized by a narrow mouth, long neck, widening body, stem foot, and no handles is a defining Hellenistic form throughout the Mediterranean world. The fusiform shape was the defining feature; later, in the first century BC and Roman times, the piriform bulbous unguentarium without a foot, but with a flat base, took over until it was replaced by glass. The vessel was widely manufactured throughout the classical world from as far west as Spain through the Mediterranean, to the east to Palestine and Mesopotamia.[9] Although it has been suggested that unguentaria were produced exclusively by a small number of workshops, "the wide variety of fabrics and shapes present at

various sites does not support the idea of only a few centers of production" (Anderson-Stojanović 1987: 115). To establish a typology, clay analysis is needed, and as Rotroff has said, "each fabric undergoes its own idiosyncratic development and therefore must be studied separately in order to establish a chronology for the shape" (1984: 258). Anderson-Stojanović thinks it probable that there is a mixture of imported and locally produced vessels in the typical ceramic assembly from most sites. The usual Palestinian unguentarium, at least at inland sites, is probably of local ware, and typologies among various local traditions need to be considered.

As early as the fourth century, a short, solid based unguentarium appeared in the Eastern Mediterranean, but in the Near East they do not occur prior to the conquest of Alexander the Great (Berlin 1995: 58–59). The slender and tall form was common in Palestine by the second century BC, but there are now stratified specimen from the late fourth and third century BC (Berlin 1995: 59, n. 142).[10]

At Balâṭah, the base of a fusiform unguentarium, pl. 3.25:1, was found above a IV surface and may be in IIIB fill, but it was not a closed locus. The top of another, pl. 3.25:2, was found beneath IIIA floor 1227–1511. In the second century BC, a fair number of fragments and several whole forms (fig. 3.16) were found in Stratum II occupational debris (pl. 3.25:3–5), II fill (pl. 3.25:6, 7), and other fills and surface debris (pls. 3.25:8–12, 3.26:1–10). A more bulbous and heavier form is represented by pl. 3.25:4 and 11 (fig. 3.17).[11] The short foot of pls. 3.25: 5 and 12 is similar to those of Berlin's banded fusiform type (Berlin 1995: 64, PW 85–93), but it is doubtful that the Balâṭah examples had the red painted bands. The rest of the Balâṭah unguentaria probably belongs to Berlin's most popular type: semifine elongated fusiform, tall and slender, with long neck, oval to globular body, and everted rim with slight overhang. Both the Anafa types are dated c. 125 BC, which fits the Balâṭah evidence. Many parallels are listed by Berlin (1995: 64–65; see also P. Lapp 1961: Corpus type 91).

There were no fragments of piriform unguentaria at Shechem, as the piriform unguentarium does not appear until the first century BC (Anderson-Stojanović 1987: 110; Berlin 1995: 59; P. Lapp 1961: Corpus type 92).

BOWLS

Small Bowls

The small bowl with an incurved rim is a typical Hellenistic vessel. At Balâṭah, the common local ware bowls have a flat base, occasionally a slight disc. The side is gently rounded, with the bowl's widest diameter just below the rim.

Berlin (1997: 72–73) reviews the history of these "imitation fine ware bowls" and traces them to the incurved rim bowls that were first produced in Athens and appear in fourth-century-BC contexts. These were always black-glazed, and early versions often had stamped designs on the inside. They continued to be produced in Hellenistic times, but were often replaced in the wider Hellenistic world by local wares and imported Terra Sigillata. In the Levant, locally produced incurved rim bowls appeared early in the Hellenistic period, shortly after the conquests of Alexander the Great. Early versions were faithful imitations with thin walls, evenly applied slip, well finished ring bases, and sometimes rouletted or stamped designs on the interior. As at other Palestinian sites, bowls with these characteristics have been uncovered at

111/116 **292**

FIG. 3.17 *Fragments from heavy unguentaria, B60 111/116 and B57 292.*

Samaria (Kenyon 1957: fig. 38). At Tarsus these are traced back to imports of the late fourth century BC. There the earliest Hellenistic bowls had a gradual slope and only slight curve in the lip, but during the course of the third century the walls had a tendency to sag, the incurved rim became more pinched, and the bowl usually became smaller (Jones 1950: 151, fig. 180). These bowls are described as "glazed," and all have ring bases. Briend dates the incurved rim bowls at Keisan to the third and the beginning of the second century on the basis of the Tarsus discussion (Briend 1980: 109, pl. 13:1–11). The two disc bases (pl. 13:18) he dates later, and he does not think the disc base appeared before the middle of the second century (p. 109).

At Shechem, only a few sherds may represent local attempts at the earliest fine ware. A bowl with a simple plain rim (pl. 3.27:1) has the remains of a fine black slip and is finely levigated. Another, pl. 3.27:2, exhibits fine workmanship, and the rim is barely incurved. These two bowls probably had ring bases that had paint or slip (see ring bases, below). They are both from fill for Stratum IVB and thus fit easily within an Early Hellenistic framework.

According to Berlin, the later development of the small incurved rim bowl, made from a less well-levigated plain ware, unslipped, and with a heavy disc base, appeared at the beginning of the

FIG. 3.18 *Some of the crudely made small incurved-rim bowls from the Stratum I occupation of the Hellenistic House excavated in 1957. Back row: 1080, 1193, 1078, 1076, 1069, 1062; front: 1967, 1075, 1045, 1081, 1068.*

second century. This type did not appear at Anafa and other northern sites (where the production of the earlier form continued), and Berlin limits its appearance to Mesopotamia and southern Palestine (1996: 73), although this has to include Samaria and Shechem.[12] At Dor there was a small percentage of the small bowls, and they were thought to be early Hellenistic and used as lids (Gus-Zilberstein 1995: 290), although three of the five bowls published seem to be from late Hellenistic loci (fig. 6.1.34–38).

It is this latter type of the incurved rim bowl, sometimes sharply turned in, only occasionally slipped, and with flat string-cut bases, that is very popular at Shechem (pls. 3.27:3–22; 28:1–13; figs. 3.18, 3.19). Although most popular in the later Hellenistic Strata II and I of the second century BC, there are a number of these vessels from Stratum III, so we know they were produced at least by the third quarter of the third century. A small number of these bowls had flattened or squared off incurved rim tips (pl. 3.28:13).[13] This may be just the result of poorer workmanship. There were occasional disc or concave bases of better workmanship than the usual string-cut base (pls. 3.27:6; 3.29:12), but other bases were left very rough (pl. 3.29:15).

A large number of these bowls came from what may have been a storage area of some sort in the Stratum I Hellenistic House in Field II (pls. 3.27:11–22; 3.28:1–3). These are very carelessly

FIG. 3.19 *String-cut disc bases from small incurved-rim bowls, carelessly finished, B60 787, 2890, 2216.*

shaped and fired, perhaps due to mass production. Some are very lopsided (pl. 3.27:14), and some bases were left very rough. This cache shows that small variations in the rim, from slightly tapered to sharply incurved, are not chronologically significant by the late Hellenistic period at Balâṭah and do not justify type separation (contrast Gitin, types 193–96, 199, 211).

The ware of the Early Hellenistic vessels is usually described as reddish yellow, according to the Munsell charts. In Stratum I, lighter colors are common: pinks, grays, and light reddish browns. (Compare the buff wares described from Samaria and Beth-zur in second-half-of-second-century-BC contexts; P. Lapp 1961: 32). Gray cores, particularly common near the base of these vessels, indicate poor firing. The surface treatment, if present, is often described as a slip, although in some cases it could be paint or wash. It is almost always very worn and has mostly disappeared. The few cases of better finishes are noted. The inclusions are small and sometimes tiny, and they are not plentiful. Ceramic, limestone, and organic inclusions are indicated in the ware descriptions, but they cannot be readily distinguished. The levigation is never coarse, but there are only a few examples of fine levigation. The latter are possibly Hellenistic Sigillata or Attic imports (see below).

The small bowl with incurved rim is that of PCC, Corpus 51.1, and the early types 51.2.A–C: small, deep, hemispherical bowls (P. Lapp 1961). They are dated in the corpus from its earliest date, 200 BC, to the latest, AD 68 (pp. 172–73). The Balâṭah material and that from other sites extend this bowl type's early history (cf. N. Lapp 1964: 18, 20, 22). At Tel Michal, the bowl first appears in Stratum V, the third century BC (Fischer 1989: 177, fig. 13.1:1), and is very common in Stratum IV, second century BC (fig. 13.2:1–14). At Samaria, many of these bowls had "poor glazes" or "washes" and ring or disc bases, and in comparing these with the Tarsus bowls Kenyon dated the Samaria bowls toward the middle of the second century BC (Kenyon 1957: 225, fig. 38); the Tarsus bowls seem to have determined the date for the local ware bowl with disc bases up to that time.[14]

At Gezer, the various bowl types similar to Balâṭah's incurved rim bowls are dated from the beginning of the second century to the early first century BC (Gitin 1990: pls. 33:14–16; 34:10; 35:1–5; 38:1–8; 40:1–4; 42:1–5; 43:6–8; 44:7; 48:11). Most of the second-century incurved rim bowls from Beth-zur had poor paint or wash (Beth-zur Stratum II; P. and N. Lapp 1968: fig. 24:10, 11), although they also appeared without (fig. 28:5). They appeared without decoration and with flat bases at Tell el-Fûl in the late second century (period IVB; N. Lapp 1981: 103, fig. 77:15–18). Among the small collec-

tion of Hellenistic sherds from ʿAraq el-ʿEmir were two roughly made small bowl flat bases (N. Lapp 1983: fig. 30:15, 16) and one with fair-quality black paint (fig. 32:57). These are dated to the second century (p. 68). The small bowls considered Late Hellenistic and published from Pella which are complete have ring bases and usually a mat black or red slip (McNicoll, Smith, and Hennessy 1982: 136, pl.128:7–10; McNicoll et al. 1992: 108, 112–13, pls. 75: 11, 14; 81:7; 82:6). There are a few bowl fragments published from Jerash said to date toward the end of the second century BC (Braemer 1986: 63, fig. 15: 4–6), but a ring or flat base cannot be determined by the fragments.

The incurved rim bowl is one of the most typical forms found at Hellenistic sites. The collections that are important for third-century dating have been cited above. Most of the bowls belong to the second century BC and add little to the typology or chronology.[15]

The shallow bowl or plate with an everted or drooping rim, often called a fish plate, is another typical Hellenistic form. Many of these have a slip or paint and well-formed ring bases. Some have a characteristic depression in the center inside of the bowl. At Balâṭah, rims of these vessels appear in late-third-century Stratum IIIA and bases in Stratum IIIB. One rim fragment came from fill for Stratum IVB (pl. 3:28:14), which is early for Balâṭah, but the fish plate appeared as early as 400 BC at Dor on the coast (Guz-Zilberstein 1995: 291). Most of the Balâṭah stratified examples belong to Stratum II, the first part of the second century BC. Many of these plates have the remains of a slip or paint. The bowls with complete profiles have flat bases (pl. 3.28:21, 25, 26) and are undecorated, but some of the ring bases presented below that have a slip or paint probably belong to fish plates. The variety in sizes of these plates should be noted (cf. diameters of pl. 3.28:15, 19 with pl. 3.28: 17, 18).

At Anafa, the earliest shallow bowls appear in Hellenistic IB, 198–125 BC, but most appear in IIA, about 125 BC, and it was thought that all had the depressed centers, ring bases, well-defined ledges, and slips (Berlin 1997: 77–78). It was not a popular form at Keisan, but there were slipped ring-base plates (Briend 1980: 109, pl. 13:12, 15, 16). At Tel Michal there were Stratum V (third century) and

Stratum IV (second century) slipped and ring base examples (Fischer 1989: 179, 181, fig. 13.1:2 and 13.2:15, 16). They were very common at Samaria in the pre-150-BC Hellenistic Fort Wall deposit, with the usual slip or wash and ring bases (Kenyon 1957: 220–22, fig. 37:1–7, 11–13). In the later deposits the rim is more turned down, and some vessels that Kenyon considers a local imitation of the fish plates have flat bases (p. 234, fig. 43:1–3). A variety of shallow bowls with turned down rims and glazes or slips are published from second-century areas at Pella (McNicoll, Smith, and Hennessy 1982: 136, pl. 128:3–6), as are a number with the hollowed-out center of "fishplates" (McNicoll et al. 1992: pls. 75:1–5; 77:7–9). One upper plate fragment with slip and a fishplate base are published from Jerash (Braemer 1986: fig. 15:2, 3).

Two kitchen ware undecorated shallow plates came from Beth-zur II (175–165 BC) and were rather carelessly made (P. and N. Lapp 1968: fig, 23:10, 12). More often, the plates were painted or slipped, and the slipped ring bases probably belong to these plates (P. and N. Lapp 1968: Beth-zur Stratum II, fig. 24:13–17, and Beth-zur Stratum I, fig. 27:8, 9). The slipped vessels exhibit careless workmanship, but the clay levigation was finer than that of the plain wares (p. 74).

At Balâṭah, the drooping rims and slipped vessels thus continue into the second century, but then a variant type of shallow plates with a simple, ledged, or flattened rim appeared, always in the local ware and without slip or paint (pl. 3.28: 22–26). These have flat bases (cf. P. Lapp 1961: Corpus 53), carelessly made like those of the small incurved rim bowls (pl. 3.28:25). The ware is similar to that of the small incurved rim bowls, often reddish yellow, but also lighter colors of pink and gray. One rim, pl. 3.28:23, seems to be of the Anafa type with grooves (Berlin 1997: 78, fig. 156–59), which occurred from the second century BC to the first century AD. As with other saucers at Anafa, this type always has a slip, center depression, and ring base. This bowl type occurred at Keisan (Briend 1980: 109, pl. 13:20) and Samaria (Kenyon 1957: fig. 37:8, 9), but the Balâṭah sherd seems to be from a simpler plain ware vessel.

There were a few stratified sherds from plates with incurved or folded-over rims, which were neatly made and usually slipped (pl. 3.28:27). Three had very fine ware and may be from Terra Sigillata vessels (see below). The three of local ware were perhaps imitations of these. The Balâṭah sherds are from Strata IIIA through I.

The bases of these incurved-rim bowls and the plates are always important chronological indicators of Hellenistic occupation. If whole profiles are not present, it is often difficult to determine whether they are from bowls or plates. There are two distinct types: ring bases (pl. 3.29:1–6) and string-cut flat or disc bases (pl. 3.29: 7–19; fig. 3.19). The ring bases are usually slipped or painted. As noted above, slipped plates were common, so most of the ring bases probably belong with them. Four of the bases had impressed designs on their interior, but only one is probably locally made (pl. 3.29:4). Local imitations of the Greek prototypes were often rouletted and/or stamped on their interiors at Anafa (Berlin 1997:73). The bases with impressed designs from Balâṭah that were probably Terra Sigillata or Attic imports are discussed below.

The small incurved rim bowls in local ware from Balâṭah were usually undecorated, and, except for the earliest rather plain bowls, it is doubtful that any of the ring bases belonged to them. The many local ware flat or disc bases, sometimes very crudely finished or hardly finished at all, probably belong with the often poorly constructed small incurved rim bowls. Occasionally the base was slightly concave.

Handle fragments of very worn or poor black and red glaze or wash were recovered. The ware is generally hard and of fairly fine levigation, with few inclusions. Some of these may have belonged to bowls with horizontal handles, rounded or flat (pl. 3.29:20). These are probably imitations of Attic forms that appeared in the fourth and fifth century. At Athens, Thompson considered the second-century bowls the Hellenistic version of the "cup-kotyle with well rounded side wall and plain, horizontal loop handles" (Thompson 1934: 372, D 16–18, fig. 118; E 52, 53). From Oboda, "bowls with horizontal strap handles" may be similar; they are dated to the late second century and the turn of the first (Negev 1986: 8, fig. 28, 29). Some handle fragments may be from juglets, but most are too fragmentary to point to parallels.

Imported Bowls

Attic

A few pieces of pottery with a glossy black glaze are possibly imports of Attic ware. Several of the black-glazed fragments were from small bowls with slightly everted rims and rounded sides (pl.3.30:1, also pottery no. 11095 and object #292, listed). A bowl of this type from the Agora, bowl A9, dated ca. 260 BC, was of "good black glaze" (Thompson 1934: 317, figs. 9, 117). Similar forms came from the Middle Hellenistic Unit (third century to beginning of the second) at Tarsus (Jones 1950: fig. 179: h) and the post-Hellenistic Fort Wall at Samaria (Kenyon 1957: fig. 43:6), dated to the last half of the second century BC. The Balâṭah fragments are from Strata IIIA/II, II, and I, and thus date with the Tarsus and Samaria bowls.

An incurved rim bowl of rather heavy ware, pl. 3.30:2, is similar to one from the Agora, A20, a bowl of "heavy fabric, careful workmanship, good black glaze" (Thompson 1934: 318, figs. 4, 117). The lower filling of deposit A is now dated to ca. 260 BC.[16] The Balâṭah fragment is from late unstratified fill.

A very plain, simple rim from Balâṭah, #145, is similar to that of an Agora bowl, E46, of "metallic black glaze" (Thompson 1934: 396, figs. 84, 117). Group E at the Agora was deposited about 110 BC. The Balâṭah rim is unstratified, and came from the north in Field II.

A glossy black base fragment from Balâṭah, pl. 3.30:3, has two palmette impressions on the interior. The footed base is rather elaborate, similar to that on a bowl from Anafa (Slane 1997: pl. 3:FW21), dated to Hellenistic Strata 2B and 2C, end of second century through first quarter of the first century BC, and to kantharoi with profiled bases from Samaria, dated to the end of the fourth century BC (Crowfoot, Crowfoot, and Kenyon 1957: fig. 46: 8–10, pp. 241–42). The Balâṭah fragment was from Pit 1514, probably belonging to Stratum IIIA.

Eastern Terra Sigillata

The designation of twelve bowl fragments as Terra Sigillata was made on the basis of ware: reddish yellow and pink to light red in color (Munsell readings), very fine levigation, no visible inclusions, and slips of red or black that were both glossy and dull, well-adhered and flaky. Unfortunately, none of the sherds were subject to chemical analysis, the most accurate way of classifying Terra Sigillata (Gunneweg, Perlman, and Yellin 1983: 5–9).[17] All the Balâṭah sherds belong to the class of Eastern Terra Sigillata I (ETS I), whose provenience is believed to be eastern Cyprus (pp. 10–13).

Four rim fragments are from small bowls with neatly rounded incurved rims (pl. 3.30:4, 5, and two more listed, nos. 754 and 10166). One was from Stratum IIIA, two were from Stratum II, while one was unstratified; their dates parallel those of Gunneweg, Perlman, and Yellin, 220–100 BC (1983: fig. 21:1), who base their chronology on this form found at Gezer, Tarsus, Anafa, and Samaria (p. 93).

Only one rim was from a plate with an everted rim and overhang (pl. 3.30:6). It came from the black earth debris in Area 2 of Field II; the material from this deposit is from Stratum II or earlier and fits the chronology for this form, 190–100 BC, as found at Ashdod, Samaria, Anafa, and Tarsus (Gunneweg, Perlman, and Yellin 1983: 93).

There were three fragments of a plate type with an inverted rim (pl. 3.30:7, 8, and no. 10938), a form not listed by Gunneweg, Perlman, and Yellin. There were three Balâṭah sherds of this form in local ware, not as well made (pl. 3.28: 27). The form is published from Dor as Eastern Terra Sigillata (Rosenthal-Heginbottom 1995: fig. 5.7.2). Various dates are suggested (p. 218), but none as early as the Balâṭah example from Stratum IIIB. The three Balâṭah Terra Sigillata rims were from stratified contexts, the earliest from beneath a IIIB floor (pl. 3.30:7). Another ETS I ware fragment, no. 837, was from this locus, possibly, but not certainly, from the same vessel. The other two inverted rim fragments were from Strata IIIA/II and II loci. Stratum IIIB is dated 250–225 BC; this is an early date for ETS I, if these sherds would prove to be ETS I. The locally made sherds were from Strata IIIA through I.

Three ring bases (pl. 3.30:9, 10, no. 391 [listed]) could be from the same vessel types as above, either bowls or plates. Two of the fragments have rouletting, and one of these has a visible palmette, which is a common feature on these bowls or plates.

Megarian Ware

Two small connecting fragments from the side of a Megarian bowl were found, one below IIIA floor 1227 and the other in the fill beneath (pl. 3.30:11). The fragmentary molded design is of petals or ovoli and X's in squares. Megarian bowls appear in Palestine in the second century BC (P. Lapp 1961: Corpus 158; Gitin 1990: 251, type 213A, late second century). At Dor, referring to recent studies, these bowls are called Ionian mould-made relief bowls. They are believed to come from the Greek coastal settlements of Asia Minor and were produced during a relatively short period of time, 169–166 BC (Rosenthal-Heginbottom 1995: 209). They sometimes are classed as ETS I, beginning about 150 BC (Gunneweg, Perlman, and Yellin 1983: fig. 22:2; and at Gezer, Gitin 1990: 251), but the Balâṭah fragments do not appear to be Terra Sigillata.

Medium Bowls

A medium-sized bowl type had a rounded "rolled" rim forming a groove below where the rim met the exterior of the bowl, and then turned out to rounded sides (pl. 3.31:1–11). These bowls probably had disc or shallow ring bases. The type appears first beneath IVB floors in Field VII, with several examples from IIIB loci, one from a IIIA locus, and several from loci of Stratum III constructions. The diagnostic rims did not appear in the Strata II and I deposits of Field II. It is probable that the form can be limited to the Early Hellenistic period, the third century BC, perhaps not made after the IIIB occupation.

At Gezer, bowl type 191A (Gitin 1990: 245, pl. 32:15–17), described as round-sided with simple rounded rim and incised lines, was one of the most popular Early Hellenistic bowl types and dated to the mid-third century BC. Two sherds that were not from closely dated contexts at Balâṭah were probably of this type (pl. 3.31:12, 13). The Balâṭah rounded rim bowls may be related but are without the incised lines, and the rolled rim is generally more rounded and everted. Both types are probably dated to around the middle of the third century BC.

Without complete forms of this bowl type, we do not know what kind of base it had. Possible flat or ring bases for medium bowls are illustrated (pl. 3.31:14, 15).

Medium to Large Bowls

There are a number of deep and shallow bowls that are Hellenistic in ware but do not seem possible to type. Varieties are shown in pl. 3.32. Rather deep medium to large bowls have varied rims (pl. 3.32:1–10). Some have rather plain or unthickened rims (pl. 3.32:1, 8); other rims are everted or thickened (pl. 3.32:3, 5–7, 10). These were generally limited to Strata IV and III; the one from the Stratum I Hellenistic House in Field II could be out of its earlier context.

A few large shallow bowl rims and bases have been separated from the mortaria because they are generally not as heavy or thickened (pl. 3.32:11–23). It would have been difficult for them to serve the purpose of mortaria, that is, as vessels for grinding. It should be noted that the Hellenistic mortaria Gitin publishes (his types 229–231) might better be considered as large shallow bowls than grinding utensils. We have discussed the Gezer bowls in the section on mortaria, since Gitin classifies them as mortaria, but the data mentioned there could belong in this section. Note that they do not appear at Gezer after the middle of the second century BC, as is likely for Balâṭah Hellenistic shallow bowls.

The Balâṭah large shallow bowls can be divided into those with unthickened rims (pl. 3.32:11–16) and those with everted and rounded rims (pl. 3.32:17–21). Most of these belong to Strata IV and III; the one designated from Stratum II is from above a IIIA floor and could represent the IIIA occupation. No stratified large shallow bowls (or mortaria) came from Field II, where Strata II and I were defined.

From Beth-zur two large shallow bowls are published from Stratum II, 175–165 BC (P. and N, Lapp 1968: fig. 23:4, 6), but they are not common at sites with late Hellenistic occupation.

KRATERS

Kraters were common in the Early Hellenistic Strata IV and III, in fills of Field VII and in Field I, but they were almost completely lacking in Field II,

FIG. 3.20 *Hellenistic kraters with grooved rims and handles, B57 123/61, B62 1058/329, and B57 274.*

which was limited to Late Hellenistic occupation (Strata II and I). Kraters are generally infrequent or missing from Late Hellenistic corpora.

Grooved

The Balâṭah Hellenistic kraters had high necks. A common type at Balâṭah had a high neck and flat rim with three or four grooves on the top of its rim (pl. 3.33 and fig. 3.20). The rim forms varied, but the type is defined by the grooves and a high neck, usually straight and sometimes quite tall. Although no complete vessels of this type were recovered, several large fragments indicate that these kraters had thick, wide handles, also with two or three grooves. One vessel could be sufficiently reconstructed to show that it had four handles (pl. 3.33:14), and the numerous handles of this type recovered indicate that this may not have been unusual. This krater type is usually of light or pale gray, pink, brown, or yellow ware and does not appear in stratified contexts prior to Stratum IV; [18] it was common through Stratum III. Though frequent in unstratified contexts, it was probably not produced later than the third century BC. It was absent from Field II, except for one example from the Black Earth layer (fill) in Area 2 where there was other earlier material.

Comparable grooved kraters are hardly known from other sites. Grooved kraters were found in a disturbed Persian period cistern at Qadum in Samaria (Stern and Magen 1984: fig. 6:1–5), where there is pottery dated to the very end of the Persian period comparable to that from the Wâdī ed-Dâliyeh cave (see Chapter 2 above, n. 7). These kraters could date with the late material in this mixed Persian group. A krater fragment from a Persian fortress north of Ashdod may be similar (Porath 1974: fig. 4:13).[19] A "large bowl" from the Yoqne'am Hellenistic level may have similar grooves on the top of its rim (Avissar 1996: fig. X.2.3). The handles from Keisan (Briend 1980: 108, pl. 10:9), dated about 300 BC, and that shown from Ramat Raḥel (Aharoni 1964: fig.13:4), found in refuse pit 484 which contained mainly material dating to the Persian-Hellenistic transitional period (pp. 18–19), may be grooved; however, they are horizontal handles, a grooved rim is not indicated, and the krater form appears to be quite different. All the grooved Balâṭah handles are vertical. An Early Hellenistic krater rim at Gezer (Gitin 1990: pl. 32:22) had grooves on the side, but the krater is of a different type. The late Persian examples may be the beginning of this type.

Varied Rims

The other high-necked kraters had varied rims, difficult to classify. A number of squared rims may be noted (pl. 3.34:1–9); though first appearing in Stratum IV, they have become popular in Stratum IIIB. Other rims with everted overhangs or exterior thickening were varied in form (pl. 3.34:10–23) and appeared in Strata IV and III, with those in later contexts probably belonging to earlier occupation. Some have a groove on the exterior part of the rim or below the rim (pl. 3.34:6, 9, 13–14, 17–18). A few rims exhibit little or no thickening (pl. 3.34:24–25). Note the variety of high-necked kraters that appeared in Locus 22.002, the fill below a IIIB floor in Field VII (pls. 3.33:8; 3.34:15–19).[20]

Hellenistic krater forms published from Samaria are mainly imitations of vessels in West Slope technique with poor matte "glazes" (Kenyon 1957: fig. 39:1–2; Crowfoot, Crowfoot, and Kenyon 1957: fig. 45:1–7). To be noted, however, is that the kraters have high necks and some of the rims are squared, similar to those in local ware at Balâṭah. The krater in Greek tradition is a deep open vessel for mixing or serving food or drink; it is of fine fabric, glazed (technically a thick, polished black slip), and often with figured decoration. According to Berlin, at Corinth the "column" krater tradition was continued in plain wares through the classical and Hellenistic periods and became the model for the eastern Mediterranean kraters (1997: 133). The slipped and decorated vessel in West Slope ware continued the Greek tradition at some sites, such as Samaria, but plain ware high-necked kraters may also have developed.

Overhang rims are found on kraters at Keisan (Briend 1980: pl. 12:4–6, 10). The everted rims from refuse pit 484 at Ramat Raḥel (Aharoni 1964: fig. 13:1–6, 8) do not have high necks. At Gezer, high-necked kraters with everted rims appeared in the Persian period (Gitin 1990: 234, type 147), and in the mid-third century BC (type 224, p. 254).

The krater rims with vertical necks from Stratum V (pl. 2.5:1–10) and those previously published should be noted (N. Lapp 1985: 23, fig. 5:17–24). A Persian-period high-necked krater is published from Tel Mevorakh (Stern 1978: fig. 5:7) and one with Persian–Early Hellenistic pottery

from Beth-zur (P. and N. Lapp 1968: fig. 21:19). As noted, these early high-neck kraters continued to appear in Stratum IV fills, but their Stratum V date can usually be determined by their reddish brown ware. The colorless pale wares of these high-necked kraters with varied rim types in Strata IV and III at Balâṭah indicate that the form continued throughout the Early Hellenistic period. A few fragments that could possibly belong to the second century are of thinner ware (pl. 3.34:20–23); compare the thinner ware kraters of the second century BC at Gezer (Gitin 1990: pl. 37:22, 24; 40:13). Note the absence of kraters from the Late Hellenistic material at Beth-zur Strata I and II, 'Araq el-'Emir, Tell el-Fûl, and Bethel. When the krater reappears very late in the Hellenistic period, it is generally of a different type. It is a deep rounded bowl with an overhanging rim, probably unrelated to the earlier type (cf. Berlin 1997: 133; and the Qumran kraters, P. Lapp 1961: Corpus type 45).

MORTARIA

Mortaria are large, rough bowls with relatively thick walls, a thickened or extended rim, coarse fabric, roughened undersides and often worn interiors, indicating their use for grinding (Berlin 1997: 123–24). Stone mortars were probably used for pounding, while clay mortaria could be used for rubbing and grinding.

The characteristic Persian mortarium, often in white or pale wares with a thick, out-folded D-shaped rim, is discussed with the Stratum V material.[21] It is believed that these are imported, probably from a manufacturing center in Northern Syria or southwestern Anatolia (Blakely and Bennett 1989: 59). Here the concern is the Hellenistic mortaria types, the large heavy bowl forms that certainly continued into at least early Hellenistic times. They are not nearly as standardized and were carelessly made when compared with the earlier Persian mortaria. Does this mean that they are now locally produced and that standardized shapes are no longer needed for shipping and storage?

Hellenistic mortaria from Balâṭah were included in Glanzman's study (Glanzman 1993; see Chapter 2, Mortaria).[22] Since the Stratum V and Hellenistic sherds were studied as a group, his general conclusions concerning manufacturing refer to the Hellenistic pottery as well as the Persian. While the Persian mortaria were limited to a few of his morphotypes (see above Ch. 2, n. 14), the Hellenistic sherds included seventeen different forms, and only three types were represented by two examples. One fabric group was more common, though seven groups were represented.[23] The variety of forms may speak to local production, whereas one fabric group may indicate a single source.[24]

The Balâṭah Hellenistic mortaria are generally classed together as those with rims that are thickened and those with variously rounded rims (pls. 3.35:1–22; 3.36:1–17).[25] As far as we can tell, bases were varied: ring, concave, and flat (pl. 3.36:18–20). One complete profile form (pl. 3.35:22) had a heavy ring base, the other (pl. 3.36:8) a concave base. A few large shallow bowls have been separated out and put in the bowl class because they are lighter and generally not as thick as those classed here as mortaria.

The closely dated Wâdī ed-Dâliyeh mortarium (N. Lapp 1964: pl. 23:1), about 331 BC, does not have any exact parallels from Balâṭah, but the Balâṭah mortaria are certainly in the same tradition.[26] At From pre-150-BC deposits at Samaria come a plain rim mortarium (Kenyon 1957: fig 40:2) and also several with everted rims (Zayadin 1966: pl. 28:28–29). No mortaria are published from 'Araq el-'Emir, Bethel, or Tell el-Fûl, which suggests their lack of popularity in the Late Hellenistic period. From Beth-zur there is a Stratum II mortarium (P. and N, Lapp 1968: fig. 23:4), but the vessels fig. 23:5–7 could better be classed as deep and shallow bowls (cf. P. Lapp 1961, Corpus 41.A–D and above, discussion of medium and large bowls).

From Keisan, mortarium rims are published from Hellenistic level 2 (Briend 1980: pl. 12:1,2,a–n), and a number of them are the Persian type that Briend claims continued to the beginning of the second century (p. 108). Their contexts, however, are dated broadly from the early fourth century to 150 BC (p. 27). A number of the Keisan forms may be related to the variety of Balâṭah Hellenistic mortaria (pl. 12: e, h, k, and perhaps others). From Yoqne'am two probable Hellenistic mortaria are published; there the Hellenistic occupation is believed to have started at the end of the third century BC and continued through the second (Avissar 1996:59; fig. X.2.4–5). Excavations at Dor yielded a variety of Hellenistic mortaria or large bowls, and they are found in loci of early Hellenistic phases (Guz-Zilberstein 1995: 295, fig. 6.9). Some of the forms can be compared to the Balâṭah assortment.

Gitin designates three types of Hellenistic mortaria at Gezer (1990: 96): a slightly flanged rim with groove below (type 229), a plain rim (230), and an everted rim (231). He considers these degenerate forms of the common Persian mortaria with folded and D-shaped rims (Gitin 1990: 255), but this is disputed by Blakely and Bennett (1989:60). They are assigned to the first half of the Hellenistic period and do not occur after the mid-second century BC (Gitin 1990: 255). Gitin finds parallels to his type 231 at Samaria (Kenyon 1957: fig. 40:3 and Zayadin 1966: pl. 28:29), dated pre-150 BC and early in the Hellenistic period, and at Balâṭah (N. Lapp 1964: fig. 1:30, or pl. 3.35:10 here) from Stratum IIIB (Gitin 1990: 255). Other Balâṭah mortaria with thickened rims can be compared with his types 229 and 231. His plain rim type 230 is also found at Samaria (Kenyon 1957: fig. 40:2), and is parallel to the Balâṭah large shallow bowls with plain rims (see bowls discussion above and pl. 3.32:11–16).

Berlin distinguishes nine types of mortaria, but only her second type has parallels in Early Hellenistic Palestine (see n. 25 above). It has a thickened, sometimes triangular-shaped rim, formed by pulling or finger molding, a shallow body, and walls that are roughly smoothed (Berlin 1997: 127). A variety of forms are reflected, and the Balâṭah thickened rims are comparable. There were three types of mortarium rims occurring in the Late Hellenistic strata at Anafa, but these all have very distinctive characteristics and are paralleled only by forms from the Anafa area.

COOKING POTS

Cooking pot sherds were generally very fragmentary, but some diagnostic rims and handles can be considered. Most of the pots were globular in form (pls. 3.38:15, 3.39:4); a few with lid devices may belong to a more shallow, casserole type.[27]

As has been noted, cooking pots were generally lighter and of thinner ware and better levigated as the Hellenistic period progressed (P. Lapp 1961: 184, Gitin 1990: 256); their fragility probably contributed to the fragmentary nature of the finds. Handles deteriorated from smooth oval sections to flattened and irregular forms with poor attachments. A few rim and neck types may be of chronological significance.

Rim with Overhang (or flanged Rim)

Most of the Stratum IV cooking pot rims were of a type with an everted overhang, sometimes called a flanged rim, with a fairly long neck before the outward turn (pl. 3.37:1–7). A few continued to appear in Stratum III (pl. 3.37:8–11) and by Stratum II, examples were of very thin ware (pl. 3.37:12–13, 15). The high neck and "thin tapered long flanged rim" was the dominant cooking pot form in the second half of the third century BC at Gezer (Gitin 1990: 256). Rims with an overhang are published from Samaria, some probably from the first half of the third century (Zayadin 1966: pl. 30:85–86) and some that probably pre-date 200 BC (Kenyon 1957: fig. 41:3–7; cf. P. Lapp 1961: 28; Zayadin 1966: 54).

Flanged rims appeared on Persian cooking pots at Gezer (type 154A; Gitin pls. 25:22; 31:11–13), Tel Mevorakh (Stern 1978: fig. 5:12, 14, 16), Tell Michal (Singer-Avitz 1989: figs. 9.1.3, 4 [Stratum XI], 9.2.4 [Stratum IX]), 9.8.5 [Stratum VII]), Keisan (Briend 1980 pl. 21:9, 9a), and Taanach (Rast 1978: fig. 79:6), but their popularity probably reached its zenith in the Early Hellenistic period. The rim with an overhang rim is infrequent in the second-century-BC cooking pot collections at Tell el-Fûl (N. Lapp 1981: figs. 78–79; only fig. 78:14, 15, both of very thin ware) and at Beth-zur (P. and N. Lapp 1968: fig. 26:9, thin ware); other isolated examples appear in Late Hellenistic times (for example, Ashdod: Dothan 1971: fig. 10:7; Yoqne'am: Avissar 1996: fig. X.3.15, with very thin ware).

Plain Rim

The most common Hellenistic cooking pot was the globular form with a plain rim (pls. 3.38 through 3.40:1–10). Sometimes it was leveled flat or squared (pl. 3.38:1–4), perhaps really a deteriorated flange or everted form. Usually, especially in Stratum III and later, it was rounded. By the middle of the third century BC (Stratum IIIB) it was the principal type and perhaps the only form of cooking vessel manufactured. After the usually flattened rims on an out-turned neck of Stratum IV, the Stratum III rims were characteristically rounded and the necks were generally more vertical (pl. 3.38:7–12, 16; with 13–15 showing slight variations). The type was plentiful to the end of the Hellenistic occupation at Balâṭah, that is, Strata II and I, the second century BC (pls. 3.39, 3.40:1–10).

Parallels to the plain rim cooking pot are very common, and it is the usual cooking pot at almost any Hellenistic site. In the Lapp corpus it is type 71.1.A, C, D, K, L with many parallels cited (P. Lapp 1961). Since that publication, more have been reported from Tell el-Fûl (N. Lapp 1981: pl. 78:1–10), Beth-zur (P. and N. Lapp 1968: figs, 26:8; 27:1–4), Heshbon (Sauer 1973: fig. 1:1), Pella (McNicoll 1982: pls. 127:2–6; 131:4), Tel Michal (Herzog et al. 1989: fig. 13.3:18–19), Yoqne'am (Avissar 1996: fig. X.3.1–8), Dor (Guz-Zilberstein 1995: 298–99, cooking pots types 1 and 3), and Jerusalem French Hill (Strange 1975: fig. 14:3–13). Most of these parallels are from second-century and Late Hellenistic contexts, but early parallels should be noted: from the Persian period, Gezer (Gitin 1990: pl. 31:14–15) and Wâdī ed-Dâliyeh (N. Lapp 1974: pl. 23:2–3); and from the Early Hellenistic period, Samaria (Zayadin 1966: pls. 30:82–83; 31:91; Kenyon 1957: fig. 41:1–2) and Gezer (Gitin 1990: pls. 33:21; 35:14–15).

Concave Neck

By Stratum II at Balâṭah (second century BC), the ware becomes thinner and the neck is somewhat concave with a slight out-turn (pl. 3.40:11–14). This was a common second-century-BC characteristic at Tell el-Fûl (N. Lapp 1981: 104, fig. 79:1–8, 16–17) and it is present in the second-century-BC corpus (P. Lapp 1961: corpus 71.1: F–G). Examples are found at Ashdod (Dothan 1971: figs. 24:1, 5; 80:5–6). At Gezer, the closest parallels may be Gitin's type 239, which he describes as with a "short beveled neck" probably used as a lid device.[28] The type does not appear before the mid-second century BC (Gitin

FIG. 3.21 *Stratum I cooking pot fragment with lid device B57 1066, and two unstratified lids, B57 1221 and B57 64.*

1990: 258); with the shorter necks and varied rim treatment, this may be a later development of the Balâṭah form. An earlier Gezer pot from the mid-third century may be closer to the Balâṭah type; it has a concave neck but the rim is not plain. Gitin considers it unique and unusual (Gitin 1990: 258, type 241, pl. 32:21). A type with concave neck was popular at Dor (Guz-Zilberstein 1995: 299, fig. 6:19), where some appeared in the third century BC but were more popular in the second.

Shallow Pot with Lid Device

A shallow cooking pot or casserole with a probable lid device (pl. 3.41:1–17; fig. 3.21) appeared first in Stratum IIIA, probably close to 200 BC. The form is probably influenced by the Greek casseroles, which had a long tradition from the sixth century BC on (Guz-Zilberstein 1995: 299), but it is the late Hellenistic period before they are popular in Palestine. The examples from Balâṭah are very fragmentary and differ considerably. It may be possible to speak of flared rims, either concave or straight on the interior with a rounded angle to hold a lid (pl. 3.41:2, 5, 9–10, 12–13, 16; cf. Guz-Zilberstein's types 5 and 6 at Dor, 1995: 299–300), and those with a sharp or angular lid seating (pl. 3.41:1, 3–4, 6–8, 11, 14–15, 17; Guz-Zilberstein's type 8). None of the

Balâṭah fragments appear to be from shouldered casseroles, a type that does not appear before the first century AD (see P. Lapp 1961: corpus type 72.2; Kahane 1952a: 130–31). Some are smaller pots (pl. 3.41:1), and these had carinated sides. In Lapp's corpus (type 72) they do not appear before 200 BC, although those from the Hellenistic Fort Wall at Samaria could be earlier. Balâṭah rims pl. 3.41:1, 3–4 are similar to one from Samaria (Kenyon 1957: fig. 41:19), whereas Balâṭah pl. 3.41:2 and 5 can be compared to others from there (fig. 41:11–14). Bar handles are indicated on pl. 3.41:3 and 4 as on some of the Samaria examples. At Gezer, the few examples of shallow cooking pots with lid devices do not appear before the second century BC (Gitin 1990: 259). Quite a number of these pots come from Ashdod, generally from Late Hellenistic contexts (Dothan and Freedman 1967: figs. 2:6–9; 6:7 [whole form]; 11:1, 2; 13:3; Dothan 1971: 8:18; 24:2–5, 7). Some casseroles are shown from Yoqne'am, where there was second-century-BC occupation (Avissar 1996: X.4.1–6). At Anafa, Berlin has three classes of casseroles, "Grooved Rim," "Beveled Lip," and "Squared Lip," which appear in Hellenistic Stratum 2A (ca. 125 BC). At Dor, the casseroles are fairly common; they are found in mid-fourth- and third-century contexts, but become plentiful in the second century (Guz-Zilberstein 1995: 299–300, fig.6:21–22). Those from Tel Mevorakh (Stern 1978: fig. 2:6–9) are discussed with the Roman pottery (p. 15), but this material does not seem closely stratified. A Bethel pot (P. Lapp 1968a: 79, pl. 71:6) is assigned a second-century-BC date.

Handles for globular Pots

Early Hellenistic cooking pot handles are usually well formed and tend to be wide and thick (Stratum IV: pl. 3.37:6–7, 9). As the period progresses, more oval handles are common (Stratum III: pl. 3.38:13, 15–16). By late Hellenistic times, handles are usually thin and often carelessly formed and sloppily attached (pls. 3.39:4–9; 3.40:14; 3.41:9, 12–13).

Lids

Fragments of a few forms in cooking pot ware appear to be cooking pot lids (pl. 3.41: 18–19; fig. 3.21). What may be similar lids are published from Yoqne'am (Avissar 1996: fig. X.4.7) and Dor (Guz-Zilberstein 1995: fig. 6.24:5–9).

LAMPS

Attic

Although not stratigraphically important, a number of Attic black-glazed lamp fragments were uncovered (pl. 3.42:1–6). At least two types of Attic lamps could be distinguished. The fragments are all of fine pink clay with a good black glaze.

Rim fragment pl. 3.42:3, with rounded sides separated from the rim by a deep groove, and base pl. 3.42:4, raised and somewhat concave with a thick bottom rising on the interior to a hump, belong to Howland's type 25A, dated by him to about 350–275 BC (1958: 68).[29] This fits Corinth type VII, dated late fifth century to the beginning of the third century (Broneer 1930: 46), Isthmia type VII, especially types VIIA and B, dated the second half and late fourth century (Broneer 1977: 15), and Tarsus Type 2, mainly third century (Jones 1950: 88). A good example also comes from Samaria (Crowfoot, Crowfoot, and Kenyon 1957: 366, fig. 85:3).

Fragments pl. 3.42:5–6 and no. 397 (listed) represent an earlier type, Howland's type 23C, with flat rims, tall, slightly curved sides meeting the rim at a sharp angle, and a horizontal banded handle. At Athens, they are dated to the first half of the fourth century (Howland 1958:59). They belong to Corinth type VI, dated to the fifth century (Broneer 1930:44). At Samaria, a similar lamp type is thought to be a little later but the earliest Hellenistic type found (Crowfoot, Crowfoot, and Kenyon 1957: 366, fig. 85:1). At Balâṭah, as imported lamps, they must belong with the Stratum IV occupation.

The vertical handle fragment pl. 3.42:2 must belong to a lamp like Howland type 33A, which dates from the last quarter of the third century to the third quarter of the second (Howland 1958: 101). The sherd is from pit 1522, probably related to the IIIB occupation (*Shechem III.1*: 325). Spout no. 47 could be related to any of the above types.

Delphiniform

The most common locally made Hellenistic lamp at Balâṭah is a plain delphiniform type (fig. 3.22; pls. 3.42:7–16, 3.43:1–12; cf. P. Lapp 1961: Corpus 83.1). The bodies of these lamps were wheelmade with the handmade nozzle fitted into a hole on the side. (The added nozzle is undoubtedly the reason detached nozzles are frequent finds in Hellenistic levels, as well as bodies that have lost their nozzles.) The delphiniform lamps usually had a flat, carelessly finished base, sometimes slightly concave, a somewhat lengthened spout, and a thin groove a half-centimeter or so from the oil hole. There were no other marks or decoration, except when there was a slip, paint, or wash, usually quite patchy and worn. A complete lamp was found in the removal of IIIB wall 1506 (pl. 3.42:10; fig. 3.22, #496). Another IIIB rim and body sherd was definitely of this type (pl. 3.42:11), and there were IIIB spout and rim fragments probably from similar lamps (pl. 3.42:7– 9, and listed lamp nos. 927, 1539, and 1540). Another complete lamp (pl. 3.42:12 and fig. 3.22, #425A) appeared near IIIB bench 1518, but the locus is not sealed.

The Balâṭah evidence establishes this form in Palestine by the second half of the third century BC. A rim fragment with remains of a slip found above IIIB surface 22.002, pl. 3.42:15, was one of the few fragments with a tiny side protrusion or lug. According to Howland, the pierced lug was first added to these small, heavy lamps to replace the unstable band handle. A string could be inserted through the hole for hanging in storage. At first the lug was carefully placed on the left side at right angles to the spout, so that any oil left in the lamp would not spill (Howland 1958: 72). As time went on, Howland thought, the lug became nonfunctional and was no longer pierced. Broneer, on the other hand, thought the primary use of the knob was to provide a secure grip on the lamp, with the knob shaped as to fit the tip of the finger when the lamp was held in the right hand (Broneer 1977: 17 and n. 18). The lug on Balâṭah pl. 3.42:15 was not pierced through; the unstratified lamp shown in fig. 3.22, #424, seems to be pierced through, but the lamp was not available to check. One was pierced through from the Stratum III pit (pl. 3.43:1). In this pit, left from the robbing of Wall B, several fragments of these lamps were found (pl. 3.43:1–2, 5–6, nos. 820 and 767), as well as a nearly complete lamp (pl. 3.43:3). Also to be noted is the complete lamp that was in the storage jar found not far from the Stratum III pavement near the Hellenistic tower in Field I (pl. 3.43:4).

The delphiniform lamp's appearance in Strata II and I loci confirms its continual use. One with the spout missing, pl. 3.43:7, was found in Stratum II pit 1205–1207; a large fragment, pl. 3.43:8, from the removal of Stratum II wall 1103, had remains of black slip on the interior. In fill below the surface in Field VII two complete lamps were uncovered: a typical lamp of this type (fig. 3.22, #424) and a very plain whole lamp without the usual groove around the oil hole, rather heavy and crude, with the remains of red slip (pl. 3.43:9; fig. 3.22, #735). The latter's short stubby spout may indicate a late-second-century-BC form. Fragments of these delphiniform lamps appeared in the Stratum I loci of the Hellenistic House in Field II. Unstratified pieces were found in all fields with Hellenistic remains. It was the main type of lamp in use throughout Balâṭah's Hellenistic occupation.

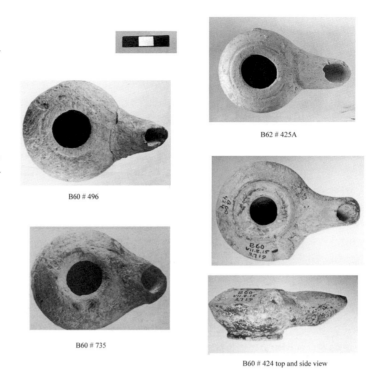

B60 # 496

B62 # 425A

B60 # 735

B60 # 424 top and side view

FIG. 3.22 *Hellenistic delphiniform lamps from Stratum IIIB (B60 496) and later contexts.*

Stratified second-century-BC delphiniform lamps were recognized at Beth-zur Stratum II, 175–165 BC (P. and N. Lapp 1968: 73, fig. 24:5; cf. p. 73, n. 167 for other published lamps of this type up to that time). A number appeared in Period IV at Tell el-Fûl, mainly IVB, ca. 135–100 BC (N. Lapp 1981: 104–5, pl. 80:3–10); to be noted is that all these have spouts that are short and stubby, while the Balâṭah lamp spouts tend to be more lengthened, particularly those from third-century-BC contexts. At Samaria, this popular type was considered a local imitation of the Greek type of the fourth–third centuries BC (Crowfoot, Crowfoot, and Kenyon 1957: 367, fig. 85:4; Zayadin 1966: pl. 31:96–99). It was the main type of Hellenistic lamp at Keisan (Briend and Humbert 1980: 110, pl. 14:1–3), where it dated to the third century.

These lamps are comparable to Broneer's Type IX from Corinth, dated to the early third century BC (Broneer 1930: 48). Those had somewhat flattened or angular bodies, a groove near the rim, a long and pointed nozzle, a finished, usually concave base, and no handle but a left side knob.

His later Type X (through second century) had smaller, rounded bodies, no handle or knob, and although early bases were trimmed, the later ones were not carefully finished (Broneer 1930: 50–51). Howland's Types 28A and B from the Athenian Agora, have similar characteristics, but also a number of differences (Howland 1958: 91–93). He calls them "Blister Ware Lamps," with curved profile (Type 28A, last quarter fourth century into second quarter of the third) and angular profile (Type 28B, early to late third century). The clay is thin, gritty, and hard but sometimes brittle; the lamps vary in color depending on firing conditions and do not have the ordinary glaze but a thin wash or slip, inside and outside but inconsistently. The handmade nozzles are long and narrow, nearly flat on top with rounded termination and a small oval wick hole at the end. The early bases are ring or concave, while the later are flat or only slightly concave. While only a few of the Balâṭah lamps have lugs, all the Agora lamps have them; the early ones are pierced while later the feature has deteriorated. Agora Type 28A has a groove where the body meets the top; Type 28B has a groove or ridge around the filling hole similar to lamps from Balâṭah. Later lamps from the Agora (last quarter of the third century through the second century), which reflect the general degeneration of wheel-made examples, are relegated to Howland's Type 33A and 34A, called "Poor Relations." The molded lamp was introduced in the early years of the third century, while the wheel-made lamps decline in workmanship (Howland 1958: 101, 104).

Molded with Relief Motifs

There are a few small molded fragments with designs in relief (pl. 3.43:13–22). Some patterns were quite elaborate and the fragments are often slipped. They may not have been produced locally. Only one

fragment, which is unstratified, is large enough to suggest a possible lamp type (pl. 3.43:22). It has a shallow ray design around the center hole, similar to some lamps in Howland's type 48A, dated from the last quarter of the third into the last quarter of the second century BC (Howland 1958: 158, pl. 48:620–34).

It is noteworthy that most of these fragments with relief motifs are of black or dark gray metallic ware (see ware descriptions, pl. 3.43: 13, 15–17, 19–21). They were very fragmentary, so not much can be said with certainty. If they were made locally, they may represent the first use of molds for lamps at Balâṭah. Rim pl. 3.43:16 and base pl. 3.43:15 came from Stratum IIIA (as well as spout fragment, pl. 3.43:14, with a red slip). From a pit belonging to the Stratum II occupation, comes a black metallic lamp spout with slight remains of a motif (pl. 3.43:17). Small unstratified sherds with evidence of molded relief (pl. 3.43:19–21) are of the gray metallic ware. The lamp fragment pl. 3.43:13 is from a pit with mainly Stratum IV pottery, but there is some later material. At Gezer, Gitin considers his delphiniform lamp sherds as "type 247 with molded relief design," and most were of a dark gray well-levigated ware, which is not described as metallic (cf. Gitin 1990: 40:20; 48:28). The metallic Balâṭah sherds with relief motif appeared late in the third century BC, while the plain delphiniform lamps were popular by the second half of the third century. Gitin did not recognize his "molded relief design Delphini Type 247" before the second-century-BC horizon (Gitin 1990: 260).

White Ware

From below a possible IIIB floor came a spout with a large hole in white ware, pl. 3.43:23, which may represent a unique Balâṭah type in ware and form.

NOTES

1 See Chap. 1, final section, concerning the publication of the pottery and the pottery charts for full discussion of the way the pottery is presented and the listings in the charts. For convenience, it is summarized here:

Representations of the various pottery forms (types and subtypes) are illustrated in the plates.

Usually a number of examples are illustrated representing the stratum in which they appear. They are listed in an accompanying chart by stratum; included are some sherds that are not in closed loci but are important for comparative purposes (indicated by "cf." in the lists). Some unstratified examples are shown or listed; this is because they are fairly complete examples that help define the type, or because they are from Fields I, II, or III and indicate the chronological occupation in these Fields. Note that the charts also list sherds of the types or subtypes that are not illustrated in the plates, these also listed by stratum. The lists for each type present most of the stratified pottery available for study; if not all the pottery excavated is listed, what is listed does suggest the proportional representation for the sherd type.

As mentioned in Chapter 1, in the charts, unless otherwise noted, Area and Basket are from 1960 for Field VII, except for areas 21–23, which were not excavated until 1962; 1957 for Field II and III (unless 1968 is indicated for Field II); 1962 for Field IX. For Field I the year is noted: "56" = 1956, "57" = 1957, "64 = 1964. Sometimes the charts note the year for a group of listed sherds.

2 As noted above, the other popular storage jar type at Keisan was the conical form, still common in the Hellenistic period in northern and coastal Palestine (Briend 1980: 105). Likewise, the jar and amphora assemblage at Anafa was entirely different from that of central and southern Palestine, and the cylindrical jar did not appear there (Berlin 1997: 149–50).

3 The recent publication from Herodian Jericho classes Balâṭah jars type D as their types J-SJ3 and J-SJ4, and does not want to place them before the end of the second century BC, in spite of the evidence from Tell el-Fûl and Beth-zur (Bar-Nathan 2002: 28; n. 3 is confusing and must contain a misprint). The Balâṭah evidence points irrevocably to at least an early-second-century date for the appearance of this type jar rim. However, some of Bar-Nathan's type J-SJ4A2, especially pl. 4:24 with its greater length

collar and the distinguishing rib, most certainly do point to at least the first century BC. Cf. P. Lapp 1968: 79 and pl. 70:2–23.

4 With appreciation to William J. Fulco, S. J., Loyola Marymount University, Los Angeles, California.

5 Liddell, Scott, Jones, and McKenzie 1996: 129a.

6 Guz-Zilberstein 1995b: 309 (in the publication of the pottery from Dor) actually distinguishes only one class of jugs, though it is remarked that, "Among all the varieties of local undecorated jugs, this type…." Other forms, such as flasks, juglets, and amphoriskoi, may be considered these other "varieties." It is also probable that unless a fragment actually had one handle preserved, indicating a pitcher, he has classed jar and jug rim forms together. Another factor is that in spite of his very detailed publication, complete or fairly significant fragments of vessels (particularly jars and jugs) are his main consideration.

7 At Paphos, Hayes classes this with his "Hellenistic colour-coated wares," usually with a partial slip-coating, all of local origin (1991: 26). More usual vessels in these wares are small bowls with incurved rims, small plates with drooping or flat rims, and saucers with rolled or flat rims – the forms that were imitated in local wares throughout the Mediterranean. It is possible that the Balâṭah parallels of this jug form may be purely coincidental.

In Transjordan a jug fragment with ridged neck appears in Stratum IV (eighth? through fifth century) at Saidiyeh (Pritchard 1985: 80; fig. 17:16), and many appear in late Iron II/Early Persian contexts at 'Umayri (Herr et al. 1991: figs. 4.9:15; 7.6:1–10; 8.13:7–14). Careful examination of the Persian and Hellenistic sherds together might help determine whether the type developed in Transjordan during the Persian period but was later adopted in western Palestine; however, the lapse in time is several centuries.

Although a ridged-neck jug is not common in Palestine, it appears often enough at Balâṭah in third- to second-century-BC contexts that it must have been an intentionally manufactured form.

8 P. Lapp actually considered pl. 3.24:4 the base of a heavy unguentarium (1961: Corpus 91.1.A), but it may belong to a "bottle."

9 The most complete study in recent years on unguentaria is by Anderson-Stojanović (1987).

10 In earlier Palestinian studies, the earliest unguentaria could not be traced further back than the

second century BC (Kahane 1952a: 132; P. Lapp 1961: 197).

11 The Balâṭah fragment, Corpus 91.1.A, is included with the bottles, above. See n. 8, above.

12 The small incurved rim bowl, both shallow and deep, continued at classical sites into Late Hellenistic times, but always with the ring base (for example, at the Agora in Athens: Rotroff 1997: figs. 62–63). At Paphos in Cyprus, the incurved rim bowl, as well as "debased 'fish plates' with drooping or flat rim, and small dishes/saucers with simple rolled or flat-topped rim" were very common in locally made "Hellenistic Colour-coated Wares," all with ring bases (Hayes 1991: 26: fig. 13). At Nea Paphos, the Colour-Coated ware was represented by innumerable incurved rim bowls in third- and second-century-BC loci (Papuci-Władyka 1995: 278, pls. 1:14; 3:198, 196; 4:216, 317). Throughout the classical world and the Levant, the small incurved rim bowl is almost always found at any site occupied in Hellenistic times. It is probably the most universal vessel form that can be traced to classical roots; it is imitated in local wares and in parts of Palestine and the Near East with a flat, string cut base.

13 Three of these sherds were identified with what may be the construction of the Hellenistic House, perhaps at the end of Stratum IIIA (nos. 10,498; 11,005; 11,008; listed, not shown).

14 This must also have been the basis for Briend's dating (cf. 1980: 109 and above).

15 For other parallels see P. Lapp 1961: 172–173, 201; Gitin 1990: 199, 247; Berlin 1997: 73, fns. 173, 174.

16 The revised dates for the Agora groups used here and elsewhere are according to Rotroff 1987: 6.

17 The designations were made by the author but confirmed by Seymour Gitin, who had a number of the sherds he published from Gezer analyzed and is familiar with diagnostic features.

18 It is to be noted that this type was not common in IV fill, as was usual for Stratum V forms.

19 There is also a krater fragment from Dor that may be of this type (Stern et al. 1995a: fig. 2.34 = 2.22.3), and, according to Stern, dated later in the Persian period (p. 35); however, the stratigraphic contexts noted in the charts for most of the kraters are early Persian loci.

20 Campbell does not consider this surface as sealed (*Shechem III.1*: 325b).

21 Blakely and Bennett (1989) have presented a lengthy discussion of mortaria, tracing them back to the last quarter of the seventh century (p. 59). More reference to this report is in the Stratum V discussion.

22 Shechem Hellenistic sherds included in Glanzman's study include pls. 3.33:1–6, 8, 10, 13–17, 19–22; 3.34:5, 7–9, 18.

23 Twelve sherds belonged to Glanzman's fabric group 5. There were none in group 8, which was the most common group for the Persian mortaria. See table 3 for fabric group, table 5 for morphotypes (Glanzman 1993).

24 Glanzman hypothesizes that the fabrics reflect products from several geologically different regions. The various regions account for variations in raw materials (1993: 41). The compositional characteristics used to define the fabric group are the sherd's inclusions, determined by kind, size, shape, color, and distribution visually discernible (1993: 7).

25 The variety of Hellenistic mortarium forms makes it difficult to divide them into types. Gitin (1990:96) has three rim types, but distinctions between types 229 and 231 are not always clear. Berlin (1997: 124–26) stratigraphically distinguishes nine mortarium types from the Persian through the Roman period. She claims that typologies are possible (see n. 276), but her type 2 is the only one of the early Hellenistic period. It is described as the thickened rim mortarium, and the rim forms are quite varied: "no two vessels are identical" (Berlin 1997: 127). Except for type 1, which is the Persian white ware mortarium, she finds parallels to the other types only in the Anafa area or further north; they do not seem to be Palestinian types. However, it would seem that most of the Balâṭah mortaria could be classed with Berlin's type 2.

26 Blakely and Bennett (1989: 60 and n.1) point to fifth- and fourth-century examples of a type different from the Levantine mortaria under discussion there. As further significant studies are made, it will be interesting to see whether these are local adaptations of the imported mortaria.

27 Distinctions as to more squat or more rounded pots can seldom be determined by fragments, and an assumption that they are at least somewhat globular in form cannot be wrong. Contrast Gitin's distinctions in his cooking pot types 233–242 (Gitin 1990: 255–58, and figures cited). P. Lapp, in his Hellenistic corpus, distinguished globular pots (type 71) and shallow pots or casseroles (type 72).

28 Gitin's description of necks and rims is confusing, since they differ in his various subtypes, and it is hard to visualize the pots, since all the examples published are small rim sherds (1990: 98, 258).

29 Howland's lamp types have been adjusted somewhat in Rotroff's Agora publication (1997) in Appendix

III (Working Suggestions for Adjustments of the Chronology of Hellenistic Lamps). It usually involves a narrowing of the dates based on data from the deposits, but she notes that the range of a type may have been longer: "The lists are provided not as a chronological revision but as more or less raw data for the use of other researches" (p. 493). For example, for this type, Howland type 25A, which he dates about 350–275 BC, Rotroff's suggested date, based on the revised chronology of the contexts, is ca. 275 BC. Generally, this makes little difference when dealing with the Palestinian lamps either imported or patterned on the Agora types.

Chapter 4

Summary of Pottery Types

The stratified material that can contribute to the development of particular ceramic types is considered in this summary of the Strata V–I pottery at Shechem. Only forms that may be confidently designated as diagnostic types for the Early Persian, Early Hellenistic, or Late Hellenistic periods will be mentioned. Details of their classification and analysis are found in Chapters 2 and 3.

EARLY PERSIAN TYPES

In the discussion of Stratum V pottery attention is given to those ceramic types that can be placed in the late sixth and early fifth century BC. First is the bag-shaped jar with a variant profiled rim, a modification or less pronounced form of a late Iron II form (fig. 4.1.1).[1] Parallels at other hill country sites indicate that this is a diagnostic form for this period. There are other jar types, but not enough Stratum V evidence to identify any that are significant diagnostically. The *ṭêt* stamped handles, however, should be mentioned as a unique feature of this period and apparently of this site (fig. 4.1.2).

A characteristic Early Persian jug is wide-mouthed with an out-turned rim and a ridge on the neck (fig. 4.1.3). This form is also related to the Iron II tradition, continuing a kind known from late Iron II pottery groups. There are also narrow-necked jug, decanter, or flask fragments (without whole forms the vessel form cannot be distinguished), but none are particularly typical, unless some are like those of the "Gibeon jar" (fig. 4.1.4).

There are no distinctive bowl types, but large deep bowls or kraters fall into several categories. High-necked kraters are common, and also typical of the Iron II and Hellenistic periods, but the ware and their findspots point some to Stratum V at Shechem (fig. 4.1.5). More distinctive and unique to Balâṭah are ledged kraters and bowls with lug handles (fig. 4.1.6, 7). As stated in Chapter 2, without clarity about the pottery of Stratum VI, these forms may be assigned to Stratum V at least for the present. More certain is the assignment of the kraters with wedged and circle impressions to the late sixth or early fifth centuries of Stratum V (fig. 4.1.8).

The vessel known as the Persian mortarium is probably the most clearly diagnostic form of this period (fig. 4.1.9). Variations soon appear, but early in the Persian period the "Persian mortarium" is the usual form. Typically, these vessels are of white to yellowish or greenish white ware, with a long folded-over rim, about 30 cm in diameter, and made in a mold. (Fig. 4.1:9 has a smaller diameter than the typical Persian mortarium, but it is shown here because it is the most complete form we have.) They are imported probably from northern Syria or southwestern Anatolia. Although at the beginning of the Persian period the flat-based type, which appeared in Palestine as early as the seventh century BC, continued, the high ring base emerged in

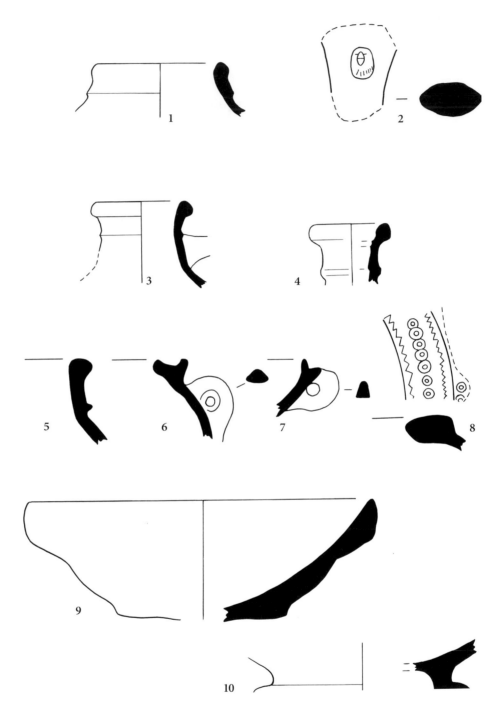

FIG. 4.1 *Diagnostic Early Persian Types.*

	TYPE	SEE PL.		TYPE	SEE PL.
1	degenerate Iron II jar rim	2.1.7	6	ledged krater	2.6.4
2	ṭêt handle	2.2.10	7	ledged bowl	2.6.6
3	wide-mouthed jug	2.3.1	8	wedged krater	2.7.3
4	"Gibeon" jug	2.3.12	9	Persian mortarium	2.8.1
5	high-necked krater	2.5.4	10	mortarium footed base	2.9.3

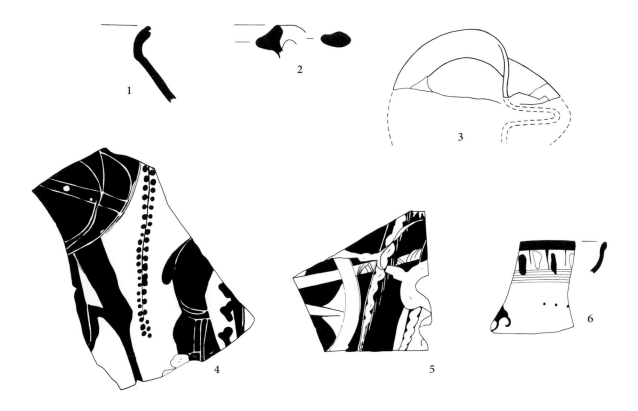

FIG. 4.2 Diagnostic Early Persian Types.

	TYPE	SEE PL.			TYPE	SEE PL.
1	grooved cooking pot rim	2.10.7		4	Attic black-figured	2.12.5
2	heavy cooking pot rim	2.10.30		5	Attic red-figured	2.13.1
3	Persian lamp	2.11.5		6	Attic cup	2.14.3

the sixth century and was in use through the fifth century (fig. 4.1.10).

The globular high-necked cooking pot of the Iron Age undoubtedly continued into the Persian and even into the Hellenistic period, but ware and form are too similar throughout these periods to designate this a diagnostic form in Stratum V. The globular pot with an everted grooved rim, forming a rounded or pointed interior angle (fig. 4.2.1), is a more easily distinguished Iron II form, and it undoubtedly continued at least through the sixth century at a number of sites. A variation of this rim of much heavier ware (fig. 4.2.2) probably belonged to a more shallow or squat cooking pot.

It is perhaps related to Iron II shallow pots, but without the evidence of Stratum VI it has been assigned to Stratum V.

The "Persian lamp" is the other well-known Persian form (fig. 4.2.3). It is an open flat lamp with a flat base and wide rim, often burnished. At other sites they have been assigned to the entire Persian period, but Balâṭah may present its earliest appearance in Palestine.

It is the closely dated imported ware that provides the definitive dates for Stratum V. The black-figured (fig. 4.2.4), early red-figured (fig. 4.2.5), and various Attic cup fragments (fig. 4.2.6) are particularly significant.

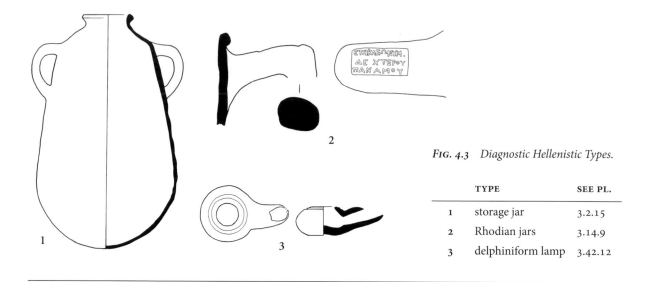

FIG. 4.3 *Diagnostic Hellenistic Types.*

	TYPE	SEE PL.
1	storage jar	3.2.15
2	Rhodian jars	3.14.9
3	delphiniform lamp	3.42.12

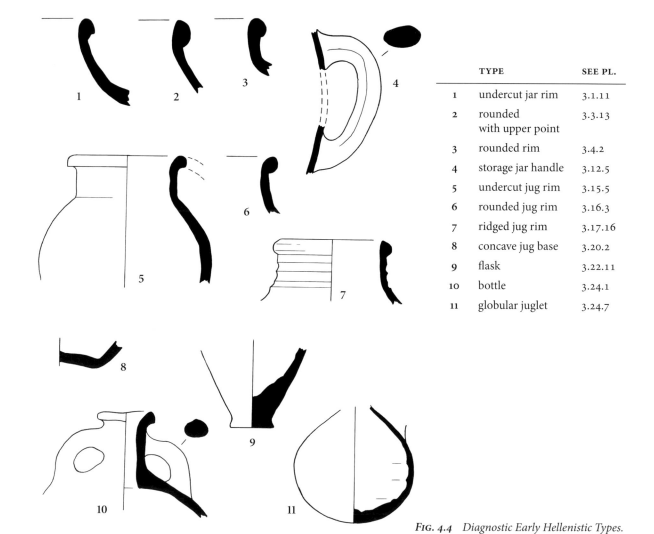

	TYPE	SEE PL.
1	undercut jar rim	3.1.11
2	rounded with upper point	3.3.13
3	rounded rim	3.4.2
4	storage jar handle	3.12.5
5	undercut jug rim	3.15.5
6	rounded jug rim	3.16.3
7	ridged jug rim	3.17.16
8	concave jug base	3.20.2
9	flask	3.22.11
10	bottle	3.24.1
11	globular juglet	3.24.7

FIG. 4.4 *Diagnostic Early Hellenistic Types.*

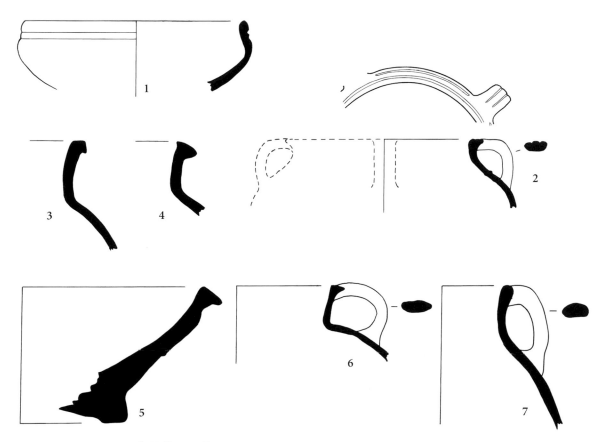

FIG. 4.5 *Diagnostic Early Hellenistic Types.*

	TYPE	SEE PL.		TYPE	SEE PL.
1	medium bowl rolled rim	3.31.1	5	Hellenistic mortarium	3.35.22
2	grooved krater	3.33.14	6	cooking pot with flanged rim	3.37.6
3	krater with squared rim	3.34.1	7	plain cooking pot	3.38.16
4	krater with overhang rim	3.34.12			

HELLENISTIC TYPES

Early Hellenistic (figs. 4.4 and 4.5) and Late Hellenistic (figs. 4.6 and 4.7) vessel types will be discussed together, but they are illustrated separately, so that they may also be examined in chronological assemblages. As noted in Chapter 1, the division between the Early Hellenistic and Late Hellenistic is usually dated about 200 BC, when the Seleucids came into Palestine. Stratum IIIA, dated to the last quarter of the third century until 190 BC, already exhibits many Late Hellenistic characteristics in its pottery. Some forms from Strata IV and III that were absent from Field II, which was not occupied

before Stratum II, indicate their probable dating to Early Hellenistic times. Although Late Hellenistic pottery is fairly well known in Palestine, Balâṭah offers some new diagnostic forms for the Early Hellenistic period. A few forms known throughout the Hellenistic period are shown in fig. 4.3.

The jar type from Hellenistic times at Balâṭah is consistently cylindrical or bag-shaped (fig. 4.3.1). The rims, however, exhibit development and changes that have chronological significance. A rim that curves or turns outward to a lower point and then meets the neck at another point, often crescent-shaped or with an undercut (jar type A, fig. 4.4.1), is the most characteristic Early Hellenistic

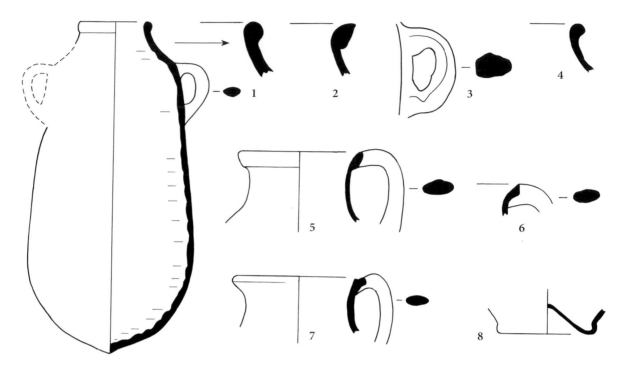

FIG. 4.6 *Diagnostic Late Hellenistic Types.*

	TYPE	SEE PL.			TYPE	SEE PL.
1	rounded jar rim	3.5.2		5	out-turned jug rim	3.17.6
2	collar rim	3.9.5		6	squared jug rim	3.18.7
3	storage jar handle	3.12.16		7	ledged jug rim with groove	3.19.6
4	rounded jug rim	3.16.15		8	concave jug base	3.20.12

form. Some forms have upper points, and a short neck is usual. A rim that rounds out and down to meet the neck develops in Early Hellenistic times; the earliest of these tend to have an inner upper point (jar type B, fig. 4.4.2), first with the rounded point at the top of neck or shoulder; later, the rim begins to turn out. The rounded rim that curves out and down to meet the neck (jar type C) appeared in Stratum IV; it was popular throughout the third century (fig. 4.4.3) and then continued into the Late Hellenistic period, particularly Stratum IIIA (fig. 4.6.1).

The most characteristic Late Hellenistic jar rim in Palestine is the collar rim (jar type D, fig. 4.6.2), an everted rim that goes out to a point, then lengthens to a lower point or angle. Some are still somewhat rounded, others flattened, and some quite depressed. Jar handles, placed vertically from the shoulder to the side wall of the jar, usually

formed an "ear shape" (fig. 4.3.1). Early Hellenistic handles are usually well made, round or oval in cross-section, with fairly neat attachments (fig. 4.4.4); in Late Hellenistic times they are sometimes carelessly formed and have sloppy attachments (fig. 4.6.3). Rhodian jars with inscriptions appear throughout the Hellenistic period (fig. 4.3.2).

Most Hellenistic jugs were wide-mouthed. Earlier jugs tend to be heavier; thinner and lighter ware increases in Late Hellenistic times. Like the jar rims, one rim type of the Early Hellenistic jugs was rounded with an undercut (jug type b, fig. 4.4.5). The rounded rim (jug type c., fig. 4.4.6), similar to the jar with rounded rim, was also popular in the third century BC; like the jar, it continued well into the Late Hellenistic period (fig. 4.6.4). The jug rim that turned out to a point (jug type d) appeared in the third century (Stratum IIIB), but it was mainly a Late Hellenistic form when it flat-

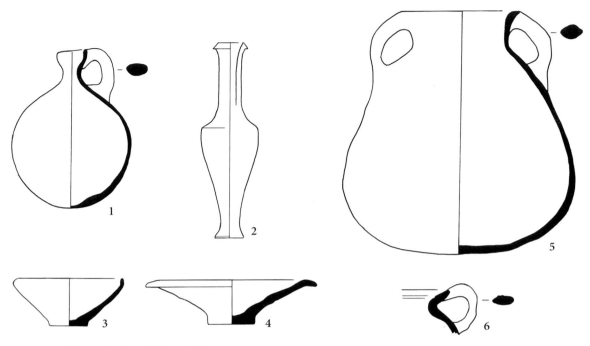

FIG. 4.7 Diagnostic Late Hellenistic Types.

	TYPE	SEE PL.		TYPE	SEE PL.
1	globular juglet	3.24.9	4	fishplate	3.28.21
2	unguentarium	3.25.3	5	plain cooking pot rim	3.39.4
3	small incurved rim bowl	3.27.21	6	cooking pot rim with lid device	3.41.9

tened and lengthened (fig. 4.6.5). Another Stratum IIIB jug type had a ridged neck (type e, fig. 4.4.7). This type is seldom found at other sites, so we are dependent on Balâṭah for its dating; it may not have been made after the Stratum IIIB occupation and can be assigned to the latter part of the Early Hellenistic period. A typical Late Hellenistic jug rim is a squared form (type f, fig. 4.6.6). A rim with a ledge that may have a groove (type g, fig. 4.6.7) is Late Hellenistic and approaches a form that becomes popular in Early Roman times. The concave base is a diagnostic feature for some Hellenistic jugs. Earlier examples tend to be heavier and less concave (fig. 4.4.8), while later they become thinner and sometimes more angular (fig. 4.6.8), though not as sharp as in the first century BC.

Most of the flask fragments from Balâṭah came from Early Hellenistic contexts (fig. 4.4.9). The banded, wider rims tended to be from early in the period, while the narrower rims were later. But the evidence is not conclusive. The few bottle fragments could also be confined to the Early Hellenistic period (fig. 4.4.10). Although not stratigraphically certain, heavy and crude globular juglets can probably be dated Early Hellenistic (fig. 4.4.11), whereas the lighter juglet with a cup-shaped rim (fig. 4.7.1) is paralleled by Late Hellenistic juglets at other sites. The first-century-BC twisted handles on this type of juglet do not appear at Balâṭah. At Balâṭah, the fusiform unguentarium (fig. 4.7.2) is characteristic of the Late Hellenistic period.

Although finer small bowls appeared in the Early Hellenistic period at Balâṭah and other sites, the crudely made small bowls with incurved rim and disk base are the typical Late Hellenistic forms (fig. 4.7.3). They are plentiful in both Late Hellenistic strata at Balâṭah, Strata II and I. The shallow bowl or plate with an everted or drooping rim, often called a fishplate, is also typical of the late strata (fig. 4.7.4), although slipped or painted shallow bowls or those with ring bases probably made their appearance late in the Early Hellenistic period at Balâṭah. A medium-size bowl with rolled rim (fig. 4.5.1) appeared in fourth- and third-century-BC contexts and is an Early Hellenistic form. Larger bowls were too varied to type.

Several high-necked kraters are Early Hellenistic forms. One type has a grooved rim, and sometimes as many as four handles that are wide and also grooved (fig. 4.5.2). Other high-necked kraters have varied rims, some squared (fig. 4.5.3), others with an overhang or exterior thickening (fig. 4.5.4). A variety of high-necked kraters have been dated to Stratum V, but the Hellenistic kraters appear in the typical Hellenistic colorless buff ware. A few kraters of thinner ware may date to Late Hellenistic times, but generally kraters do not appear in later strata and are lacking at second-century-BC sites.

Hellenistic mortaria are large, heavy bowls used for grinding, but their forms are no longer standardized like the typical Persian mortaria. The rims are often rounded, and they may be variously thickened (fig. 4.5.5), but like the kraters, they were not popular after the Early Hellenistic period. Most likely, the variety of large bowls served the mortarium's purpose along with stone vessels.

Cooking pot fragments indicated several types of deep globular vessels. Rims of an Early Hellenistic globular pot usually have a flange or an overhang (fig. 4.5.6). The most common Hellenistic form is that with plain rounded rims; the earliest were often flattened, but in the third century it is distinctly rounded and the neck becomes more vertical (fig. 4.5.7); perhaps by then it was the only type used. The type continues into Late Hellenistic times (fig. 4.7.5), usually with thinner ware and sometimes with a concave neck and slight outturn. A shallow cooking pot or casserole with a ledge that was probably a lid device (fig. 4.7.6) and which varied in form also appears in the Late Hellenistic period.

The plain delphiniform lamp is the typical Hellenistic lamp at Balâṭah (fig. 4.3.3). It appears by the middle of the third century and continues through the second century BC. Except for a few Attic lamp fragments, which most likely date early in the Hellenistic period, and tiny fragments of molded lamps that appear in Late Hellenistic times, the delphiniform lamp must have been the common Balâṭah Hellenistic lamp type.

Other forms may prove to be diagnostic, particularly as more stratified material is excavated and published, but the corpus presented here makes a significant contribution.

NOTES

1   For scales of the individual drawings, as well as locus and ware descriptions, refer to the respective pottery plate listed in the figure caption.

Appendix I: Locus Lists

Stratified loci are listed with descriptions and the pottery from each, along with publication references. Stratified coins are also included. All of the Strata V–I pottery available for study is included, not just what is illustrated in this volume. In the lists, the loci are separated by Field and listed chronologically, beginning with the earliest stratum, Stratum V. Vessels from Stratum V are noted, otherwise the pottery is all Hellenistic in date. Within each stratum the loci are listed, sometimes first by segment of the Field (i.e., north, south, southwest) and then by Locus type (e.g., fill, above floor, below wall). Unstratified pottery is included at the end, either because it is unique, because it illustrates complete forms, or because its presence may indicate occupation in a Field (particularly I, II, and III) that is unattested by stratified deposits. (Note that not all of the column headings are used for every list of unstratified deposits.)

The columns headings, 1–7, for the stratified deposits are as follows:

(1) Locus.
(2) Locus Description.
(3) Publication References. These include both published and unpublished field reports. The unpublished field reports have appendices that list sherds by area and basket. Further references to these unpublished appendices appear thus: "app. I" and so forth. See the Bibliography for complete references.

(4) Area and Basket. Unless otherwise noted, Area and Basket are from 1960 for Field VII, except for Areas 21–23, which were not excavated until 1962; from 1957 for Field II and III (unless 1968 is indicated for Field II); and from 1962 for Field IX. For Field I the year is noted: "56" = 1956, "57" = 1957, "64" = 1964. Sometimes the year is noted for a group of sherds listed below.

(5) Pottery Registry Number. If the sherd or vessel has an object registry number, "#" is inserted before it. This object registry number may appear in column 6.

(6) Vessel Type. Abbreviations are as follows: cp = cooking pot, med = medium, misc = miscellaneous, fig = figured. Fuller information on vessel types is found in the pottery discussions in the text and in the plate descriptions. Coins are listed also with their registration number in column 5 in the locus from which they came.

(7) Plate number in this volume, if illustrated.

Locus	Description	Publication Reference	yr/area/bkt		No.	Type	Pl.
FIELD I							
Stratum IV							
4	L. 4 fill below	Shechem III: 315a	56	1	4	jar C	
	Pavement	Wright 1956: 13	56	1	6	krater handle, grooved	
			56	1	8	jar A-3	
			56	1	9	H mortarium	
			56	1	17	bowl, med rolled	
			56	1	22	jar A-1	
			56	1	23	krater, grooved	
			56	1	24	jar A-1	
			56	1	25	jar A-1	
			56	1	27	jar A-1	
			56	1	30	krater, grooved	
			56	1	32	jar A-1	
4	L. 4	Shechem III: 315a	56	1	102	H mortarium	3.35:7
	below Hellenistic Tower		56	1	110	jar A-3	3.2:6
			56	1	115	jar A-1	3.1:5
			56	1	116	V medium bowl	
			56	1	119	jar C	
			56	1	122	jar A-2	3.1:15
			56	1	124	jar Cv	
			56	1	128	bowl, rolled, base	
205	in lower IV Floor 205	Shechem III: 333a	57	7b.56	317	V lamp	2.11:5
			57	7b.56	326	V jug	2.3:6
			57	7b.56	328	bowl, med rolled	
			57	7b.56	331	jar A-1	3.1:4
			57	7b.56	332	krater, squared	
			57	7b.56	333	jar Cv	3.7:5
			57	7b.56	337	V medium bowl	
			57	7b.56	340	jar A-2	3.1:14
			57	7b.56	341	jug b	
205	below lower	Shechem III: 333a	57	7b.57	342	V jar	2.1:13
	IV Floor 205		57	7b.57	346	V krater-wedged	2.7:2
205	on Floor 205 below	Shechem III: 333a	57	7	**#93**	**Alexander the Great coin**	
204	Burn 204						

Locus	Description	Publication Reference	yr/area/bkt		no.	type	Pl.
FIELD I							
cf Stratum IV							
	Fill at foot of tower	Shechem III: 315 Wright 1975, 171, n. 2 Wright 1956: 13	**56**	1.1	#18-25	**Ptolemy I coins**	
17.481	Fill 481 below H walls	Lance 1964:3	64	17.34	38,900	V jar handle-ṭêt	
			64	17.36	38,880	V jar handle-ṭêt	
FIELD I							
Stratum IV/III							
Wall B	layers against Wall B	Shechem III: 313b	57	5.8	35	V mortarium	2.8:18
			57	5.10	83	jug c	3.16:3
			57	5.11	82	jar handle 1	3.12:3
			57	5.11	84	jar B	
204	lower H Floors 205 &	Shechem III: 333,	57	7.21	122	V Attic cup	
205	206, covered by	ill. 17	57	7.23	135	V medium bowl	
206	Burn 204		57	7.23	136	jar handle 3	3.12:13
			57	7.23	138	jar D-1	3.8:1
			57	7.23	139	V jug	2.3:7
			57	7.23	140	jar D-1	3.8:2
FIELD I							
Stratum III							
3	L. 3 on Pavement	Shechem III.1:	56	1	8	jar B	
		315a	56	1	11	jar A-3	
			56	1	13	jar C	
			56	1	15	krater, grooved	
			56	1	23	jar A-3	
			56	1	24	H mortarium	
			56	1	25	jar A-1	
			56	1	30	jar A-3	
			56	1	31	krater handle, grooved	
			56	1	39	H mortarium base	
			56	1	60	jar A-1	

Locus	Description	Publication Reference	Yr/Area/Bkt		No.	Type	Pl.
			56	1	64	H mortarium	
			56	1	65	jar B	
			56	1	76	jar C	
			56	1	80	jar A-1	
			56	1	82	jar B	
			56	1	86	jar A-1	
			56	1	88	bowl, large shallow	
			56	1	89	krater, thickened	
203	burn above Floor 203	Shechem III.1: 334b;	57	6.10	15	jar C	3.4:16
152-153	between Walls 152-153	2: ill. 17	57	6.10	34	jar C	3.4:17
			57	6.11	14	krater, grooved	
			57	6.11	62	jug f	3.18:8
			57	6.11	66/	jar D-1	3.8:6
			57	6.15	/38	(Floor 203)	
			57	6.11	71	V krater-wedged	2.7:7
			57	6.12	16	jar C	3.4:18
			57	6.12	21	cp, plain	
			57	6.12	22	jar Dv	3.11:4
			57	6.12	32	jar B	3.3:17
203	Floor 203	Shechem III.1: 334b	57	6.15	39	bowl, med to large deep	3.32:7
			57	6.15	41	jar C	3.4:19
			57	6.22	117	bowl, med to large deep	3.32:8
203	below Floor 203	Shechem III.1: 334b	57	6.17	97	H mortarium	3.36:1
			57	6.18	101	jar Dv	3.11:5
204	above Lower Burn 204	Shechem III.1: 334a	57	7b.41	206	bowl, small, disk base	3.29:14
			57	7b.41	207	jar D-2	3.9:5
			57	7b.47	274	krater, grooved	3.33:12
			57	7b.55	318	jar A-3	3.2:13
			57	7b.55	321	jar A-3	
			57	7b.55	323	jug c	

FIELD I

cf Stratum III

Locus	Description	Publication Reference	Yr/Area/Bkt		No.	Type	Pl.
202	between Floors 202 & 206	Shechem III.1: 334b	57	7.8	104	jar Dv	3.11:8
206			57	7.14	108	jar D-2	3.9:6

LOCUS	DESCRIPTION	PUBLICATION REFERENCE	YR/AREA/BKT	NO.	TYPE	PL.
			57 7.14	109	cp, plain	3.39:1
			57 7.14	111/113	cp, plain	3.39:2
Wall B	pit in wall B	Shechem III.1: 313a, 316; 2: ill. 20:1A	57 6.34	818	V large bowl	
			57 6.55	453	jar C	3.4:20
			57 6.55	454	jar A-1	3.1:6
			57 6.55	455	cp, plain	
			57 6.55	457	jar C	3.4:21
			57 6.55	458	jug a	
			57 6.57	459	bowl, large shallow	3.32:20
			57 6.57	460	V jar	2.1:14
			57 6.59	463	cp, plain	3.38:15
			57 6.59	464	jug d	
			57 6.60	466	flask	3.23:7
			57 6.60	468	V mortarium	
			57 6.72	637	jar C	3.4:22
			57 6.72	640	juglet	3.24:3
			57 6.72	641	krater, overhang	3.34:21
			57 6.72	641A	jar Dv	3.11:6
			57 6.72	642	lamp, delphiniform	3.42:17
			57 6.76	644	krater, grooved	3.33:11
			57 6.77	646	V lamp	
			57 6.79	648	lamp, delphiniform	3.43:1
			57 6.82	762	H mortarium	3.36:2
			57 6.82	763	cp, plain	
			57 6.82	764	jar Dv	3.11:7
			57 6.82	765	jar C	3.4:23
			57 6.82	766	flask	3.22:11
			57 6.82	2103	jar base	3.13:4
			57 6.84	814	jar B	3.3:18
			57 6.84	815	jar handle 1	3.12:8
			57 6.84	817	jug d	3.17:7
			57 6.84	820	lamp, delphiniform	
			57 6.84	821	flask	3.23:4
	"heavy organic matter & clay near bottom"	Toombs 1957: 9	57 6.91	767	lamp, delphiniform	3.43:1
			57 6.91	768	cp, plain	3.38:16
			57 6.91	769	lamp, delphiniform	3.43:2
			57 6.93	771	jar D-3	3.10:5
			57 6.93	772	jug c	3.15:13
			57 6.95	823	lamp, delphiniform #246	3.43:3
			57 6.98	822	lamp, delphiniform	3.42:18

Locus	Description	Publication reference	Yr/Area/Bkt		No.	Type	Pl.
	near Pavement	Toombs 1957: 3	56	1	#15	jar D-2	3.9:7
			56	1	#16	lamp, delphiniform	3.42:4
Wall A	striated makeup over Wall	Shechem III.1: 312b	57	9.9	123/	krater, grooved	3.33:14
			57	9.7	/61	(surface)	
			57	9.9	124	cp, plain	3.39:3
			57	9.9	125	jar D-1	
			57	9.9	126	jug b	

FIELD I

Unstratified

Locus	Description	Publication reference	Yr/Area/Bkt		No.	Type	Pl.
	unstratified		56	1	90	bowl, small simple	
	top of Tower		56	3	118	unguentarium	3.26:10
	unstratified		57		#29A	jug, unique handle	
	unstratified		57	2.2	55	V Attic cup	
	surface		57	5.3	74	bowl, large shallow	
	surface		57	6	#44A	V Attic cup	
	surface		57	6.7	3	flask	3.22:12
	surface		57	6.8	64	cp, lid device	3.41:19
	surface		57	6.9	7	krater, grooved	
	top of wall B robber pit		57	6.25	134	H mortarium	3.36:10
	striated fill over wall		57	6.40	289	lamp, delphiniform #115	3.43:8
	surface		57	7.3	12	cp, plain	3.40:8
	unstratified		57	7.4	11	cp, lid device	3.41:17
	unstratified		57	7.70	469	V jar	2.1:15
	surface		57	7a.34	198	H mortarium	
	surface to west		57	7b.31	172	jar handle 4	
	surface to west		57	7b.31	174	jar C	3.6:2
	surface to west		57	7b.31	202	bowl, med to large deep	
	surface to west		57	7b.31	203	H mortarium	3.36:11
	surface		57	7b.38	199	H mortarium	3.36:12
	surface		57	9.4	54	cp, plain	3.40:9
	surface		57	9.5	58	H mortarium	3.36:13
	surface		57	9.7	46/	jar Dv	3.11:12
	top of H Tower mixed		57	9.19	/175	jar D-v	
	balk		57	9.12	142	bowl, small, disk base	
	top of H Tower mixed with		57	9.13	145	H mortarium	
	debris from German trench		57	9.19	176/	jar D-v	3.11:11
	top of H Tower mixed with		57	9.19	/179	jar D-v	

LOCUS	DESCRIPTION	PUBLICATION REFERENCE	YR/AREA/BKT	NO.	TYPE	PL.
	debris from German trench		57 9.19	177	jar A-2	3.1:23
	top of H Tower mixed with		57 9.19	178	jar C	
	debris from German trench		57 9.19	180	jar A-1	
	top of H Tower mixed with		57 9.19	181	jar A-3	
	debris from German trench		57 9.19	182	bowl, med to large deep	
	top of H Tower mixed		57 9.19	184	bowl, large shallow	3.32:10
	surface		57 10.3	49	V medium bowl	2.4:8
	unstratified		57 10.4	48	bowl, small incurved	3.28:12
	unstratified		57 10.8	127	cp, overhang	3.37:15
	unstratified		57 10.9	128	V krater-high neck	
	unstratified		57 10.12	161	H mortarium	3.36:14
	unstratified		57 10.12	162	H mortarium	3.36:15
	unstratified		57 10.12	163	H mortarium	3.36:16
	trench along east side of Tower		57 10.15	185	H mortarium	
	surface		57 11a&b.1	397	lamp-Attic #140	
	unstratified		57 11b.5a	885	jar handle 1	
	huwwar to small stones		57 11b.5a	886	V large bowl	
	huwwar to small stones		57 11b.5a	888	jar D-1	3.8:12
	huwwar to small stones		57 11b.5a	889	V mortarium	2.8:26
	unstratified		57 11b.5a	890	jar handle 2	
	unstratified		57 11b.5a	892	V large bowl	
	surface		57 11b.5a	893	V jar	
	huwwar to small stones		57 17a.38	189	V lamp	
	surface		64 17.5	38,605	lamp, delphiniform	
	surface		64 17.19	38,766	krater, grooved	

FIELD II

Stratum IIIA/II

1968

LOCUS	DESCRIPTION	PUBLICATION REFERENCE	YR/AREA/BKT	NO.	TYPE	PL.
7036	in Foundation Trench	Shechem III.1:	1.18	10,366	flask	
7006	7036 for Walls 7006	336b, 337a	1.18	10,376	jug d	
7008	& 7008					
7048	beneath Flagstone	Shechem III.1:	1.37	10,496	plate, ledge/simple	
	7048	336b, 337, 340b	1.37	10,498	bowl, small flattened	
			1.37	10,500	bowl, small, ring base	

Locus	Description	Publication Reference	Year Area/Bkt	No.	Type		Pl.
7049	embedded in Plaster 7049 of Hellenistic House	Shechem III.1: 336b, 337b, 340b, 341a	1.47	10,938	bowl-ETS I		
			1.47	10,940	bowl, small incurved		
7083	Fill 7083 in robber trench of Iron age Wall 7051 sub Floor 7049	Ross 1968: 11; app. I	1.53	11,002	plate, inverted		
			1.53	11,005	bowl, small flattened		
			1.54	11,008	bowl, small flattened		
			1.54	11,009	lamp, delphiniform		
			1.54	11,010	bowl, small incurved		
			1.54	11,011	bowl, base-ETS I		3.30:9
			1.54	11,012	bowl, ring base		
			1.64	11,095	bowl, Attic		

1957

Locus	Description	Publication Reference	Year Area/Bkt	No.	Type		Pl.
7013	140-160 cm below Wall 7013 in Room 2	Lapp 1961: 48-49	1.98	931	jar D-2		3.9:8
				932	jar C		3.4:24
				933	jug g		
	below 160 cm in Room 2	Lapp 1961: 49 Richardson 1957: 15	1.105	923	krater, overhang		
				924	jar A-2		
				925	jug b		
				926	jar A-2		3.1:21

FIELD II

Stratum II

1957

Locus	Description	Publication Reference	Year Area/Bkt	No.	Type		Pl.
Room 1	HH black earth layer Room 1 (1957)	Shechem III.1: 336b; fig. 300 Lapp 1961: 42, 45, n. 212 Wright 1965: 40–41	1.6	148	jar handle 1		
			1.10	151	bowl, small, disk base		
			1.10	152	bowl, small incurved		
			1.14	154	jar C		3.5:5
			1.15	156	jug g		
			1.15	157	jug e		3.17:22
			1.15	158	jar A-3		3.2:16
			1.25	262	cp, lid device		
			1.25	263	jar D-1		3.8:8
			1.25	264	krater, overhang		3.34:23
			1.25	265	bowl-ETS I	#63	3.30:5
			1.9	150	V krater-ledged		2.6:5
			1	#147	**Ptolemy I coin**		

Locus	Description	Publication reference	Year Area/Bkt	No.	Type	Pl.
N. balk	black earth layer		1.36	391	bowl, base-ETS I	
	North Balk (1957)		1.37	293	jar handle 4	3.12:21
			1.37	294	jar handle 4	3.12:18
			1.48	396	jar rim C	3.6:1
			1.48/49	581	plate, inverted	3.28:27
			1.50	583	cp, lid device	3.41:6
			1.50	584	bowl, small incurved	
			1.50	1,747	jar base	3.13:10
			1.50	1,748	jar base	3.13:11
			1.51	587	bowl-ETS I	3.30:8
			1.51	588	cp, lid device	3.41:7
			1.51	589	flask	
			1.51	590	juglet	3.24:4
			1.52	778	V large bowl	
			1.52	779	jug-unique	3.31:3
			1.52	781	cp, lid device	3.41:8
			1.53	592	bowl base, Attic #186	
			1.56	593	jug c	3.16:14
			1.56	595	jug d	3.17:11

1968

Locus	Description	Publication reference	Year Area/Bkt	No.	Type	Pl.
7041	Foundation Trench 7041	Ross 1968: app. I	68 2.24	#265	coin	
7043	for Walls 7043, 7006,					
7006	Buttress 7045					
7045						
7100	Make-up 7100 for II	Shechem III.1: 340a,	2.78	11,405	jug d	
	Floor 7099	fig. 265; 2: ill. 34:	2.78	11,407	cp, lid device	
		center 3	68 2.78	#720	coin	
7101	Make-up 7101 for II	Ross 1968: app. 1	2.79	11,423	bowl, small incurved	
	Floor 7099 sub 7100					
7052	Fill 7052 in Rooms 2 & 3	Ross 1968: app. 1	2.64	11,233	V mortarium	2.8:25

FIELD II

cf Stratum II

1957

Locus	Description	Publication reference	Year Area/Bkt	No.	Type	Pl.
Area 2	black earth layer Area 2	Shechem III.1: 336	2.25	298	cp, lid device	3.41:11
	(1957)	Lapp 1961: 49	2.27	281	bowl, small, disk base	
			2.29	300/301	cp, plain	3.39:6

Locus	Description	Publication Reference	Year Area/Bkt	No.	Type	Pl.
			1.23	10,427	plate, fish	
			1.23	10,430	jar D-2	
			1.23	10,431	bowl, small incurved	
			1.23	10,436	bowl, small incurved	
7046	Fill 7046 for Bin 7011	Shechem III.1: 337b	1.32	10,468	lamp, delphiniform	
7011		Ross 1968: 14	1.32	10,474	lamp, delphiniform	
			1957			
Room 1	Room 1 occupation	Shechem III.1: 337	1.109	922	bowl, small incurved #255	3.27:11
	(1957)	Lapp 1961: 45	1.109	1042/	cp, plain	3.39:8
			1.120	/1181		
			1.109	1043	cp, lid device	3.41:12
			1.109	1045	bowl, small incurved	3.27:12
			1.109	1046	jar handle 3	
			1.109	1047	bowl, small varied	3.28:25
			1.109	1048	jar D-3	3.10:9
			1.110	1049/	jar D-2	3.9:10
			1.109	/1051		
			1.111	1053	cp, plain	3.39:9
			1.111	1054	jug base-angular	3.20:13
			1.111	1055	bowl, small incurved	3.27:13
			1.111	1057	jar D-2	3.9:11
			1.111	1058	jar D-2	
			1.111	1059	Rhodian handle	3.14:6
			1.113	1060/	jug g	3.19:6
			1.113	/1061		
			1.113	1062	bowl, small incurved	3.27:14
			1.113	1063	bowl, med to large deep	3.32:9
			1.113	1064/	cp, lid device	3.41:13
			1.114	/1066		
			1.114	1067	bowl, small incurved #298	3.27:15
			1.114	1068	bowl, small incurved #297	3.27:16
			1.114	1069	bowl, small incurved	3.27:17
			1.114	1070	bowl, small incurved	3.27:18
			1.116	1071	jar D-2	3.9:12
			1.116	1072	jar handle 3	
			1.116	1073	jug f	
			1.116	1074	bowl, small incurved	3.27:19
			1.116	1075	bowl, small incurved #299	3.27:20
			1.117	1076	bowl, small incurved	3.27:21
			1.117	1077	bowl, small incurved	3.27:22

Locus	Description	Publication reference	Year area/bkt	No.	Type	Pl.
			1.117	1078	bowl, small incurved	3.27:23
			1.117	1079	bowl, small incurved	3.28:1
			1.117	1080	bowl, small incurved	3.28:2
			1.117	1081	bowl, small incurved	3.28:3
			1.117	1082	cp, plain	
			1.117	1083	jug base-angular	3.20:14
			1.117	1084	jar handle 1	
			1.117	1086	jar B	
			1.117	1087	krater, squared	3.34:9
Room 1	deeper in Room 1	Lapp 1961: 45	1.120	1183	jar Dv	
			1.120	1184	jar handle 4	
			1.120	1186	jar D-3	3.10:11
			1.120	1188	jar D-3	3.10:12
			1.120	1189	jug-unique #317	3.21:4
			1.120	1190	jar A-2	3.1:22
			1.120	#292	bowl, Attic	
		Shechem III.1: 338a	**1.123**	**#321**	**Antiochus VIII coin**	
			1.124	1192	jar handle 3	
			1.124	1193	bowl, small incurved	3.28:4
			1.124	1194	jar A-1	3.1:7
			1.124	1195	jar D-1	
			1.124	1196	jar D-1	3.8:10
			1.124	1198	jug e	
			1.124	#293	V black-glazed	

FIELD II

cf Stratum I

1957

Locus	Description	Publication reference	Year area/bkt	No.	Type	Pl.
Room 1	higher in Room 1		1.31	292	unguentarium body #116	3.25:11
	(1957)		1.32	279	jar Dv	
			1.32	280	bowl, small, disk base	
			1.32	282	bowl, small, disk base	3.29:19
			1.32	283	bowl, small incurved	
			1.32	285	bowl, small incurved	
			1.33	287	jar D-2	3.9:13
			1.33	288	plate, fish	
			1.33	290	bowl, small incurved	3.28:5
			1.33	291	bowl, small incurved #103	3.28:6
			1.33	316	bowl, base-ETS I #107	3.30:10

LOCUS	DESCRIPTION	PUBLICATION REFERENCE	YEAR AREA/BKT	NO.	TYPE	PL.
			1.34	369	bowl, small, disk base	
			1.34	370	cp, plain	
			1.34	371	bowl, small incurved	
			1.34	372	jug rim d	3.17:12
			1.34	373	cp, plain	3.40:1
			1.35	299	bowl, small incurved #255	3.28:7
			1.35	376	jar D-2	3.9:14
			1.35	377	bowl, small incurved	3.28:8
			1.35	378	bowl, small incurved	3.28:9
			1.35	379	cp, lid device	
			1.35	380	cp, lid device	3.41:14
			1.35	382	cp, plain	3.40:2
			1.35	383	bowl, small, disk base	
			1.35	385	jar D-3	3.10:13
			1.35	386	V Jar	
			1.35	387	jar D-1	3.8:11
			1.35	428	cp, plain	3.40:3
			1.35	#106	V Attic black & red	

FIELD II

Stratum IA

1957

7104	below IA Wall 7104	Shechem III.1.1: 336a, 341a; 2: ill. 34; fig. 303	1.96	#243	**Caliphate coin**	

1968

7074	I Debris 7074 to Wall 7072	Shechem III.1.1: 341a; 2: ill. 35	2.56	11,134	plate, ledge/simple	
			2.56	11,138	bowl, small, disk base	
			2.56	11,139	bowl, small, disk base	
			2.58	11,168	bowl, small incurved	
			2.58	11,171	bowl, small, ring base	
			2.58	11,173	bowl, small incurved	
			2.51	#558	**bronze coin**	

LOCUS	DESCRIPTION	PUBLICATION REFERENCE	YEAR AREA/BKT	NO.	TYPE	PL.
FIELD II						
Unstratified						
			1957			
	surface		1	#1	**Roman coin**	
	top of H Wall		1	#50	V Attic black & red	
	north balk		1	#145	bowl, Attic	
7106	Storage Bin 7106	Shechem III.1: 341a	1.45b	393	jar C	3.6:4
	north of Hellenistic House		1.45b	394	bowl, med rolled	3.31:11
			1.45b	395	lamp, delphiniform	
	below yard's surface	Shechem III.1: 328b	**1.66**	**#348**	**Ptolemy I or II coin**	
	unstratified		1.70	2120	jar C	3.6:5
	unstratified		2.23	296	V mortarium base	2.9:9
	German dump		2.29	#123	V black on brown	
7071	German dump		**68.2.48**	**#556**	**bronze coin**	
	balk		2.69	1221	cp, lid	3.42:18
7016	Probe Trench 7016	Ross 1968: app. 1	68 2.1	10,166	bowl-ETS I	
	Probe Trench 7016		68 2.2	10,177	cp, lid device	
	unstratified		6.14 ?	198	Rhodian	3.14:8
FIELD III						
Stratum III/II						
			1957			
Wall B	pit between Walls B	Shechem III.1:	4.9A	2122	jar base	3.13:5
606	& 606, incl. storage jar	316a; 335b	4.9B	2123	jar C with potter's mark	3.5:1
	cache	2: ills. 40, 42	4.9C	2117	jar C	3.5:2
			4.9G	2113	jar base	3.13:6
			4.9H	2128	jar base	3.13:7
			4.12	2127	jar base	3.13:8
			4.15A	2102	jar base	3.6:16
			4.15C	2116	jar A-3	3.2:15
			4.15E	2126	cp, plain	3.39:4

Locus	Description	Publication Reference	Year Area/Bkt	No.	Type	Pl.
FIELD III						
Stratum II						
1	foundation of plastered Bin of upper phase	Shechem III:1: 335b	3.13	235	jar D-1	3.8:8
			3.13	236/	plate, fish	3.28:16
			3.4	/426	(debris over bin)	
FIELD III						
Unstratified						
	surface		3.1	131	cp, lid device	3.41:15
			3.3	132	cp, plain	3.40:10
			3.5	186	flask rim - one handle	
			3.10	232	jug g	3.19:7
			3.10	233	bowl, small incurved	3.28:11
	debris over Bin		3.4	425	storage jar Dv	3.11:13
	Hellenistic House		3.11	234	bowl, med rolled	
	east balk		3.16	356	cp, plain	3.40:7
	surface		4.1	427/ 237	jar D-1	3.8:13
			4.1	241	cp, lid device	
			4.1	242	H mortarium	3.36:17
			4.1	243	lamp, delphiniform	
			4.4	245	lamp, relief #90	3.43:22
			4.5	247	jar A-3	3.2:17
			4.16	952	flask	3.22:13
	MB fill/glacis		5.20	802	lamp, delphiniform	3.43:11
	outside Wall A		6.1	687	plate, fish	3.28:21
			6.1	689	cp, lid device	3.41:15
FIELD IV						
	unstratified		1.1	1541	lamp, delphiniform	3.42:12

Locus	Description	Publication Reference	Year Area/Bkt	No.	Type	Pl.
FIELD VII						
Stratum V						
1127	sub V Installation 1127	Shechem III.1: 301, 307; fig.272 Lapp 1985: 38, n. 1 Wright 1965: 167	62 2.50	643	V small bowl	2.4:1
1537 1544 1545	removal V Stone Circle =1544-1545	Lapp 1985: 19 Shechem III.1: 301; fig. 271 Horn & Campbell 1962: app.I:46	62 4.109 62 4.109	1026 1028	V jar-misc V small bowl	2.1:16
FIELD VII						
cf Stratum V						
1530 1229 1232 1234 1230	in fill below IV metalled Surface 1530- 1229-1232-1234 (above and on 1230)	Shechem III.1: 301 Lapp 1985: 19	62 1.2 62 1.92 62 1.92 62 1.92 62 1.92 62 1.92 62 1.93 62 1.99 62 1.93 62 1.95 62 1.100 62 1.101 62 1.103	7 1128 1130 1131 1188 1186 1187 1201 1266 1267 1636	V lamp V jar V jar V small bowl V medium bowl V med bowl base V large bowl krater, grooved V red-fig krater V black-fig krater V black-glazed V Attic black & red V Attic cup	2.1:8 2.13:2 2.12:1
1230 1231	sub 2nd IVB metalled Surface 1230 Surface 1231 in 1230	Shechem III.1: 301, 317b; 2: ill. 113: n 11 Lapp 1985: 19	62 1.8 62 1.9 62 1.110 62 1.21 62 1.21	11 1121 94 95	V jar-misc V lamp V Attic black & red V cooking pot V jar	2.10:3 2.1:3
1243 1245 1230	IVB Fill 1243-45 sub Surface 1230	Lapp 1985: 19 Campbell 1964: 1, app. I:1	64 1.5 64 1.8	32 80	V jar V jar	2.1:4 2.1:5

LOCUS	DESCRIPTION	PUBLICATION REFERENCE	YEAR AREA/BKT	NO.	TYPE	PL.
1556	IVB Fill 1556 sub	Shechem III.1: 301,	62 1.17	86/87	V black-fig krater	2.12:2
	Surface 1530	307, 317b; 2: ill.	62 1.17	88	V black/red-fig krater	2.13:12
		113:10-11	62 4.6	52	V jar-misc	2.1.17
		Lapp 1985: 19-20	62 4.6	57	V cooking pot-heavy	2.10:21
			62 4.6	58	V jar handle	2.2:1
			62 4.38	199	V krater-sloping shoulder	2.5:12
			62 4.38	200	V black-glazed	
			62 4.39	240	V krater-high neck	2.5:7
			62 4.44	244	V cooking pot	2.10:4
			62 4.44	245	V jar	2.1:6
			62 4.45	275	V jar handle	2.2:2
			62 4.45	276	V medium bowl	
			62 4.52	285	V cooking pot-heavy	2.10:22
			62 4.53	399	V krater-high neck	
			62 4.54	400	V jug	
			62 4.54	401	V flask	2.3:12
			62 4.54	404	V jar handle	
			62 4.55	405	V jar handle	2.2:3
			62 4.56	406	V jar-misc	2.1:18
			62 4.56	407	V jar	2.1:7
			62 4.58	408	V jar handle	2.2:4
			62 4.58	409	V cooking pot	2.10:5
			62 4.58	410	V cooking pot	2.10:6
			62 4.58	412	V small bowl	2.4:3
			62 4.58	413	V flask	2.3:13
			62 4.112	1033	V cooking pot	2.10:17
1542	IVB soil Layer 1542 in	Lapp 1985: 20	62 4.151	1775	V black-glazed	
	Fill 1558	Horn & Campbell				
		1962: app. I:47				
1127	inside V Installation	Shechem III.1: 301,	62 2.10	251	V jug	2.3:1
	1127	307; Lapp 1985: 19	62 2.15	269	V mortarium	
		Horn & Campbell	62 2.15	270	V cooking pot	
		1962: app. I:38				
1247	V? Pit 1247	Campbell 1964: 1;	64 1.48	2721	V large bowl	
		app. I:1,2				
1248	Debris 1248 of V?	Campbell 1964:	64 1.11	126	V jar	
1247	Pit 1247	app.I:2				

Locus	Description	Publication reference	Year Area/Bkt	No.	Type	Pl.
1257	L. 1257 of V? Pit 1247 or collapse in it		64 1.31	662	V mortarium	2.8:2
1259	V? Hardpack 1259	Campbell 1964: 1; app. I:3	64 1.43	743	V mortarium	2.8:3
			64 1.54	2297	V jug	
1260	V? Hardpack 1260	Campbell 1964: 1; app. I:3	64 1.71	20754	V lamp	

FIELD VII

Levelling Fills for Stratum IVB

Locus	Description	Publication reference	Year Area/Bkt	No.	Type	Pl.
1228	in Probe 1228 below IV installations	Shechem III.1: 318a	1.114	6894	V Attic cup	
			1.115	7300	V lamp	
			1.115	7301	H mortarium	3.35:1
			1.115	7304	V jar-misc	
			1.115	7305	bowl, small simple	3.27:2
			1.115	7306	V lamp	2.11:1
			1.116	7307	krater, plain	3.34:24
			1.117	7312	V krater-ledged	2.6:1
			1.117	7313	V mortarium base	
1123A	L. 1123A levelling below IV installations	Shechem III.2: ill.116:9	2.131	6907	V jar	
			2.131	6908/	bowl, med rolled	3.31:1
		Lapp 1985: 20	2.135	/7327		
		Campbell 1960a:	2.131	6914	V krater-high neck	2.5:4
		xxxiv	2.131	6915	jar A-1	
			2.134	7323	V stamped jar handle	
			2.134	7324	V krater-high neck	2.5:5
			2.135	7328	jar A-3	
			2.135	7329	V krater-ledged	2.6:2
			2.135	7331	V cooking pot	2.10:10
1029A	Fill 1029A below IV installations in area 3	Shechem III.1: 318a	3.138	5619	V jar	
		Lapp 1985: 20	3.138	5623	V jar	
			3.145	5648	jar B	3.3:1
			3.145	6307	jar B	3.3:2
			3.149	6251	jar A-2	3.1:4
			3.149	6253	V large bowl	
			3.150	6260/64	jar A-1	3.1:1
			3.150	6265	cp, overhang	3.37:2

LOCUS	DESCRIPTION	PUBLICATION REFERENCE	YEAR AREA/BKT	NO.	TYPE	PL.
			3.151	6268	bowl, small simple	3.27:1
			3.151	6270	V Attic lid handle	2.15:1
			3.154	6285	jar A-3	3.2:1
			3.154	6290	jar A-3	
			3.155	6292	jar A-3	
			3.158	6303/	V Attic cup	2.14:8
			62 3.29	/215/	(unstratified)	
			9.13	/2373	(surface fill)	
			3.158	6305	krater, overhang	
			3.158	6308	jar A-1	
			3.158	6309	jar A-1	
1030	Probe 1030 beneath IV levels along north balk area 3	Shechem III.1: 318a Lapp 1985: 20	3.172	6640	krater, overhang	3.34:11
			3.175	6804	cp, overhang	3.37:3
			3.178	6925	V cooking pot-heavy	2.10:23
1424	Fill 1424 west of IVB Wall 1415 down to VII Installations	Shechem III.1: 318a	5.147	6544	jar A-1	3.1:2
1415			5.147	6545	jar A-2	3.1:10
1311	Probe 1311 in brick debris to VII house Wall 1323	Shechem III.1: 318a Lapp 1985: 20	6.123	2170	jar B	
			6.123	2171	jar handle 2	
			6.123	2172	jar A-2	
			6.123	2175	jar handle 1	3.12:1
			6.123	2177	V jar	2.1:12
			6.123	2181	V jar	
			6.124	2956	jar handle 1	
			6.126	2961	jar A-2	
1836	Fill 1836-1841 below IV strata Area 7	Shechem III.1: 318a; 2: ill 112:9,10 Lapp 1985: 20	7.91	4669	V lamp	
1841			7.122	5995	V cooking pot	2.10:13
			7.125	6002	jar A-3	3.2:2
			7.126	6008	V black-glazed	
			7.126	6013	jar A-3	
			7.127	6213	V mortarium	2.8:5
			7.129	6226	V cooking pot	2.10:14
			7.132	6241	V cooking pot-heavy	2.10:24
			7.136	6322	V krater-high neck	
			7.138	6324	V cooking pot	
			7.138	6325	plate, fish	3.28:14
			7.142	6846	V krater-ledged	2.6:3

Locus	Description	Publication Reference	Year Area/Bkt	No.	Type	Pl.
			7.142	6847	V cooking pot	
			7.145	6870	jar B	
			7.146	7139	jar A-1	
1609	Fill 1609-10,1612-15 in	Shechem III.1: 318a;	9.46	3232	krater, grooved	3.33:1
1610	brick debris above Iron	2: ill 112:11	9.48	4038	juglet	3.24:1
1612	II installations (Area 9)	Lapp 1985: 20	9.48	4040	jug b	3.15:7
1613			9.49	4048	V mortarium	2.8:6
1614			9.51	4054	V Attic black & red	
1615			9.51	4056	V lamp	
			9.51	4057/	krater, squared	3.34:1
			9.51	/4059		
			9.52	4065	flask	3.22:1
			9.57	4076	V mortarium	2.8:7
			9.57	4078	jar B	
			9.67	4102	krater, squared	
			9.67	4105	jar A-1	
			9.67	4106	jug b	3.15:8
			9.70	4119	V mortarium base	2.9:1
			9.86	4199	V Attic black & red	
			9.86	4200	V krater-ledged	
			9.87	4203	V Attic black & red	
1630	Fill 1630 down to Iron	Lapp 1985: 20	9.94B	5911A	V lamp	2.11:2
	II house		9.95	5917	V lamp	2.11:3

FIELD VII

Stratum IVB Complexes — South Complex

Locus	Description	Publication Reference	Year Area/Bkt	No.	Type	Pl.
1123	removal IVB Wall 1123	Shechem III.1: 318b;	2.126	6249	V red-fig krater	2.13:8
		2: ill. 106	2.126	6250	V mortarium	2.8:4
		Lapp 1985: 21	2.127	6588	jar A-1	
			2.128	6592	jar A-3	
			2.128	6598	krater, overhang	3.34:10
			2.128	6599	V jar	
1415	removal IVB Wall	Shechem III.1: 318b;	2.130	6897	krater, grooved	
1117	1415-1117	2: ill. 106	2.130	6899	V jug	2.3:2
		Lapp 1985: 21	2.130	6900	V cooking pot	2.10:9
			2.130	6903	V jar	2.1:9

LOCUS	DESCRIPTION	PUBLICATION REFERENCE	YEAR AREA/BKT	NO.	TYPE	PL.
			2.130	6904	jug a	3.25:1
			5.137	6399	V jug	
			5.137	6400	V mortarium	
			5.142	6418	flask	
			5.144	6421	bowl, large shallow	3.20:11
1426	removal IVB Wall 1426	Shechem III.1: 318b;	5.152	6569	krater, overhang	
		2: ill. 1	5.154	6575	jar handle 2	3.12:9
1517	sealed in IV Wall 1517	Shechem III.2:	62 4.2	21	V jar	
		ill. 107	62 4.2	24	V jar	
			62 4.4	28	V cooking pot	2.10:11
			62 4.4	32	V krater-high neck	2.5:6
1529	Hardpack 1529 sub IV	Shechem III.2:	62 4.18	101	V jar	2.1:10
1517	Wall 1517	ill. 107	62 4.18	103	V jar	2.1:11
		Lapp 1985: 21	62 4.18	104	V medium bowl	
			62 4.18	105	V jug	
			62 4.19	112	V small bowl base	2.4:5
			62 4.19	113	V jar handle	
			62 4.19	117	V jar	
1521	under IVB Floor 1521	Shechem III.1: 318b, fig. 271; 2: ill. 113:9 Lapp 1985: 22	62 4.26	187	V cooking pot	2.10:12
1232	on IVB metalled	Shechem III.1: 301,	1.29	263	jug b	3.15:5
1530	Surface 1530-1232	317b-318;	62 1.65	807	V red-fig krater	2.13:3
1521	(sub 1521)	Lapp 1985: 19	62 1.89		V black-glazed	
			62 4.22	141	V mortarium	
1236	sub IVB Surface 1236	Shechem III.1: 318b	62 1.69	890	V large bowl	
1216	(sub IVB Surface 1216)	Lapp 1985: 21, 40	62 1.69	891	V jug	
			62 1.85	1110	V Attic cup	
			62 1.85	1111	cp, overhang	3.37:1
1236	on IVB Surface 1236	Shechem III.1: 318b	62 1.18	89	V cooking pot	2.10:8
1216	(sub 1216 and 1521)	Lapp 1985: 21	62 1.64	804	krater, squared	
1521			62 1.66	808	V mortarium base	
			62 1.80	1103	V jar	
			62 1.84	1106	V mortarium	2.8:9

Locus	Description	Publication Reference	Year Area/Bkt	No.	Type	Pl.
			62 1.84	1107	V black-glazed	

FIELD VII

Stratum IVB Complexes — North Complex

Locus	Description	Publication Reference	Year Area/Bkt	No.	Type	Pl.
1817	removal IV Wall 1817	Shechem III.1: fig. 270; 2: ill. 106, 107 Lapp 1985: 21	7.119	5982	V Attic black & red	
1818	removal stones for IVB Jar Stand 1818	Shechem III.1: 319a; 2: ill. 106	7.114	5850	jug b	3.15:6
1828	around V Tannur 1828 sub IV Installations	Shechem III.1: 319a, fig. 270; 2: ill. 106	7.103 7.103	5251 5252	jar base V lamp	

FIELD VII

Other Loci

Locus	Description	Publication Reference	Year Area/Bkt	No.	Type	Pl.
21.013	sub IVB Floor 21.013	Shechem III.1: 321a	21.93	714	bowl, med rolled	3.31:2
1133 1232	Pit 1133 sealed by Surface 1232	Shechem III.1: 318a	62 1.98	1200	V Attic black & red	
1239 1237	IVB pit 1239 includes rockfall 1237	Shechem III.1: 320b Lapp 1985: 22	62 1.62 62 1.63	800 801	V black-fig krater V cooking pot-heavy	2.12:4 2.10:31

FIELD VII

cf. Stratum IVB

Locus	Description	Publication Reference	Year Area/Bkt	No.	Type	Pl.
1529	Hardpack 1529 sub IV Wall 1517	Horn & Campbell 1962: app. I:45	62 4.28	189	V mortarium	2.8:15

FIELD VII

Stratum IVA — Northeast Complex

Locus	Description	Publication Reference	Year Area/Bkt	No.	Type	Pl.
1826	removal IVA Floor 1826	Shechem III.1: 319b	7.112	5846	jug g	
1824	removal IVA Cobbling 1824	Shechem III.1: 319b Lapp 1985: 21	7.110 7.110	5840A 5841	jar handle 3 V cooking pot	3.12:12 2.10:16

LOCUS	DESCRIPTION	PUBLICATION REFERENCE	YEAR AREA/BKT	NO.	TYPE	PL.
			7.112	5845	V mortarium	2.8:11
			7.115	5853	V mortarium	2.8:12
			7.115	5855	V cooking pot-heavy	2.10:26
1716	removal IVA Wall 1716	Shechem III.1: 320b, 2: ill. 107; Lapp 1985: 21, 40	8.105	5869	V Attic cup	

FIELD VII

Stratum IVA — South Complex

LOCUS	DESCRIPTION	PUBLICATION REFERENCE	YEAR AREA/BKT	NO.	TYPE	PL.
1521	on IVB Floor 1521	Shechem III.1: 318b; 2: ill. 113:9; Lapp 1985: 22	62 4.136		V black/red fig krater	
			62 4.136		V black-glazed	
1527	removal IVA Floor 1527	Shechem III.1: 319b, fig. 286; 2: ill. 113:8	4.110	5537	bowl, large shallow	3.32:12
			4.110	5540	H mortarium	3.35:4
			4.110	5541	jar Cv	3.7:3
			4.110	5546	V cooking pot-heavy	2.10:25
1527 1523	on IVA Floor 1527 sub IVA Floor 1523	Shechem III.1: 319b; 2: ill. 113:8; Lapp 1985: 21	4.9	5015	V krater-ledged	2.6:4
1525	removal IVA Press 1525	Shechem III.1: 319b, 320a, fig. 286; 2: ill. 113	4.111	5553	V jar	
			4.111	5555	V lamp	
			4.111	5556	V lamp	
			4.111	5557	jar B	
1526	L. 1526 removal large jar	Shechem III.1: 319b, fig. 286; 2: ill. 112:7	4.102, 113A	7448/A	jar A-2	3.1:12
	removal IVA Cobbling 1421 and hardpack north		62 4.20	120	V cooking pot	2.10:15
			62 4.50	282	V cooking pot-heavy	
1419	sub IVA Wall 1419	Shechem III.1: 321b; 2: ill. 107 Lapp 1985: 21	5.136	6398	V Attic cup	
			5.146	6542	V krater-sloping shoulder	2.5:14
			5.148	6547	jar Cv	
			5.148	6548	jar A-1	
			5.150	6559	jar Cv	3.7:4
			5.150	6567	jar A-3	

Locus	Description	Publication Reference	Year Area/Bkt		No.	Type	Pl.
1420	removal IVA Wall 1420 of bin	Shechem III.1: 321b	5.132		6164	jar A-1	
			5.132		6165	V mortarium	2.8:10
			5.132		6166	krater, overhang	3.34:12
1421	removal IVA Cobbling 1421 & hardpack north	Shechem III.1: 321b Lapp 1985: 21	5.133		6167	V black on brown	2.15:9
			5.133		6168	V black on brown	2.15:10
			5.135		6395	handle 2	
			5.135		6396	jar A-1	
1216	on IVB plastered Surface 1216 cf IVB	Shechem III.1: 318b Lapp 1964:14 Lapp 1985: 22	1.62		5319	krater, squared	3.34:2
			1.62		5310A	V black-fig krater	2.12:5
			1.62		5330A/ /928A	V black-fig krater	2.12:3

FIELD VII

Stratum IVA — Southern Edge Complex

Locus	Description	Publication Reference	Year	Area/Bkt	No.	Type	Pl.
1129A 1026	Fill 1129A sub IVA Wall 1026	Shechem III.1: 320b; 2: ill. 107; Campbell 1964: 2; app. I:4	64	2.3	144	jar A-1	
			64	2.4	146	V jug	
			64	2.5	171	V med bowl base	
1130A 1026	Hardpack 1130A sub IVA Wall 1026	Campbell 1964: 2; app. I:4	64	2.7	323	V jar	
			64	2.8	339	V cooking pot-heavy	
1025 1308	removal IVA Wall 1025-1308	Shechem III.1: 320b, 321a; 2: ill. 107 Lapp 1985: 21	3.140		5629	jar handle 1	3.12:2
			3.140		5631	jar C	3.4:2
			3.140		5633	jar B	3.3:4
			6.205		5587	V jug	2.3:4
1028	removal IVA Drain 1028	Shechem III.1: 320b;2: ill.107	3.143		5668	jar A-2	
1024	removal IVA Oven 1024A	Shechem III.1: 321a; fig. 287 Lapp 1985: 21	3.134b		5607/ /3804	flask [IIIA]	3.23:1
			3.118				
			3.134b		5608	jar Cv	3.7:4
			3.134b		5609	jar A-3	3.2:3
			3.134b		5610/11/ /1773	jar C	3.4:1
			3.96a			(from hardpack of oven [cf IV])	

LOCUS	DESCRIPTION	PUBLICATION REFERENCE	YEAR AREA/BKT	NO.	TYPE	PL.
			3.134b	5612	jar handle 1	
			3.136	5615	jug base, concave	3.20:1
21.011	sub IVA Floor 21.011	Shechem III.1: 321a;	21.82	607	jar C	3.4:3
		2: ill. 117:10	21.82	608	jug b	3.15:9
		Lapp 1985: 21	21.82	609	cp, overhang	3.37:4
			21.83	612	V lamp	2.11:4
			21.87	706	krater, grooved	3.33:2
			21.87	707	cp, overhang	3.37:5
			21.87	708	cp, plain	3.38:1
21.012	sub IVA or IVB Floor 21.012	Shechem III.1: 321a	21.89	709	jar B	3.3:5
			21.89	710	bowl, med to large deep	3.32:2
			21.89	711	bowl, med rolled	3.31:3
			21.89	713	jar C	

FIELD VII

Stratum IVA — Northwest (and see cf IV, below)

LOCUS	DESCRIPTION	PUBLICATION REFERENCE	YEAR AREA/BKT	NO.	TYPE	PL.
23.008	sub IVA Floor 23.008	Shechem III.1: 322b	23.56	477	V krater-wedged	2.7:1
		Lapp 1985: 21	23.56	479	bowl, med rolled	3.31:4
			23.57	481	jar C	
			23.56	482	jug b	3.15:10
			23.56	483	flask	3.23:2
23.009	above IVB Floor 23.009, sub 23.008	Shechem III.1: 322b; fig. 288	23.62	489	jar A-1	3.1:3
			23.63	492	V mortarium	2.8:13
			23.63	493	jar A-2	3.1:13
			23.63	494	flask	3.22:3
			23.64	495	H mortarium	3.35:5
			23.64	497	jar C	
			23.64		V black-glazed	
23.016	Fill 23.016 below	Shechem III.1: 322b	23.66	499	V mortarium	
23.005	IV Floor 23.005	Lapp 1985: 22	23.66	501	V mortarium base	
			23.67	502	cp, plain	3.38:2
			23.67		V Attic cup	
			23.101	882	V mortarium base	2.9:2

LOCUS	DESCRIPTION	PUBLICATION REFERENCE	YEAR AREA/BKT	NO.	TYPE	PL.
FIELD VII						
cf Stratum IV						
21.036	Pit 21.036 dug in III	Shechem III.1: 321a;	21.106	867	jar A-1	
	or II	2: ill. 117:3	21.106	868	jar A-1	
			21.106	869	jar B	3.3:7
			21.106	870	jar A-1	
			21.110	875	bowl, med rolled	
			21.123	1044	jar A-1	
			21.123	1045	jar A-1	
			21.126	1048	cp, overhang	
			21.127	1049	jar A-2	
			21.127	1050	jar A-1	
			21.131	1155	jar A-1	
			21.132	1157	V black-glazed	
			21.209	2011	lamp, relief	3.43:13
22.010	IV Pit 22.010	Shechem III.1: 321b;	22.121		V Attic cup	
		2: ill. 117:13	22.129	1053	V black-glazed	
		Lapp 1985: 22	22.132	1058/	krater, grooved	3.33:4
			22.440	/329	(sub possible IIIB Floor 22.002)	
			22.145	1256	bowl, large shallow	3.32:18
23.004	around IV Column	Shechem III.1:	23.51	475	V mortarium	2.8:16
	Base 23.004	322b; fig. 288	23.51	476	jar B	
23.005	above IV Floor 23.005	Shechem III.1: 322b	23.48	472	jar A-1	
			23.50	473	jar B	
			23.50	474	jug c	3.16:2
23.010	IV Stonefall 23.010	Shechem III.1: 322b	23.69	530	V jar handle-têt	
		Lapp 1985: 22	23.69	532	V krater,-wedged	2.7:4
			23.70	535	V jug	
			23.71	536	V jar handle-têt	
			23.76	538	V mortarium base	2.9:10
			23.76	540	V mortarium	2.8:17
			23.70		V black-glazed	
21.014	stone Installation	Horn & Campbell	21.98	722	V krater-wedged	2.7:3
	21.014	62: app. I:3				

LOCUS	DESCRIPTION	PUBLICATION REFERENCE	YEAR AREA/BKT	NO.	TYPE	PL.
			1.63	930	jar B	
			1.63	931	jar B	
			1.63	933	jar C	
			1.63	935	jar A-3	3.2:8
			1.63	938	H mortarium	3.35:9
			1.63	942	jar handle 1	
			1.64	944	bowl, med rolled	3.31:5
			1.64	945	V krater-ledged	
			1.64	947/	jar B	3.3:9
			1.61	/5296		
			1.64	949	jar C	3.4:7
			1.64	950	jar C	
			1.64	951	jar A-3	
			1.64	953	jar C	3.4:8
			1.65	955	jar C	3.4:9
			1.65	959	jar Cv	
			1.65	959A	jar C	3.4:10
			1.66	961	jug base, concave	3.20:2
			1.66	963	jar A-3	
			1.66	965	V black-glazed	
			1.66	966	jar B	
			1.66	967	jar B	
			1.66	968	H mortarium	3.35:10
			1.66	972	jar A-2	
			1.68	2850	bowl, small, disk base	3.29:7
			1.71	2860	krater, overhang	3.34:13
			1.71	2861	jar D-2	3.9:2
			1.71	2862	krater, grooved	
			1.72	2863	jar A-3	
			1.74	2865	krater, squared	3.34:5
			1.75	2866	bowl, med to large deep	3.32:4
			1.76	2870	jar A-3	
			1.76	2871	jar A-2	
			1.77	2874	bowl, med rolled	3.31:6
			1.77	2875	jar A-3	
			1.77	2876	jar C	
			1.77	2877	jar A-3	
			1.77	2878	lamp, delphiniform	3.42:9

Locus	Description	Publication reference	Year area/bkt	No.	Type	Pl.
1214	beneath IIIB Floor 1214	Shechem III.1: 325a	1.43	805	jug e	3.17:14
		Lapp 1964: 14-19	1.43	806	jar handle 2	
			1.43	809	jar D-2	3.9:1
			1.43	810	jug a	
			1.44	811	lamp, delphiniform	3.42:7
			1.44	812	jar Cv	3.7:8
			1.44	813	V jug	
			1.44	814	cp, plain	3.38:6
			1.44	815	bowl, small incurved	
			1.44	817	jar handle 4	
			1.44	819	jar handle 1	
			1.44	821	jug b	3.15:12
			1.45	822	jar handle 1	
			1.45	825A	V black-glazed	
			1.45	826	jar C	
			1.45	827	jug b	
			1.45	829	jar C	
			1.46	832	jar B	3.3:8
			1.46	833	jar C	
			1.46	834	jar Cv	3.7:7
			1.46	835	flask rim	3.23:6
			1.46	837	bowl-ETS I	
			1.53	868	jar handle 2	3.12:10
			1.53	869	bowl, small incurved	3.27:3
			1.53	870	bowl-ETS I	3.30:7
			1.53	871	jar A-2	3.1:16
			1.54	873	jar C	3.4:5
			1.54	874	jar C	
			1.55	875	jug base, ring	3.19:15
			1.55	879	jar Dv	
			1.55	878/	jar Cv	3.7:8
			1.56	/884		
			1.55	880	jar A-3	
			1.55	881	jar C	3.4:6
			1.56	882	jar handle 4	
			1.56	885	jar A-2	
			1.56	886	bowl, small, disk base	
			1.56	887	flask	3.22:-5
			1.68	2853	V mortarium base	2.9:3
			1.90	2920	jar A-3	3.2:7
			1.90	2922	bowl, small, ring base	3.29:1

LOCUS	DESCRIPTION	PUBLICATION REFERENCE	YEAR AREA/BKT	NO.	TYPE	PL.
			1.90	2923	lamp, delphiniform	3.42:8
			1.91	2925	jar D-1	
			1.91	2926	jug e	3.17:15
			1.92	2927	Rhodian jar handle	3.14:1
			1.92	2929	jar Cv	3.7:9
1715	beneath IIIB Cobbling 1715	Shechem III.1: 325a	8.54	3862	jar B	3.3:12
			8.55	3863	jar A-2	
			8.55	3865	jar C	
			8.56	3867	jar A-3	
			8.56	3869	jar A-2	
			8.56	3870	jar C	
			8.56	3871	jar C	
			8.56	3872	V jug	2.3:8
			8.57	3873	V lekythos	2.15:2
1719	sub IIIB Cobbling 1719	Shechem III.1: 325a, 327b; 2: ill. 108	8.47	3501	jar C	
			8.47	3502	bowl, small, disk base	
			8.47	3504	jar Cv	
			8.47	3506	krater, squared	3.34:6
			8.47	3507	jug base, ring	
			8.77	4583	jar handle 1	3.12:6
			8.77	4584	jar B	3.3:13
			8.77	4585	H mortarium	3.35:12
			8.77	4586	jar A-3	
			8.78	4587	bowl, large shallow	3.32:13
			8.78	4588	jar handle 1	
			8.78	4589	bowl, med rolled	
			8.78	4590	bowl, small, handle	3.29:20
			8.79	4591	H mortarium	3.35:13
			8.79	4592	bowl, large shallow	3.32:19
			8.79	4593	jar Dv	3.11:3
			8.79	4594	krater, grooved	3.33:5
			8.79	4595	jar handle 1	
			8.80	4596	V mortarium base	2.9:4
			8.80	4597	jar base	3.13:1
			8.80	4598	jar C	
			8.80	4599	jar C	
			8.80	4600	flask	
			8.81	4601	jug a	3.15:3
			8.82	4603	jar A-3	

Locus	Description	Publication reference	Year Area/Bkt	No.	Type	Pl.
			8.82	4606	V Attic cup	2.14:11
			8.83	4607	krater, grooved	3.33:6
			8.83	4608	V mortarium	2.8:20
			8.83	4609	jar A-2	3.1:18
			8.84	4612	jar C	3.4:7
			8.84	4613	bowl, large shallow	3.32:14
			8.85	4614	Rhodian jar handle	3.314:2
			8.85	4615	jar A-3	
			8.85	4616	jar A-1	
			8.85	4617	jar A-1	
			8.86	4618	jar A-1	
			8.86	4619	jug b	3.15:13
			8.86	4620	V mortarium	2.8:21
			8.86	4621	juglet	3.24:13
			8.87	4623	V jug	2.3:9
			8.89	4628	jar A-2	3.1:19
			8.90	4631	V Attic black and red	
			8.90	4632	jar Cv	
			8.90	4633	krater, plain	
			8.90	4634	jar C	
			8.90	4635	bowl, large shallow	3.32:15
			8.90	4636	jar C	3.4:12
			8.90	4637	krater, grooved	3.33:7
			8.91	5098	lamp, delphiniform	3.42:11
			8.91	5100	jar Cv	
			8.93	5108	jar C	
			8.93	5109	jar handle 3	
			8.104	5863	krater, squared	3.34:7
1506	removal III Wall 1506	Shechem III.1: 323b, 324a; 2: ills. 108, 109	4.76	4958	jar B	3.3:10
			4.76	4960	juglet	3.24:12
			4.78	3844	lamp, delphiniform	3.42:10
			4.78	4961	jar A-2	
			4.78	4963	jar B	3.3:11
			4.78	4964	jug base, concave	3.20:3
1516	removal IIIB Wall 1516	Shechem III.1: 324a; 2: ill. 108	4.79	4966	jar A-3	
			4.79	4967	flask	3.22:8
			4.79	4968	H mortarium	3.35:11
1513	removal IIIB Wall 1513 of Room A	Shechem III.1: 323b, 324a; 2: ill. 108	4.80	4969	bowl, small, ring base	
			4.80	4970	jar A-2	3.1:17
			4.80	4972	jar C	

Locus	Description	Publication Reference	Year Area/Bkt		No.	Type	Pl.
			4.80		4973	V lamp	
			4.80		4974	jar A-3	
1414	removal III Wall 1414	Shechem III.1: 323b; 2: ills. 108, 109	4.73		3842	bowl, small incurved	
1803	removal III Wall 1803-	Shechem III.1:	7.75		4017	bowl, rolled, base	3.31:14
1807	1807, 1813 of Room A	323b, fig. 289;	7.75		4018	jar Dv	3.11:2
1813		2: ills. 108, 109	7.79		4028	jug d	3.17:1
			7.79		4029	bowl, small, disk base	3.29:8
			7.79		#494a	**Ptolemy II coin**	
1816	Resurfacing 1816 of IIIB Floor 1816A in Area D	Shechem III.1: 323b; 2: ill. 112:4	7.62		3991	bowl, small, ring base	3.29:2
1824	on IVA Cobbling 1824	Shechem III.1: 319b	7.106		5259A	jar A-3	3.2:10
1523	above IV Floor 1523	Shechem III.1: 319b; fig. 286; 2: ill. 113:8	4.83		4985	flask	
1523	on IV Floor 1523 (cf. IV)	Shechem III.1: 319b; fig. 286; 2: ill. 113:8	4.86		4996	jug f	
			4.86		4997	jug d	
			4.86		#573	**Ptolemy II coin**	
1525	cleaning IV Press 1525	Shechem III.1: 319a,	4.11		5521	jug e	3.17:16
1520	sub IIIB Installation 1520	324a, figs. 286, 290	4.11		5523	jar handle 3	3.12:14
1522	sealed in Pit 1522	Shechem III.1: 318,	62	4.141	1538	juglet	3.24:2
		325a, fig. 271	62	4.142	1539	lamp, delphiniform	
		Campbell and Horn	62	4.142	1540	lamp, delphiniform	
		1962: app l:44-45	62	4.142	1541	jar A-3	
	sealed = 4:8,11,12,17,23,		62	4.142	1542	lamp-Attic	3.42:2
	27,83,85,87,88,141,142,		62	4.8	61	V mortarium base	
	14 4,146,147,157; 1:10,		62	4.8	62	V jug	2.3:14
	12-16,44, 45		62	4.8	65	V krater-wedged	2.7:6
	(for unsealed see cf		62	4.88	635	jar A-3	
	IIIB below)		62	4.88	639	V mortarium	
			62	4.141	1536/	V black/red fig krater	2.13:10
			1.61		/5309	(IIIB Fill 1216)	
			62	4.157	1783	V Attic cup	
			62	1.15	78	V cooking pot	

LOCUS	DESCRIPTION	PUBLICATION REFERENCE	YEAR AREA/BKT	NO.	TYPE	PL.
			62 1.45	542	V krater-wedged	2.7:5
			62 1.45	543	V krater-ledged	
1235	Stone Heap 1235	Horn and Campbell	62 1.91	1123/	V black/red fig krater	2.13:9
1522	probably part of Pit 1522	1962: app. I:36	1.60	/5291A	(IIIB Fill 1216)	
1106	sub unrelated IIIB Surface 1106	Shechem III.1: 327b	2.49	1006	jar B	
1017	sub IIIB Hardpack	Shechem III.1: 328b	3.62	1641	jar handle 1	
1019	1017-1019		3.62	1642	jar A-3	3.2:9
			3.62	1646	jar C	
			3.62	1647	cp, plain	3.38:8
			3.65	1667	V cooking pot	2.10:17
			3.65	1669	flask	3.22:6
			3.107	1802	V Attic cup	
			3.107	1803	jar B	
			3.107	1805	V mortarium	2.8:19
			3.107	1808	V black-glazed	
			3.107	1809	V black-glazed	

FIELD VII

cf Stratum IIIB

LOCUS	DESCRIPTION	PUBLICATION REFERENCE	YEAR AREA/BKT	NO.	TYPE	PL.
1522	unsealed in Pit 1522	Shechem III.1: 318,	62 4.132	1529	jug e	3.17:17
		325a, fig. 271	62 4.132	1530	krater, grooved	
		Horn and Campbell	62 4.138	1533	lamp-Attic	3.42:1
	(for sealed see IIIB	1962: 44	62 1.36	357	V black-glazed	
	above)		62 1.45	543	V krater-ledged	
1518	to IIIB Installation 1518	Shechem III.1:	62 4.134	1532	lamp, delphiniform	3.42:12
		324b, fig. 291	**62 4.134**	#416	**Ptolemy II or later coin**	
1018	Probe 1018 from III to	Campbell 1960b:	3.78	1720	Attic lamp	3.42:3
	IV levels	xxxiv	3.79	928B	V black on brown	
			3.79	928B	V black-glazed	
			3.80	928B	V black-glazed	
1021	above IV Surface 1021-	Shechem III.1:	3.77	1717	H mortarium base	3.36:20
1023	1023	321a, fig. 287	3.93	1763	krater, overhang	3.34:14

Locus	Description	Publication Reference	Year Area/Bkt	No.	Type	Pl.
		Campbell 1960b:	3.93	1764	unguentarium	3.25:1
		xxxv	3.93	1765	jar B	
			3.94	1769	flask	3.23:2
1808	sub IIIB Surface 1808-1507 level	Shechem III.1: 324a	7.139	6839	jar B	
			7.139	6840	V cooking pot	2.10:18
1808	on IIIB Surface 1808	Shechem III.1: 324a Campbell 1960b: xxiii	7.67	#479	**Seleucid ? Coin**	
1717 1720	unsealed IIIB Fill 1717-20, sub IIIB level western half of field	Campbell 1960b: xxx	8.60	3875	cp, overhang	3.2:6
			8.70	4193	krater, grooved	3.27:9
			8.88	4625/	V Attic cup	
			8.105	/5068	(unstratified)	2.14:1
			8.88	4626	V Attic cup	
			8.96	5124A	V jar handle-ṭêt	2.14:4
			8.96	5125	V Attic cup	
			8.107	5874	V Attic cup	2.14:5
1712 1713	L.1712-1713 unsealed but sub level of IIIB Surface 1719	Campbell 1960b: xxvi	8.68a	3897	V jar handle-ṭêt	3.2:5
1822 1823	IIIB Fill 1822-1823 above IV Installations	Lapp 1985: 40 Campbell 1960b: xxvii	7.95a	4684	V Attic cup	
22.002	sub possible IIIB Floor 22.002	Shechem III.1: 325b	22.40	235	jug b	3.15:14
			22.42	317	H mortarium	3.35:14
			22.42	325	jug c	
			22.42	342	jug b	
			22.44	322	H mortarium	3.35:15
			22.44	323	H mortarium	3.35:16
			22.44	329/	krater, grooved	3.33:4
			22.132	/1058	(see Pit 22.010 cf IV)	
			22.45	330	flask	3.23:3
			22.45	332	krater, overhang	3.34:15
			22.45	333	jug c	3.16:4
			22.47	453	krater, overhang	3.34:16
			22.48	457	jar B	
			22.49	460	krater, grooved	3.33:8
			22.50	463	krater, overhang	3.34:17
			22.50	464	krater, overhang	3.34:18

Locus	Description	Publication Reference	Year Area/Bkt	No.	Type	Pl.
			22.50	465	krater, overhang	3.34:19
			22.50	466	cp, plain	3.40:9
			22.50	467	krater, grooved	
			22.50	469	H mortarium	3:35:17
			22.50	471	jar A-1	
			22.51	337	lamp, white ware	3.43:23
			22.52	343	cp, overhang	3.37:8
			22.52	344	jar B	
			22.49	461	V jug	
			22.51	503	V juglet	2.3:15

FIELD VII

Stratum IIIA

Locus	Description	Publication Reference	Year Area/Bkt	No.	Type	Pl.
1203	sub IIIA Floor 1203 in Courtyard F	Shechem III.1: 327a Lapp 1964: 14-15, 19-21	1.40	769	lamp, delphiniform	
			1.40	770	cp, plain	
			1.40	771	juglet	3.24:14
			1.40	772	cp, plain	3.38:10
			1.40	773	jar C	
			1.40	774	cp, plain	
			1.40	775	jug d	3.26:2
			1.40	777	bowl, small, disk base	
			1.40	778	bowl, small, disk base	3.29:9
			1.40	779	cp, plain	3.39:11
			1.40	782	bowl, small incurved	
			1.40	786	cp, plain	
			1.40	787	bowl, small, disk base	3.29:10
			1.41	791	jar C	
			1.41	792	plate, fish	
			1.41	794	jar handle 3	
			1.62	795	V small bowl	
			1.41	796	jar A-3	
			1.41	797	jar handle 4	
			1.41	799	jar base	3.13:2
			1.50	848	jar A-2	
			1.50	850	jar C	
			1.51	852	cp, overhang	
			1.51	853	jug f	3.18:2
			1.51	855	jar D-3	
			1.51	856	jug base-angular	3.20:10

Locus	Description	Publication Reference	Year Area/Bkt	No.	Type	Pl.
			1.51	857	cp, lid device	3.41:1
			1.51	858	V large bowl	
			1.88	2903	bowl, small, disk base	
			1.88	2904	krater, squared	3.34:8
			1.88	2905	lamp, relief	3.42:15
			1.88	2906	jar D-3	3.10:1
			1.88	2907	jar D-1	
			1.88	2908	D-2	
			1.88	2909	cp, plain	
1214	on IIIB Floor 1214	Shechem III.1: 327a	1.52	861	jar D-2	3.9:3
1203	below IIIA Floor 1203		1.52	862	jug d	3.17:3
			1.52	864	jar handle 2	3.12:11
			1.52	866	bowl, small, disk base	
			1.89	2911	jar C	
			1.89	2912	jar D-1	3.8:3
			1.89	2913	jug g	3.19:1
			1.89	2915	jug e	3.17:18
			1.89	2916	plate, fish	3.28:15
			1.89	2917	jar D-2	3.9:4
1227	sub IIIA Floor 1227-	Shechem III.1: 326b;	1.43	1839	jar Cv	3.7:10
1511	1511 in Room E	2: ill. 109	62 1.20	93/ /588	Megarian bowl ware (below 1530 fill)	3.30:11
		Lapp 1964: 14-15	4.30	1832	lamp, delphiniform	3.42:13
			4.39	1834	jar handle 3	
			4.42	1838	unguentarium	3.26:2
			4.44	1840	jar D-1	3.8:4
			4.44	1842	jar A-3	3.2:11
	embedded in Floor 1227		62 1	#8	**Antiochus III coin**	
1530	Fill 1530 sub Floor 1227	Horn and Campbell	62 4.107	911	flask	3.22:9
		1962: app.I:46	62 4.70	588/ /93	Megarian bowl ware (sub 1511 above)	3.30:11
1107	removal IIIA Walls	Shechem III.1: 326a;	2.69	1121	jar A-2	
1109	1107-1109	2: ill. 109	**2.69**	**#247**	**Ptolemy II coin**	
			2.70	1123	bowl, small incurved	3.27:4
			2.70	1124	jar C	
			2.70	1127	jar C	
			2.120	5501	jar A-2	

LOCUS	DESCRIPTION	PUBLICATION REFERENCE	YEAR AREA/BKT	NO.	TYPE	PL.
			2.120	5505	V cooking pot	
			2.120	5506	jar D-2	
			2.120	5507	cp, overhang	3.37:10
1110	removal IIIA Buttress	Shechem III.1: 326a;	1.35	763	cp, plain	3.38:14
1211	1110-1211	2: ill. 109	1.35	764	jug b	
			2.56	1043	jar A-2	
			2.56	1045	jar C	
1206	removal IIIA Walls	Shechem III.1: 326a;	1.48	839	H mortarium	3.35:18
1210	1206-1210	2: ill. 109	1.48	840	krater, overhang	
			1.48	842	jar B	
			1.111	5246	jar B	
			1.112	6246	lamp, relief	3.43:16
			1.112	6247	bowl, small, disk base	3.29:11
1408	removal IIIA Wall	Shechem III.1: 325b,	5.85	3978	jar A-3	
	1408	326a; 2: ill. 109	5.86	3980	jug c	3.16:7
			5.86	3981	jug d	3.17:4
			5.86	3982	V black/red fig krater	
			5.87	5227	V Attic black and red	
			5.88	5228	jug d	3.17:5
			5.88	5229	jug c	3.16:8
1505	removal IIIA Walls	Shechem III.1: 326a;	4.62	3828	jug c	3.26:6
1510	1505-1510 of Room E	2: ill. 109	4.62	3829	jar B	
			4.62	3877	jar C	
			4.77	3847	V jar handle-*ṭêt*	2.3:9
			4.62	3831	V Attic cup	
1509	cleaning IIIB Tannur	Shechem III.1: 324,	4.37	1828	jar D-3	3.10:2
1528	1509 and Plaster 1528	326a, fig. 291;	4.37	1830	jar C	
	(cf IIIB)	2: ill. 108;	4.37	1831	jar handle 1	3.12:7
1802	sub IIIA Floor 1802-	Shechem III.1: 327a;	7.30	2286	jar D-1	
1508	1508, Rooms G and H	2: ill. 113:6	7.30	2287	jar handle 3	3.12:15
			7.30	2288	jug f	3.18:5
			7.30	2289/90/91	jar D-3	3.10:3
			7.30	2292	jug g	3.19:2
			7.57	3120	jar D-3	3.10:4
			7.57	3121	bowl, small, disk base	3.29:13

LOCUS	DESCRIPTION	PUBLICATION REFERENCE	YEAR AREA/BKT	NO.	TYPE	PL.
			7.57	3122	bowl, small incurved	
			7.57	3123	cp, plain	3.39:13
			7.57	3124	jar B	
			7.57	3125	krater, grooved	
			7.57	3126	jug c	3.16:9
			7.57	**#526**	**Ptolemy II coin**	
			7.60	3133	H mortarium	3.35:19
			7.60	3135	jug b	3.15:16
			7.60	3137	cp, lid device	3.41:2
			7.60	**#89**	**unidentified coin**	
			7.58	3185	V Attic cup	
1801	sub IIIA Floor 1801 in Room J	Shechem III.1: 327a	7.25	2244/47/59 2263/65	jug d	3.17:6
			7.25	2249	bowl, small, disk base	
			7.25	2251/46/ /2250/58	jug-unique	3.21:2
			7.25	2252	jar D-1	3.8:5
			7.25	2253	jug f	3.18:4
			7.25	2254	jar A-3	
			7.25	2256	jar D-2	
			7.25	2257	lamp, delphiniform	
			7.25	2260	jar D-2	
			7.25	2261	jar D-2	
1815	cleaning above IIIB Surface 1815	Shechem III.1: 324a; 2: ill. 108	7.88	4664	V cooking pot-heavy	2.10:28
1806	removal IIIA Wall 1806	Shechem III.1: 326b; 2: ill. 109	7.66 7.66	3995 3996	jar handle 3 V Attic black and red	3.12:16
1811	removal IIIA Wall 1811 facing	Shechem III.1: 325b; 2: ill. 109	7.58 7.73	4001 3139	lamp, delphiniform jar C	
1805N	removal IIIA Wall 1805N Room J	Shechem III.1: 323, 325b; 2: ills. 109, 112	7.77 7.77 7.82 7.82 7.82 7.82 7.82	4022 4024 4644 4645 4646 4647 4648	bowl, small, handle jar A-3 V Attic cup jar C jar B cp, plain krater, squared	

Locus	Description	Publication Reference	Year Area/Bkt	No.	Type	Pl.
			7.82	4649	jar C	
			7.82	4650	jar A-2	
1810	removal IIIA Walls	Shechem III.1: 323b,	7.74	4014	bowl, small incurved	
1812	1810, 1812 and Threshold	326; 2: ill. 109	7.74	4015	lamp, relief	3.43:14
1814	1814, Room J		7.74	#463	**Ptolemy II coin**	
			7.80	4032	flask	
1701	removal IIIA Structure	Shechem III.1: 327b;	8.41	2799	jar B	
1705	1707-1705-1701-1601	2: ill. 109	8.41	2800	jug base, concave	3.20:4
1707			8.50	3512	jar C	3.4:14
1601			9.43	3208	jar handle 1	
			9.43	3213	jar C	
			9.43	3215	V jar	
			9.44	3216	jar B	3.3:16
			9.44	3217	jar A-3	
			9.44	3218	cp, overhang	3.37:11
			9.44	3219	bowl-ETS I	3.30:4
			9.44	3222	jar A-3	
			9.44	3223	V krater-ledged	
			9.45	3231	jar B	
1604	removal IIIA Cobbling	Shechem III.1: 327b	9.39	3190A	juglet	3.248
	1604		9.42b	3202	V cooking pot-heavy	2.10:29
			9.42b	3205	jar C	
1703	sub IIIA Cobbling	Shechem III.1: 325a,	8.44	3483	jar C	
1602	1703-1602	327b; 2: ill. 116:4	8.44	3484	jar A-2	3.1:20
1715	on IIIB Cobbling 1715	Shechem III.1: 325a	8.52	3516	bowl, med to large deep	3.32:6
	sub IIIA Cobbling		8.52	3517	krater, grooved	3.33:10
	1703-1602					
1007	removal IIIA Wall	Shechem III.1:	3.61a	1632	jug f	3.18:3
	1007	328b; 2: ill. 109	3.63b	1652	jug c	3.16:5
			3.64	1657	V cooking pot-heavy	2.10:27
			3.64	1660	V mortarium	2.8:22
1008	removal IIIA Wall	Shechem III.1:	3.63a	1648	jar B	3.3:15
21.007	1008-21.007	328a; 2: ill. 109	3.63a	1649	jug b	

LOCUS	DESCRIPTION	PUBLICATION REFERENCE	YEAR AREA/BKT	NO.	TYPE	PL.
21.006	removal IIIA Wall 21.006	Shechem III.1: 328; 2: ill. 109	21.44	313	jug d	
1010	removal IIIA Wall 1010	Shechem III.1: 328b	3.116	3797	jar Dv	
			3.117	3800	jar C	
			3.118	3802	V black-glazed	
			3.118	3803	jar C	
			3.118	3804/	flask	
			3.134b	/5607	(removal IVA Oven 1024A)	
1015	removal IIIA Drain	Shechem III.1:	3.60	1623	V krater-high neck	2.5:9
1016	1015-1016	328b; ill. 109	3.60	1624	jar C	
21.004	21.004 sidewalls		3.60	1625	jar C	3.4:13
			3.60	1626	jar A-3	
			3.60	1629	jar B	3.3:14
			3.60	1630	jar B	
	continuing removal		21.51	431	V krater-ledged	
21.034	IIIA Fill 21.034 below	Shechem III.1: 328b;	21.52	435	V lamp	
21.009	Floor 21.009	2: ill 117:4,5	21.55	# 136	**Ptolemy II coin**	
		Horn and Campbell	21.58	439	V lamp	
		1962: app. I:6	21.61	451	V lamp	2.11:6
			21.62	452	V mortarium	2.8:23
			21.71	593	V Attic cup	
			21.71	598	lamp, delphiniform	3.42:16
			21.79	599	V mortarium base	2.9:6
			21.100	723	V Attic black and red	
			21.117	999	V Attic black and red	
			21.117	1000	V black-glazed	
21.035	Debris 21.035 sub IIIA	Shechem III.1: 328b	21.64	506	jug c	3.16.10
21.031	walls and Floor 21.031	Horn and Campbell	21.67	511	bowl, large shallow	3.32:16
		1962: app. I:7, 8	21.67	512	bowl, med rolled	3.31:7
			21.68	517	V lamp	
			21.145	1242	V jug	
			21.156	1327	V cooking pot	
			21.156	1329	V jar	
22.001	sub IIIA Floor 22.001	Shechem III.1:	22.34	228	H mortarium	3.35:20
	above Floor 22.002	325b, 327b	22.34	229	lamp, delphiniform	3:42:15
			22.34	230	V black-glazed	

LOCUS	DESCRIPTION	PUBLICATION REFERENCE	YEAR AREA/BKT	NO.	TYPE	PL.
22.002	above possible IIIB Floor 22.002; sub IIIA Floor 22.001	Shechem III.1: 325b	22.28	224	V cooking pot-heavy	2.10:30
			22.25	**#133**	**Ptolemais-Ake coin**	
23.001	23.001a sub IIIA Hardpack 23.001	Shechem III.1: 327b	23.37	171	V black-glazed	
			23.37	172	V black-glazed	
1017	on IIIB Hardpack	Shechem III.1: 328b	3.106	1796	jar A-3	
1019	1017-1019		3.106	1797	jar handle 2	
			3.106	1798	bowl, med to large deep	3.32:5
			3.106	1800	jar C	
1306	sub IIIA Cobbling	Shechem III.1:	6.72	1949	jug b	3.15:15
1307	1306 and 1307	327b, fig. 294	6.74	1955	jar A-3	3.2:12
			6.74	1957	bowl, small, disk base	3.29:12
			6.75	1960	krater, plain	
			6.75	1961	krater, overhang	3.34:20
			6.75	1963	krater, squared	
			6.77	1965	jar B	
			6.77	1966	krater, grooved	3.33:9
			6.78	1971	jar D-1	
			6.78	1972	jar C	
1006	sub unrelated IIIA Wall 1006	Shechem III.1: 328b	3.55	1597	flask	3.22:10

FIELD VII

cf Stratum IIIA

LOCUS	DESCRIPTION	PUBLICATION REFERENCE	YEAR AREA/BKT	NO.	TYPE	PL.
1204	removal Mortar 1204 of IIIA occupation	Shechem III.1: 326b cf Lapp 1964: 14, 15, 24-26	1.22	91	cp, lid device	3.41:3
			1.22	92	simple plate	3.28:22
			1.22	94	jug f	3.18:6
			1.22	95	jug c	3.16:11
			1.22	97	juglet	3.24:10
			1.49	844	jug base, concave	3.20:7
			1.49	847	jar handle 1	
1106	on unrelated IIIB Surface 1106	Shechem III.1: 327b	2.44	991	jar C	
			2.44	992	jug e	

LOCUS	DESCRIPTION	PUBLICATION REFERENCE	YEAR AREA/BKT	NO.	TYPE	PL.
1802	sub IIIA Floor 1802-	Campbell 1960a:	7.24	2243	jug-unique	3.21:1
1508	1508 - unsealed	xii	7.24	#240	**Ptolemais-Ake**	
1719	over IIIB Surface 1719	Shechem III.1: 327b	8.46	3490	bowl, med rolled	3.31:10
1520	on IIIB Bin 1520	Shechem III.1: 324a, fig. 290; 2: ill. 108 Campbell 1960a: app. I:xxii	4.64	#481	**Antiochus III coin**	
22.001	on IIIA Floor 22.001	Shechem III.1: 327b	22.23	166	H mortarium	3.35:22
1009	L. 1009 around IIIA Drain 1015-16	Campbell 1960a: app. I:xx	3.28	186	bowl, med rolled	3.31:8
			3.28	187	V mortarium	2.8:24
			3.28	188	bowl, med rolled	3.31:9
			3.29	191	jug c	3.16:12
			3.43	1542	jug c	
			3.46	1551	jug c	
			3.48	1562	H mortarium	3.35:21
			3.48	1567	bowl, small, disk base	
			3.51	1583	jar base	3.13:3
			3.61b	1639	cp, plain	
			3.66	1670	lamp, delphiniform	3.42:16
1514	Pit 1514	Shechem III.1: 327a	4.29	1827	cp, plain	
			4.84	4986	jar base	
			4.84	4989	jar C	
			4.85	4991	cp, plain	
			4.85	4992	jug g	
			4.85	4993	lamp, delphiniform	
			4.88	5003	jar D-2	
			4.100	5377	jug b	
			4.100	5378	jug f	3.18:7
			4.100	5383	jug e	3.17:19
			4.100/	5379/	jug base-concave	3.20:6
			4.101	5382		
			4.101	5380	krater, grooved	3.33:11
			4.101	5381	bowl, med rolled	
			4.101	5383	jug e	3.17:19
			4.101	5385	jar D-1	
			4.103	5267	V krater-wedged	
			4.103	5268	bowl-Attic, base	3.30:3

Locus	Description	Publication Reference	Year Area/Bkt	No.	Type	Pl.
1477	Pit 1477	Shechem III.1: 322a	62 5.54	681	V krater-ledged	
			62 5.55	686	V black on brown	2.15:12
			62 5.55	686b	V black on brown	
			62 5.55	685	V black-glazed	
			62 5.55		V black-glazed	
			62 5.57	687	jug c	
1531	pit top courses of Wall	Horn and Campbell	62 1.51	541	jar C	3.4:15
1544	1531, west wall V	1962: app. I:45	62 1.51	572	V black-glazed	
1545	Installation 1544-45	cf Shechem III.1: 301b				
23.017	Pit 23.017 near column base	Shechem III.1: 322b	23.93	883	jug g	3.19:3
		Horn and Campbell 1962: app. I.19	23.93	1068	jug base, concave	3.20:7

FIELD VII

Stratum II

Locus	Description	Publication Reference	Year Area/Bkt	No.	Type	Pl.
1103	removal II Wall 1103	Shechem III.1: 329b	2.53	1033	H mortarium	3:36:5
			2.53	1038	jug b	
			2.53	1040	jar B	
			2.53	1041	jar C	3.5:4
			2.54	1019	jar handle 1	
			2.54	1022	jar handle 4	3.12:19
			2.54	1024	H mortarium	3.36:6
			2.54	1025	bowl, small, ring base	3.29:3
			2.54	1026	jar A-2	
			2.54	1028	jar B	
			2.54	1032	lamp, delphiniform	3.43:8
1227	above IIIA Floor 1227 in Room E	Shechem III.1: 326b	1.23	110	jug base, angular	3.20:12
		Lapp 1964: 14-15,	1.23	111/	unguentarium	3.25:3
		24-26	1.26	/116		
			1.25	#22	**Antiochus III coin**	
			1.26	114	unguentarium	3.25:4
			1.26	115	bowl, small, disk base	3.29:15
			1.30	748	jar handle 4	
			1.30	749	bowl, small, disk base	
			1.30	750	bowl, small incurved	3.27:5
			1.30	753	jug d	3.17:8

Locus	Description	Publication reference	Year Area/Bkt	No.	Type	Pl.
			1.33	761	plate, ledge/simple	3.28:23
			1.33	#57	**Ptolemy III coin**	
			1.101	3744	bowl, large shallow	3.32:21
			1.101	3745	lamp-Attic	3.42:4
			1.101	3747	krater, overhang	3.34:22
			1.101	3748	jug e	3.17:21
			2.25	41	jar handle 1	
			2.25	#17	**Ptolemy II coin**	
	cf IIIA		2.27a	291	jug b	3.15:17
			2.27a	293	krater, plain	3.34:25
			2.31	309	H mortarium	3.36:4
			2.31	#20	**Demetrius II coin**	
			2.41	988	jar C	
			2.41	989	cp, overhang	3.37:12
			4.27	1821	jar handle 4	3.12:20
			4.27	1822	jar D-2	
			4.32a	2453	jar D-3	3.10:7
			4.59	3824	jar D-3	
			4.59	3825	bowl, small flattened	3.28:13
			4.59	3826	bowl, small incurved	
			4.59	#434	**Antiochus IV coin**	
			4.59	#448	**Antiochus III coin**	
			4.115	7369	bowl, small, disk base	
			4.115	7370	jar D-3	
			4.115	7369A	V Attic cup	
1203	on IIIA Surface 1203 in Courtyard F	Shechem III.1: 325a Lapp 1964:14-15, 21-24	1.18	83	jar D-3	3.10:6
			1.18	85	H mortarium	3.36:3
			1.18	86	plate, fish	3.28:18
			1.19	89A	unguentarium	3.255
			1.29	732	jar D-2	
			1.29	734	jar D-2	
			1.29	735	jar C	
			1.29	736	jar C	
			1.29	737	jar D-1	3.8:7
			1.29	741	plate, fish	3.28:17
			1.29	743	jar D-1	
			1.29	744	jar C	
			1.29	745	bowl, small, disk base	
			1.29	746	jug base, angular	3.20:11
			1.87	2890	bowl, small, disk base	3.29:17

Locus	Description	Publication reference	Year area/bkt	No.	Type	Pl.
			1.87	2892	jug base, concave	3.20:8
			1.87	2894	bowl, small, disk base	
			1.87	2895	jar C	
			1.87	2896	jug d	
			1.87	2898	bowl, small, disk base	
			1.87	2899	cp, concave	3.40:13
			1.87	2902	fish plate	
			1.102	3749	cp, lid device	3.41:4
			1.87	2891	V krater-ledged	
1802	above IIIA Floor 1802-	Shechem III.1: 327a;	7.22	2213	unguentarium	3.25:6
1508	1508	2: ill. 113:6	7.22	2214	unguentarium	3.25:7
		Lapp 1964: 14-15,	7.22	2216	small bowl disk base	3.29:18
		21-24	7.22	2217	jar D-2	3.8:9
			7.22	2220	bowl, small incurved	3.27:6
			7.22	2221	jug base, ring	
			7.22	2222	jar C	
			7.22	2224	bowl, small incurved	
			7.22	2225	jar D-3	
			7.22	2226	bowl, small incurved	3.27:7
			7.22	2227	bowl, Attic	3.30:1
			7.46	3162	cp, concave	3.40:11
			7.46	3164	cp, concave	3.40:12
			7.46	3165	jug g	3.19:4
			7.58	3127	jar D-3	3.10:8
			7.58	3129	plate, fish	
			7.58	3131	jug d	3.17:10
			7.58	3132	bowl, small incurved	
			7.58	3187	bowl, small incurved	
			7.20	2186	V krater-ledged	
			7.58	3185	V black/red fig krater	4.13:14
1703	above IIIA Cobbling 1703	Shechem III.1: 327b	8.26	2745	jar C	
1205	II occupation Pit 1205-	Shechem III.1:	1.21	98	jar Dv	3.11:9
1207	1207	330b, 327a	1.21	99	plate, ledge/simple	3.28:24
			1.21	102	plate, fish	3.28:19
			1.21	106	jug f	3.18:9
			1.21	108	lamp, delphiniform	3.43:7
			1.24	120	cp, plain	
			1.24	122	flask	3.23:5

LOCUS	DESCRIPTION	PUBLICATION REFERENCE	YEAR AREA/BKT	NO.	TYPE	PL.
			1.28	117	jar C	3.5:3
			1.28	118	lamp, relief	3.43:17
			1.28	119	cp, lid device	3.41:5
			1.28	**#36**	**Ptolemy II coin**	
			1.32	754	bowl-ETS I	
			1.32	755	jug e	3.17:20
			1.32	758	bowl, small, disk base	3.29:16
			1.81	2887	cp, overhang	3.37:13
			1.81	2888	jug d	3.17:9
			1.81	2889	plate, fish	3.28:20
1820	L. 1820 pit of IIIA Floor	Shechem III.1.1:	7.55	3117A	jar base	3.13:9
1801	1801 with II storage jar	327a, 330b; 2: ill. 112	7.55	3118	cp, plain	
	3117A in Room J					

FIELD VII

cf Stratum II

LOCUS	DESCRIPTION	PUBLICATION REFERENCE	YEAR AREA/BKT	NO.	TYPE	PL.
1103	around & on II Wall	Shechem III.1: 328b	2.26	286	jug c	3.16:15
	1103		2.27b	294	Rhodian jar handle	3.13:3
			2.28	297	H mortarium base	3.36:21
1108	Rockfall 1108 south of	Campbell 1960a:	**2.35**	**#21**	**Cleopatra/Ant.VIII coin**	
	Room E above IIIA level	viii	**2.39**	**#47**	**Antiochus III coin**	
1300	above & on Hardpack	Shechem III.1: 330	4.21	278	unguentarium	3.25:8
1400	1500-1400-1300		4.49	2937	jug f	3.18:10
1500			5.30	2316	juglet	3.24:11
1702	above possible IIIA	Shechem III.1: 327b	8.25	2742	V stamped jar handle	
	Surface 1702		**8.61**	**#528**	**Ptolemy II coin**	

FIELD VII

Unstratified

LOCUS	DESCRIPTION	PUBLICATION REFERENCE	YEAR AREA/BKT	NO.	TYPE	PL.
	unstratified		62 VII		black/red fig krater	2.13:1
	unstratified		62 VII	629	black/red fig krater	2.13:13
	surface		64 1.6	61	V krater-ledged	
	surface		62 1.2		V black-glazed	

Locus	Description	Publication reference	Year Area/Bkt	No.	Type	Pl.
	unstratified		62 1.31	268	V krater-ledged	
	unstratified		62 1.32	47	lamp-Attic	
	unstratified		VII.1.71		V Attic black & red	
	unstratified		VII.1.75		V black-glazed	
	balk cleaning		62 1.77	898	Rhodian jar handle	3.14:7
	unstratified		1.87	1114	V Attic black & red	
	surface fill		1.99	3736	cp, plain	3.40:4
	surface fill		1.100	3741	jar D-1	
	surface fill		1.108	5236	lamp, delphiniform	3.43:9
	surface fill		1.108	5238	juglet	3.24:15
	surface fill		1.109	5239	lamp, relief	3.42:18
	surface fill		1.109	5240	jug base, concave	
	unstratified		1.118	7322	V lamp	
	unstratified		2.4	160	V Attic black & red	
	surface		2.7	14	unguentarium	3.26:9
	unstratified		62 2.11	253	V krater-high neck	2.5:10
	unstratified		2.20	34	V krater-wedged	2.7:8
	unstratified		62 2.25	358	V jar	
	unstratified		62 2.25	359	V jar	
	unstratified		2.33	310	V bottle	2.3:18
	rockfall		2.39	980	unguentarium	3.26:5
	unstratified		2.51	1013/A	jug-unique	3.21:5
	probe trench		2.60	1069/	Attic lamp	3.42:5
	unstratified		2.117	/5221		
	L. 1112 down to IV floor		2.62	1081	V jar handle-ṭêt	2.2:8
	probe trench		2.66	1095	juglet	3.24:5
	down to IV		2.68	1115	V juglet	2.3:17
	contaminated Stone Pile 1161		62 2.70	1132	V jar handle-lion stamp	2.2:9
	Fill 1113		2.72	1139	V black-glazed	
	unstratified		2.75	1283	V Attic cup	2.14:9
	unstratified		2.87	4938	V black-glazed	
	unstratified		2.99	4952	V lekythos	
	unstratified		2.101	4955	V Attic cup	2.14:6
	surface fill		2.113	5209	V krater-wedged	
	unstratified		62 2.113	1840	V cooking pot	
	unstratified		2.114	5216	V Attic cup	
	unstratified		2.117	5222	V lekythos	
	unstratified		2.118	5498	V krater-ledged	
	unstratified		2.119	4673/	V lekythos	
	unstratified		5.29	/2759		

Locus	Description	Publication Reference	Year Area/Bkt	No.	Type	Pl.
	unstratified		2.119	5225	V lekythos	
	unstratified		2.129	6500	V cooking pot	
	surface		3.4	44	lamp, relief	3.43:19
	unstratified		3.6	57	unguentarium	3.26:8
	unstratified		3.7	97	jug-unique	3.21:6
	unstratified		62 3.10	98	V cooking pot-heavy	2.10:32
	surface		3.11	67	unguentarium	3.26:7
	surface fill		3.18	149	V black-glazed	
	surface fill		3.19	151	jar base	
	surface fill		3.19	156	jar handle 2	
	unstratified		3.23	172	lamp-Attic	3.42:6
	surface fill		3.25	175	flask	3.23:9
	surface fill		3.25	178	jar handle 1	
	surface fill		3.27	182	H mortarium	3.36:7
	surface fill		62 3.27	254	V Attic cup	2.14:13
	unstratified		62 3.29	/215/	V Attic cup	2.14:8
	unstratified		62 3.29		V black-glazed	
	unstratified		62 3.30	317	bowl, small, handle	
	unstratified		62 3.53	1151	V Attic cup	2.14:12
	unstratified		62 3.56	671	unstratified	2.10:33
	unstratified		62 3.84	1388	V cooking pot-heavy	2.10:34
	unstratified		62 3.96	1455	V cooking pot	
	unstratified		3.131	5593	V mortarium base	2.9:7
Pit 1029B			3.152	6271	black/red fig krater	
	surface		4.8	260	V krater-ledged	
	surface fill		4.18	265	unguentarium	3.25:12
	surface fill		4.19	267	bowl, Attic	3.30:2
	surface fill		4.22	1812	bowl, med rolled	
	unstratified		4.47	1844	V krater-wedged	
	surface fill		4.55	2948	V black-glazed	
	surface fill		4.56	2952	jar D-1	
	unstratified		4.72	3848	black/red fig krater	2.13:6
	unstratified		4.83	4983	V krater-ledged	
	unstratified		4.89	5008	bowl, small incurved	3.28:10
	unstratified		4.116	7371	V krater-ledged	
	unstratified		4.116	7382	V black-glazed	
	unstratified		4.145	1774	V black on brown	
	surface		5.1	220	black/red fig krater	2.13:15

Locus	Description	Publication Reference	Year Area/Bkt	No.	Type	Pl.
	unstratified		62 5.8	123	V cooking pot	2.10:19
	surface		5.9	227	jug-unique	3.21:7
	surface		5.9	228	unguentarium rim	
	unstratified		62 5.10	144	V krater-wedged	
	1485 rockfall or pit		62 5.28	421	V lamp	
	1485 rockfall or pit		62 5.28	422	V mortarium base	2.9:8
	1485 rockfall or pit		62 5.28	424	cp, overhang	3.37:14
	disturbed debris of street		5.22	7441A	V jar-misc	2.1:20
	disturbed debris of street		5.40	2328	V lekythos	2.15:6
	disturbed debris of street		5.69a	3914	jug-unique	3.21:8
	disturbed debris of street		5.70	3943A	juglet #531	3.24:7
	unstratified		5.79	3963A	plate, ledge/simple	3.28:26
	unstratified		5.98	4951	V krater-wedged	2.7:10
	disturbed debris of street		5.117	5825	V Attic cup	
	disturbed debris of street		5.124	5838	V krater-wedged	
	disturbed debris of street		5.124	5839	black/red fig krater	2.13:11
	unstratified		5.129	6162	bowl, small, handle	
	unstratified		5.161	6778	V krater-ledged	
	unstratified		6.159	4173	juglet	
	unstratified		62 6.26	420	V Attic black & red	
	unstratified		6.31	295	V Attic cup	
	unstratified		6.56	1859	V krater-wedged	
	unstratified		6.60	1877	V Attic black & red	
	unstratified		6.64	1901	V krater-wedged	
	unstratified		6.68	1935	V lamp	
	unstratified		6.80	1982	V lamp	
	unstratified		6.85	2001	bowl, small, handle	
	unstratified		6.101	2148	V krater-ledged	
	unstratified		6.104	2020	H mortarium	3.36:8
	unstratified		6.109	2054	V krater-wedged	
	unstratified		6.155	4161	V krater-wedged	2.7:10
	surface fill		6.169	4185	V krater-wedged	
	surface fill		6.171	4186	V Attic cup	
	surface fill		6.172	5035	V lamp	
	unstratified		6.185	5065	black/red fig krater	
	unstratified		62 7.11		V Attic cup	
	surface fill		7.21	2187	unguentarium	3.26:1
	surface fill		7.21	2188	unguentarium	3.26:2
	surface fill		7.21	2189	unguentarium	3.26:3

LOCUS	DESCRIPTION	PUBLICATION REFERENCE	YEAR AREA/BKT	NO.	TYPE	PL.
	surface fill		7.21	2190	unguentarium	3.26:4
	unstratified		7.28	944	V jar-misc	
	unstratified		62 7.22	840	V jar	
	unstratified		7.37	2295	V krater-ledged	
	unstratified		62 7.41	1214	V jug	
	surface fill		7.52	3169	H mortarium	3.36:9
	surface fill		7.53	3176	jar handle 3	
	surface fill		7.54	3177	V krater-ledged	2.6:6
	surface fill		7.54	3179	jar D-1	
	surface fill		7.54	3181	V lekythos	
	unstratified		7.58	3188	V krater-ledged	
	surface fill		7.73	3138	V lekythos	
	unstratified		7.95A	4679	V black-glazed	
	unstratified		7.107	5261	V krater-wedged	
	probe trench		7.149	7374	jug base, concave	3.20:9
	probe trench		7.149	7378	cp, plain	
	probe trench		7.149	7377/	jug e	3.17:23
	unstratified		7.151	7381		
	unstratified		7.151	7385	V cooking pot-heavy	
	unstratified		8.21	1527	flask	3.23:10
	unstratified		8.31	2764	V lekythos	2.15:3
	unstratified		8.33	2775	V juglet	2.3:16
	unstratified		8.43	3478	V krater-ledged	
	unstratified		8.64	3884	V krater-wedged	
	unstratified		8.87	3890	V Attic cup	
	unstratified		8.92	5105	V lekythos	2.15:4
	unstratified		8.102	5142	V krater-ledged	2.6:7
	surface fill		8.108	5878	V black on brown	
	surface fill		9.10	2375	V black-glazed	
	surface fill		9.11	2368	V krater-ledged	
	surface fill		9.13	/2373	V Attic cup	
	unstratified		9.24	2398	V krater-ledged	
	unstratified		9.25	2400	V Attic cup	
	unstratified		9.27	2410	V Attic cup	
	unstratified		9.38	3189	V lekythos	
	surface fill		9.42A	3201	V lamp	
	unstratified		9.43	3228	V cooking pot	2.10:20
	surface		9.60	2366	bowl, small, handle	
	unstratified		9.79	5894	juglet	3.24:6

Locus	Description	Publication reference	Year area/bkt	No.	Type	Pl.
	unstratified		21.2	146	V krater-wedged	
	unstratified		21.10	74	V cooking pot	
	surface		21.10	75	Rhodian jar handle	3.14:9
	unstratified		21.22	129	V lamp	
	above & around VII Wall 21.015		21.97	719	V krater-ledged	2.6:8
	unstratified		22.5	76	V krater-wedged	
	surface		22.20	40	lamp, relief	3.43:20
	unstratified		22.23	167	V jug	2.3:10
	unstratified		22.57	520	jug d	3.17:13
	unstratified		22.71	615	V Attic cup	2.14:14
	unstratified		22.73	617	V mortarium base	
	unstratified		22.85	737	V lamp	
	unstratified		23.5	41	V lamp	
	surface		23.13	43	V krater-wedged	2.7:11
	surface		23.14	44	lamp, relief	3.43:21
	around Stones 23.002		23.32	164	V lekythos	
	around Stones 23.002		23.32	165	V Attic cup	
	unstratified		23.33	153	V krater-wedged	
	around Wall 23.003		23.40	236	V Attic cup	
	around Wall 23.003		23.40	237	V Attic black & red	2.15:8
	unstratified		23.87	753	jug e - large fragment	
	unstratified		23.91	757	jug f	3.18:11
	around VII Wall (?) 23.012		23.92	763	jar D-3	3.10:15
	around VII Wall (?) 23.012		23.92	766	V cooking pot - heavy	
	around VII Wall (?) 23.012		23.92	768	V jar handle-*têt*	
	near column base		23.95	1067	cp, concave	3.40:5

FIELD IX

Stratum VI

1962

Locus	Description	Publication reference	Year area/bkt	No.	Type	Pl.
9043	fragment. Wall Base 9043	Callaway 1962: xxi	1.101	465/	V mortarium	2.8:1
	unstratified		1.90-91	/366		

LOCUS	DESCRIPTION	PUBLICATION REFERENCE	YEAR AREA/BKT	NO.	TYPE	PL.
FIELD IX						
Stratum V						
9034	V compact gray Layer 9034	Lapp 1985: 19 Callaway 1962: xv	1.69 1.73	213 249	V krater-sloping shoulder V krater-high neck	2.5:11 2.5:1
9037	V Surface 9037	Shechem III.1: 299; fig. 269; 2: ills. 143:11,144:12 Lapp 1985: 19	1.76	261	V jar	2.1:1
9273 9274	V Surface 9273 outside Wall 9274	Shechem III.1: 299; 2: ill. 144:11 Lapp 1985: 19 Callaway 1962: xvi	2.56 2.56 2.56 2.57 2.57 2.60	176 179 180 183 184 215	V cooking pot V jar V jar V small bowl V jar V cooking pot	2.10:2 2.4:2 2.10:1
9278	V Fill 9278 over VI remains	Shechem III.1: 300 Lapp 1985: 19	2.69 2.69	276 277	V medium bowl V large bowl	2.4:6 2.4:10
9524	V Debris 9524	Shechem III.1: 300; 2: ills. 141:13, 143:11 Lapp 1985: 19	3.87 3.87	287 288	V krater-high neck V krater-high neck	2.5:2 2.5:3
9531	V (probably) Rubble 9531	Callaway 1962: xvi	3.104	382	V cooking pot	
9768	V Layer 9768	Lapp 1985: 19 Callaway 1962: xvii	4.6	245	V flask	2.3:11
9770	V Layer (floor?) 9770	Shechem III.1: 299 Lapp 1985: 19	4.63	246	V jar	2.1:2
9774 9768	V Layer 9774 =V Layer 9768	Callaway 1962: xvii	4.67	293	V jar	
9778 9774	V Layer 9778=9774	Callaway 1962: xvii	4.74	311	V med bowl base	2.4:9

LOCUS	DESCRIPTION	PUBLICATION REFERENCE	YEAR AREA/BKT	NO.	TYPE	PL.
FIELD IX						
Stratum IVB						
9024	grayish rubbly Fill 9024	Shechem III.1: 331a; 2: ill. 144:9	1.48 1.48 1.48 1.58	97 98 101 148	jug a jar A-2 V medium bowl H mortarium	3.15:2 3.1:11 3.35:2
9026 9024	Layer 9026 under IVB Layer 9024	Callaway 1962: xi	1.55	153	V jar	
9033	grayish rubbly Soil 9033	Shechem III.1: 331a	1.68	212	bowl, med to large deep	3.32:-1
9035	Rubble 9035 over V Floor 9037	Shechem III.1: fig. 209; 2: ill. 144:10; Callaway 1962: xiv	1.7	214	V mortarium	2.8:8
9264	grayish rubbly Soil 9264	Shechem III.1: 331b	2.46	106	H mortarium	3.35:13
9266	Layer 9266 sub Soil 9264	Shechem III.2: ill. 142:9 Callaway 1962: viii	2.43	104	bowl, large shallow	3.32:17
9269	IVB Fill 9269	Lapp 1985: 21	2.47 2.49	109 111	V small bowl V jar	2.4:4
9270 9264 9265	Layer 9270 under IVB Layers 9265 & 9264	Callaway 1962: xiv	2.50 2.50 2.54	112 116 169	V large bowl V small bowl V cooking pot-heavy	
9271 9270	Layer 9271 along s. balk, sub 9269 = IVB Layer 9270	Callaway 1962: xiv	2.51	119	V jar	
9272	stony Layer 9272 below IVB Layer 9270	Callaway 1962: xiv	2.52	161	jar A-3	
9280 9270	stony Surface 9280 sub IV Layer 9270	Callaway 1962: xvi	2.71	281	V jar	

Locus	Description	Publication Reference	Year Area/Bkt	No.	Type	Pl.
9517	occupation Debris 9517C	Shechem III.2: ill. 141:9	3.47	80	jar-B	3.3:3
			3.48	82	jar Cv	3.7:1
		Lapp 1985: 21, fig. 2	3.53	120	V jar	
			3.53	121	V krater-high neck	
			3.53	122	V cooking pot	
9521 9517C	occupation Debris 9521 as 9517C	Lapp 1985: 21, fig. 2	3.49	83	red-fig krater	2.13:4
			3.56	123	V black-glazed	
			3.59	125	V cooking pot	
9522A	IVB stony Layer 9522A	Lapp 1985: 21	3.65	189	V jar	
		Callaway 1962: xii	3.65	190	V jug	2.1:3
			3.65	191	V krater-high neck	
	intrusive?		**3.63**	**#263**	**Antiochus IV coin**	
9522B	bricky Earth 9522B sub 9522A	Callaway 1962: xii	3.64	187	V jar-misc	
9523	IVB Fill 9523	Shechem III.2: ill. 141:12	3.71	196	V medium bowl	
			3.71	197	V jar handle	
			3.71	198	V medium bowl	
			3.72	200	V jar	
			3.73	202	V jar	
			3.75	205	V krater-ledged	
			3.75	207	flask	3.22:7
			3.75	208	V cooking pot	
			3.76	218	jar-B	
			3.76	219	V cooking pot	
			3.77	220	V jar	
			3.77	221	V jar	
			3.82	284	bowl, large shallow, base	3.32:22

FIELD IX

Stratum IVA

Locus	Description	Publication Reference	Year Area/Bkt	No.	Type	Pl.
9016	decomposed Brick 9016	Shechem III.1: 331b; 2: ills. 144:3; 143:3	1.26	29	jar A-3	3.2:4
			1.26	30	V Attic black & red	2.15:7
9018 9016	soil Layer 9028, sub 9016	Shechem III.1: 332a; Callaway 1962: viii	1.35	66	jug c	3.16:1
			1.35	67	jug b	3.15:11
			1.35	69	V krater-ledged	

LOCUS	DESCRIPTION	PUBLICATION REFERENCE	YEAR AREA/BKT	NO.	TYPE	PL.
9019	compact gray Layer	Shechem III.2:	1.39	89	jug b	
9018	9019, sub 9018	ill. 143:5;	1.39	91	jar C	3.4:4
		Callaway 1962: viii	1.43	93	krater, grooved	3.33:4
9020	L. 9020 = 9018	Callaway 1962: viii	1.40	92	H mortarium	3.35: 6
9018	removing large stones					
9021	Debris 9021, sub Layer	Callaway 1962: viii	1.44	94	V medium bowl	
	9019					
9022	L. 9022 removing upper	Callaway 1962: viii	1.45	95	cp, plain	
9514	courses of Wall 9514					
9029	occupation Debris	Callaway 1962: ix	1.61	155	V krater-high neck	
	9029		1.62	156	cp, overhang	3.37:6
			1.64	158	V jug	2.3:5
9262	silty Soil 9262	Shechem III.1: 332a;	2.28	36	V mortarium base	
		2: ill. 142:6	2.28	38	jar-B	3.3:6
			2.28	39	bowl, med to large deep	3.32:3
			2.29	40	V mortarium	2.8:14
			2.31	41	V krater-high neck	
			2.31	42	flask	3.22:4
			2.31	43	V medium bowl	
9263	silty Soil 9263	Shechem III.1: 332a;	2.33	45	jar A-3	
		2: ill. 142:6				
9268	pottery from Wall 9267	Callaway 1962: viii	2.45	105	V krater-high neck	3.34:8
9514	pottery from Wall 9514	Shechem III.1: 331;	3.58	124	jug base, ring	3.20:15
		2: ills. 159, 141, 144				
9517A	IVA Layering 9517A	Callaway 1962: vii	3.39	50	V Attic cup	
	outside Wall 9514					
9517B	probable Surface 9517B	Shechem III.1: 332a;	3.40	51	jar-B	
		2: ills. 141:7, 143:7	3.45	79	cp, plain	3.38:3
			3.52	84	jug a	
			3.52	85	jar-B	
			3.60	126	V medium bowl	

LOCUS	DESCRIPTION	PUBLICATION REFERENCE	YEAR AREA/BKT	NO.	TYPE	PL.
9759	Locus 9759	Shechem III.1: 332	4.29	53	V krater-ledged	
9760	resurfacing Cobbling	Callaway 1962:	4.29	55	V Attic cup	
	9760	viii, p.6; x	4.30	57	jar A-3	3.2:5
			4.31	60	flask	3.23:8
			4.32	86	V krater-sloping shoulder	2.5:13
9760	stony Surface 9760 sub	Callaway 1962:	4.33	87	cp, overhang	3.37:7
9769	9759	x, p. 7	4.38	130	V medium bowl	
9763	IVA Layering 9763	Callaway 1962: x	4.39	132	V lekythos	2.15:5
9764	Rubble 9764		4.47	128	V mortarium	
9765	on which IV Wall 9765					

FIELD IX

Unstratified

LOCUS	DESCRIPTION	PUBLICATION REFERENCE	YEAR AREA/BKT	NO.	TYPE	PL.
	unstratified		1.15	10	V lekythos	
	unstratified		1.83	332	V mortarium	2.8:27
	unstratified		1.99	421	V mortarium base	
	unstratified		2.18	16	V Attic cup	
	unstratified		2.72	314	V Attic black and red	
	German dump		3.4	1	V krater-wedged	
	unstratified		3.33	25	V lamp	
	unstratified		3.93	359	V mortarium	2.8:28
	unstratified		4.14	7	V black/red fig krater	
	unstratified		4.15	8	V Attic black and red	

FIELD X

Unstratified

LOCUS	DESCRIPTION	PUBLICATION REFERENCE	YEAR AREA/BKT	NO.	TYPE	PL.
	unstratified		1.38	10261	V krater-wedged	2.7:12

Appendix II: Locus Indices

All Persian-Hellenistic loci referred to in this volume or *Shechem III* are listed sequentially by Fields. Strata are indicated in column 3. For complete descriptions, references, and pottery, the reader is referred to the appropriate Stratum in the Locus Lists (Appendix I). Since loci without pottery are not listed in Appendix I, references to these appear here in column 4. The columns in Appendix II are:

(1) locus number
(2) locus description
(3) stratum

Abbreviations for loci without pottery are as follows:

nhp = no helpful pottery
np = no pottery
npa = no pottery available
nps = no pottery saved
nex = not excavated
preH = pre-Hellenistic pottery
unstr = unstratified

(4) In loci where no pottery appeared as noted in column 3, published references to the loci are given.

LOCUS	DESCRIPTION	STRATUM	REFERENCES	(REFERENCES FOR STRATIFIED LOCI APPEAR IN APPENDIX I)
Locus Index Field I				
3	on Pavement	III		
4	fill below Pavement	IV		
4	below Hellenistic Tower	IV		
152	burn above Floor 203 between Walls 152-153	III		
153	burn above Floor 203 between Walls 152-153	III		
202	between Floors 202 and 206	cf III		
203	burn above Floor 203	III		
203	Floor 203	III		
203	below Floor 203	III		
204	on Floor 205 below Burn 204	IV		
204	lower H Floors 205 & 206 covered by Burn 204	IV/III		
204	above Lower Burn 204	III		
205	below lower IV Floor 205	IV		
205	in lower IV Floor 205	IV		
205	on Floor 205 below Burn 204	IV		
205	lower H Floors 205 & 206 covered by Burn 204	IV/III		
206	lower H Floors 205 & 206 covered by Burn 204	IV/III		
206	between Floors 202 and 206	cf III		
481	Fill 481 below H walls	cf IV		
Wall A	striated makeup	cf III		
Wall B	layers against Wall B	IV/III		
Wall B	pit in wall B	cf III		

LOCUS	DESCRIPTION	STRATUM	REFERENCES	(REFERENCES FOR STRATIFIED LOCI APPEAR IN APPENDIX I)
	Fill at foot of tower (coins)	cf IV		
	near Pavement	cf III		

Locus Index Field II

LOCUS	DESCRIPTION	STRATUM	REFERENCES	
7000	Sellin dump	nhp	Shechem III.1: 365; 2: ill. 34:left 1	
7005	Hellenistic House north wall Room 2	nex	Shechem III.1: 336a, 338b, 339a; 2: ills. 31, 34	
7006	Hellenistic House west wall Room 1 see 7041	nex	Shechem III.1: 336b, 337, 338b, 340b, figs. 227, 300; 2: ill. 31	
7007	Hellenistic House north wall Room 1	nex	Shechem III.1: 336b, 337a, 338; figs. 255, 227, 300; 2: ill. 31	
7008	Hellenistic House south wall Room 1	nex	Shechem III.1: 336b, 337a, 338b, figs. 227, 300; 2: ill. 31	
7009	Hellenistic House south wall Room 3	nex	Shechem III.1: 339; 2: ill. 31, 34,35	
7010	foundation course of Wall 7009	nex	Shechem III.1: 339; 2: ill. 31	
7011	Bin 7011 in Hellenistic House Room 1	npa	Shechem III.1: 337b	
7012	Hellenistic House east wall Room 1	nex	Shechem III.1: 337; 2: ill. 31; 300	
7013	Hellenistic House west wall Room 2	nex	Shechem III.1: 338b, 339; 2: ills. 31, 35	
7013	140-160 cm. below Wall 7013 in Room 2	IIIA/II		
7014	foundation course of Wall 7013	nex	Shechem III.1: 339; 2: ills. 31, 35	
7015	dividing wall between Rooms 2 and 3	nex	Shechem III.1: 339, 340a, fig. 301	
7016	Probe Trench 7016	unst		
7017	buttress east side Wall 7013-7014	nex	Shechem III.1: 339a; 2: ill. 35	
7024	Floor 7024 of Iron age	Iron Age		
7025	in Fill 7025 for Str. I surface	I		
7031	Room 1 makeup	nhp	Shechem III.1: 336b	
7033	Room 1 makeup	nhp	Shechem III.1: 336b	
7036	in Foundation Trench 7036 for Walls 7006 & 7008	IIIA/II		
7039	in Fill 7039 above Flagstone 7048	I		
7041	Foundation Trench 7041 (coin) for Walls 7043, 7006, Buttress 7045	II		
7042	Room 1 makeup	nhp	Shechem III.1: 336b	
7043	southern east wall of Hellenistic House Room 3 see 7041	nex	Shechem III.1: 339a	
7044	Room 1 makeup	nhp	Shechem III.1: 336b	
7045	buttress west end of Wall 7008; see 7041	nex	Shechem III.1: 338b	
7046	fill or Foundation Trench 7046 for Bin 7011	I	Shechem III.1: 337b	
7048	beneath flagstone Floor 7048	IIIA/II		
7049	embedded in Plaster 7049	IIIA/II		
7050	occupation Debris 7050 over Floor 7049	I		
7051	Iron age Wall 7051	Iron Age		
7052	Fill 7052 in Rooms 2 and 3	II		
7058	Sellin dump	nhp	Shechem III.1: 365; 2: ill. 34:left 1	

LOCUS	DESCRIPTION	STRATUM	REFERENCES	(REFERENCES FOR STRATIFIED LOCI APPEAR IN APPENDIX I)
7065	Sellin dump	nhp	Shechem III.1: 365; 2: ill. 34:left 1	
7070	Sellin dump	nhp	Shechem III.1: 365; 2: ill. 34:left 1	
7071	Sellin dump	nhp	Shechem III.1: 365; 2: ill. 34:left 1	
7072	IA wall near surface	nex	Shechem III.1: 341a; 2: ill. 34:left	
7074	I Debris 7074 to Wall 7072	IA		
7078	fallen stones from Wall 7072	nhp	Shechem III.1: 341a; 2: ill. 34:left 2	
7080	Fill 7080 sub Surface 7098 in Room 2	cf II		
7083	Fill 7083 in robber trench of Iron age Wall 7051	IIIA/II		
7084	Rockfall 7084 in Room 3	nhp	Shechem III.1: 340	
7089	destruction Debris 7089 over II Floor 7099	cf II		
7098	IA surface with Fill 7080 below	npa	Shechem III.1: 341a; 2: ill. 34:left 3	
7099	in ash on II Floor fragment 7099	cf II		
7100	Make-up 7100 for II Floor 7099	II		
7101	Make-up 7101 for Floor II 7099 sub 7100	II		
7104	below IA Wall 7104 (coin)	IA		
7105	IA wall near surface	npa	Shechem III.1: 341a; 2: ill. 34:right	
7106	IA storage Bin 7106 north of HH	unstr	Shechem III.1: 341a	
7107	buttress south end Wall 7043	nex	Shechem III.1: 339a; 2: ill. 31	
7108	skin Wall north Wall 7005	npa	Shechem III.1: 339a; 2: ill. 34:center	
7109	skin Wall south Wall 7005	npa	Shechem III.1: 339a; 2: ill. 34:center	
7111	IA Wall east of Wall 7008	nex	Shechem III.1: 341a	
Room 1	Hellenistic House black earth layer Room 1	II		
	black earth layer north balk	II		
Area 2	black earth layer Area 2	cf II		
	black earth layer west balk	cf II		
Room 1	Hellenistic House Room 1 occupation	I		
Room 1	Hellenistic House deeper in Room 1	I		
Room 1	Hellenistic House deeper in Room 2	cf I		
Room 2	below 160 cm in Room 2	IIIA/II		
	top of Hellenistic wall	unstr		
	north balk	unstr		
	balk	unstr		

Locus Index Field III

LOCUS	DESCRIPTION	STRATUM	REFERENCES	
601	walls of animal pens or walls of uncertain date	npa	Shechem III.1: 335a	
602	walls of animal pens or walls of uncertain date	npa	Shechem III.1: 335a	
603	wall of lower phase ?	npa	Shechem III.1: 335a	
605	wall of later phase	npa	Shechem III.1: 335b	

LOCUS	DESCRIPTION	STRATUM	REFERENCES	(REFERENCES FOR STRATIFIED LOCI APPEAR IN APPENDIX 1)
606	wall of later phase	npa	Shechem III.1: 335b	
607	wall of later phase	npa	Shechem III.1: 335b	
608	wall of later phase	npa	Shechem III.1: 335b	
609	wall of lower phase	npa	Shechem III.1: 335a	
610	wall of lower phase	npa	Shechem III.1: 335a	
611	wall of lower phase	npa	Shechem III.1: 335a	
612	wall of lower phase	npa	Shechem III.1: 335a	
Wall B	pit between Walls B & 606	III/II	Shechem III.1: 316a; 335b; 2: ills. 40, 42	
606	including storage jar cache			
1	foundation of plastered Bin of upper phase	II	Shechem III.1: 335a	

Locus Index Field VII

LOCUS	DESCRIPTION	STRATUM	REFERENCES	
1005	removal II Wall 1005	nps	Shechem III.1: 329b; 2: ill. 110	
1006	sub unrelated IIIA Wall 1006	IIIA		
1007	removal IIIA Wall 1007	IIIA		
1008	removal IIIA Wall 1008-21.007	IIIA		
1009	L. 1009 around IIIA Drain 1015-16	cf IIIA		
1010	removal IIIA Wall 1010	IIIA		
1012	IIIA Stone Pile 1012	nps	Shechem III.1: 328b	
1013	below III Hardpack 1013	nps	Shechem III.1: 328b	
1015	removal IIIA Drain 1015-1016	IIIA		
1016	removal IIIA Drain 1015-1016	IIIA		
1017	sub IIIB Hardback 1017-1019	IIIB		
1017	on IIIB Hardpack 1017-1019	IIIA		
1018	Probe 1018 from III to IV levels	cf IIIB		
1019	sub IIIB Hardpack 1017-1019	IIIB		
1019	on IIIB Hardpack 1017-1019	IIIA		
1021	Hardpack 1021-1023	cf IV		
1021	above IV Surface 1021-1023	cf IIIB		
1023	Hardpack 1021-1023 in which Oven 1024A appeared	cf IV		
1023	above IV Surface 1021-1023	cf IIIB		
1023	earth Surface 1023A	np	Shechem III.1: 320b; 2: ill. 116:8	
1024	removal IVA Oven 1024A	IVA		
1025	removal IVA Wall 1025-1308	IVA		
1026	IVA Wall 1026 over Fill 1129A and 1130A	IVA		
1027	IVB Wall 1027 sub IVA Wall 1025-1308	nhp	Shechem III.1: 321a, fig. 287; 2: ill.107	
1028	removal IVA Drain 1028	IVA		
1028	cleaning IV Drain 1028-1116	cf IV		
1029	Fill 1029A below IV installations	IVB		
1029	Pit 1029B	unstr	Campbell 1960b: app. xxxvi	

LOCUS	DESCRIPTION	STRATUM	REFERENCES	(REFERENCES FOR STRATIFIED LOCI APPEAR IN APPENDIX I)
1030	Probe 1030 beneath IV levels	IVB		
1042	Stonefall 1042 in balk	cf IV		
1103	removal II Wall 1103	II		
1103	around and on II Wall 1103	cf II		
1106	sub unrelated IIIB Surface 1106	IIIB		
1106	on unrelated IIIB Surface 1106	cf IIIA		
1107	removal IIIA Walls 1107-1109	IIIA		
1108	Rockfall 1108 south of Room E above IIIA level (coins)	cf II		
1109	removal IIIA Walls 1107-1109	IIIA		
1110	removal IIIA Buttress 1110-1211	IIIA		
1112	L. 1112 down to IV floor	unstr		
1113	Fill 1113	unstr		
1116	cleaning IV Drain 1028-1116	cf IV		
1117	removal IVB Wall 1415-1117	IVB		
1123	removal IVB Wall 1123	IVB		
1123	L. 1123A levelling below IV installations	IVB		
1124	on and above IV Surface 1124	cf IV		
1125	IVA Wall 1219-1125	nhp	Shechem III.1: 320; 2: ill. 107	
1127	sub V Installation 1127	V		
1127	inside V Installation 1127	cf V		
1128	V curb wall of Installation 1127	nps	Shechem III.1: 301, 307; 2: fig. 272	
1129	Fill 1129A sub IVA Wall 1026	IVA		
1130	Hardpack 1130A sub IVA Wall 1026	IVA		
1133	Pit 1133 sealed by Surface 1232	IVB		
1203	sub IIIA Floor 1203	IIIA		
1203	on IIIA Surface 1203 in Courtyard F	II		
1204	removal Mortar 1204 of IIIA occupation	cf IIIA		
1205	II occupation Pit 1205-1207	II		
1206	removal IIIA Walls 1206-1210	IIIA		
1207	II occupation Pit 1205-1207	II		
1208	loose Rockfall 1208 with II pottery	nps	Shechem III.1: 330	
1209	Stones 1209 on IIIA Surface 1227	np	Shechem III.1: 327a	
1210	removal IIIA Walls 1206-1210	IIIA		
1211	removal IIIA Buttress 1110-1211	IIIA		
1212	extensions of II Wall 1103	nps	Shechem III.1: 329b	
1212	II Wall 1005-1103-1212	nps	Shechem III.1: 329b; 2: ill. 110	
1214	beneath IIIB Floor 1214	IIIB		
1214	on IIIB Floor 1214 below Floor 1203	IIIA		
1216	on IVB plastered Floor 1216	IVA		
1216	IVB plaster Floor 1216	npa	Shechem III.1: 318a; Lapp 1985: 21, 40	
1216	Fill 1216,1217,1220-1224,1226	IIIB		
1219	IVA Wall 1219-1125	nhp	Shechem III.1: 320; 2: ill. 107	
1227	sub IIIA Floor 1227-1511	IIIA		

LOCUS	DESCRIPTION	STRATUM	REFERENCES	(REFERENCES FOR STRATIFIED LOCI APPEAR IN APPENDIX I)
1227	above IIIA Floor 1227 in Room E	II		
1228	in Probe 1228 below IV Installations	IVB		
1229	in fill below IV metalled Surface 1530-1229-1232-1234	cf V		
1230	sub 2nd IVB metalled Surface 1230	cf V		
1231	Surface 1231 in 1230	cf V		
1232	in fill below IV metalled Surface 1530-1229-1232-1234	cf V		
1232	on IVB metalled Surface 1530-1232	IVB		
1233	metalled Surface 1233 in balk	cf IV		
1234	in fill below IV metalled Surface 1530-1229-1232-1234	cf V		
1235	Stone Heap 1235 part of Pit 1522	IIIB		
1236	sub IVB Surface 1236 (sub 1216)	IVB		
1236	on IVB Surface 1236	IVB		
1237	Rockfall 1237 part of IVB Pit 1239	IVB		
1239	IVB Pit 1239	IVB		
1243	IVB Fill 1243-1245 beneath Surface 1230	cf V		
1245	IVB Fill 1243-1245 beneath Surface 1230	cf V		
1247	V? Pit 1247	cf V		
1248	Debris 1248 of V? Pit 1247	cf V		
1257	L. 1257 of V? Pit 1247 or collapse into it	cf V		
1259	V? Hardpack 1259	cf V		
1260	V? Hardpack 1260	cf V		
1300	above and on Hardpack 1500-1400-1300	cf II		
1303	1303-1304 west in area 6	unstr		
1304	robber Pit 1304A east IIIA complex	nhp	Shechem III.1: 327b	
1306	sub IIIA Cobbling 1306 and 1307	IIIA		
1307	sub IIIA Cobbling 1306 and 1307	IIIA		
1308	removal IVA Wall 1025-1308	IVA		
1310	above unrelated IV Surface 1310	cf IV		
1311	Probe 1311 in brick debris	IVB		
1312	IV Wall 1312	nps	Shechem III.1: 320b; 2: ill. 107	
1400	above and on Hardpacked 1500-1400-1300	cf II		
1403	unrelated metalled Surface 1403	nhp	Shechem III.1: 327b	
1408	removal IIIA Wall 1408	IIIA		
1412	IIIA Blocking 1412 of III Wall 1414	nhp	Shechem III.1: 325b	
1414	removal III Wall 1414	IIIB		
1415	removal IVB Wall 1415-1117	IVB		
1419	sub IVA Wall 1419	IVA		
1420	removal IVA Wall 1420 of bin	IVA		
1421	removal IVA Cobbling 1421 and hardpack north	IVA		
1423	IV Wall 1423 west from 1415	nhp	Shechem III.1: 322a	
1424	Fill 1424 west of IVB Wall 1415	IVB		
1426	removal IVB Wall 1426	IVB		
1476	to possible IVB Surface 1476-1548	cf IV		
1477	Pit 1477	cf IIIA		

LOCUS	DESCRIPTION	STRATUM	REFERENCES	(REFERENCES FOR STRATIFIED LOCI APPEAR IN APPENDIX I)
1485	rockfall or Pit 1485	unstr		
1500	above and on Hardpacked 1500-1400-1300	cf II		
1505	removal IIIA Walls 1505-1510	IIIA		
1506	removal III Wall 1506	IIIB		
1507	sub IIIB Surface 1808-1507 level	cf IIIB		
1508	sub IIIA Floor 1802-1508	IIIA		
1508	sub IIIA Floor 1802-1508 - unsealed	cf II!A		
1508	above IIIA Floor 1802-1508	II		
1509	cleaning IIIB Tannur 1509	IIIA		
1510	removal IIIA Walls 1505-1510	IIIA		
1511	sub IIIA Floor 1227-1511	IIIA		
1513	removal IIIB Wall 1513	IIIB		
1514	Pit 1514	cf IIIA		
1516	removal IIIB Wall 1516	IIIB		
1517	sealed in IV Wall 1517	IVB		
1518	to IIIB Installation 1518	cf IIIB		
1520	sub IIIB Installation 1520	IIIB		
1520	on IIIB Bin 1520 (coin)	cf IIIA		
1521	under IVB Floor 1521	IVB		
1521	on IVB Floor 1521	IVA		
1522	sealed in Pit 1522	IIIB		
1522	unsealed in Pit 1522	cf IIIB		
1523	IVA Floor 1523 above IVA Floor 1527	IVA		
1523	above IV Floor 1523	IIIB		
1523	on IV Floor 1523	IIIB		
1525	removal IV Press 1525	IVA		
1525	cleaning IV Press 1525	IIIB		
1526	L. 1526 removal large jar	IVA		
1527	removal IVA Floor 1527	IVA		
1527	on IVA Floor 1527 sub IVA Floor 1523	IVA		
1528	removal IIIB Surface 1528 sub 1509	preH	Shechem III.1: 324b, fig. 291; 2: ill. 108	
1528	cleaning Plaster 1528 of IIIB Tannur 1509	IIIA		
1529	Hardpack 1529 sub IV Wall 1517	IVB		
1529	Hardpack 1529 north of sub IV Wall 1517	cf IVB		
1530	in fill below IV metalled Surface 1530–1229–1232–1234	cf V		
1530	on IVB metalled Surface 1530–1232	IVB		
1530	Fill 1530 sub Floor 1227	IIIA		
1531	Wall 1531 with Stone Circle 1544-1545 and Surface 1530	nps	Shechem III.1: 301	
1531	pit top courses of Wall 1531	cf IIIA		
1536	IVB ash in Fill 1556	nhp	Shechem III.1: 317a	
1537	removal V Stone Circle 1537=1544–1545	V		
1542	IVB soil Layer 1542 in Fill 1556	cf V		
1544	removal V Stone Circle 1544–1545=1527	V		
1545	removal V Stone Circle 1544–1545=1527	V		

LOCUS	DESCRIPTION	STRATUM	REFERENCES	(REFERENCES FOR STRATIFIED LOCI APPEAR IN APPENDIX I)
1547	IIIB Wall 1547	nps	Shechem III.1: 324b-325a	
1548	to possible IVB Surface 1476–1548	cf IV		
1556	IVB Fill 1556 sub Surface 1530	cf V		
1601	removal IIIA Structure 1707–1705–1701–1601	IIIA		
1602	sub IIIA Cobbling 1703–1602	IIIA		
1604	removal patch of IIIA Cobbling 1604	IIIA		
1609	Fill 1609–10,1612–15 in brick debris	IVB		
1610	Fill 1609–10,1612–15 in brick debris	IVB		
1612	Fill 1609–10,1612–15 in brick debris	IVB		
1613	Fill 1609–10,1612–15 in brick debris	IVB		
1614	Fill 1609–10,1612–15 in brick debris	IVB		
1615	Fill 1609–10,1612–15 in brick debris	IVB		
1622	IVB pocket of fill	nhp	Shechem III.1: 318a	
1630	Fill 1630 down to Iron II house	IVB		
1701	removal IIIA Structure 1707–1705–1701–1601	IIIA		
1702	above possible IIIA Surface 1702	cf II		
1703	sub IIIA Cobbling 1703–1602	IIIA		
1703	above IIIA Cobbling 1703	II		
1704	1704-1706-1708 street?	unstr		
1705	removal IIIA Structure 1707–1705–1701–1601	IIIA		
1706	1704-1706-1708 street?	unstr		
1707	removal IIIA Structure 1707–1705–1701–1601	IIIA		
1708	IIIB Cobbling 1708 in street	npa	Shechem III.1: 327b	
1709	IIIB Cobbling 1709 in street	npa	Shechem III.1: 327b	
1712	L.17128/17/20081713 unsealed but sub level of IIIB Surface 1719	cf IIIB		
1713	L.17128/17/20081713 unsealed but sub level of IIIB Surface 1719	cf IIIB		
1715	beneath IIIB Cobbling 1715	IIIB		
1715	on IIIB Cobbling 1715 sub IIIA Cobbling 1703–1602	IIIA		
1716	removal IVA Wall 1716	IVA		
1717	unsealed IIIB Fill 1717–20 sub IIIB level	cf IIIB		
1719	sub IIIB Cobbling 1719	IIIB		
1719	L. 1712-1713 unsealed but sub level of IIIB Surface1719	cf. IIIB		
1719	over IIIB Surface 1719	cf IIIA		
1720	unsealed IIIB Fill 1717–20 sub IIIB level	cf IIIB		
1723	IVA Wall 1723	nps	Shechem III.1: 319b. 320b; 2: ill. 107	
1727	IVB pockets in brick debris	nhp	Shechem III.1: 318a	
1732	IVB pockets in brick debris	nhp	Shechem III.1: 318a	
1734	IIIA Wall 1734A in balk	np	Shechem III.1: 327b; fig. 292	
1801	sub IIIA Floor 1801	IIIA		
1802	sub IIIA Floor 1802–1508	IIIA		
1802	sub IIIA Floor 1802–1508, unsealed	cf IIIA		
1802	above IIIA Floor 1802–1508	II		

LOCUS	DESCRIPTION	STRATUM	REFERENCES	(REFERENCES FOR STRATIFIED LOCI APPEAR IN APPENDIX I)
1803	removal III Wall 1803–1807, 1813	IIIB		
1804	IIIB Floor 1804	np	Shechem III.1: 323b; 2: ill. 112:5	
1805	IIIB Wall 1805	np	Shechem III.1: 323b, 325b; 2: ills. 108-9, 112	
1805	removal IIIA Wall 1805N	IIIA		
1806	removal IIIA Wall 1806	IIIA		
1807	removal III Wall 1803–1807, 1813	IIIB		
1808	on IIIB Surface 1808 (coin)	cf IIIB		
1808	sub IIIB Surface 1808–1507 level	cf IIIB		
1810	removal IIIA Walls 1810, 1812	IIIA		
1811	removal IIIA Wall 1811 facing	IIIA		
1812	removal IIIA Walls 1810, 1812	IIIA		
1813	removal III Wall 1803–1807, 1813	IIIB		
1814	removal IIIA Threshold 1814	IIIA		
1815	cleaning above IIIB Surface 1815	IIIA		
1816	IIIB Floor 1816A	np	Shechem III.1: 323b	
1816	Resurfacing 1816 of IIIB Floor 1816A	IIIB		
1817	removal IV Wall 1817	IVB		
1818	removal stones for IVB Jar Stand 1818	IVB		
1820	Pit 1820 of IIIA Floor 1801 with jar	II		
1821	IVB Cobbling 1821	nhp	Shechem III.1: 319	
1822	IIIB Fill 1822–1823 above IV	cf IIIB		
1823	IIIB Fill 1822–1823 above IV	cf IIIB		
1824	removal IVA Cobbling 1824	IVA		
1824	on IVA Cobbling 1824	IIIB		
1826	removal IVA Floor 1826	IVA		
1826	around IVA Cobbling 1826	cf IV		
1828	V Tannur 1828 over VI complex	npa	Shechem III.1: 301, fig. 270	
1828	around V Tannur 1828	IVB		
1829	IVB Wall 1829	nhp	Shechem III.1: 319	
1830	IVA Floor 1830	np	Shechem III.1: 319b	
1831	IVB hardpacked Surface 1831	nhp	Shechem III.1: 319	
1832	IVB plaster Floor 1832	npa	Shechem III.1: 319a; 2: ill. 106	
1834	possible IV Wall 1834 in balk	nhp	Shechem III.1: 321b	
1836	Fill 1836–1841 below IV strata	IVB		
1841	Fill 1836–1841 below IV strata	IVB		
1845	IV or III Pit 1845	nhp	Shechem III.1: 321b	
1845	? Pit in balk	npa	Shechem III.1: 321b-322a	
21.003	Wall 21.003 with IIIA drain	nps	Shechem III.1: 328; 2: ill. 109	
21.004	removal IIIA drain Sidewalls 21.004	IIIA		
21.005	Wall 21.005 with IIIA drain	nhp	Shechem III.1: 328; 2: ill. 109	
21.006	removal IIIA Wall 21.006	IIIA		
21.007	removal IIIA Wall 1008-21.007	IIIA		
21.008	Wall 21.008 with IIIA drain	nhp	Shechem III.1: 328; 2: ill. 109	
21.009	IIIA Fill 21.034 below Floor 21.009	IIIA		

LOCUS	DESCRIPTION	STRATUM	REFERENCES	(REFERENCES FOR STRATIFIED LOCI APPEAR IN APPENDIX 1)
21.011	sub IVA Floor 21.011	IVA		
21.012	sub IVA or IVB Floor 21.012	IVA		
21.013	sub IVB Floor 21.013	IVB		
21.014	stone Installation 21.014	cf IV		
21.015	above and around VII Wall 21.015	unstr	Horn and Campbell 1962: app. 1:3	
21.031	Debris 21.035 sub IIIA walls and Floor 21.031	IIIA		
21.034	IIIA Fill 21.034 below Floor 21.009	IIIA		
21.035	Debris 21.035 sub IIIA walls and Floor 21.031	IIIA		
21.036	Pit 21.036 dug in III or II	cf IV		
22.001	sub IIIA Floor 22.001 above Floor 22.002	IIIA		
22.001	on IIIA Floor 22.001	cf IIIA		
22.002	sub possible IIIB Floor 22.002	cf IIIB		
22.002	above possible IIIB Floor 22.002 sub IIIA Floor 22.001	IIIA		
22.003	Pit 22.003	unstr	Horn and Campbell 1962: app. 1:11	
22.010	IV Pit 22.010	cf IV		
22.020	IVB Fill 22.020 around VII Wall 22.005	npa	Shechem III.1: 318a	
23.001	23.001a below IIIA Hardpack 23.001	IIIA		
23.002	around Stones 23.002	unstr		
23.003	around Wall 23.003	unstr		
23.004	around IV Column Base 23.004	cf IV		
23.005	Fill 23.016 below IV Floor 23.005	IVA		
23.005	above IV Floor 23.005	cf IV		
23.006	IV Floor 23.006	nps	Shechem III.1: 322b	
23.008	sub IVA Floor 23.008	IVA		
23.009	flagstone IVB Floor 23.009	npa	Shechem III.1: 322b, fig. 288	
23.009	above IVB Floor 23.009 sub IVA Floor 23.008	IVA		
23.010	IV Stonefall 23.010	cf IV		
23.012	around Wall (?) 23.012	unstr	Horn and Campbell 1962: app. 1:18	
23.016	Fill 23.016 below IV Floor 23.005	IVA		
23.017	Pit 23.017 near Column Base 23.004	cf IIIA		

Locus Index Field IX

9016	decomposed Brick 9016 outside IV Wall 9514	IVA		
9017	compact gray inside IV Wall 9514	nps	Shechem III.1: 331b; 2: ill. 144:3; Callaway 1962: vii	
9018	soil Layer 9018, sub L. 9016	IVA		
9019	compact gray Layer 9019, sub Layer 9018	IVA		
9020	L. 9020 = Layer 9018 removing large stones	IVA		
9021	Debris 9021, sub L. 9019	IVA		
9022	L. 9022 removing upper courses of Wall 9514	IVA		
9024	grayish rubbly Fill 9024	IVB		
9026	Layer 9026 under IVB Layer 9024	IVB		
9029	occupation Debris 9029	IVA		

LOCUS	DESCRIPTION	STRATUM	REFERENCES	(REFERENCES FOR STRATIFIED LOCI APPEAR IN APPENDIX I)
9033	grayish rubbly Soil 9033	IVB		
9034	V compact gray Layer 9034	V		
9035	Rubble 9035 over V floor 9037	IVB		
9037	V Surface 9037	V		
9043	fragmentary Wall base 9043	VI		
9262	silty Soil 9262	IVA		
9263	silty Soil 9263	IVA		
9264	grayish rubbly Soil 9274	IVB		
9265	IVB Layer 9265	IVB		
9266	Layer 9266 sub 9264	IVB		
9267	IV Wall 9267	np	Shechem III.1: 332a; 2: ill. 139	
9268	pottery from IVA Wall 9267	IVA		
9269	Layer 9269 sub 9264	IVB		
9270		IVB		
9271	Layer 9271 along S balk, sub 9269 = 9270	IVB		
9272	stony Layer 9272 below 9270	IVB		
9273	V Surface 9273 outside Wall 9274	V		
9274	Wall 9274	nps	Shechem III.1: 299; 2: Ill. 144:11; Callaway 1962: xvi	
9278	V Fill 9278 over VI remains	V		
9280	stony Surface 9280 sub IVB Layer 9270	IVB		
9514	pottery from IVA Wall 9514	IVA		
9517	IVA Layering 9517A outside Wall 9514	IVA		
9517	probable Surface 9517B	IVA		
9517	occupational Debris 9517C	IVB		
9521	occupational Debris 9521 as 9517C	IVB		
9522	IVB stony Layer 9522A	IVB		
9522	bricky Layer 9522B sub 9522A	IVB		
9523	IVB Fill 9523	IVB		
9524	V Debris 9524	V		
9531	V (probably) Rubble 9531	V		
9758	IVA firepit set into L. 9759	nps	Shechem III.1: 332a	
9759	L. 9759.29-32 resurfacing Surface 9760	IVA		
9760	stony Surface 9760 sub 9759	IVA		
9763	IVA Layering 9763.39.40	IVA		
9764	Rubble 9764 on which Wall 9765 stood	IVA		
9765	stone heap - IV wall	nhp	Shechem III.1: 332a; 2: ill. 139	
9768	V ashy and brick Layer 9768	V		
9769	V ashy and brick Layer = 9768	nps	Callaway 1962: xvii	
9770	V Layer (floor?) 9770	V		
9774	V ashy & brick Layer 9774 = V Layer 9768	V		
9778	V Layer 9778 = Layer 9774	V		

Appendix III: Coins

All identifiable and/or stratified coins from the 1956, 1957, 1960, and 1964 campaigns are listed in this appendix. Each year is listed separately, with stratified coins first, followed by unstratified ones. Coin reports (especially that by O. R. Sellers for the 1960 coins), registration books, published reports, and field reports were used to compile the lists. Where conflicting data was found, the more reliable, usually the subsequent report, has been accepted.

The columns include:
(1) Object Registration Number
(2) Field, Area, and Basket
(3) Stratum (or indication if unstratified)

(4) Locus
(5) Locus Description
(6) Publication References. For coins from the 1960 campaign, the numbers assigned by Sellers are given in parenthesis. In his 1962 *Biblical Archaeologist* article, he used only these numbers to identify the coins. In his 1960 unpublished report, Sellars gives the equivalent Shechem object registration number. This 1960 report also gives more details about each coin—measurements, obverse and reverse descriptions, and references.
(7) Identification
(8) Date

No.	Field, Area, Basket	Stratum	Locus	Locus Description	Publication References	Identification	Date BC
1956							
#8							
#18-25	I.1	cf IV		coin hoard; fill at foot of tower	Shechem III.1: 315 Wright 1975, 171, n. 2 Wright 1956: 13 Sellers 1962: 88		305–285
#18	I.1	cf IV		coin hoard		Ptolemy I	
#19	I.1	cf IV		coin hoard		Ptolemy I	
#20	I.1	cf IV		coin hoard		Ptolemy I	
#21	I.1	cf IV		coin hoard		Ptolemy I	
#22	I.1	cf IV		coin hoard		Ptolemy I	
#23	I.1	cf IV		coin hoard - 2 coins		Ptolemy I	
#24	I.1	cf IV		coin hoard - 3 coins		Ptolemy I	
#25	I.1	cf IV		coin hoard - 5 indistinct coins		Ptolemy I	
#6	I.4	unstr		mixed debris over East Gate	Shechem III.1: 307b Wright 1965: 168–69; fig. 95 Wright 1956: 6, 19; fig. 6 Wright 1957b: 29, fig. 10; 32 Toombs & Wright 1961:52 Sellers 1962: 88	Thasos electrum	560–465

No.	Field, Area, Basket	Stratum	Locus	Locus Description	Publication References	Identification	Date BC
#8	I.1	unstr	3	E end near & above pavement	Wright 1956: 13	Antiochus IV Epiphanes	175–164
#10	I.2	unstr	3	corner just above fallen brick		silver - unidentified	
#17	I.2	unstr		surface -20 cm; digging steps	Wright 1956: 13	Antiochus VII Euergetes	138–129
#26	I.4	unstr		West end, 90 cm below oil press		corroded	
#46	surface	unstr		NE edge of SE gate pier	1956 Object Registration Book	Neapolis mint or Agrippa	
#47	I.4	unstr		surface debris	1956 Object Registration Book	Roman - Neapolis mint	
#48		unstr		SE corner of tower			

1957

No.	Field, Area, Basket	Stratum	Locus	Locus Description	Publication References	Identification	Date BC
#93	I.7	IV		on Floor 205 below Burn 204	Shechem III.1: 333a Toombs & Wright 1961:41 n.32 Toombs 1957: 12 Sellers 1962: 88	Alexander the Great silver to Department of Antiquities	
#147	II.1.	II		black earth level	Wright 1957: 27 Toombs & Wright 1961:40 n.31 Lapp 1961: 42, n. 181 Sellers 1962: 88	Ptolemy I	312–247
#321	II.1.123	I	4	Hellenistic House	Shechem III.1: 338a, 311b Wright 1957: 27 Toombs & Wright 1961:40 n.31 Lapp 1961: 41 n. 172 Sellers 1962: 88–89	Antiochus VIII to Department Antiquities	121–120
#243	II.1.96	IA		below IA Wall 7104	Shechem III.1: 336a, 341a; 2: ill. 34; fig. 303 Richardson 1957: 11 Sellers 1962: 88–89	Caliphate	
#348	II.1.160		11	below yard's surface	Shechem III.1: 338 Wright 1957: 27 Toombs & Wright 1961:40 n.31 Lapp 1961: 41, n. 174 Sellers 1962: 88–89	Ptolemy II	
#4	I.6	unstr		45 cm below surface	Toombs 1957: 10		
#20	I.9	unstr		in and around tower	Anderson & Farmer 1957: 5		
#23	I.10	unstr		in and around tower	Anderson & Farmer 1957: 5		
#25	I.10	unstr		in and around tower	Anderson & Farmer 1957: 5		

No.	Field, Area, Basket	Stratum	Locus	Locus Description	Publication References	Identification	Date BC
#26	I.9	unstr		in and around tower	Anderson & Farmer 1957: 5		
#49	I.7	unstr		probably planted	Toombs 1957: 11		
#56	I.7	unstr		first burn layer	Toombs 1957: 11	Antiochus IV	
#32	III.3.5	unstr		to phase A walls	Funk 1957: app: 6		
#33	III.3.5	unstr		to phase A walls	Funk 1957: app: 6		
#48	III.1.12	unstr	1	inside circular wall a	Funk 1957: app: 1	bronze	
#58	III.1.15	unstr	1	inside circular wall a	Funk 1957: app: 1	bronze	
#59	III.1.16	unstr	1	inside circular wall a	Funk 1957: app: 1	bronze	
#82	III.4.6	unstr		surface to -50 cm.	Funk 1957: app: 9	Ptolemy I or II; to Dept of Antiq	
#109	III.3.14			in hole in brick wall in balk between 3 and 4	Funk 1957: app: 6	Seleucid?	
#148	III.6.2		1	trench outer face wall A1	Shechem III.1: 311b Wright 1957: 27	Antiochia (Ptolemais)	112–111
#162	III.6.2			trench outer face wall A1	Wright 1957: 27	Demetrius II	145–144

1960

No.	Field, Area, Basket	Stratum	Locus	Locus Description	Publication References	Identification	Date BC
#494a	VII.7.79	IIIB	1803-1807, 1813	removal III Wall 1803-1807, 1813	Shechem III.1: 323b–324a; fig. 289; 2: ill. 108 Sellers 1962: 92 (29) Toombs & Wright 1961:44	Ptolemy II	285–247
#573	VII.4.86	IIIB	1523	on IV Floor 1523	Shechem III.1: 319a; fig. 286; 2: ill. 113:8 Sellers 1962: 92 (36) Toombs & Wright 1961:48	Ptolemy II	285–247
#479	VII.7.67	cf IIIB	1808	on IIIB Surface 1808	Shechem III.1: 324a Sellers 1962: 96 (87) Campbell 1960b: xxiii	Ptolemais-Ake	ca. 126
#89	VII.7.60	IIIA	1802-1508	sub IIIA Floor 1802-1508	Shechem III.1: 329a Toombs & Wright 1961:44	unidentified	
#247	VII.2.69	IIIA	1107-1109	removal IIIA Walls 1107-1109	Shechem III.1: 329a;2: ill. 109 Toombs & Wright 1961:44 Sellers 1962: 92, fig. 11 (42)	Ptolemy II	285–247
#463	VII.7.74	IIIA	1810, 1814	removal IIIA Walls 1810, 1812	Shechem III.1: 329a;2: ill. 109 Toombs & Wright 1961:44 Sellers 1962: 92, fig. 11 (28)	Ptolemy II	285–247
#526	VII.7.57	IIIA	1802-1508	sub IIIA Floor 1802-1508	Shechem III.1: 329a Toombs & Wright 1961:44 Sellers 1962: 92, fig. 11 (26)	Ptolemy II	285–247

No.	Field, Area, Basket	Stratum	Locus	Locus Description	Publication References	Identification	Date BC
#240	VII.7.24	cf IIIA	1802-1508	sub IIIA Floor 1802-1508-unsealed	Sellers 1962: 96, fig. 12 (85) Campbell 1960b:xii	Ptolemais-Ake	ca. 126
#481	VII.4.64	cf IIIA	1520	on IIIB Bin 1520	Campbell 1960b: xxii Toombs & Wright 1961:44 Sellers 1962: 94, fig. 12 (64)	Antiochus III	223–187
#17	VII.2.25	II	1227	above IIIA Floor 1227 in Room E	Shechem III.1: 329a Sellers 1962: 92 (33)	Ptolemy II	285–247
#20	VII.2.31	II	1227	above IIIA Floor 1227 in Room E	Shechem III: 329a Sellers 1962: 94, fig. 12 (75)	Demetrius II	128
#22	VII.1.25	II	1227	above IIIA Floor 1227 in Room E	Shechem III.1: 329a Toombs & Wright 1961:44 Sellers 1962: 92, fig. 12 (63)	Antiochus III	223–187
#36	VII.1.28	II	1205-1207	II occupation Pit 1205-1207	Shechem III.1: 330a	Ptolemy II	285–247
#57	VII.1.33	II	1227	above IIIA Floor 1227 in Room E	Shechem III.1: 329a Toombs & Wright 1961:44 Sellers 1962: 92, fig. 11 (46)	Ptolemy III	246–221
#434	VII.4.59	II	1227	above IIIA Floor 1227 in Room E	Shechem III.1: 329a Toombs & Wright 1961:44 Sellers 1962: 94, fig. 12 (72)	Antiochus IV	175–164
#448	VII.4.59	II	1227	above IIIA Floor 1227 in Room E	Shechem III.1: 329a Toombs & Wright 1961:44 Sellers 1962: 94, fig. 12 (69)	Antiochus III	223–187
#21	VII.2.35	cf II	1108	Rockfall 1108 south of Room E	Sellers 1962: 96, fig. 12 (86) Campbell 1960b: viii	Ptolemais-Ake	ca. 126
#47	VII.2.39	cf II	1108	Rockfall 1108 south of Room E	Campbell 1960b: viii Toombs & Wright 1961:44 Sellers 1962: 92–94 (67)	Antiochus III	223–187
#528	VII.8.61	cf II	1702	above possible IIIA Surface 1702	Campbell 1960b: xv Toombs & Wright 1961:44 Sellers 1962: 92 (32)	Ptolemy II	285–247
#1	VII.1.2	unstr		surface	Shechem III.1:330b Toombs & Wright 1961:41 Sellers 1962: 94, fig. 12 (76)	Demetrius II	127
#2	VII.3.7	unstr		surface	Shechem III.1:330b Toombs & Wright 1961:41 Sellers 1962: 94, fig. 12 (74)	Antiochus VII	138–129
#3	VII.2.1	unstr		surface	Shechem III.1:330b Sellers 1962: 96 (79)	Alexander Zebina	128–123

No.	Field, Area, Basket	Stratum	Locus	Locus Description	Publication References	Identification	Date BC
#4	VII.3.11	unstr		surface	Shechem III.1:330b Toombs & Wright 1961:41 Sellers 1962: 92 (4)	Ptolemy I	312–285
#5	VII.1.2	unstr		surface	Shechem III.1:330b Toombs & Wright 1961:41 Sellers 1962: 92 (39)	Ptolemy II	285–247
#6	VII.2.4	unstr		surface	Shechem III.1:330b Sellers 1962: 96 (88) Campbell 1960b: i	Ptolemais-Ake	ca. 126
#8	VII.2.13	unstr		surface fill	Campbell 1960b: iv Sellers 1962: 92 (7)	Ptolemy I	312–285
#52	VII.4.4	unstr		surface	Toombs & Wright 1961:41 Sellers 1962: 92–94 (66)	Antiochus III	223–187
#62	VII.4.4	unstr		surface	Toombs & Wright 1961:41 Sellers 1962: 92–94 (65)	Antiochus III	223–187
#64	VII.4.11	unstr		surface	Shechem III.1:330b Toombs & Wright 1961:41 Sellers 1962: 96, fig. 12 (81)	Alexander Zebina	128–123
#85	VII.4.18	unstr		surface fill	Shechem III.1:330b Toombs & Wright 1961:41 Sellers 1962: 96, fig. 12 (78)	Alexander Zebina	128–123
#86	VII.4.20	unstr		surface fill	Shechem III.1:330b Sellers 1962: 94, fig. 12 (73)	Demetrius I	162–160
#167	VII.6.49	unstr	1303-1304	unstratified	Campbell 1960b: xix Sellers 1962: 92, fig. 11 (8)	Ptolemy I	312–285
#221	VII.5.42	unstr	1403-1404-1406	disturbed debris of street	Campbell 1960b: xiv Sellers 1962: 96 (80)	Alexander	128–123
#222	VII.5.42	unstr	1403-1404-1406	disturbed debris of street	Campbell 1960b: xiv	unidentified	
#250	VII	unstr		dump - railroad car	Sellers 1962: 92, fig. 11 (62)	Ptolemy V	204–181
#251	VII.5.48	unstr	1402-04-06-1407	disturbed debris of street	Sellers 1962: 96 (84) Campbell 1960b: xxiv	Ptolemais-Ake	ca. 126
#266	VII.8.22	unstr	1704-1706-1708	L. 1704-06-08 street?	Shechem III.1:330b	Seleucid	2nd cen
#267	VII.8.22	unstr	1704-1706-1708	L. 1704-06-08 street?	Shechem III.1:330b Sellers 1962: 92 (40)	Ptolemy II	285–247

No.	Field, Area, Basket	Stratum	Locus	Locus Description	Publication References	Identification	Date bc
#293	VII.8.27	unstr	1704- 1706- 1708	L. 1704-06-08 street?	Shechem III.1:330b Sellers 1962: 92 (6)	Ptolemy I	312–285
#306	VII.5.43	unstr	1403- 1404- 1406	disturbed debris of street	Campbell 1960b: xiv Sellers 1962: 92 (30)	Ptolemy II	285–247
#307	VII.5.43	unstr	1403- 1404- 1406	disturbed debris of street	Campbell 1960b: xiv Sellers 1962: 92 (38)	Ptolemy II	285–247
#308	VII.5.43	unstr	1403- 1404- 1406	disturbed debris of street	Campbell 1960b: xiv Sellers 1962: 92 (9)	Ptolemy I	312–285
#309	VII.5.43	unstr	1403- 1404- 1406	disturbed debris of street	Campbell 1960b: xiv Sellers 1962: 92, fig. 11 (29)	Ptolemy II	285–247
#314	VII.6.116	unstr	1305	unstratified	Campbell 1960b: xvii	Ptolemy I	312–285
#325	VII.8.15	unstr		surface fill	Campbell 1960b: vi Sellers 1962: 92, fig. 11 (11)	Ptolemy I	312–285
#343	VII.9	unstr		surface	Shechem III.1:330b Toombs & Wright 1961:41 Sellers 1962: 94, fig. 12 (70)	Antiochus IV	175–164
#358	VII	unstr		steps	Toombs & Wright 1961:41 Sellers 1962: 92–94 (64)	Antiochus III	223–187
#378	VII.7.54	unstr		surface fill	Campbell 1960b: vi Sellers 1962: 92 (35)	Ptolemy II	285–247
#464	VII.4.97	unstr	1227	Room E (balk 4/5 cleaning)	Shechem III.1:329b Sellers 1962: 92 (31)	Ptolemy II	285–247
#527	VII.I.103	unstr		balk	Sellers 1962: 92 (34)	Ptolemy II	285–247
#529	VII.4.97	unstr	1227	Room E (balk 4/5 cleaning)	Shechem III.1: 329a Toombs & Wright 1961:48 Sellers 1962: 92, fig. 11 (12)	Ptolemy I	312–285
#532- 555, 557- 567	VII.5.5.70	unstr	1402- 1404- 1406- 1407	disturbed debris of street coin hoard in juglet #531	Shechem III.1: 329; fig. 295 Campbell 1960a: 105: fig. 2 Toombs & Wright 1961:44 Sellers 1960; 1962: 89		
#532					Sellers 1962: 90 (23)	Ptolemy II	285–246
#533					Sellers 1962: 90, fig. 10 (2)	Ptolemy I	312–285
#534					Sellers 1962: 90 (43)	Ptolemy II (?)	285–246
#535					Sellers 1962: 90, fig. 10 (3)	Ptolemy I	312–285
#537					Sellers 1962: 90 (24)	Ptolemy II	254

No.	Field, Area, Basket	Stratum	Locus	Locus Description	Publication References	Identification	Date BC
#538					Sellers 1962: 90, fig. 10 (20)	Ptolemy II	257
#539					Sellers 1962: 90, fig. 10 (21)	Ptolemy II	256
#540					Sellers 1962: 90 42)	Ptolemy II (?)	285–246
#541					Sellers 1962: 90 (49)	Ptolemy IV (?)	221–204
#542					Sellers 1962: 90, fig. 10 (1)	Ptolemy I	312–285
#543					Sellers 1962: 90, fig. 10 (4)	Ptolemy I	312–285
#544					Sellers 1962: 90 (18)	Ptolemy II	285–246
#545					Sellers 1962: 90 (13)	Ptolemy II	285–246
#546					Sellers 1962: 90, fig. 10 (53)	Ptolemy V	204–181
#547					Sellers 1962: 90–92 (52)	Ptolemy V	204–181
#548					Sellers 1962: 90, fig. 10 (47)	Ptolemy IV	221–204
#549					Sellers 1962: 90, fig. 10 (45)	Ptolemy III	245
#550					Sellers 1962: 90 (15)	Ptolemy II	285–246
#551					Sellers 1962: 90 (16)	Ptolemy II	285–246
#552					Sellers 1962: 90 (19)	Ptolemy II	285–246
#553					Sellers 1962: 90 (17)	Ptolemy II	285–246
#554					Sellers 1962: 90, fig. 10 (14)	Ptolemy II	285–246
#555					Sellers 1962: 90 (22)	Ptolemy II	256
#557					Sellers 1962: 90 (48)	Ptolemy IV	221–204
#558					Sellers 1962: 92, fig. 10 (54)	Ptolemy V	204–181
#559					Sellers 1962: 92 (55)	Ptolemy V	204–181
#560					Sellers 1962: 92 (56)	Ptolemy V	204–181
#561					Sellers 1962: 92 (57)	Ptolemy V	204–181
#562					Sellers 1962: 92 (58)	Ptolemy V	204–181
#563					Sellers 1962: 92 (59)	Ptolemy V	204–181
#564					Sellers 1962: 92 (60)	Ptolemy V	204–181
#565					Sellers 1962: 92 (61)	Ptolemy V	204–181
#566					Sellers 1962: 90, fig. 10 (50)	Ptolemy V	198
#567					Sellers 1962: 90, fig. 10 (51)	Ptolemy V	193
#556	VII.7.37	unstr		east balk	Sellers 1962: 90, fig. 10 (25)	Ptolemy II	285–247
#576	VII.4.97	unstr	1227	Room E (balk 4/5 cleaning)	Shechem III.1: 329a; Sellers 1962: 96, fig. 12 (83); Campbell 1960b:xxx	Ptolemais-Ake	ca. 126
#610	VII.2.106	unstr		surface fill	Toombs & Wright 1961:41; Sellers 1962: 94, fig. 12 (77)	Alexander Zebina	128–123
#652	VII.5.94	unstr		surface fill	Campbell 1960b: v; Toombs & Wright 1961:41; Sellers 1962: 94 (71)	Antiochus IV	175–164
#656	VII.5	unstr		balk	Campbell 1960b: xlv; Sellers 1962: 92 (41)	Ptolemy II	285–247

No.	Field, Area, Basket	Stratum	Locus	Locus Description	Publication References	Identification	Date BC
1962							
#416	VII.4.134	cf IIIB	1518	to IIIB Installation 1518	Shechem III.1: 324b	Ptolemy II or later	284–?
#8	VII.1.	IIIA	1227	embedded in IIIA Floor 1227	Shechem III.1: 329a Toombs & Wright 1963:33	Antiochus III	223–187
#133	VII.22.25	IIIA	22.002	above possible IIIB Floor 22.002, sub IIIA Floor 22.001	Shechem III.1: 325b	Ptolemais-Ake	late 2nd
#136	VII.21.55	IIIA	21.034	IIIA Fill 21.034 below Floor 21.009	Shechem III.1:328; 2:ill. 117:4,5 Campbell & Horn 1962: app. 6	Ptolemy II	284–247
#6	VII.23.6	unstr		surface	Campbell & Horn 1962: app.16	Philisto-Arabian	5th–4th
#31	VII.6.6	unstr		balk removal	Campbell & Horn 1962: app.29		
#61	VII.6.10	unstr		balk removal	Campbell & Horn 1962: app.29	Antiochus IV	
#62	VII	unstr		unstratified		Antiochus VII	
#106	VII.3.39	unstr		surface	Campbell & Horn 1962: app.23	Antiochus VII	
#135	VII.22.36	unstr	22.003	Pit 22.003	Campbell & Horn 1962: app.11	bronze	?
#213	VII.4/7	unstr		balk		Ptolemy II	
#214	VII.5.36	unstr		balk removal		Ptolemaic	
#215	VII.21	unstr		balk removal		Ptolemy I	
#251	VII.5.56	unstr		balk removal	Campbell & Horn 1962: app.50	Philisto-Arabian? silver - as #6 ?	5th–4th
#263	IX.3.63	intrus.	9522A	IVB stony Layer 9522A	Callaway 1962: 9, xii	Antiochus IV	175–164
1968							
#265	II.2.24	II	7041	foundation trench Walls 7043, 7006, Buttress 7045	Ross 1968: app. I	coin?	
#720	II.2.78	II	7100	Make-up 7100 for II Floor 7099	Shechem III.1: 340a; 2: ill. 34:center 3; fig. 265	coin?	
#125	II.1.12	I	7025	in Fill 7025 for str. I surface	Ross 1968: 11	bronze	
#126	II.1.12	I	7025	in Fill 7025 for str. I surface	Shechem III.1: 338a Ross 1968: 11	Cleopatra Thea	122–21
#192	II.1.21	I	7039	ph. 1 occupation	Ross 1968: 11	bronze	
#558	II.2.51	IA	7074	debris 7074 to Wall 7072	Shechem III.1: 341a; 2: ill. 35	bronze	
#83	II.2.48	unstr	7018	surface, Room A		bronze	
#556	II.2.48	unstr	7071	German dump	Ross 1968: app. I	bronze	

Bibliography

Aharoni, Y.

1956a Excavations at Ramat Raḥel, 1954: Preliminary Report—I. *Israel Exploration Journal* 6: 102–11.

1956b Excavations at Ramat Raḥel, 1954: Preliminary Report—II. *Israel Exploration Journal* 6: 137–57.

1962 *Excavations at Ramat Raḥel: Seasons 1959 and 1960.* Rome: Centro di Studi Semitici.

1964 *Excavations at Ramat Raḥel: Seasons 1961 and 1962.* Rome: Centro di Studi Semitici.

Albright, W. F.

1932 *The Excavations of Tell Beit Mirsim, I.* Annual of the American Schools of Oriental Research 12. New Haven, CT: American Schools of Oriental Research.

1943 *The Excavations of Tell Beit Mirsim, III.* Annual of the American Schools of Oriental Research 21–22. New Haven, CT: American Schools of Oriental Research.

Amiran, R.

1969 *Ancient Pottery of the Holy Land.* Jerusalem: Masada.

1975 A Note on the "Gibeon Jar." *Palestine Exploration Quarterly* 107: 129–32.

Anderson, B., and W. Farmer

1957 Field Report: 1957 Season, [Field I] Areas 8–9–10. Unpublished manuscript archived in the Semitic Museum, Harvard University, Cambridge, MA.

Anderson, W. P.

1988 *Serapta I: The Late Bronze and Iron Age Strata of Area II, Y.* Beyrouth: Université Libanaise.

Anderson-Stojanović, V.

1987 The Chronology and Function of Ceramic Unguentaria. *American Journal of Archaeology* 91: 105–22.

1992 *Stobi: The Hellenistic and Roman Pottery.* Princeton, NJ: Princeton University.

Artzy, M.

1980 The Utilitarian "Persian" Storejar Handles. *Bulletin of the American Schools of Oriental Research* 238: 69–73.

Avissar, M.

1996 The Hellenistic and Early Roman Pottery. Pp. 48–59 in *Yoqneʿam: The Late Period*, eds. A. Ben-Tor, M. Avissar, and Y. Portugali. Qedem Reports 3. Jerusalem: The Institute of Archaeology, Hebrew University.

Avi-Yonah, M.

1966 *The Holy Land From the Persian to the Arab Conquests (536 B.C. to A.D. 640): A Historical Geography.* Grand Rapids, MI: Baker.

Bar-Nathan, R.

2002 *Hasmonean and Herodian Palaces at Jericho: Final Reports of the 1973–1987 Excavations.* III: The Pottery. Jerusalem: Israel Exploration Society.

Beazley, J. D.

1932 Little Master Cups. *Journal of Hellenic Studies* 52: 167–204.

Beazley, J. D., and Payne, H. G. G.

1929 Attic Black-figured Fragments from Naucratis. *Journal of Hellenic Studies* 49: 253–72.

Bennett, W. J., and Blakely, J. A.

1989　*Tell el-Hesi: The Persian Period (Stratum V).* Winona Lake, IN: Eisenbrauns.

Berlin, A.

1997　The Plain Wares. Pp. 1–211 in *Tel Anafa II: The Hellenistic and Roman Pottery*, ed. S. Herbert. Journal of Roman Archaeology Supplementary Series 10. Ann Arbor, MI: Kelsey Museum.

Blakely, J. A., and Bennett, W. J.

1989　Levantine Mortaria of the Persian Period. Pp. 45–65 in *Analysis and Publication of Ceramics: The Computer Data-Base in Archaeology*, eds. J. A. Blakely and W. Bennett. British Archaeology Reports International Series 551. Oxford: British Archaeology Reports.

Braemer, F.

1986　Etudes stratigraphiques au N.E. de la façade du temple de Zeus. Pp. 61–66 in *Jerash Archaeological Project, 1981–1983*, ed. F. Zayadine. Amman: Department of Antiquities.

Briend, J.

1980　Vestiges hellenistiques. Pp. 101–16 in *Tell Keisan (1971–1976): une cité phénicienne en Galilée*, by J. Briend and J.-B. Humbert. Fribourg: Éditions Universitaires.

Briend, J., and Humbert, J.-B.

1980　*Tell Keisan (1971–1976): une cité phénicienne en Galilée.* Fribourg: Éditions Universitaires.

Broneer, O.

1930　*Terracotta Lamps. Corinth IV, 2.* Cambridge, MA: Harvard University.

1977　*Terracotta Lamps. Isthmia III.* Princeton, NJ: American School of Classical Studies at Athens.

Callaway, J. A.

1962　Report of Field IX, 1962 Drew-McCormick Expedition to Shechem. Unpublished man-uscript archived in the Semitic Museum, Harvard University, Cambridge, MA.

Campbell, E. F.

1960a　Excavations at Shechem 1960. *Biblical Archaeologist* 1960: 102–26.

1960b　Field Report, Field VII, Shechem, 1960. Unpublished manuscript archived in the Semitic Museum, Harvard University, Cambridge, MA.

1964　Probe in Area 1, Field Report, Field VII, Balâṭah 1964. Unpublished manuscript archived in the Semitic Museum, Harvard University, Cambridge, MA.

Campbell, E. F., and Wright, G. R. H.

2002　*Shechem III: The Stratigraphy and Architecture of Shechem/Tell Balâṭah.* Vol. 1: Text (E. F. Campbell), Vol. 2: Illustrations (G. R. H. Wright). Boston, MA: American Schools of Oriental Research.

Cole, D. P.

1984　*Shechem I: The Middle Bronze IIB Pottery.* Winona Lake, IN: American Schools of Oriental Research.

Cross, F. M.

1962　Epigraphical Notes on Hebrew Documents of the Eighth-Sixth Centuries B.C.: III. The Inscribed Jar Handles from Gibeon. *Bulletin of the American Schools of Oriental Research* 168: 18–23.

1969　Judean Stamps. *Eretz-Israel* 9: 20–27.

Crowfoot, J. W., Crowfoot, G. M., and Kenyon, K. M.

1957　*The Objects from Samaria (Samaria-Sebaste III).* London: Palestine Exploration Fund.

Dornemann, R.

1990　Preliminary Comments on the Pottery Traditions at Tell Nimrin, Illustrated from the 1989 Seasons of Excavations. *Annual of the Department of Antiquities of Jordan* 34: 153–82.

Dothan, M.

1971   *The Second and Third Season of Excavations 1963, 1965.* 'Atiqot 9–10. Jerusalem: Israel Department of Antiquities and Museums.

Dothan, M., and Freedman, D. N.

1967   *Ashdod I: The First Season of Excavations 1962.* 'Atiqot 7. Jerusalem: Israel Department of Antiquities and Museums.

Edwards, P.; Bourke, S.; DaCosta, K.; Tidmarsh, J.; Walmsley, A.; and Watson, P. M.

1990   Preliminary Report on the University of Sydney's Tenth Season of Excavations at Pella (Tabaqat Fahl) in 1988. *Annual of the Department of Antiquities of Jordan* 34: 57–93.

Elgavish, J.

1968   *Archaeological Excavations at Shikmona.* Field Report No. 1: The Levels of the Persian Period, Seasons 1963–1965. Haifa: City Museum of Ancient Art.

Fantalkin, A.

2001   Meṣad Ḥashavyahu: Its Material Culture and Historical Background. *Tel Aviv* 28: 3–165.

Fischer, M.

1989   Hellenistic Pottery (Strata V–III). Pp. 177–87 in *Excavations at Tel Michal, Israel,* eds. Z. Herzog, G. Rapp, and O. Negbi. Minneapolis, MN: University of Minnesota and Tel Aviv University.

Flanagan, J. W.; McCreery, D. W.; and Yassine, K.

1994   Tell Nimrin: Preliminary Report on the 1993 Season. *Annual of the Department of Antiquities of Jordan* 38: 205–44.

Folsom, R. S.

1975   *Attic Black-figured Pottery.* Park Ridge, NJ: Noyes.

Funk, R. W.

1957   Excavations at Tell Balâṭah, 1957. Field Report Field III. Unpublished manuscript archived in the Semitic Museum, Harvard University, Cambridge, MA.

Geraty, L. T.; Herr, L. G.; and LaBianca, Ø. S.

1989   *Madaba Plains Project 1: The 1984 Season at Tell el-ʿUmeiri and Vicinity and Subsequent Studies.* Berrien Springs, MI: Andrews University/Institute of Archaeology.

Geraty, L. T.; Herr, L. G.; LaBianca, Ø. S.; Battenfield, J.; Christopherson, G. L.; Clark, D. R.; Cole, J. A.; Daviau, P. M.; Hubbard, L. E.; Lawlor, J. I.; Low, R.; and Younker, R. W.

1990   Madaba Plains Project: A Preliminary Report of the 1987 Season at Tell el-ʿUmeiri and Vicinity. Pp. 59–88 in *Bulletin of the American Schools of Oriental Research Supplement* 26, ed. W. E. Rast. Baltimore: American Schools of Oriental Research.

Gitin, S.

1990   *Gezer III: A Ceramic Typology of the Late Iron II, Persian and Hellenistic Periods at Tell Gezer.* Annual of the Nelson Glueck School of Biblical Archaeology 3. Jerusalem: Hebrew Union College.

Glanzman, W.

1993   Mortaria from Balâṭah (Shechem) and Tell el-Hesi: A Study of Their Manufacture and Its Significance, Being the Results of an Initial Phase of Research. Burnaby. Unpublished manuscript archived at Simon Fraser University, British Columbia.

Grace, V.

1953   The Eponyms Named on Rhodian Amphora Stamps. *Hesperia* 22.2: 116–28.

Graef, B.

1909–1933 *Die Antiken Vasen von der Akropolis zu Athens.* 2 vols. Berlin: de Gruyter.

Grant, E., and Wright, G. E.

1938   *Ain Shems Excavations, IV (Pottery).* Haverford, CT: Haverford College.

1939   *Ain Shems Excavations, V (Text).* Haverford, CT: Haverford College.

Gunneweg, J.; Perlman, I.; and Yellin, J.

1983   *The Provenience, Typology, and Chronology of Eastern Terra Sigillata.* Qedem 17. Jerusalem: Institute of Archaeology/Hebrew University of Jerusalem.

Guz-Zilberstein, B.

1995   The Typology of the Hellenistic Coarse Ware and Selected Loci of the Hellenistic and Roman Periods. Pp. 289–433 in *Excavations at Dor, Final Report: Volume I B, Areas A and C: The Finds*, eds. E. Stern, J. Berg, A. Gilboa, B. Guz-Zilbertein, A. Raban, R. Rosenthal-Heginbottom, and I. Sharon. Qedem Reports 1. Jerusalem: Institute of Archaeology/Hebrew University of Jerusalem.

Hadidi, A.

1970   The Pottery from the Roman Forum at Amman. *Annual of the Department of Antiquities of Jordan* 15: 11–15.

Hamilton, R. W.

1934   Excavations at Tell Abu Hawām. *Quarterly of the Department of Antiquities in Palestine* 4: 1–69.

Hayes, J. W.

1991   *Paphos. Vol. III: The Hellenistic and Roman Pottery.* Nicosia: Department of Antiquities of Cyprus.

Hennessy, J. B.

1970   Excavations at Samaria-Sebaste, 1968. *Levant* 2: 1–21.

Henschel-Simon, E.

1945   Note on the Pottery of the 'Amman Tombs. *Quarterly of the Department of Antiquities in Palestine* 11: 75–80.

Herr, L. G.

1989   The Pottery Finds. Pp. 299–354 in *Madaba Plains Project 1: The 1984 Season at Tell el 'Umeiri and Vicinity and Subsequent Studies*, eds. L. T. Geraty, L. G. Herr, Ø. S. LaBianca, and R. W. Younker. Berrien Springs, MI: Andrews University/Institute of Archaeology.

Herr, L. G.; Geraty, L. T.; Younker, R. W.; and LaBianca, Ø. S.

1991   *Madaba Plains Project 2: The 1987 Season at Tell el-'Umeiri and Vicinity and Subsequent Studies.* Berrien Springs, MI: Andrews University/Institute of Archaeology.

1997   *Madaba Plains Project 3: The 1989 Season at Tell el-'Umeiri and Vicinity and Subsequent Studies.* Berrien Springs, MI: Andrews University/Institute of Archaeology.

Herr, L. G.; Clark, D R..; Geraty, L. T.; Younker, R. W.; and LaBianca, Ø. S.

2000   *Madaba Plains Project 4: The 1992 Season at Tall al-'Umayri and Subsequent Studies.* Berrien Springs, MI: Andrews University/ Institute of Archaeology.

2002   *Madaba Plains Project: The 1994 Season at Tall al-'Umayri and Subsequent Studies.* Berrien Springs, MI: Andrews University/ Institute of Archaeology.

Herzog, Z.; Rapp, G.; and Negbi, O.

1989   *Excavations at Tel Michal, Israel.* Minneapolis: University of Minnesota/Tel Aviv: Sonia and Marco Nadler Institute of Archaeology, Tel Aviv University

Hiller von Gaertringen, F.

1931   Rhodes. *Pauly Real-Encyclopädie der Classischen Altertumswissenschaft, Supplementband* 5, cols. 818–40. Stuttgart: Metzler.

Howland, R. H.

1958   *Greek Lamps and their Survivals.* Athenian Agora 4. Princeton, NJ: American School of Classical Studies at Athens.

Horn, S. H., and Campbell, E. F.

1962   Report on the Excavation of Field VII at Balâṭah, 1962. Unpublished manuscript archived in the Semitic Museum, Harvard University, Cambridge, MA.

Ji, C-H. C.

1998 ʿIraq al-ʿAmir and the Hellenistic Settlements in Central and Northern Jordan. *Studies in the History and Archaeology of Jordan* 6: 379–89.

1999 The 1998 Season of Archaeological Survey in the regions of ʿIrāq al-ʿAmīr and Wādī al-Kafrayn. A Preliminary Report. *Annual of the Department of Antiquities of Jordan* 43: 521–39.

Johns, C. N.

1932 Excavations at ʿAthlit (1930–31): The South-East Cemetery. *Quarterly of the Department of Antiquities of Palestine* 2: 41–104.

Jones, F. F.

1950 The Pottery. Pp. 49–296 in *Excavations at Gözlü Kule, Tarsus I. The Hellenistic and Roman Periods*, ed. H. Goldman. Princeton, NJ: Princeton University.

Kahane, P.

1952a Pottery Types from the Ossuary-Tombs around Jerusalem—I. *Israel Exploration Journal* 2: 125–39.

1952b Pottery Types from the Ossuary-Tombs around Jerusalem—II. *Israel Exploration Journal* 2: 176–82.

1953 Pottery Types from the Ossuary-Tombs around Jerusalem—III. *Israel Exploration Journal* 3: 48–54.

Kee, H., and Toombs, L.

1957 The Second Season of Excavation at Biblical Shechem. *Biblical Archaeologist* 20: 82–105.

Kelso, J. L.

1968 *The Excavations of Bethel (1934–60)*. Annual of the American Schools of Oriental Research 39. Cambridge, MA: American Schools of Oriental Research.

Kenyon, K. M.

1957 Israelite Pottery: Stratified Groups; Hellenistic Pottery: Stratified Groups. Pp. 94–134, 217–35 in *The Objects from Samaria (Samaria-Sebaste III)*, by J. W. Crowfoot, G. M. Crowfoot, and K. M. Kenyon. London: Palestine Exploration Fund.

Kerkhof, V.

1969 Catalogue of the Shechem Collection in the Rijksmuseum van Oudheden in Leiden. *Oudheidkundige Mededelingen* 50: 28–109.

Lamon, R., and Shipton, G.

1939 *Megiddo I: Seasons of 1923–34, Strata I–V*. Oriental Institute Publications 62. Chicago: University of Chicago.

Lance, H. D.

1964 Field Report, Field I, Areas 16 and 17, 1964. Unpublished manuscript archived in the Semitic Museum, Harvard University, Cambridge, MA.

Lapp, N. L.

1964 Pottery From Some Hellenistic Loci at Balâṭah (Shechem). *Bulletin of the American Schools of Oriental Research* 175: 14–26.

1974 The Late Persian Pottery. Pp. 30–32 in *Discoveries in the Wâdī ed-Dâliyeh*, eds. P. W. Lapp and N. L. Lapp. Annual of the American Schools of Oriental Research 41. Cambridge, MA: American Schools of Oriental Research.

1981 The Pottery in the 1964 Campaign. Pp. 79–107 in *The Third Campaign at Tell el Fûl: The Excavations of 1964*, ed. N. L. Lapp. Annual of the American Schools of Oriental Research 45. Cambridge, MA: American Schools of Oriental Research.

1983 Hellenistic Pottery from the Qasr and Square Building. Pp. 63–74 in *The Excavations of ʿAraq el-ʿEmir, I*, ed. N. L. Lapp. Annual of the American Schools of Oriental Research 47. Winona Lake, IN: American Schools of Oriental Research.

1985 The Stratum V Pottery from Balâṭah (Shechem). *Bulletin of the American Schools of Oriental Research* 257: 19–43.

Lapp, P. W.

1961 *Palestinian Ceramic Chronology, 200 B.C.–A.D. 70*. New Haven, CT: American Schools of Oriental Research.

1963 Ptolemaic Stamped Handles from Judah. *Bulletin of the American Schools of Oriental Research* 172: 22–25.

1968a Bethel Pottery of the Late Hellenistic and Early Roman Periods. Pp. 77–80 in *The Excavations of Bethel (1934–60)*, ed. J. L. Kelso. Annual of the American Schools of Oriental Research 39. Cambridge, MA: American Schools of Oriental Research.

1968b Review of J. B. Pritchard, *Winery, Defenses, and Soundings at Gibeon. American Journal of Archaeology* 72: 391–93.

1970a The Pottery of Palestine in the Persian Period. Pp. 179–97 in *Archäologie und Altes Testament: Festschrift für Kurt Galling*, eds. A. Kuschke and E. Kutsch. Tübingen: Mohr.

1970b The Tell Deir ʿAllā Challenge to Palestinian Archaeology, review of H. Franken, *Excavations at Tell Deir ʿAllā I: A Stratigraphical and Analytical Study of the Early Iron Age Pottery, Vetus Testamentum* 20: 243–56.

Lapp, P. W., and Lapp, N. L.

1968 Iron II-Hellenistic Pottery Groups. Pp. 54–79 in *The 1957 Excavation at Beth-Zur*, eds. O. R. Sellers, R. W. Funk, N. L. Lapp, P. W. Lapp, and R. L. McKenzie. Annual of the American Schools of Oriental Research 38. Cambridge, MA: American Schools of Oriental Research.

Liddell H. G.; Scott, R.; Jones, H. S.; and McKenzie, R.

1996 *A Greek-English Lexicon*. New York: Oxford University Press.

Lugenbeal, E., and Sauer, J. A.

1972 Pottery from Heshbon. *Andrews University Seminary Studies* 10: 21–69.

Mazar, B., Dothan, T., and Dunayevsky, I.

1966 *En-Gedi: The First and Second Seasons of Excavations, 1961–62.* ʿAtiqot 5 (English Series). Jerusalem: Israel Department of Antiquities and Museums.

Mazar, B., and Dunayevsky, I.

1967 En-Gedi: The Fourth and Fifth Seasons of Excavations (Preliminary Report). *Israel Exploration Journal* 17: 133–43.

McNicoll, A.; Edwards, P.; Hanbury-Tenison; Hennessy, J. B.; Potts, T.; Smith, R. H.; Walmsley, A.; and Watson, P.

1992 *Pella in Jordan 2*. Sydney: Meditarch.

McNicoll, A.; Smith, R. H.; and Hennessy, J. B.

1982 *Pella in Jordan 1*. Canberra: Australian National Gallery.

Mitchel, L.

1992 *Hellenistic and Roman Strata: A Study of the Stratigraphy of Tell Hesban from the 2nd Century B.C. to the 4th Century A.D.* Hesban 7. Berrien Springs, MI: Institute of Archaeology, Andrews University.

Munsell Soil Color Charts

1975 Baltimore, MD: Munsell Color Macbeth.

Naveh, J.

1962 The Excavations at Meṣad Ḥashavyahu, Preliminary Report. *Israel Exploration Journal* 12: 89–113.

1963 Old Hebrew Inscriptions in a Burial Cave. *Israel Exploration Journal* 13: 74–92.

Negev, A.

1986 *The Late Hellenistic and Early Roman Pottery of Nabatean Oboda*. Qedem 22. Jerusalem: Institute of Archaeology, Hebrew University of Jerusalem.

Nilsson, M. P.

1909 *Timbres amphoriques de Lindos*. Exploration archéologique de Rhodes 5. Copenhagen: Lunos.

Nodet, E.

1980   Le Niveau 3 (Periode Perse). Pp. 117–129 in *Tell Keisan (1971–1976): une cité phénicienne en Galilée*, by J. Briend, J. and J.-B. Humbert. Fribourg: Éditions Universitaires.

Papuci-Władyka, E.

1995   Hellenistic Pottery from New Paphos—First Results of Scientific Analysis. Pp. 247–53 in *Hellenistic and Roman Pottery I the Eastern Mediterranean—Advances in Scientific Studies*. Acts of the II Nieborów Pottery Workshop, eds. H. Meyza and J. Mlynarczyk. Warsaw: Research Centre for Mediterranean Archaeology, Polish Academy of Sciences.

Porath, J.

1974   A Fortress of the Persian Period. ʿAtiqot 7: 43–55, 6*–7* (in Hebrew).

Prag, K.

1989   Preliminary Report on the Excavations at Tell Iktanu, Jordan, 1987. *Levant* 21: 33–45.

Pritchard, J. B.

1959   *Hebrew Inscriptions and Stamps from Gibeon*. Philadelphia, PA: University Museum.

1975   *Sarepta: A Preliminary Report on the Iron Age*. Philadelphia, PA: University Museum.

1985   *Tell es-Saʿidiyeh: Excavations on the Tell, 1964–1966*. Philadelphia, PA: University Museum.

1988   *Sarepta IV: The Objects from Area II, X*. Beyrouth: Université Libanaise.

Rast, W. E.

1978   *Taanach I: Studies in the Iron Age Pottery*. Cambridge, MA: American Schools of Oriental Research.

Reisner, G. R.; Fisher, C. S.; and Lyon, D. G.

1924   *Harvard Excavations at Samaria, 1908–1910, I: Text*. Cambridge, MA: Harvard University.

Richardson, H. N.

1957   Field II. Unpublished manuscript archived in the Semitic Museum, Harvard University, Cambridge, MA.

Rosenthal-Heginbottom, R.

1995   Imported Hellenistic and Roman Pottery. Pp. 183–288 in *Excavations at Dor, Final Report: Volume I B, Areas A and C: The Finds*, eds. E. Stern, J. Berg, A. Gilboa, B. Guz-Zilbertein, A. Raban, R. Rosenthal-Heginbottom, and I. Sharon. Qedem Reports 1. Institute of Archaeology, The Hebrew University of Jerusalem: Israel.

Ross, J. R.

1968   Field II–1968. Unpublished manuscript archived in the Semitic Museum, Harvard University, Cambridge, MA.

Rotroff, S. I.

1984   The Origins and Chronology of Hellenistic Gray Unguentaria. *American Journal of Archaeology* 88: 258.

1987   Two Centuries of Hellenistic Pottery, Preface. Pp. 1–8 in *Hellenistic Pottery and Terracottas*, eds. H. and D. Thompson. Princeton, NJ: American School of Classical Studies.

1997   *The Athenian Agora*. Vol. 29: *Hellenistic Pottery: Athenian and Imported Wheelmade Table Ware and Related Material*. Princeton, NJ: American School of Classical Studies at Athens.

Sauer, J. A.

1973   *Heshbon Pottery 1971*. Berrien Springs, MI: Andrews University.

1994   The Pottery at Hesban and its Relationships to the History of Jordan: An Interim Hesban Pottery Report, 1993. Pp. 225–81 in *Hesban After 25 Years*, eds. D. Merling and L. T. Geraty. Berrien Springs, MI: Institute of Archaeology.

Sellers, O. R.

1960 Coins of the 1960 Excavation at Balâṭah. Unpublished manuscript archived in the Semitic Museum, Harvard University, Cambridge, MA.

1962 Coins of the 1960 Excavations at Shechem. *Biblical Archaeologist* 25: 87–96.

Sinclair, L.

1960 *An Archaeological Study of Gibeah (Tell el-Fûl).* Annual of the American Schools of Oriental Research 24–25. Cambridge, MA: American Schools of Oriental Research.

Singer-Avitz, L.

1989 Local Pottery of the Persian Period (Strata XI–VI). Pp. 115–44 in *Excavations at Tel Michal, Israel,* eds. Z. Herzog, G. Rapp, and O. Negbi. Minneapolis, MN: University of Minnesota and Tel Aviv University.

Slane, K. W.

1997 The Fine Wares. Pp. 247–393 in *Tel Anafa II: The Hellenistic and Roman Pottery,* ed. S. Herbert. Journal of Roman Archaeology Supplementary Series 10. Ann Arbor, MI: Kelsey Museum.

Smith, R. H.

1990 The Southern Levant in the Hellenistic Period. *Levant* 22: 123–30.

Sparkes, B. A., and Talcott, L.

1970 *Black and Plain Pottery of the Sixth, Fifth, and Fourth Centuries B.C.* Athenian Agora 12. Princeton, NJ: American School of Classical Studies.

Stern, E.

1970 Excavations at Gil`am (Kh. er-Rujm). ʿAtiqot 6 (Hebrew series): 31–55, 4*–6*.

1978 *Excavations at Tel Mevorakh (1973–1976). Part One: From the Iron Age to the Roman Period.* Qedem 9. Jerusalem: Institute of Archaeology, Hebrew University.

1980 Achaemenian Tombs from Shechem. *Levant* 12: 90–111.

1982 *Material Culture of the Land of the Bible in the Persian Period 538–332 B.C.* Warminster, England: Aris and Phillips.

Stern E.; Berg, J.; Gilboa, A.; Guz-Zilberstein, B.; Raban, A.; Rosenthal-Heginbottom, R.; and Sharon, I. (eds.)

1995a *Excavations at Dor, Final Report: Volume I A, Areas A and C: Introduction and Stratigraphy.* Qedem Reports 1. Jerusalem: Institute of Archaeology, Hebrew University.

1995b *Excavations at Dor, Final Report: Volume I B, Areas A and C: The Finds.* Qedem Reports 2. Jerusalem: Institute of Archaeology, Hebrew University.

Stern, E., and Magen, Y.

1984 A Pottery Group of the Persian Period from Qadum in Samaria. *Bulletin of the American Schools of Oriental Research* 253: 9–27.

Stewart, A., and Martin, S. R.

2005 Attic Imported Pottery at Tel Dor, Israel: An Overview. *Bulletin of the American Schools of Oriental Research* 337: 79–94.

Strange, J. F.

1975 Late Hellenistic and Herodian Ossuary Tombs at French Hill, Jerusalem. *Bulletin of the American Schools of Oriental Research* 219: 39–67.

Thompson, H.

1934 Two Centuries of Hellenistic Pottery. *Hesperia* 3: 311–480.

Toombs, L.

1957 Field I, Areas 5, 6, and 7. Unpublished manuscript archived in the Semitic Museum, Harvard University, Cambridge, MA.

Toombs, L., and Wright, G. E.

1961 The Third Campaign at Balâṭah (Shechem). *Bulletin of the American Schools of Oriental Research* 161: 11–54.

1962 The Fourth Campaign at Balâṭah (Shechem). *Bulletin of the American Schools of Oriental Research* 169: 1–60.

incised designs 27, 33, 35, 60
inscription 23, 36, 45–46, 78
'Iraq al-'Emir. *See* 'Araq el-'Emir
ivy pattern 35

J

jar
  bag-shaped 19–20, 41, 73, 77
  collar rim 42–45, 78
  conical 41
  cylindrical 19–20, 41, 44, 77
  Gibeon 22–23, 73–74
  grooved neck 42
  profile-rimmed 19–20, 73
  Rhodian 45–46, 76, 78
  "sausage" 20
Jericho (Herodian) 49, 51, 54
jug
  narrow-necked 23, 47, 73
  ridge-necked 22–23, 48–49, 73, 76, 79
  wide-mouthed 22, 47, 54, 73–74, 78

K

Keisan, Tell 24, 31, 41, 44, 55, 57–58, 61–64, 67
knob 36, 67–68
krater
  grooved 61, 77
  high-necked 25, 27, 61–62, 73–74, 80

L

Lachish 19, 22, 26
lamp
  Attic 66
  delphiniform 6, 33, 66–67, 76, 80
  molded 68
  spout 31, 33, 66–68
Lapp, P. W. 6, 11, 13, 20–22
ledged rim 25, 48–49, 57–58, 73–74, 78–80
lekythos 34, 36
lid 26, 30, 34, 36, 48, 49, 56, 63, 64, 65–66, 79, 80
lion 2, 22
lug handle 25, 67–68, 73

M

Madaba 33
Mediterranean 54
Megarian ware 60
Megiddo 25–26
Mesopotamia 27, 54, 56
Mevorakh, Tel 20, 23–25, 31, 62, 64, 66
Michal, Tel 19, 23, 25, 29, 31, 57, 64

N

Naṣbeh, Tell en- 19–20, 22–25
Nimrin, Tell 30

O

Oboda 58

P

painted pottery 24, 32–35, 51, 54–55, 57–58, 66, 79
Phoenician stamp. *See ṭêt* handle
piriform shape 46, 54–55
Ptolemy
  I 2–3
  II 3
  V 3
pylix 36

Q

Qadum 61
Qasr al-Hamrā' 27

R

Ramat Raḥel 22, 24–25, 61–62
relief motif 68
Rhodes 23
Rotroff, S. I. 54

S

Saidiyeh, Tell es- 29–30, 53
Samaria 20, 25–26, 29, 48, 51, 55–59, 61–67
  Hellenistic Fort Wall 44, 48, 52, 58–59, 65
Sarepta 31
seal (sealing) 2, 22
Shephela 19–20
Shiqmona 22, 24, 41
slipped pottery 51, 54–59, 62, 66–68, 79
Stern, E. 25

T

Taanach 20, 22, 25, 64
tannur 5, 7, 9
Tarsus 55, 57, 59, 66
Terra Sigillata 57, 59–60
ṭêt handle 9, 20–22, 73–74
Theudōros 45
Thompson, H. 58
Transjordan 19, 27, 29–30, 33, 45, 53

U

'Umayri, Tell al- 25, 27, 29, 31
undercut rim 20, 22, 29, 41, 44–45, 47, 76–78

W

Wâdī ed-Dâliyeh 41, 42, 44, 46–49, 51, 53, 61, 63–64
wedge impressions 26–27, 73–74
West Slope ware 62
Wright, G. E. 1, 2, 6, 22

Y

Yoqne'am 51, 61, 63–66

Z

Zorn, J. 27

Pl. 2.1   Stratum V Jars   (cont.)

Pl	Str	Fld, Ar,Bkt	No.	Locus D
	cf IV	62 VII.1.113	1640	above me
	cf IV	VII.3.141	5635	cleaning
	IIIA	VII.9.43	3215	removal
	IIIA	VII 21.156	1329	Debris 21
2.1:14	cf III	57 I.6.57	460	pit in Wa
	cf I	57 II.1.35	386	Hellenist
	unstr	62 VII.2.25	358	unstratifi
	unstr	62 VII.2.25	359	unstratifi
	unstr	62 VII.7.22	840	unstratifi
15	unstr	I.7.70	469	unstratifi
	unstr	I.llb.5a	893	unstratifi

Other Jars

Pl	Str	Fld, Ar,Bkt	No.	Locus D
2.1:16	V	62 VII.4.109	1026	removal V
	cf V	62 VII.1.8	11	sub 2nd I
17	cf V	62 VII.4.6	52	IVB Fill 1
18	cf V	62 VII.4.56	406	IVB Fill 1
	IVB	VII.1.115	7304	in Probe
	IVB	IX.3.64	187	bricky Lay
	unstr	VII.7.28	944	unstratifi
19	IVA	VII.3.143	5667	cleaning I
20	unstr	VII.5.22	7441A	disturbed

POTTERY PLATES AND DESCRIPTIONS

Pl. 2.1   Stratum V Jars   (cont.)

PL	STR	FLD, AR,BKT	NO.
2.1:9	IVB	VII.2.130	6903
	IVB	62 VII.4.2	21
	IVB	62 VII.4.2	24
10	IVB	62 VII.4.18	101
11	IVB	62 VII.4.18	103
	IVB	62 VII.4.19	117
12	IVB	VII.6.123	2177
	IVB	VII.6.123	2181
	IVB	IX.1.55	153
	IVB	IX.2.49	111
	IVB	IX.2.51	119
	IVB	IX.2.71	281
	IVB	IX.3.53	120
	IVB	IX.3.65	189
	IVB	IX.3.72	200
	IVB	IX.3.73	202
	IVB	IX.3.77	220
	IVB	IX.3.77	221
	IVA	64 VII.2.7	323
	IVA	VII.4.111	5553
2.1:13	IV	I.7b.57	342

Pl. 2.2   Stratum V Jar Handles

PL	STR	FLD, AR,BKT	NO.	LOCUS DESCRIPTION	WARE DESCRIPTION
Handles					
2.2:1	cf V	62 VII.4.6	58	IVB Fill 1556 sub Surface 1530	5YR 4/1 gray, 2.5YR 6/8 light red surfaces; very few small and large inclusions
2	cf V	62 VII.4.45	275	IVB Fill 1556 sub Surface 1530	2.5Yr 3/0 very dark gray, 5/8 red surfaces; many small to very large inclusions
	cf V	62 VII.4.54	404	IVB Fill 1556 sub Surface 1530	5YR 5/1 gray; many small inclusions
3	cf V	62 VII.4.55	405	IVB Fill 1556 sub Surface 1530	5YR 4/1 dark gray, 6/6 reddish yellow surfaces
4	cf V	62 VII.4.58	408	IVB Fill 1556 sub Surface 1530	10YR 6/4 light yellowish brown; very few large inclusions
	IVB	62 VII.4.19	113	Hardpack 1529 sub IV Wall 1517	2.5YR N6/ gray, 6/6 light red exterior surface; medium and large inclusions
Ṭêt Handles					
5 fig. 2.1 (p. 21)	cf IV	62 VII.23.69	530	IV Stonefall 23.010	2.5YR N4/ dark gray, 5/6 red surfaces; medium inclusions
6 fig. 2.1	cf IV	62 VII.23.71	536	IV Stonefall 23.010	5YR 5/1 gray; medium and large inclusions
fig. 2.2 (p. 21)	cf IV	64 I.17.34	38,900 #450	Fill 481 below H walls	not available; to Dept. of Antiquities
	cf IV	64 I.17.36	38,880 #454	Fill 481 below H walls	not available
7 fig. 2.1	cf IIIB	60 VII.8.68a	3897 #506	L.1712-1713 unsealed but sub level of IIIB Surface 1719	2.5YR N4/ dark gray, 5/6 red surfaces; few large inclusions
8 fig. 2.1	cf IIIB	60 VII.8.96	5124A #620	unsealed IIIB Fill 1717-20 sub IIIB level	5YR 3/3 dark reddish brown & 3/1 very dark gray; 4/1 dark gray surfaces; medium inclusions
9 fig. 2.1	IIIA	60 VII.4.77	3847 #505	removal IIIA Walls 1505-1510	5YR 3/1 very dark gray, with thin layer of 4/3 reddish brown below 3/1 very dark gray surfaces; many small & few large inclusions
10 fig. 2.1	unstr	60 VII.2.62	1081 #277	L. 1112 down to IV floor	5YR 4/1 dark gray, 4/8 yellowish red surfaces; medium inclusions
11 fig. 2.1	unstr	62 VII.23.92	768	around VII Wall (?) 23.012	2.5YR N3/ very dark gray, N4/ dark gray surfaces; medium and large inclusions
12	unstr	1964-68		unknown	5YR 4/1 dark gray, 5/8 yellowish red surfaces; medium and few large inclusions
	?	1926-27		no record	not available; PAM 1.979
	?	1926-27		no record	not available; PAM 1.995
	?	1926-27		no record - 5 or 6 more	not available; Lieden: Kerkhof 1969: fig. 15:21
Other stamped Handles					
	IVB	VII.2.134	7323	L. 1123A levelling below IV installations	5YR 6/6 reddish yellow with 5/1 gray core; medium and large inclusions; empty circle imprint
	IVB	IX.3.71	197	IVB Fill 9523	5YR 6/1 gray, 2.5YR 6/6 light red slip int.; many medium incl; somewhat like ṭêt stamp, but smaller

Pl. 2.2 Stratum V Jar Handles.

Pl. 2.2 Stratum V Jar Handles (cont.)

Pl	Str	Fld, Ar,Bkt	No.	Locus Description	Ware description
	cf II	VII.8.25	2742 #426	above possible IIIA Surface 1702	5YR 7/4 pink, 7/3 pink exterior surface; many small inclusions; Hellenistic ware, but small stamp somewhat like ṭêt stamp
2.2:13 fig 2.3 (p. 22)	unstr	62 VII.2.70	1132 #349	contaminated Stone Pile 1161	7.5YR 6/4 light brown, 5YR 7/4 pink exterior surface, 7/2 pinkish gray interior surface; many medium inclusions; lion stamp

Pl. 2.3   Stratum V Jugs and Juglets

PL	STR	FLD, AR,BKT	NO.	LOCUS DESCRIPTION	WARE DESCRIPTION
Wide-mouth Jugs					
2.3:1	cf V	62 VII.2.10	251	inside V Installation 1127	5YR 6/1 light gray, 7.5YR 7/4 pink exterior surface; some medium inclusions
	cf V	64 VII.1.54	2297	V? Hardpack 1259	5YR 6/1 gray, 7/8 reddish yellow interior & 7/6 reddish yellow exterior surfaces; large & small incl
	cf V	62 VII.4.54	400	IVB Fill 1556 sub Surface 1530	2.5YR 5/0 gray, 10R 6/6 light red exterior surface; small and few large inclusions
	IVB	62 VII.1.69	891	sub IVB Surface 1236 (sub 1216)	2.5YR 4/0 dark gray, 5YR 4/2 dark reddish gray int & 10R 6/6 light red ext surfaces; many small incl
2	IVB	VII.5.137	6399	removal IVB Wall 1415-1117	5YR 5/3 reddish brown; some large inclusions
	IVB	VII.2.130	6899	removal IVB Wall 1415-1117	5YR gray, 2.5YR 6/6 light red interior & 10R6/6 light red exterior surfaces; small & few large inclusions
	IVB	62 VII.4.18	105	Hardpack 1529 sub IV Wall 1517	2.5YR 5/0 gray, 5/6 red exterior surface; few incl
3	IVB	IX.3.65	190	IVB stony Layer 9522A	2.5YR 5/0 gray, 5YR 6/6 reddish yellow surfaces; many small and few extra large inclusions
	IVA	64 VII.2.4	146	Fill 1129A sub IVA Wall 1026	5YR 6/1 gray, 2.5YR 6/6 light red exterior surface; few small inclusions
4	IVA	VII.6.205	5587	removal IVA Wall 1025-1308	5YR 6/6 reddish yellow, 5/1 gray core; some medium and large inclusions
5	IVA	IX.1.64	158	occupation Debris 9029	2.5YR 5/0 gray, 5/6 light red exterior surface; some large inclusions
6	IV	I.7b.56	326	in lower IV Floor 205	5YR 5/1 gray, 7/3 pink exterior surface; some medium inclusions
	cf IV	62 VII.1.67	885	above metalled Surface 1233 in balk	2.5YR 5/0 gray, 6/3 light red interior & 6/4 light reddish brown ext surface; small & many large incl
	cf IV	VII.23.70	535	IV Stonefall 23.010	5YR 6/1 gray, 7/3 pink interior & 7/4 pink exterior to 10YR 8/3 very pale brown exterior surfaces; few large & many small inclusions
7	IV/III	I.7.23	139	lower H Floors 205 & 206	2.5YR 5/0 gray, 5/6 light red exterior surface; some large inclusions
	IIIB	VII.1.44	813	beneath IIIB Floor 1214	5YR 6/1 gray, 7.5YR 6/4 light brown interior & 5YR 7/4 pink exterior surfaces; small inclusions
8	IIIB	VII.8.56	3872	beneath IIIB Cobbling 1715	5YR 6/1 gray, 2.5YR 6/4 light reddish brown exterior surfaces; many small inclusions
9	IIIB	VII.8.87	4623	sub IIIB cobbling 1719	5YR 6/1 gray, 7/3 pink exterior surface; few smaller inclusions
	cf IIIB	VII.22.49	461	sub possible IIIB Floor 22.002	5YR 6/1 gray, 8/4 pink exterior surface; few large and many small inclusions
	IIIA	VII.21.145	1242	Debris 21.035 sub IIIA walls & Floor 21.031	5YR 7/2 pinkish gray, 2.5YR 6/4 light reddish brown interior & 10YR 8/3 very pale brown exterior surfaces; large and many small inclusions

(continued on p. 179)

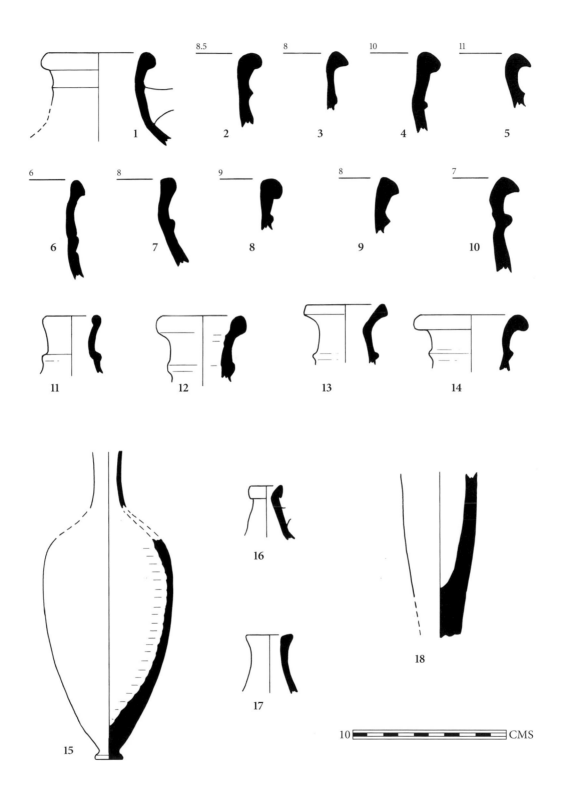

Pl. 2.3 Stratum V Jugs and Juglets.

Pl. 2.3 Stratum V Jugs and Juglets (cont.)

Pl	Str	Fld, Ar, Bkt	No.	Locus Description	Ware description
	unstr	62 VII.7.41	1214	unstratified	2.5YR 4/0 dark gray, 5/4 reddish brown interior and 5YR 6/2 pinkish gray exterior surfaces; small and few large inclusions
2.3:10	unstr	VII.22.23	167	unstratified	10R 6/6 light red, 7.5YR 5/0 gray core; few med incl

Narrow-necked Jugs, Decanters, or Flasks

11	V	IX.4.60	245	V ashy and brick Layer 9768	7.5YR 7/4 pink; very few medium to large inclusions
12	cf V	62 VII.4.54	401	IVB Fill 1556 sub Surface 1530	7.5YR 7/4 pink; very few medium to large inclusions
13	IVB	62 VII.4.58	413	IVB Fill 1556 sub Surface 1530	10R 5/6 red exterior, 5YR 5/2 reddish gray interior; very many medium to large inclusions
14	IIIB	62 VII.4.8	62	sealed in Pit 1522	not accessible

Juglets or Bottles

15 fig 2.4 (p. 23)	cf IIIB	VII.22.51	503	sub possible IIIB Floor 22.002	5YR 5/1 gray, 10YR 5/3 brown interior & 5YR 5/6 yellowish red exterior surf; some very small incl
16	unstr	VII.8.33	2775	unstratified	2.5YR 7/2 light gray; few very small inclusions
17	unstr	VII.2.68	1115	down to IV	5YR 7/4 pink, 6/4 light reddish brown exterior surface; few small inclusions
18	unstr	VII.2.33	310	unstratified	10YR 6/2 light brownish gray, 6/2 light brownish gray exterior surface; many very small inclusions

Pl. 2.5 Stratum V Kraters

Pl	Str	Fld, Ar,Bkt	No.	Locus Description	Ware description
High-necked					
2.5:1	V	IX.1.73	249	V compact gray Layer 9034	10R 4/1 dark reddish gray, 2.5YR 6/8 light red surfaces; some small to medium inclusions
2	V	IX.3.87	287	V Debris 9524	6YR 5/ gray, 6/6 reddish yellow surfaces; few very small inclusions
3	V	IX.3.87	288	V Debris 9524	2.5YR 5/6 red; few medium to large inclusions
4	cf V	62 VII.4.39	240	IVB Fill 1556 sub Surface 1530	5YR 6/4 light reddish brown
	cf V	62 VII.4.53	399	IVB Fill 1556 sub Surface 1530	5YR 5/1 gray, 5/8 yellowish red surfaces; medium and small inclusions
5	IVB	VII.2.131	6914	L. 1123A levelling below IV installations	5YR 6/1 gray, 7/4 pink exterior surface; large ceramic & many large organic, & few limestone incl
6	IVB	VII.2.134	7324	L. 1123A levelling below IV installations	not accessible
7	IVB	62 VII.4.4	32	sealed in IV Wall 1517	5YR 6/6 reddish yellow, 7.5YR 6/4 light brown exterior surface; many small inclusions
	IVB	VII.7.136	6322	Fill 1836-1841 below IV strata	6YR 5/1 gray, 10R 6/6 light red exterior surface, some large and many small inclusions
	IVB	IX.3.53	121	occupational Debris 9517C	5YR 5/1 gray, 10R 6/6 light red interior, 2/5YR 6/6 light red exterior, large and many small inclusions
	IVB	IX.3.65	191	IVB stony Layer 9522A	10YR 5/1 gray, 2.5YR 6/4 light reddish brown, 10R 6/8 light red exterior, large and many small incl
	IVA	IX.1.61	155	occupation Debris 9029	5YR 6/1 light gray, 7/4 pink exterior surface; many small and few large inclusions
	IVA	IX.2.31	41	silty Soil 9262	5YR 5/1 gray with 10R light red core, 5YR 7/3 pink exterior surface; large and many small inclusions
8	IVA	IX.2.45	105	pottery from IVA Wall 9267	5YR 6/2 gray, 7/6 reddish yellow exterior surface; some medium inclusions
9	IIIA	VII.3.60	1623	removal IIIA Drain 1015-1016	2.5YR 5/6 red, 5/4 reddish brown interior & 6/6 light red exterior surfaces; some small and large incl
10	unstr	62 VII.2.11	253	unstratified	not accessible
	unstr	I.10.9	128	surface	2.5YR 5/0 gray, 10YR 8/4 very pale brown exterior surface; small and few large inclusions
Sloping-shoulder					
11	V	IX.1.69	213	V compact gray Layer 9034	2.5YR 6/6 light red with 5YR 7/4 pink core, 2/5YR 6/8 light red interior & 6/6 light red exterior surfaces; many large and small inclusions
12	cf V	62 VII.4.38	199	IVB Fill 1556 sub Surface 1530	5YR 7/4 pink, 6/3 light reddish brown core; many medium to large inclusions
13	IVA	IX.4.32	86	L. 9759.29-32 resurfacing Surface 9760	10R 5/1 reddish gray, 2.5YR 6/6 light red surfaces; very few small to large inclusions
14	IVA	VII.5.146	6542	sub IVA Wall 1419	2.5YR 6/6 light red to 5YR light reddish brown, 5YR 6/2 pinking gray core; very few small to large incl

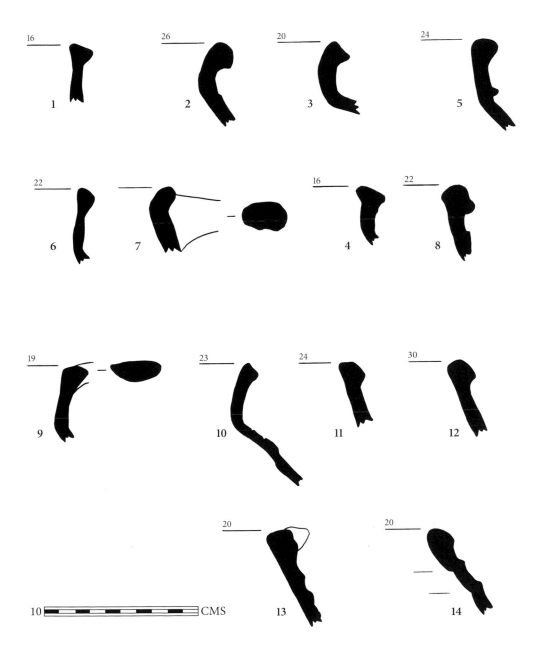

Pl. 2.5 Stratum V Kraters.

Pl. 2.8   Stratum V Mortaria

Pl	Str	Fld, Ar,Bkt	No.	Locus Description	Ware description
2.8:1	VI	IX.1.101	465/	fragmentary Wall base 9043	5YR pale olive, 7/3 pale yellow surfaces; many
fig. 2:7 (p. 28)	unstr	IX.1.90-91	/366		organic, some sand & limestone inclusions
	cf V	62 VII.2.15	269	inside V Installation 1127	7.5YR 6/4 light brown, 5YR 7/4 pink interior & 10YR 8/4 very pale brown; many inclusions
2	cf V	64 VII.1.31	662	L. 1257 of V? Pit 1247 or collapse into it	5YR 7/3 pink, 8/3 pink surfaces; many sandstone & limestone inclusions
3	cf V	64 VII.1.43	743	V? Hardpack 1259	7.5YR 7/6 reddish yellow, 5YR 8/2 white surfaces; very few limestone inclusions
4	IVB	VII.2.126	6250	removal IVB Wall 1123	7.5YR 8/4 pink, 8/3 very pale brown surfaces; many organic inclusions
	IVB	VII.5.137	6400	removal IVB Wall 1415-1117	10YR 8/4 very pale brown, 8/2 white surfaces; very few organic inclusions
5	IVB	VII.7.127	6213	Fill 1836-1841 below IV strata	5YR 7/6 reddish yellow, 8/6 yellow surfaces; few organic & limestone inclusions
6	IVB	VII.9.49	4048	Fill 1609-10,1612-15 in brick debris	5YR 4/4 reddish brown, 8/1 white surfaces; very many limestone & organic inclusions
7	IVB	VII.9.57	4076	Fill 1609-10,1612-15 in brick debris	10YR 8/2 white, 8/3 very pale brown surfaces; many organic inclusions
8	IVB	IX.1.70	214	Rubble 9035 over V floor 9037	7.5YR 8/4 pink, similar surfaces; many limestone & some organic inclusions
9	IVA	62 VII.1.84	1106	on IVB Surface 1236	10YR 7/3 very pale brown, 8/2 white surfaces; some organic inclusions
10	IVA	VII.5.132	6165	removal IVA Wall 1420 of bin	5Y 8/2 white, 8/2 white surfaces; many organic & few crystalline inclusions
11	IVA	VII.7.112	5845	removal IVA Cobbling 1824	5Y 8/2 white, 8/2 white surfaces; many organic incl
12	IVA	VII.7.115	5853	removal IVA Cobbling 1824	10YR 8/2 white, 8/3 very pale brown surfaces; many organic inclusions
13	IVA	VII.23.63	492	above IVB Floor 23.009 sub IV A Floor 23.01	2.5YR 6/4 light yellowish brown, 8/4 pale yellow surfaces; many limestone, few organic & sand incl
fig. 2:7	IVA	VII.23.66	499	Fill 23.016 below IV Floor 23.005	10YR 8/3 very pale brown, 8/2 white exterior surface; many small inclusions
14	IVA	IX.2.29	40	silty Soil 9262	7.5YR 7/6 reddish yellow, 10YR 8/4 very pale brown surfaces; very few sand inclusions
	IVA	IX.4.47	128	Rubble 9764 on which Wall 9765 stood	7.5YR 6/2 pinkish gray, 6/4 light brown exterior surface; many very small inclusions
	IVB	62 VII.4.22	141	on IVB metalled Surface 1530-1232	5YR 6/2 pinkish gray, 6/4 light reddish brown exterior surface; some large inclusions
15	cf IVB	62 VII.4.28	189	Hardpack 1529 north of where V Wall 1517 ended	5YR 8/4 pale yellow, 8/2 white surfaces; many organic inclusions
16	cf IV	VII.23.51	475	around IV Column Base 23.004	2.5YR 6/6 light red, 10YR 7/3 very pale brown surfaces; many sand & few organic inclusions

(continued on p. 197)

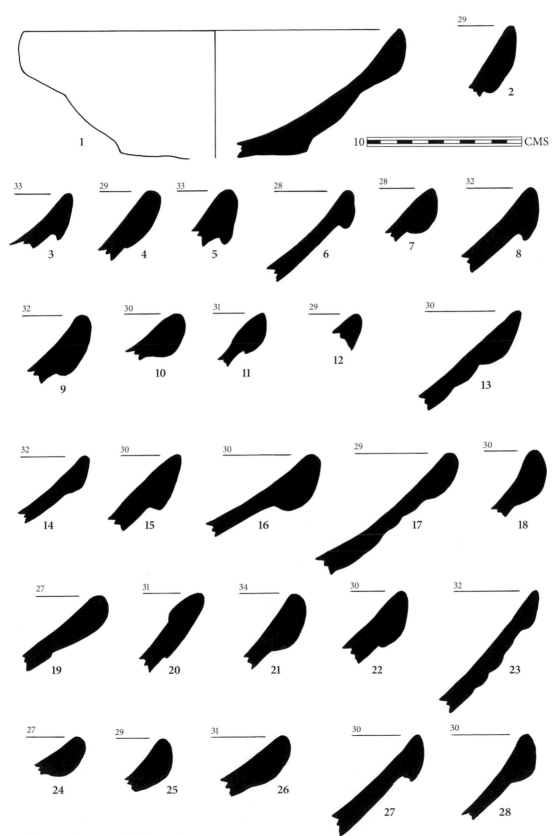

Pl. 2.8 Stratum V Mortaria.

Pl. 2.8 Stratum V Mortaria (cont.)

Pl	Str	Fld, Ar,Bkt	No.	Locus Description	Ware description
2.8:17	cf IV	VII.23.76	540	IV Stonefall 23.010	5YR 7/6 reddish yellow, 8/4 pink surfaces; many limestone & sand inclusions
18	IV/III	I.5.8	35	layers against Wall B	5YR 6/4 light reddish brown, 7/3 pink exterior surf.; limestone, many organic, & few ceramic incl
19	IIIB	VII.3.107	1805	sub IIIB Hardpack 1017-1019	7.5YR 8/2 pinkish white, 8/4 very pale brown surfaces; sandstone & very few crystalline incl
	IIIB	62 VII.4.88	639	sealed in Pit 1522	7.5YR 6/6 reddish yellow, 2.5YR 8/2 white surfaces; very few organic & sand inclusions
20	IIIB	VII.8.83	4608	sub IIIB Cobbling 1719	10YR 8/4 very pale brown, 8/2 white surfaces; many organic inclusions
21	IIIB	VII.8.86	4620	sub IIIB Cobbling 1719	2.5YR 6/8 light red, 8/3 very pale brown surfaces; many organic & limestone inclusions
22	IIIA	VII.3.64	1660	removal IIIA Wall 1007	5YR 7/1 light gray, similar surfaces; very few organic inclusions
23 fig. 2:7 (p. 28)	IIIA	VII.21.62	452	IIIA Fill 21.034 below Floor 21.009	10YR 6/2 light brownish gray, 8/2 white surfaces; many limestone inclusions
24	cf IIIA	VII.3.28	187	L. 1009 around IIIA Drain 1015-16	2.5YR 6/6 light red, 8/4 pink surfaces; many limestone & organic inclusions
	cf III	I.6.60	468	pit in Wall B	7/5 pink, 5YR 6/4 light gray core; many limestone & organic, and few small ceramic inclusions
25	I	68 II.2.64	11233	Fill 7052 in Rooms 2 and 3	5YR 8/2 pinkish white, 10YR 8/2 white surfaces; many organic & sandstone inclusions
26	unstr	I.11b.5a	889	huwwar to small stones	2.5YR 7/2 light gray, 5YR 8/1 white exterior surface; many small inclusions
27	unstr	IX.1.83	332	unstratified	5YR 7/8 reddish yellow, 7.5YR 7/6 reddish yellow surfaces; some organic & limestone inclusions
28	unstr	IX.3.93	359	unstratified	10YR 7/4 very pale brown, 5YR 8/4 pink surfaces; very many organic & crystalline inclusions

Pl. 2.9   Stratum V Mortarium Bases

Pl	Str	Fld, Ar,Bkt	No.	Locus Description	Ware description
Footed Bases					
	IVB	VII.1.117	7313	in Probe 1228 below IV installations	not accessible
2.9:1	IVB	VII.9.70	4119	Fill 1609-10,1612-15 in brick debris	2.5YR 7/4 pale yellow, 8/2 white surfaces; organic limestone & sand inclusions
	IVA	62 VII.1.66	808	on IVB Surface 1236	5YR 6/4 light reddish brown, 10YR 7/4 very pale brown int & 7/3 very pale ext surf; many small incl
	IVA	VII.23.66	501	Fill 23.016 below IV Floor 23.005	not accessible
2	IVA	VII.23.101	882	Fill 23.016 below IV Floor 23.005	5YR 6/6 olive yellow, 8/3 pale yellow surfaces; organic & sand inclusions
3	IIIB	VII.1.68	2853	beneath IIIB Floor 1214	7.5YR 6/2 pinkish gray, 8/2 pinkish white surfaces; sand & organic inclusions
4	IIIB	VII.8.80	4596	sub IIIB Cobbling 1719	5YR 7/3 pale yellow, 10YR 8/4 very pale brown surfaces; few organic inclusions
5	cf IV	VII.2.81	3764	on & above IV Surface 1124	10YR 7/1 light gray, 8/2 white surfaces; many sand & organic inclusions; thinner bottom – (shows wear?)
6	IIIA	VII.21.79	599	IIIA Fill 21.034 below Floor 21.009	5YR 8/4 pink, 10YR 8/3 very pale brown surfaces; very few sand inclusions
7	unstr	VII.3.131	5593	unstratified	2.5YR 8/6 yellow, 8/2 white surfaces; organic & limestone inclusions
8	unstr	62 VII.5.28	422	1485 rockfall or pit	5YR 5/6 olive, 8/4 pale yellow surfaces; many sand & organic inclusions
	unstr	VII.22.73	617	unstratified	2.5YR 8/2 white, 7/2 light gray exterior surface; large and many small inclusions
9	unstr	II.2.23	296	unstratified	5YR 8/2 white, 8/2 white exterior surfaces; few limestone inclusions
Flat Bases					
	IVA	IX.2.28	36	L. 9262 silty soil silty Soil 9262	5YR 7/3 pale yellow, 10YR 8/3 very pale brown surfaces; ceramic inclusions
10	cf IV	62 VII.23.76	538	IV Stonefall 23.010	5YR 8/2 white, similar surfaces; very many organic inclusions
	IIIB	VII.4.8	61	sealed in Pit 1522	10YR 8/2 white, 8/3 very pale brown exterior and 2.5YR 7/2 light gray interior surfaces; very small and few large inclusions
	unstr	IX.1.99	421	unstratified	7.5YR 7/4 pink, 5YR 7/4 pink exterior surface; few large and many small and very small inclusions

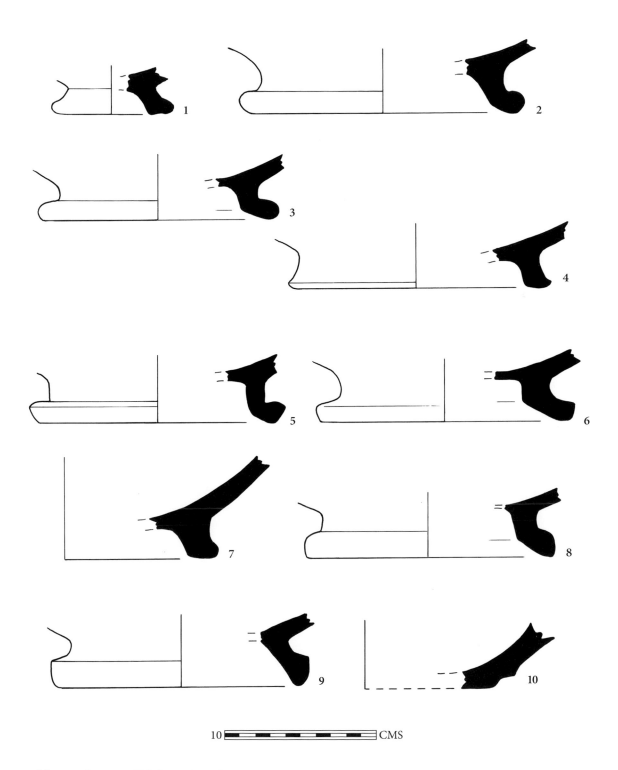

Pl. 2.9 Stratum V Mortarium Bases.

Pl. 2.10   Stratum V Cooking Pots

Pl	Str	Fld, Ar, Bkt	No.	Locus Description	Ware description
Light, grooved					
2.10:1	V	IX.2.60	215	V Surface 9273 outside Wall 9274	2.5YR 3.2 dusky red; very few small inclusions
2	V	IX.2.56	176	V Surface 9273 outside Wall 9274	2.5YR 4/6 red, 3/4 dark reddish brown toward surfaces
fig. 2:8 (p. 30)	V	IX.3.104	382	V (probably) Rubble 9531	5YR 5/6 yellowish red; many inclusions
3	cf V	62 VII.1.21	94	sub 2nd IVB metalled Surface 1230 Surface 1231 in 1230	2.5YR 5/6 red; very small inclusions
	cf V	62 VII.2.15	270	inside V Installation 1127	5YR 5/4 reddish brown with 5/1 gray core; 2.5YR 5/2 weak red ext surface; small & few large incl
4	cf V	62 VII.4.44	244	IVB Fill 1556 sub Surface 1530	2.5YR 4/8 red; 4/1 dark gray core
5	cf V	62 VII.4.58	409	IVB Fill 1556 sub Surface 1530	2.5YR 4/8 red; few medium inclusions
6	cf V	62 VII.4.58	410	IVB Fill 1556 sub Surface 1530	2.5YR 4/6 red, N 2.5/0 black core; some small to medium inclusions
7 fig. 2:8	cf V	62 VII.4.112	1033	IVB Fill 1556 sub Surface 1530	5YR 4/4 reddish brown, 4/1 dark gray core; few medium inclusions
8	IVB	62 VII.1.18	89	on IVB Surface 1236	5YR 5/4 reddish brown, 3/1 very dark gray core, 6/2 pinkish gray interior, 6/3 light reddish brown exterior; small inclusions
9	IVB	VII.2.130	6900	removal IVB Wall 1415-1117	5YR 5/4 reddish brown, 3/1 very dark gray core, 6/4 pinkish gray interior, 6/3 light reddish brown exterior; small inclusions
10	IVB	VII.2.135	7331	L. 1123A levelling below IV installations	2.5YR 4/4 reddish brown to 5/6 red; very few medium inclusions
11	IVB	62 VII.4.4	28	sealed in IV Wall 1517	5YR 5/4 reddish brown, 5/3 reddish brown exterior surface; few very small inclusions
12	IVB	62 VII.4.26	187	under IVB Floor 1521	not accessible
13	IVB	VII.7.122	5995	Fill 1836-1841 below IV strata	2.5YR 4/4 reddish brown, 5/4 reddish brown exterior surface; few small inclusions
14	IVB	VII.7.129	6226	Fill 1836-1841 below IV strata	2.5YR 5/8 red, 5/4 reddish brown exterior surface; few large inclusions
	IVB	VII.7.138	6324	Fill 1836-1841 below IV strata	2.5YR 5/8 red, 5/2 red exterior surface; few small inclusions
	IVB	VII.7.142	6847	Fill 1836-1841 below IV strata	2.5YR 5/8 red, 5/6 red exterior surface; few small inclusions
	IVB	IX.3.53	122	occupational Debris 9517C	2.5YR 5/6 red, 5/4 reddish brown exterior surface; large and few small inclusions
	IVB	IX.3.59	125	occupational Debris 9521 as 9517C	2.5YR 5/6 red, 6/4 light reddish brown exterior surface; small inclusions
	IVB	IX.3.75	208	IVB Fill 9523	2.5YR 5/6 red, 6/4 light reddish brown exterior surface; few inclusions

(continued on p. 202)

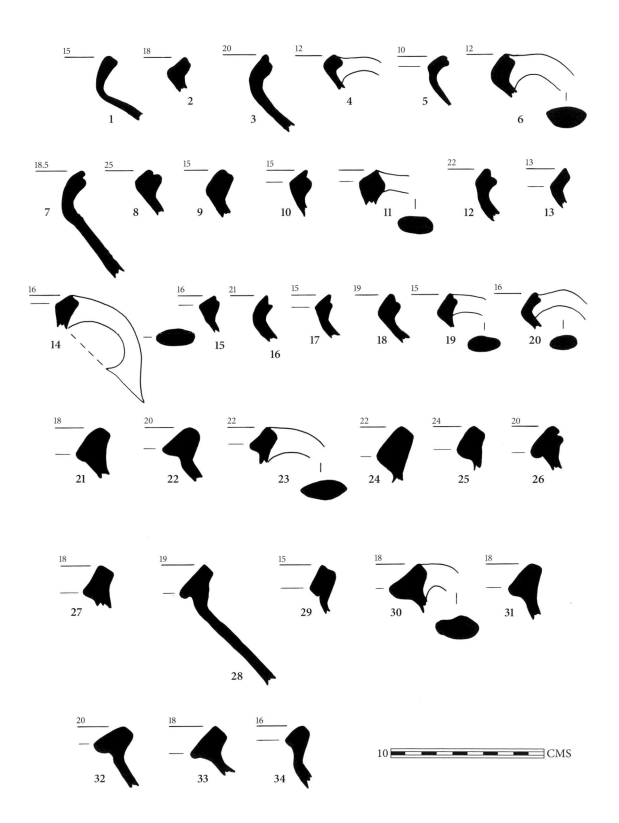

Pl. 2.10 Stratum V Cooking Pots.

Pl. 2.10   Stratum V Cooking Pots   (cont.)

Pl	Str	Fld, Ar,Bkt	No.	Locus Description	Ware description
	IVB	IX.3.76	219	IVB Fill 9523	2.5YR 4/4 reddish brown with 5YR 4/1 gray core, 2.5YR 5/4 reddish brown exterior surface; few large inclusions
2.10:15	IVA	62 VII.4.20	120	L. 1526 removal large jar	5YR 4/1 dark gray, 5/2 reddish gray exterior, 5/3 reddish brown exterior; few small incl
16	IVA	VII.7.110	5841	removal IVA Cobbling 1824	2.5YR 5/6 red, 5YR 5/3 reddish brown exterior surface; few small inclusions
17	IIIB	VII.3.65	1667	sub IIIB Hardpack 1017-1019	2.5YR 5/4 reddish brown, 5/2 weak red interior; 4/4 reddish brown exterior; few very small incl
	IIIB	62 VII.1.15	78	sealed in Pit 1522	2.5YR 4/4 reddish brown, 5/2 weak red exterior surface; many large inclusions
18	cf IIIB	VII.7.139	6840	sub IIIB Surface 1808-1507 level	5YR 5/4 reddish brown, 2.5YR 5/4 reddish brown interior, 4/2 weak red exterior; some small inclusions
	IIIA	VII.2.120	5505	removal IIIA Walls 1107-1109	2.5YR 5/6 red, 4/2 weak red exterior surface; few inclusions
	IIIA	VII.21.156	1327	Debris 21.035 sub IIIA walls & Floor 21.031	2.5YR 5/0 gray, 5/2 red exterior surface; few inclusions
	cf IIIA	62 VII.5.57	688	pit 1477	2.5YR 5/2 red, 5/0 weak red exterior surface; few inclusions
	unstr	62 VII.2.113	1840	unstratified	2.5YR 5/6 red, 10R5/6 red exterior surface; few inclusions
	unstr	VII.2.129	6500	unstratified	5YR 5/1 gray, 5/4 reddish brown exterior surface; many large and few small inclusions
	unstr	62 VII.3.96	1455	unstratified	5YR 5/6 yellowish red, many inclusions
19	unstr	62 5.8	123	unstratified	2.5YR 6/8 light red, 5/6 red exterior surface; few inclusions
20	unstr	VII.9.43	3228	unstratified	2.5YR 5/6 red, 5/4 reddish brown interior, 4/4 reddish brown exterior; some medium incl.
	unstr	VII.21.10	74	unstratified	2.5YR 5/2 weak red, 6/6 light red exterior surface; small inclusions

Thick and heavy

Pl	Str	Fld, Ar,Bkt	No.	Locus Description	Ware description
21	cf V	62 VII.4.6	57	IVB Fill 1556 sub Surface 1530	5YR 4/8 yellowish red, 2.5YR 4/0 dark gray core; many small to large inclusions
22	cf V	62 VII.4.52	285	IVB Fill 1556 sub Surface 1530	5YR 4/4 reddish brown, 3/1 very dark gray core; many small to large inclusions
23 fig. 2:8 (p. 30)	IVB	VII.3.178	6925	Probe 1030 beneath IV levels	5YR 5/4 reddish brown; some small to large inclusions
24	IVB	VII.7.132	6241	Fill 1836-1841 below IV strata	5YR 4/6 yellowish red, 4/2 dark reddish gray core; many small to large inclusions
	IVB	IX.2.54	169	Layer 9270 sub IVB Layers 9265 & 9264	5YR 5/1 gray, 2.5YR 5/6 red exterior surface; large and few small inclusions

Pl. 2.10   Stratum V Cooking Pots   (cont.)

Pl	Str	Fld, Ar,Bkt	No.	Locus Description	Ware description
	IVA	64 VII.2.8	339	Hardpack 1130A sub IVA Wall 1026	5YR 5/1 gray, 5/3 reddish brown exterior surface; few inclusions
	IVA	62 VII.4.50	282	L. 1526 removal large jar	2.5YR 5/6 red, 10R 5/6 red exterior surface; few small inclusions
2.10:25	IVA	VII.4.110	5546	removal IVA Floor 1527	5YR 4/3 reddish brown, 4/2 dark reddish gray exterior surface; few small inclusions
26	IVA	VII.7.115	5855	removal IVA Cobbling 1824	10R 3/1 dark reddish gray, many small to large inclusions
27	IIIA	VII.3.64	1657	removal IIIA wall 1007	5YR 4/1 dark gray, 4/2 dark reddish gray exterior surface; some large inclusions
28 fig. 2:8 (p. 30)	IIIA	VII.7.88	4664	cleaning above IIIB Surface 1815	not accessible
29	IIIA	VII.9.42b	3202	removal IIIA Cobbling 1604	5YR 3/1 very dark gray, 5/4 reddish brown interior, 5/3 reddish brown exterior; few large incl
30 fig. 2:8	IIIA	VII.22.28	224	above possible IIIB Floor 22.002 sub IIIA Floor 22.001	10R 2.5/1 reddish black; very many small to large inclusions
31	IVB	62 VII.1.63	801	rockfall 1237 part of IVB pit 1239	5YR 5/1 gray, 2.5YR 5/4 reddish brown exterior surface; many medium inclusions
32	unstr	62 VII.3.10	98	unstratified	2.5YR 3/4 dark reddish brown; many small to medium inclusions
33	unstr	62 VII.3.56	671	unstratified	2.5 YR 4/2 weak red, 5/4 reddish brown exterior surface; many medium and small inclusions
34	unstr	62 VII.3.84	1388	unstratified	10YR 4/2 dark grayish brown, 5YR 4/2 dark reddish gray exterior surface; many small incl
	unstr	VII.7.151	7385	unstratified	2.5YR 4/4 reddish brown, 5/6 red exterior surface; few inclusions
	unstr	VII.23.92	766	around VII Wall (?) 23.012	5YR 5/1 gray, 5/3 reddish brown exterior surface; few inclusions

Pl. 2.11   Stratum V Lamps

Pl	Str	Fld, Ar,Bkt	No.	Locus Description	Ware description
	cf V	62 VII.1.2	7	in fill below IV metalled Surface 1530-1229-1232-1234	5YR 5/6 yellowish red, remains of 5/6 yellowish red on rim; medium incl; coarse levigation
	cf V	62 VII.1.9	1121	sub 2nd IVB metalled Surface 1230	5YR 7/4 pink; large and many small inclusions
	cf V	64 VII.1.71	20754	V? Hardpack 1260	5YR 7/6 reddish yellow, few very small inclusions
	IVB	VII.1.115	7300	in Probe 1228 below IV installations	5YR 6/1 gray, 7/2 pinkish gray exterior surface; small and few large inclusions
2.11:1	IVB	VII.1.115	7306	in Probe 1228 below IV Installations	5YR 7/4 pink, 7/6 reddish yellow exterior surface; few very small inclusions
	IVB	VII.7.91	4669	Fill 1836-1841 below IV strata	5YR 6/1 gray, 6/2 pinkish gray interior, 7/3 pink exterior; few large inclusions
	IVB	VII.7.103	5252	around V Tannur 1828 sub IV installations	5YR 7/2 pinkish gray, 2.5Y 8/2 white exterior surface; small inclusions
	IVB	VII.9.51	4056	Fill 1609-10,1612-15 in brick debris above Iron II installations	5YR 6/6 reddish yellow, 5/6 yellowish red slip; medium inclusions; medium levigation
2 fig. 2.9 (p. 31)	IVB	VII.9.94B	5911A	Fill 1630 down to Iron II house	2.5YR 6/6 light red; very small inclusions
3	IVB	VII.9.95	5917	Fill 1630 down to Iron II house	5YR 6/6 reddish yellow; few very small incl
	IVA	VII.4.111	5555	removal IV Press 1525	2.5YR 5/6 red, 5/6 burnished red slip; fine incl
	IVA	VII.4.111	5556	removal IV Press 1525	5YR 6/8 reddish yellow; few medium inclusions
4	IVA	VII.21.83	612	sub IVA Floor 21.011	5YR 5/6 yellowish red, 5/8 yellowish red burnished slip; medium inclusions
5 fig. 2.9	IV	I.7b.56	317 #141	in lower IV Floor 205	5YR 6/6 reddish yellow, 6/8 reddish yellow slip; very few inclusions
	cf IV	62 VII.1.24	175	above metalled Surface 1233 in balk	5YR 7/4 pink, 7/6 reddish yellow exterior slip; few very small inclusions
	IIIB	VII.4.80	4973	removal IIIB Wall 1513	5YR 6/6 reddish yellow, 7.5YR 7/6 yellowish red exterior surface; 5YR 5/8 red slip; few incl
	IIIA	VII.21.52	435	IIIA Fill 21.034 below Floor 21.009	10YR 7/2 light gray, 5YR 7/4 reddish yellow interior surface; many large inclusions
	IIIA	VII.21.58	439	IIIA Fill 21.034 below Floor 21.009	5YR 6/1 gray, 7/4 pink exterior surface; few small inclusions
6 fig. 2.9	IIIA	VII.21.61	451	IIIA Fill 21.034 below Floor 21.009	7.5YR 5/6 strong brown, 7/6 reddish yellow surfaces; few inclusions
	IIIA	VII.21.68	517	Debris 21.035 sub IIIA walls & Floor 21.031	2.5YR 6/6 light red, 6/6 light red exterior surface; few inclusions
	cf III	I.6.77	646	pit in Wall B	5YR 6/2 light reddish brown, 7.5YR 7/4 pink exterior surface; few small inclusions
	unstr	VII.1.118	7322	unstratified	5YR 7/4 pink, 7/6 reddish yellow exterior surface; few very small inclusions
	unstr	VII.5.28	421	1485 rockfall or pit	10YR 7/2 light gray, 8/3 very pale brown exterior surface; large and small inclusions

(continued on p. 206)

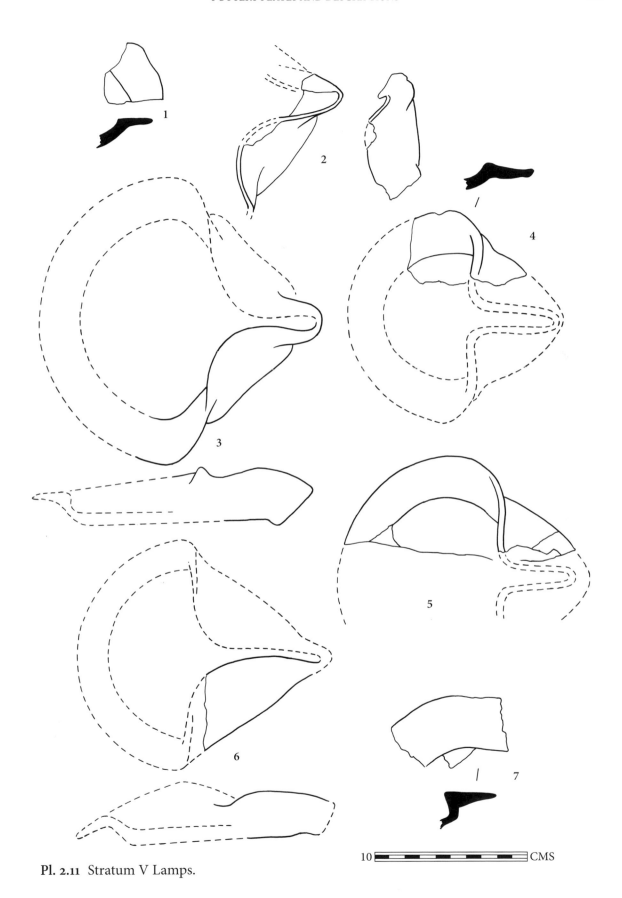

Pl. 2.11 Stratum V Lamps.

10 ▮▭▮▭▮▭▮▭▮ CMS

Pl. 2.11   Stratum V Lamps   (cont.)

PL	STR	FLD, AR,BKT	No.	LOCUS DESCRIPTION	WARE DESCRIPTION
	unstr	VII.6.68	1935	unstratified	7.5YR 7/6 reddish yellow, 7/6 reddish yellow slip; few very small inclusions
	unstr	VII.6.80	1982	unstratified	5YR 6/8 reddish yellow, 5/6 yellowish red slip; medium inclusions
	unstr	VII.6.172	5035	surface fill	5YR 7/6 reddish yellow, few inclusions
	unstr	VII.9.42A	3201	surface fill	5YR 6/2 pinkish gray, 7/4 pink exterior surface; few small inclusions
	unstr	VII.21.22	129	unstratified	5YR 7/2 pinkish gray, 7/4 pink exterior surface; few very small inclusions
	unstr	VII.22.85	737	unstratified	5YR 6/6 reddish yellow 5/6 yellowish red slip; medium inclusions
	unstr	VII.23.5	41	unstratified	5YR 7/2 pinkish gray, 2.5Y 8/2 white exterior surface; several large inclusions
2.11:7	unstr	57 I 7a.38	189	surface	5YR 6/4 light reddish brown, 7.5YR 7/4 pink surfaces, 2.5YR 5/6 red slip ; medium inclusions
	unstr	IX 3.33	25	unstratified	5YR 7/4 pink, 7.5YR 7/4 pink exterior surface; few small inclusions

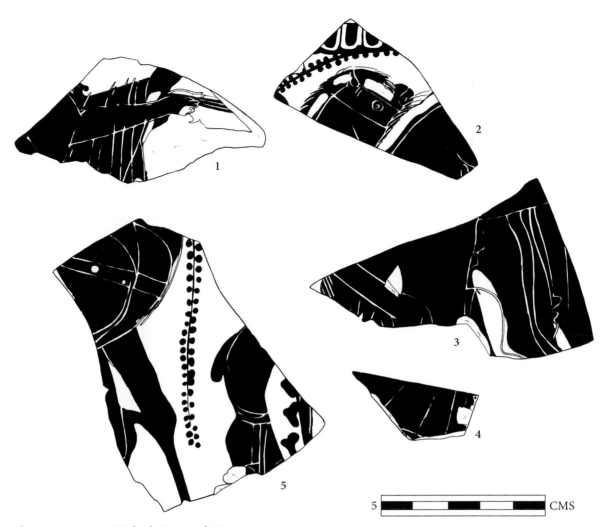

Pl. 2.12 Stratum V Black-Figured Krater.

Pl. 2.12   Stratum V Black-Figured Krater

Pl	Str	Fld, Ar,Bkt	No.	Locus Description	Ware description (surfaces with glaze, slip, paint, or wash)
2.12:2 fig. 2.10 (p. 32)	cf V	62 VII.1.17	86/87	IVB Fill 1556 sub Surface 1530	2.5YR 5/8 red; 2.5Y N2 5/0 black-figured & 10R 3/2 dusky red on 5YR 5/4 reddish brown, incised lines, exterior surf; some black interior surf
1 fig. 2.10	cf V	62 VII.1.95	1267	in fill below IV metalled Surface 1530-1229-1232-1234	2.5YR 5/8 red; 2.5Y N2 5/0 black-figured on 5YR 5/4 reddish brown, incised lines, exterior surf; 2.5Y N2 5/0 black interior surface
4 fig. 2.10	IVB	62 VII.1.62	800	rockfall 1237 part of IVB pit 1239	2.5YR 5/8 red; 2.5Y N2.5/0 black-figured, incised lines, exterior surface; worn black interior surface
5 fig. 2.10	IVA	VII.1.62	5310A #207A	on IVB plastered Floor 1216	2.5YR 5/8 red; 2.5Y N2 5/0 black-figured & 10R 3/2 dusky red on 5YR 5/4 reddish brown, incised lines, exterior surf; 2.5Y N2 5/0 black interior surface
3 fig. 2.10	IVA	VII.1.62	5330A/ /928A #206	on IVB plastered Floor 1216	2.5YR 5/8 red; 2.5Y N2 5/0 black-figured on 5YR 5/4 reddish brown, incised lines, exterior surface; 2.5Y N2 5/0 black interior surface

Pl. 2.13   Stratum V Black- and Red-Figured Kraters

Pl	Str	Fld, Ar,Bkt	No.	Locus Description	Ware description (surfaces with glaze, slip, paint, or wash)
2.13:12	cf V	62 VII.1.17	88	IVB Fill 1556 sub Surface 1530	5YR 5/6 yellowish red; 2.5Y N2.5/o black exterior worn surf
2 fig 2.10 (p. 32)	cf V	62 VII.1.93	1266	in fill below IV metalled Surface 1530-1229-1232-1234	5YR 6/6 reddish yellow; 2.5YR 5/8 red reserved & 10R 3/4 dusky red on 2.5Y N2.5/o black, incised lines, exterior surf; continuous black interior surface
4 fig 2.10	IVB	IX.3.49	83	occupational Debris 9521 as 9517C	5YR 6/6 reddish yellow; 2.5YR 6/8 light red reserved & black lines, on 2.5Y N2.5/o black exterior surface; 2.5YR 4/8 red, 6/8 light red, 3/6 dark red interior surf
8 fig 2.10	IVB	VII.2.126	6249	removal IVB Wall 1123	2.5YR 5/6 red; 2.5Y N2.5/o black-figured exterior surface; 10R 3/2 dusky red and black on rim
	IVA	62 VII.4.136		on IVB Floor 1521	5YR 6/6 reddish yellow; 2.5Y N2.5/o black on 2.5YR 5/6 red reserved, black and incised lines, exterior surf; black 2.5Y N2.5/o int surf
3 fig 2.10	IVB	62 VII.1.65	807	on IVB metalled Surface 1530-1232	5YR 6/6 reddish yellow; 2.5Y N2.5/o black on 2.5YR 5/6 red reserved, black and incised lines, exterior surf; continuous black 2.5Y N2.5/o int surf
	cf IV	62 VII.1.73	998	above metalled Surface 1233 in balk	5YR 6/6 reddish yellow; 2.5Y N2.5/o black on 8/2 pinkish white and incised lines exterior surface
5 fig 2.10	IIIB	VII.1.60	5285	Fill 1216,1217,1220-1224,1226	5YR 6/6 reddish yellow; 2.5Y N2.5/o black-figured surfaces
10 fig 2.10	IIIB IIIB	VII.1.61 62 VII.4.141	5309/ /1536	Fill 1216,1217,1220-1224,1226 sealed in Pit 1522	5YR 5/6 yellowish red; 2.5Y N2.5/o black exterior surface
9 fig 2.10	IIIB IIIB	62 VII.1.91 VII.1.60	1123/ /5291A	Stone Heap 1235 part of Pit 1522 Fill 1216,1217,1220-1224,1226	5YR 6/6 reddish yellow; 2.5Y N2.5/o black exterior surface; continuous 2.5Y N2.5/o black interior surf
	IIIA	VII.5.86	3982	removal IIIA Wall 1408	5YR 6/6 reddish yellow; 2.5YR N2.5/o black surfaces with 10R 3/2 dusky red stripes on exterior
14	II	VII.7.58	3185	above IIIA Floor 1802-1508	2.5YR 5/4 reddish brown; 2.5Y N2.5/o black exterior surf
1 fig 2.10	unstr	62 VII		unstratified	5YR 6/6 reddish yellow; 2.5YR 5/8 red reserved, 10R 3/4 dusky red and 2.5Y N2.5/o black, incised lines, exterior surface; continuous black interior surf
13	unstr	62 VII	629	unstratified	2.5YR 6/6 light red; 2.5Y N2.5/o black-figured surfaces
7 fig 2.10	unstr	62 VII.2.3	159		5YR 6/6 reddish yellow; 2.5Y N2.5/o black-figured surfaces
	unstr	VII.3.152	6271	Pit 1029B	5YR 6/6 reddish yellow; 2.5Y N2.5/o black surfaces, very worn on exterior
6 fig. 2.10	unstr	VII.4.72	3848	unstratified	5YR 6/6 reddish yellow; 2.5Y N2.5/o black-figured surfaces
15	unstr	VII.5.1	220	surface	5YR 5/3 reddish brown; 2.5Y N2.5/o black surfaces; 6/4 light reddish brown top
11	unstr	VII.5.124	5839	disturbed debris of street	2.5YR 5/4 reddish brown; 2.5Y N2.5/o black (worn) exterior surf
	unstr	VII.6.185	5065	unstratified	5YR 5/6 yellowish red; 2.5Y N2.5/o black exterior surface (base as 1535)
	unstr	IX.4.14	7	unstratified	5YR 5/6 yellowish red; 2.5Y N2.5/o black surfaces (handle)

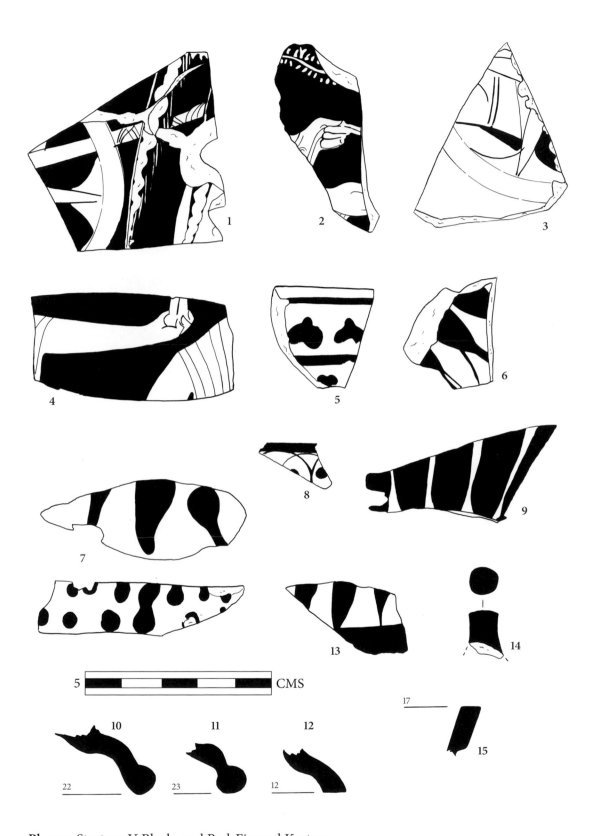

Pl. 2.13 Stratum V Black- and Red-Figured Kraters.

Pl. 2.14   Stratum V Attic Cups

PL	STR	FLD, AR,BKT	NO.	LOCUS DESCRIPTION	WARE DESCRIPTION (surfaces with glaze, slip, paint, or wash)
	cf V	62 VII.1.103	1636	in fill below IV metalled Surface 1530-1229-1232-1234	5YR 6.6 reddish yellow; 2.5Y N2.5/0 black continuous on surfaces (rim, cf 6306)
fig. 2.11 (p. 34)	IVB	VII.1.114	6894	in Probe 1228 below IV installations	(handle) 5YR 6/8 reddish yellow; 2.5/0 black surface
	IVB	62. VII.1.85	1110	sub IVB Surface 1236 (sub 1216)	(handle) 5YR 6/8 reddish yellow; 2.5/0 black surface
2.14:8 fig. 2.11	IVB	VII.3.158 62 VII.3.29 VII.9.13	6303/ /215/ /2373	Fill 1029A below IV installations unstratified surface fill	5YR 6.6 reddish yellow; 2.5Y N2.5/0 black continuous on surfaces
	IVA	VII.5.136	6398	sub IVA Wall 1419	(handle) 5YR 6/8 reddish yellow; 2.5/0 black surf
	IVA	VII.8.105	5869	removal IVA Wall 1716	5YR 6/8 reddish yellow; 2.5Y N2.5/0 black interior and over rim
	IVA	VII.23.67		fill 23.016 below IV floor 23.005	5YR 6/8 reddish yellow; 2.5Y N2.5/0 black surfaces
	IVA	IX.3.39	50	IVA Layering 9517A outside Wall 9514	5YR 6.6 reddish yellow; 5/8 yellowish red surfaces, 2.5Y N2.5/0 black (worn) on rim (form as 6303)
	IVA	IX.4.29	55	L. 9759.29-32 resurfacing Surface 9760	(handle) 2.5YR 6/4 light reddish brown; N2.5/0 black surfaces
	cf IV	VII.3.141	5639	cleaning IV Drain 1028-1116	2.5YR 6/6 light red; N2.5/0 black interior and over rim, 4/6 red interior and lower exterior surf
3 fig. 2.11	cf IV	62 VII.7.7	303	around IVA Cobbling 1826	5YR 6/6 reddish yellow; 2.5Y N2.5/0 black and 5 YR 4/4 reddish brown-figured exterior surface; continuous 2.5Y N2.5/0 black interior surface
7	cf IV	62 VII.7.7	302	around IVA Cobbling 1826	5YR 6/6 reddish yellow; 2.5Y N2.5/0 black continuous int, top edge, & exterior below carination
	cf IV	62 VII.7.7	304	around IVA Cobbling 1826	5YR 6.6 reddish yellow; 2.5Y N2.5/0 black continuous on surfaces except reserved inside rim
	cf IV	VII.22.121		IV Pit 22.010	5YR 6.6 reddish yellow; 2.5Y N2.5/0 black continuous on surfaces (rim as 6303)
	IV/III	I.7.21	122	lower H Floors 205 & 2067	5YR 7/4 light reddish brown; 4/1 dark gray (dulled) surfaces (rim)
	IIIB	VII.3.107	1802	sub IIIB Hardpack 1017-1019	2.5YR 6/6 light red; N2.5/0 worn black surface but reserved underside
	IIIB	62 VII.4.157	1783	sealed in Pit 1522	5YR 6.6 reddish yellow; 2.5Y N2.5/0 black continuous on surfaces (rim as 6303)
11	IIIB	VII.8.82	4606	sub IIIB Cobbling 1719	5YR 6/6 reddish yellow; 2.5Y N2.5/0 black upper surf
	IIIB	VII.7.95a	4684	IIIB Fill 1822-1823 above IV	5YR 7/4 pink; 2.5/0 black surfaces (rim)
1 fig. 2.11	cf IIIB cf IIIB	VII.8.88 VII.8.105	4625/ /5068	unsealed IIIB Fill 1717-20 sub IIIB level unstratified	5YR 6/6 reddish yellow; 2.5Y N2.5/0 black and 5YR 4/4 reddish brown-figured exterior surface; continuous 2.5Y N2.5/0 black interior surface

(continued on p. 212)

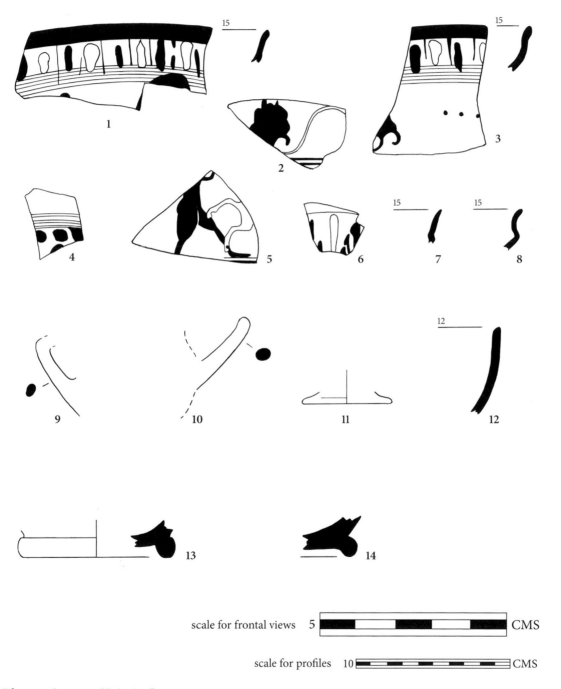

Pl. 2.14 Stratum V Attic Cups.

Pl. 2.14　　Stratum V Attic Cups　　(cont.)

PL	STR	FLD, AR,BKT	No.	LOCUS DESCRIPTION	WARE DESCRIPTION (surfaces with glaze, slip, paint, or wash)
2.14:4 fig. 2.11 (p. 34)	cf IIIB	VII.8.88	4626	unsealed IIIB Fill 1717-20 sub IIIB level	5YR 6/6 reddish yellow; 2.5Y N2.5/0 black and 5 YR 4/4 reddish brown-figured exterior surface; continuous 2.5Y N2.5/0 black interior surface
5 fig. 2.11	cf IIIB	VII.8.96	5125	unsealed IIIB Fill 1717-20 sub IIIB level	5YR 6/6 reddish yellow; 2.5Y N2.5/0 black, 5YR 4/4 reddish brown, & 5YR 8/1 white-figured exterior surf; continuous 2.5Y N2.5/0 black interior surface
2 fig. 2.11	cf IIIB	VII.8.107	5874	unsealed IIIB Fill 1717-20 sub IIIB level	5YR 6/6 reddish yellow; 2.5Y N2.5/0 black and 5 YR 4/4 reddish brown-figured exterior surface; continuous 2.5Y N2.5/0 black interior surface
	IIIA	VII.4.62	3831	removal IIIA Walls 1505-1510	5YR 6.6 reddish yellow; 2.5Y N2.5/0 black continuous on surfaces (rim)
	IIIA	VII.7.58	3185	sub IIIA Floor 1802-1508	(handle) not accessible
	IIIA	VII.7.82	4644	removal IIIA Wall 1805N	5YR 6.6 reddish yellow; 2.5Y N2.5/0 black continuous on surfaces (rim as 6303)
10 fig. 2.11	IIIA	VII.21.71	593	IIIA Fill 21.034 below Floor 21.009	5YR 6.6 reddish yellow; 2.5Y N2.5/0 black continuous on surfaces; reserved inner handle
	II	VII.4.115	7369A	above IIIA Floor 1227 in Room E	(base) 5YR 7/4 pink; 2.5/1 black exterior surface only
9 fig. 2.11	unstr	VII.2.75	1283	unstratified	5YR 6.6 reddish yellow; 2.5Y N2.5/0 black continuous on surfaces; reserved inner handle
6 fig. 2.11	unstr	VII.2.101	4955	unstratified	5YR 6/6 reddish yellow; 2.5Y N2.5/0 black and 5 YR 4/4 reddish brown-figured exterior surface; continuous 2.5Y N2.5/0 black interior surface
	unstr	VII.2.114	5216	unstratified	(handle) 5 YR 4/4 reddish brown; 2.5Y N2.5/0 black surfaces
13 fig. 2.11	unstr	62 VII.3.27	254	surface fill	5YR 6/6 reddish yellow; 2.5Y N2.5/0 black upper exterior and interior surfaces
12	unstr	62 VII.3.53	1151	unstratified	5YR 6/6 reddish yellow; 2.5Y N2.5/0 black continuous on surfaces
	unstr	VII.5.117	5825	disturbed debris of street	not accessible
	unstr	VII.6.31	295	unstratified	5YR 6/6 reddish yellow; 2.5Y N2.5/0 black continuous on surfaces (rim)
	unstr	VII.6.171	4186	surface fill	5YR 7/6 reddish yellow; 2.5/1 black surfaces (rim)
	unstr	62 VII.7.11		unstratified	5YR 6/1 light gray; 2.5/1 black surfaces with reserved stripes near rim
	unstr	VII.8.87	3890	unstratified	(handle) 5YR 6/4 pink; 2.5/1 black surfaces with reserved underside
	unstr	VII.9.25	2400	unstratified	(handle) 5YR 7/6 reddish yellow; 2.5/1 black surfaces with reserved underside
	unstr	VII.9.27	2410	unstratified	(handle) 5YR 6/6 reddish yellow; 2.5/1 black surf
14	unstr	VII.22.71	615	unstratified	(base) 5YR 6/6 reddish yellow; 2.5/1 black surfaces except lower base

Pl. 2.14   Stratum V Attic Cups   (cont.)

Pl	Str	Fld, Ar,Bkt	No.	Locus Description	Ware description (surfaces with glaze, slip, paint, or wash)
	unstr	VII.23.32	165	around Stones 23.002	(base) 5YR 7/6 reddish yellow; 2.5/1 black surfaces except lower base
	unstr	VII.23.40	236	around Wall 23.003	(base) 5YR 6/6 reddish yellow; 2.5/1 black surfaces except lower base
	unstr	IX.2.18	16	unstratified	(base) 5YR 5/8 yellowish red; 2.5/1 black on edge of base only
	unstr	I.2.2	55		(base) 5YR 6/3 light reddish brown, 2.5/1 black surf
	unstr	I.6	#44A		5YR 7/6 reddish yellow; 2.5/1 black surfaces (rim)

Pl. 2.15   Stratum V Lekythoi and other Fragments

Pl	Str	Fld, Ar,Bkt	No.	Locus Description	Ware description (surfaces with glaze, slip, paint, or wash)
Lid Handle					
2.15:1 fig. 2.11 (p. 34)	IVB	VII.3.151	6270	Fill 1029A below IV installations	5YR 6/6 reddish yellow; 2.5Y N2.5/0 black exterior surface, black-figured on top
Lekythoi					
5	IVA	IX.4.39	132	IVA Layering 9763.39.40	5YR 6/4 light reddish brown; 2.5Y N2.5/0 black (worn) upper surface
2 fig. 2.12 (p. 34)	IIIB	VII.8.57	3873	beneath IIIB Cobbling 1715	5YR 6/4 light reddish brown; 2.5Y N2.5/0 black-figured exterior surface
	unstr	VII.2.99	4952	unstratified	10YR 7/2 light gray, 2.5YR 2.5/0 black (worn) exterior surface
	unstr	VII.2.117	5222	unstratified	10YR 7/2 light gray, 2.5YR 2.5/0 black (worn) exterior surface
fig. 2.12	unstr	VII.2.119 VII.5.29	4673/ /2759	unstratified unstratified	2.5YR 6/6 light red, 6/6 light red interior and 2.5/0 black exterior surfaces with 6/6 light red stripe
	unstr	VII.2.119	5225	unstratified	2.5YR 6/6 light red, 6/6 light red interior and 2.5/0 black exterior surfaces
6	unstr	VII.5.40	2328	disturbed debris of street	5YR 7/6 reddish yellow, 7/6 reddish yellow interior 2.5YR 2.5/0 black exterior with worn areas
	unstr	VII.7.54	3181	surface fill	2.5YR 6/6 light red, 6/6 light red interior and 3/0 very dark gray worn surface
	unstr	VII.7.73	3138	surface fill	5YR 7/6 reddish yellow, 2.5YR 2.5/0 exterior worn surf
3 fig. 2.12	unstr	VII.8.31	2764	unstratified	5YR 6/4 light reddish brown; 2.5Y N2.5/0 black-figured exterior surface
4 fig. 2.12	unstr	VII.8.92	5105	unstratified	5YR 5/8 yellowish red; 2.5Y N2.5/0 black to 3/6 dark red upper surface; 2.5YR 4/8 red lower surface
	unstr	VII.9.38	3189	unstratified	5YR 7/4 pink 2.5YR 2.5/0 black worn surface with 6/6 light red stripes
	unstr	VII.23.32	164	around Stones 23.002	5YR 7/6 reddish yellow, 2.5YR 2.5/0 black exterior worn surface
	unstr	IX.1.15	10	unstratified	5YR 7/6 reddish yellow, 7/6 reddish yellow interior and 2.5YR 2.5/0 black exterior worn surface
Black-on-brown Fragments					
9 fig. 2.13 (p. 34)	IVA	VII.5.133	6167	removal IVA Cobbling 1421 & hardpack north	7.5YR 5/6 strong brown, 6/6 reddish yellow exterior surface with N2.5/0 black design
10 fig. 2.13	IVA	VII.5.133	6168	removal IVA Cobbling 1421 & hardpack north	7.5YR 5/6 strong brown, 6/6 reddish yellow exterior surface with N2.5/0 black design
11	cf IV	62 VII.1.23	96	above metalled Surface 1233 in balk	7.5YR 6/4 light brown. 10YR 6/4 light yellowish brown exterior surface with 7.5YR N2.5/0 black design and N2.5/0 black interior surface
fig. 2.13	cf IV	62 VII.5.95	1954	to possible IVB Surface 1476-1548	7.5YR 6/6 reddish yellow, 5/4 brown exterior surface with N2.5/0 black design

(continued on p. 216)

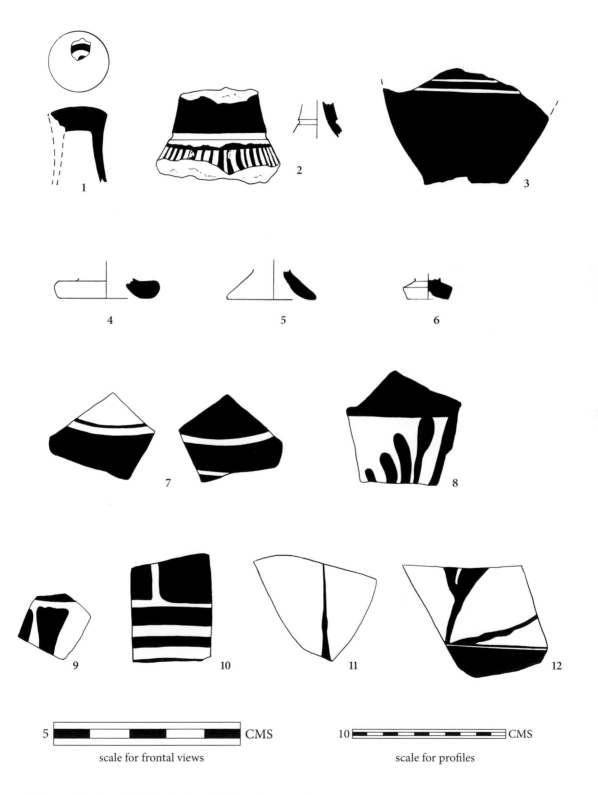

5 |▬▬▬▬▬| CMS 10 |▬▬▬▬| CMS
scale for frontal views scale for profiles

Pl. 2.15 Stratum V Lekythoi and other Fragments.

Pl. 2.15   Stratum V Lekythoi and other Fragments   (cont.)

Pl	Str	Fld, Ar,Bkt	No.	Locus Description	Ware description (surfaces with glaze, slip, paint, or wash)
fig. 2.13 (p. 34)	cf IV	62 VII.5.95	1955	to possible IVB Surface 1476-1548	7.5YR 6/6 reddish yellow, 5/4 brown exterior surface with N2.5/0 black design
fig. 2.13	cf IIIB	VII.3.79	928B #223C	Probe 1018 from III to IV levels	7.5YR 7/2 pinkish gray, 6/2 pinkish gray exterior surface, N2.5/0 worn black interior surface
2.15:12 fig. 2.13	cf IIIA	62 VII.5.55	686	Pit 1477	7.5YR 5/6 strong brown, 5/2 brown exterior surface with N2.5/0 black design
fig. 2.13	cf IIIA	62 VII.5.55	686B	Pit 1477	7.5YR 5/6 strong brown, 5/2 brown exterior surface with N2.5/0 black design
	unstr	VII.4.145	1774	unstratified	7/5YR 5/6 strong brown, 6/6 reddish yellow exterior surface with N2.5/0 black design
fig. 2.13	unstr	VII.8.108	5878	surface fill	5YR 6/8 reddish yellow, 7.5YR 5/6 strong brown with N2.5/0 black design
	unstr	II.2.29	#123	German dump	7.5YR 4/2 dark brown, 5/2 brown interior surface with N2.5/0 black circular design and N2.5/0 black exterior surface

Pl	Str	Fld, Ar, Bkt	No.	Locus Description	Ware description (surfaces with glaze, slip, paint, or wash)
Black and red Fragments					
	cf V	62 VII.1.101		in fill below IV metalled Surface 1530-1229-1232-1234	2.5YR 6/4 light reddish brown, 5YR 5/6 yellowish red faded exterior surface, 2.5YR 6/6 light red with 5YR 5/6 yellowish red slip interior surface
	cf V	62 VII.1.110		sub 2nd IVB metalled Surface 1230	5YR 7/3 pink, 2.5YR 2.5/0 black worn interior, 5YR 7/6 reddish yellow ext with 2.5YR 2.5/0 black stripe
	IVB	62 VII.1.98	1200	Pit 1133 sealed by Surface 1232	7.5YR 6/4 light brown, 5YR 7/6 reddish yellow ext surface with two bands of 5YR 5/1 gray int surface
	IVB	VII.7.119	5982	removal IV Wall 1817	5YR 7/6 reddish yellow, 2.5YR 2.5/0 black exterior stripes, 2.5/0 black interior surface
	IVB	VII.9.51	4054	Fill 1609-10,1612-15 in brick debris	5YR 7/4 pink, 7/6 reddish yellow ext with 2.5YR 2.5/0 black stripes, 4/4 reddish brown interior surf
	IVB	VII.9.86	4199	Fill 1609-10,1612-15 in brick debris	2.5YR 6/6 light red, 10R 5/6 red stripes on ext surf
	IVB	VII.9.87	4203	Fill 1609-10,1612-15 in brick debris	2.5YR 6/4 light reddish brown, 2.5/0 black on parts of interior, 5YR 7/6 reddish yellow exterior surface
2.15:7	IVA	IX.1.26	30	decomposed Brick 9016 outside IV Wall 9514	5YR 7/6 reddish yellow, with 2.5YR 2.5/0 black stripes exterior and interior surfaces
	IIIB	VII.8.90	4631	sub IIIB Cobbling 1719	5YR 7/6 reddish yellow, 5/8 yellowish red exterior surf with 2.5YR 2.5/0 black stripe and 2.5/0 black worn interior surface
	IIIA	VII.5.87	5227	removal IIIA Wall 1408	5YR 7/5 pink, 5/4 reddish brown part of interior, 4/1 dark gray worn exterior
	IIIA	VII.7.66	3996	removal IIIA Wall 1806	5YR 7/4 pink, 7/6 reddish yellow exterior surface, 2.5YR 2.5/0 black worn stripes ext & int surfaces
	IIIA	VII.21.100	723	IIIA Fill 21.034 below Floor 21.009	5YR 7/4 pink, 7/3 reddish yellow interior with 2.5YR reddish brown some places, 5/6 yellowish red exterior with 4/1 dark gray stripe
	IIIA	VII.21.117	999	IIIA Fill 21.034 below Floor 21.009	5YR 7/6 reddish yellow, 2.5 black interior surface, 2.5 black faded stripe exterior surface
	cf I	II.1.35	#106	Hellenistic House higher in Room 1	7.5YR 7/6 reddish yellow, 2.5YR 2.5/0 black int with 5YR 7/6 reddish yellow stripes, 7/6 reddish yellow exterior with 5/4 reddish brown and 2.5YR 2.5/0 black patterns
	unstr	VII.1.71		unstratified	5YR 7/6 reddish yellow, 6/8 reddish yellow exterior with 2.5YR 2.5/0 black parts and 2.5/0 black int surf
	unstr	VII.1.87	1114	unstratified	5YR 7/4 pink, 7/6 reddish yellow with 2.5YR 2.5/0 black interior & 5YR 5/4 reddish brown stripes interior surface, 2.5YR 2.5/0 black exterior surface
	unstr	62 VII.2.4	160	unstratified	5YR 7/6 reddish yellow, 2.5YR 6/6 light red surfaces with .25/0 black faded bands interior surf
	unstr	62 VII.6.26	420	unstratified	2.5YR 6/4 light reddish brown, 2.5/0 black int, 7/8 reddish yellow with some 2.5YR 2.5/0 black ext surf

Pl. 3.1   Hellenistic Jars Type A

Pl	Str	Fld, Ar,Bkt	No.	Locus Description	Ware description
	IVB	VII.2.127	6588	removal IVB Wall 1123	10YR 6/3 pale brown, 7/4 very pale brown exterior surface; few small inclusions
	IVB	VII.2.131	6915	L. 1123A levelling below IV installations	5YR 6/1 gray, 7/4 pink interior & 6/4 light reddish brown exterior surfaces; many large and small incl
3.1:1	IVB	VII.3.150	6260/ 6264	Fill 1029A below IV installations	10YR 8/2 white; 10YR8/3 very pale brown core; some limestone and ceramic inclusions
	IVB	VII.3.158	6308	Fill 1029A below IV installations	2.5YR 5/0 gray, 5YR 6/4 light reddish brown interior & 7.5YR 6/4 light brown; few large & many small incl
	IVB	VII.3.158	6309	Fill 1029A below IV installations	10YR 6/2 light brownish gray, 7/2 light gray interior surface; few small inclusions
2	IVB	VII.5.147	6544	Fill 1424 west of IVB Wall 1415	2.5YR 6/8 light red, 5YR 6/1 gray core; limestone and ceramic inclusions
	IVB	VII.7.146	7139	Fill 1836-1841 below IV strata	5YR 7/2 pinkish gray, 8/3 pink interior & 7/3 pink exterior surfaces; few small inclusions
	IVB	VII.9.67	4105	Fill 1609-10,1612-15 in brick debris	2.5YR 5/0 gray, 5/6 red interior and 6/4 light reddish brown exterior surfaces; many medium & small incl
	IVA	64 VII.2.3	144	Fill 1129A sub IVA Wall 1026	2.5YR 6/6 light red, 10YR 6/3 pale brown exterior surface; many large and very small inclusions
	IVA	VII.5.132	6164	removal IVA Wall 1420 of bin	10YR 7/2 light gray, 8/3 very pale brown interior & 7/1 light gray exterior surfaces; some small inclusions
	IVA	VII.5.135	6396	removal IVA Cobbling 1421 & hardpack north	10YR 6/2 light brown gray, 7/2 light gray exterior surface; few medium and many small inclusions
	IVA	VII.5.148	6548	sub IVA Wall 1419	10YR 6/1 gray, 7/3 very pale brown interior & 5YR 7/4 pink exterior surfaces; many large & many small incl
3	IVA	VII.23.62	489	above IVB Floor 23.009 sub IV A Floor 23.008	10YR 8/3 very pale brown, 7.5YR 8/2 pinkish white core; limestone and ceramic inclusions
4	IV	57 I.7b.56	331	in lower IV Floor 205	5YR 6/1 gray, 7/4 pink interior & 7/3 pink exterior surfaces; organic and few large ceramic inclusions
	IV	56 I.1	22	L. 4 fill below Pavement	2.5YR 3/0 gray, 5YR 7/4 pink exterior surface; some large and many very small inclusions
	IV	56 I.1	24	L. 4 fill below Pavement	10YR light gray, 7/3 very pale brown interior & 8/3 very pale brown exterior surfaces; many large & small incl
	IV	56 I.1	25	L. 4 fill below Pavement	10YR 7/2 light gray, 5YR 7/4 pink exterior surface; some medium and small inclusions
	IV	56 I.1	27	L. 4 fill below Pavement	10YR 7/2 light gray, 7/3 very pale brown exterior surface; few large and many small inclusions
	IV	56 I.1	32	L. 4 fill below Pavement	10YR 7/1 light gray; many small inclusions

A. Rim with exterior lower Point meeting Neck at Point or Angle

A-1. Shoulder slopes up to interior Point (which is usually rounded), Rim then rounds out and down to exterior Point

(continued on p. 222)

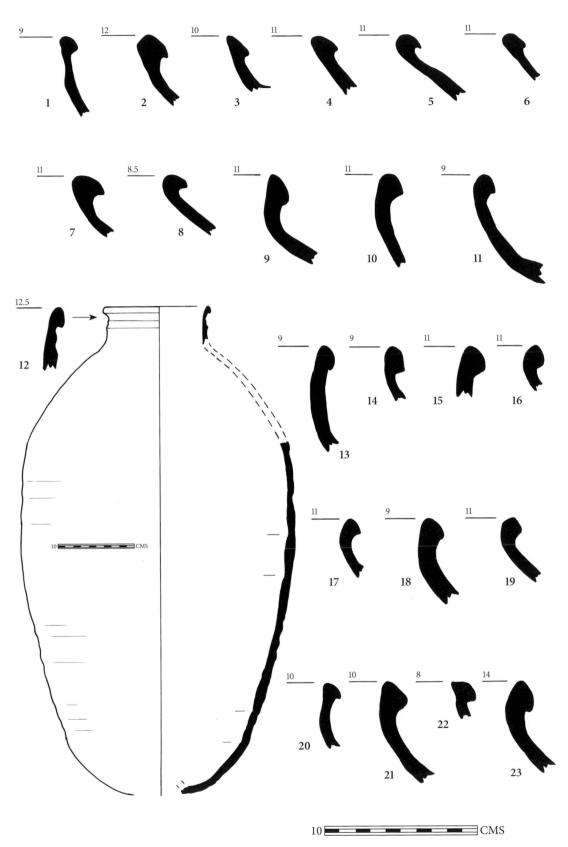

Pl. 3.1   Hellenistic Jars Type A.

Pl. 3.1   Hellenistic Jars Type A   (cont.)

Pl	Str	Fld, Ar,Bkt	No.	Locus Description	Ware description
3.1:5	IV	56 I.1	115	L. 4 below Hellenistic Tower	5YR 5/1 gray, 7/4 pink exterior surface; few ceramic and limestone inclusions
	cf IV	VII.21.106	867	Pit 21.036 dug in III or II	5YR 6/1 gray, 7/4 pink interior & 10YR 8/3 very pale brown exterior surfaces; many small inclusions
	cf IV	VII.21.106	868	Pit 21.036 dug in III or II	5YR 5/1 gray, 2.5YR 5/0 gray interior &7.5YR 7/4 pink exterior surfaces; many small inclusions
	cf IV	VII.21.106	870	Pit 21.036 dug in III or II	5YR 7/2 pinkish gray, 7/4 pink exterior surface; some smaller and very few large inclusions
	cf IV	VII.21.123	1044	Pit 21.036 dug in III or II	7.5YR 7/2 pinkish gray, 5YR 7/4 pink exterior; several large and some smaller inclusions
	cf IV	VII.21.123	1045	Pit 21.036 dug in III or II	5YR 5/1 gray, 7/4 pink exterior surface; some small inclusions, few large inclusions
	cf IV	VII.21.127	1050	Pit 21.036 dug in III or II	5YR 6/1 gray, 2.5YR 6/6 light red interior & 5YR 7/4 pink exterior surfaces; many large inclusions
	cf IV	VII.21.131	1155	Pit 21.036 dug in III or II	5YR 6/1 gray, 7/3 pink interior, 7.5YR 7/4 and 2.5YR 6/6 light red exterior surfaces; many small & large incl
	cf IV	VII.23.48	472	above IV Floor 23.005	10YR 6/1 gray, 7/4 very pale brown int & 7/3 very pale brown ext surfaces; few small & many small incl
	IIIB	VII.1.61	5308	Fill 1216,1217,1220-1224,1226	2.5YR 6/6 light red, 5YR 7/3 pink interior & 10YR 8/4 very pale brown exterior surfaces; some large incl
	IIIB	VII.8.85	4616	sub IIIB Cobbling 1719	5YR 6/1 gray, 7/4 pink interior & 2.5YR 6/6 light red exterior surfaces; many small and large inclusions
	IIIB	VII.8.85	4617	sub IIIB Cobbling 1719	7.5YR 8.2 pinkish white, 5YR 7/2 pinkish gray exterior surface; many large inclusions
	IIIB	VII.8.86	4618	sub IIIB Cobbling 1719	2.5YR 6/6 light red, 6/4 light reddish brown interior and 5YR 7/3 pink exterior surfaces; many small incl
	cf IIIB	VII.22.50	471	sub possible IIIB Floor 22.002	5YR 6/1 gray, 2.5YR 6/8 light red int and 6/4 light reddish brown ext surfaces; several small & many ceramic & limestone & few large limestone incl
	III	56 I.1	25	on Pavement	2.5YR 6/6 light red, 5YR 6/4 light reddish brown int & 7/4 pink ext surfaces; many various incl
	III	56 I.1	60	on Pavement	10YR 7/2 light gray, 7/3 very pale brown exterior surface; many smaller inclusions
	III	56 I.1	80	on Pavement	10YR 6/1 gray, 73 very pale brown interior & 5YR 7/4 pink exterior surfaces; some various inclusions
	III	56 I.1	86	on Pavement	10YR 7/1 light gray, 7/2 light gray exterior surface; some medium and smaller inclusions
6	cf III	57 I.6.55	454	pit in Wall B	2.5YR 6/6 light red, 6/4 light reddish brown ext surf; many ceramic & limestone & few large limestone incl
7	I	II.1.124	1194	Hellenistic House deeper in Room 1	5YR 6/2 pinkish gray, 7/3 pink exterior surface; many ceramic and few limestone inclusions

Pl. 3.1 Hellenistic Jars Type A (cont.)

Pl	Str	Fld, Ar, Bkt	No.	Locus Description	Ware description
3.1:8	unstr	57 I.9.19	180	top of Hellenistic tower	5YR 7/4 pink, 7/2 pinkish gray exterior surface; small limestone & many small organic & ceramic incl

A-2. Neck (usually short) or Shoulder turns out to upper Point, rounded to lower exterior Point

Pl	Str	Fld, Ar, Bkt	No.	Locus Description	Ware description
9	IVB	VII.3.149	6251	Fill 1029A below IV installations	10YR 7/1 light gray, 5YR 7/6 reddish yellow surface; small limestone and organic inclusions
10	IVB	VII.5.147	6545	Fill 1424 west of IVB Wall 1415	10YR 8/3 very pale brown, 10YR 8/2 white surface; some organic inclusions
	IVB	VII.6.123	2172	Probe 1311 in brick debris	10YR 7/3 very pale brown, 5YR 7/3 pink exterior surface; many small and few large inclusions
	IVB	VII.6.126	2961	Probe 1311 in brick debris	5YR 6/1 gray, 2.5YR 6/4 light reddish brown interior and 5/5 red exterior surfaces; some large inclusions
11	IVB	IX.1.48	98	grayish rubbly Fill 9024	5YR 6/8 reddish yellow, 7.5YR 8/2 pinkish white surfaces, 7.5YR /N4, very large dark gray core, few medium and evidence of small organic inclusions
	IVA	VII.3.143	5668	removal IVA Drain 1028	2.5YR 5/0 gray, 6/6 light red interior and 5YR 7/6 reddish yellow exterior surfaces; some small incl
12	IVA	VII.4.102, 113A	7448/A	L. 1526 removal large jar	10YR 7/3 very pale brown, 8/3 very pale brown surfaces; small or no inclusions
13	IVA	VII.23.63	493	above IVB Floor 23.009 sub IVA Floor 23.008	10YR 6/4 very pale brown exterior, 7.5YR /N5 gray interior; few medium ceramic and limestone incl
14	IV	57 I.7b.56	340	in lower IV Floor 205	2.5YR 5/6 red, 5/0 gray core, 6/6 light red interior and 10YR 6/3 pale brown exterior surfaces; ceramic and many large limestone inclusions
15	IV	56 I.1	122	L. 4 below Hellenistic Tower	5YR 7/6 reddish yellow, 10YR 7/2 light gray interior & 8/2 white exterior surfaces; many small ceramic and few large limestone incl
	cf IV	VII.6.69	1938	above unrelated IV Surface 1310	10YR 6/3 pale brown, 5YR 7/4 pink interior and 7/3 pink exterior surfaces; few large and many small incl
	cf IV	VII.21.127	1049	Pit 21.036 dug in III or II	2.5YR 6/0 gray, 5YR 8/4 pink interior and 7.5YR 7/8 reddish yellow exterior surfaces; few medium and many small inclusions
16	IIIB	VII.1.53	871	beneath IIIB floor 1214	7.5YR 7/4 pink, similar surfaces; small organic inclusions
	IIIB	VII.1.56	885	beneath IIIB floor 1214	10YR 7/2 light gray, 8/3 very pale brown exterior surface; few small inclusions
	IIIB	VII.1.61	5295	Fill 1216,1217,1220-1224,1226	5YR 6/1 gray, 7/6 reddish yellow exterior surface; many small inclusions
	IIIB	VII.1.61	5307	Fill 1216,1217,1220-1224,1226	5YR 7/2 pinkish gray, 10YR 7/3 very pale brown interior and 7/2 light gray exterior surfaces; large and many small inclusions

Pl. 3.1   Hellenistic Jars Type A   (cont.)

PL	STR	FLD, AR,BKT	NO.	LOCUS DESCRIPTION	WARE DESCRIPTION
	IIIB	VII.1.61	5311	Fill 1216,1217,1220-1224,1226	2.5YR 5/0 gray with 5/4 reddish brown, 5YR 7/4 pink exterior surface; few large and many small inclusions
	IIIB	VII.1.66	972	Fill 1216,1217,1220-1224,1226	10YR 7/2 light gray, 5YR 7/3 pink interior and 7/4 pink exterior surfaces; many small and few medium inclusions
	IIIB	VII.1.76	2871	Fill 1216,1217,1220-1224,1226	5YR 6/7 gray, 7/6 reddish yellow exterior surface; many small inclusions
	IIIB	VII.4.78	4961	removal III Wall 1506	10YR 7/1 light gray, 2.5YR 6/8 light red interior and 5YR 7/4 pink exterior surfaces; few large inclusions
3.1:17	IIIB	VII.4.80	4970	removal IIIB Wall 1513	7.5YR /N5 gray, 8/4 pink surface; few small ceramic inclusions
	IIIB	VII.8.55	3863	beneath IIIB Cobbling 1715	10YR 7/2 light gray,2.5YR 6/4 light reddish brown interior and 10YR 7/2 light gray exterior surfaces; few small inclusions
	IIIB	VII.8.56	3869	beneath IIIB Cobbling 1715	5YR 7/2 pinkish gray, 10YR 8/3 very pale brown interior and 7/2 light gray exterior surfaces; many small inclusions
18	IIIB	VII.8.83	4609	sub IIIB Cobbling 1719	7.5YR 6/8 reddish yellow, 7/4 pink surfaces; thick dark gray core; ceramic inclusions
	IIIB	VII.8.89	4627	sub IIIB Cobbling 1719	7.5YR 6.4 light brown, 5YR 7/6 reddish yellow interior surface; few medium and some small inclusions
19	IIIB	VII.8.89	4628	sub IIIB Cobbling 1719	7.5YR 6/8 reddish yellow, 7/5 pink surfaces; thick gray core; limestone and ceramic inclusions
	IIIA	VII.I.50	848	sub IIIA Floor 1203	5YR 7/2 pinkish gray, 7/4 pink interior and 10YR 7/2 light gray exterior; many small inclusions
	IIIA	VII.2.56	1043	removal IIIA Buttress 1110-1211	10YR 7/2 light gray, 8/4 very pale brown exterior surface; many small inclusions
	IIIA	VII.2.69	1121	removal IIIA Walls 1107-1109	10YR 8/2 white, 7/3 very pale brown interior & 8/3 very pale brown exterior surfaces; large and many small inclusions
	IIIA	VII.2.120	5501	removal IIIA Walls 1107-1109	5YR 7/4 pink, 6/1 gray core; 2.5YR 6/6 light red exterior surface; large and many small inclusions
	IIIA	VII.7.82	4650	removal IIIA Wall 1805N	5YR 5/1 gray, 6/1 gray interior and 7/4 pink exterior surfaces; few large and many small inclusions
20	IIIA	VII.8.44	3484	sub IIIA Cobbling 1703-1602	5YR 6/1 gray, 7/4 pink exterior surface; some large and small inclusions
	IIIA/II	II.1.105	924	below 160 cm. in Room 2	10YR 7/4 very pale brown, 7/3 very pale brown surfaces; ceramic and many limestone inclusions
21	IIIA/II	II.1.105	926	below 160 cm. in Room 2	5YR 8/4 pink, 10YR 7/3 very pale brown interior and 8/4 very pale brown exterior surfaces; small ceramic, many large limestone, and few organic inclusions

Pl. 3.1   Hellenistic Jars Type A   (cont.)

Pl	Str	Fld, Ar,Bkt	No.	Locus Description	Ware description
	II	VII.2.54	1026	removal II Wall 1103	10YR 7/2 light gray, 8/3 very pale brown interior and 8/2 white exterior surfaces; many large and small inclusions
22	I	II.1.123	1190	Hellenistic House deeper in Room 1	5YR 5/1 gray, 6/1 gray interior & 7/4 pink exterior surfaces; limestone & ceramic inclusions
23	unstr	57 I.9.19	177	top of Hellenistic tower	5YR 7/6 reddish yellow, 6/1 gray core, 7/3 pink interior and 8/4 pink exterior surfaces; limestone, few small organic, and many very small ceramic inclusions

Pl. 3.2   Hellenistic Jars Type A

Pl	Str	Fld, Ar,Bkt	No.	Locus Description	Ware description

A-3. Neck usually short and/or vertical, rounded Rim, rounded or flat to lower exterior Point

Pl	Str	Fld, Ar,Bkt	No.	Locus Description	Ware description
	IVB	VII.2.128	6592	removal IVB Wall 1123	2.5YR 5/6 red, 6/6 light red exterior surface; many medium and small inclusions
	IVB	VII.2.135	7328	L. 1123A levelling below IV installations	5YR 6/1 gray, 7/2 pinkish gray interior & 7/4 pink exterior surfaces; many small inclusions
3.2:1	IVB	VII.3.154	6285	Fill 1029A below IV installations	7.5YR 8/4 pink, 2.5YR 6/6 light red surfaces; some ceramic, few limestone, & evidence of tiny organic incl
	IVB	VII.3.154	6290	Fill 1029A below IV installations	5YR 5/1 gray 6/2 pinkish gray interior &7/6 reddish yellow exterior surfaces; some large & many small incl
	IVB	VII.3.155	6292	Fill 1029A below IV installations	2.5YR 5/6 red, 6/6 light red exterior surface; few medium and many small inclusions
2	IVB	VII.7.125	6002	Fill 1836-1841 below IV strata	10YR 8/3 very pale brown, similar surface; some organic inclusions
	IVB	VII.7.126	6013	Fill 1836-1841 below IV strata	10YR 7/2 light gray, 7.5YR 8/2 pinkish white exterior surface; many small inclusions
	IVB	IX.2.52	161	stony Layer 9272 below 9270	5YR 5/1 gray, 2.5YR 6/8 light red interior & 7.5 7/4 pink exterior surfaces; some large and small inclusions
3	IVA	VII.3.134b	5609	removal IVA Oven 1024A	5YR 7/4 pink, 10YR 8/3 exterior surface; many ceramic and few limestone inclusions
	IVA	VII.5.150	6567	sub IVA Wall 1419	5YR 6/4 light reddish brown, 2.5 light red interior and 6/4 light reddish brown exterior surfaces; many large and medium inclusions
4	IVA	IX.1.26	29	decomposed Brick 9016 outside IV Wall 9514	5YR 7/6 reddish yellow, 10YR 8/3 very pale brown surface; sand inclusions
	IVA	IX.2.33	45	silty Soil 9263	10YR 6/3 pale brown, 7/4 very pale brown interior and 8/3 very pale brown exterior surfaces; few large & many medium and small inclusions
5	IVA	IX.4.30	57	L. 9759.29-32 resurfacing Surface 9760	10YR 8/3 very pale brown; 5YR 6/3 light reddish brown core; some limestone inclusions
	IV	56 I.1	8	L. 4 fill below Pavement	7.5YR 6/4 light brown, 5YR 7/4 pink interior & 7/3 pink exterior surfaces; many large and medium inclusions
6	IV	56 I.1	110	L. 4 below Hellenistic Tower	5YR 6/1 gray, 7.5YR 8/2 pinkish white interior & 7/6 reddish yellow exterior surfaces; many small ceramic and few limestone and organic inclusions
	IIIB	VII.1.55	880	beneath IIIB Floor 1214	10YR 7/2 light gray, 7/4 very pale brown interior & 8/3 very pale brown exterior surfaces; some medium and many small inclusions
7	IIIB	VII.1.90	2920	beneath IIIB Floor 1214	10YR 5/2 grayish brown, 8/3 very pale brown surface; many sand and organic inclusions
	IIIB	VII.1.57	902	Fill 1216,1217,1220-1224,1226	10YR 5/3 brown, 7/3 very pale brown interior & 5/2 white exterior surfaces; many medium and small incl
	IIIB	VII.1.58	911	Fill 1216,1217,1220-1224,1226	2.5YR 6/6 light red; few large & many small inclusions

(continued on p. 228)

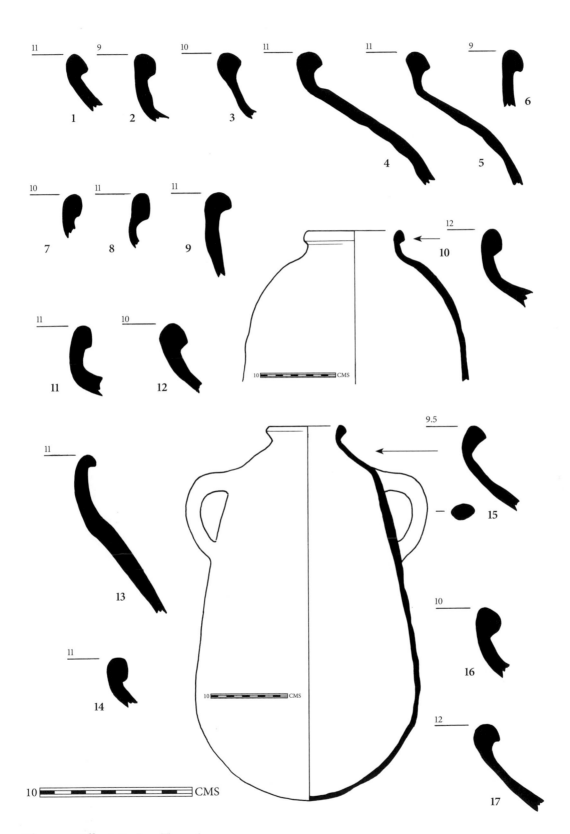

Pl. 3.2 Hellenistic Jars Type A.

Pl. 3.2   Hellenistic Jars Type A   (cont.)

Pl	Str	Fld, Ar,Bkt	No.	Locus Description	Ware description
	IIIB	VII.1.59	920	Fill 1216,1217,1220-1224,1226	2.5YR 4/0 dark gray, 7.5YR 7/4 pink interior & 6/4 light brown exterior surfaces; some large & many small incl
	IIIB	VII.1.59	924	Fill 1216,1217,1220-1224,1226	5YR 7/1 light gray, 2.5YR 6/6 light red exterior surface; few medium and many small inclusions
3.2:8	IIIB	VII.1.63	935	Fill 1216,1217,1220-1224,1226	10YR 7/4 very pale brown, 7/3 very pale brown interior, 8/2 white exterior surf; with 10 R6/3 pale red stain; small limestone, many ceramic & few large organic incl
	IIIB	VII.1.64	951	Fill 1216,1217,1220-1224,1226	5YR 5/1 gray, 7.5YR 7/4 pink exterior surface; few medium and some small inclusions
	IIIB	VII.1.66	963	Fill 1216,1217,1220-1224,1226	7.5YR 7/2 pinkish gray, 5YR 7/3 pink int and 7.5YR 8/2 pinkish white ext surfaces; few large & many small incl
	IIIB	VII.1.72	2863	Fill 1216,1217,1220-1224,1226	5YR 5/1 dark gray, 10YR 5/1 gray interior & 6/3 pale brown exterior surfaces; few large & many small incl
	IIIB	VII.1.76	2870	Fill 1216,1217,1220-1224,1226	5YR 6/1 gray, 7/4 pink exterior surface; few medium and many small inclusions
	IIIB	VII.1.77	2875	Fill 1216,1217,1220-1224,1226	10YR 7/2 light gray, 7/3 very pale brown interior & 8/3 very pale brown ext surfaces; many large & small incl
	IIIB	VII.1.77	2877	Fill 1216,1217,1220-1224,1226	2.5YR 6/6 light red, 6/4 light reddish brown exterior surface; many small inclusions
	IIIB	VII.1.61	5305	Fill 1216,1217,1220-1224,1226	5YR 7/4 pink, 8/4 pink interior & 7/3 pink exterior surfaces; many medium and small inclusions
	IIIB	VII.1.61	5315	Fill 1216,1217,1220-1224,1226	2.5YR 5/0 gray, 6/6 light red interior and 7.5YR 7/2 pinkish gray ext surfaces; few large & many small incl
9	IIIB	VII.3.62	1642	sub IIIB hardpack 1017-1019	7.5YR 7/6 reddish yellow, 8/4 pink surface; many sand, organic, and ceramic inclusions
	IIIB	VII.4.79	4966	removal IIIB Wall 1516	5YR 7/6 reddish yellow, 7/4 pink exterior surface; few large and many small inclusions
	IIIB	VII.4.80	4974	removal IIIB Wall 1513	2.5YR 5/0 gray, 5YR7/3 pink interior and 7/4 pink exterior surfaces; few large and some small inclusions
	IIIB	62 VII.4.83	635	sealed in Pit 1522	2.5YR 6/6 light red, 5YR 8/4 pink interior and 7/4 pink exterior surfaces; several large and many small incl
	IIIB	62 VII.4.142	1541	sealed in Pit 1522	10YR 7/3 very pale brown, 8/3 very pale brown int & 8/2 white ext surfaces; few large & many small incl
10	IIIB	VII.7.106	5259A	on IVA Cobbling 1824	10YR 8/4 very pale brown, similar surfaces; ceramic and organic inclusions
	IIIB	VII.8.56	3867	beneath IIIB Cobbling 1715	5YR 6/1 light gray, 8/4 pink interior and 7/3 pink exterior surfaces; few small inclusions
	IIIB	VII.8.77	4586	sub IIIB Cobbling 1719	5YR 6/1 light gray, 7/4 pink exterior surface; few large and many small inclusions
	IIIB	VII.8.82	4603	sub IIIB Cobbling 1719	10YR 7/2 light gray, 8/3 very pale brown interior and 7/2 light gray exterior surfaces; some small inclusions
	IIIB	VII.8.85	4615	sub IIIB Cobbling 1719	2.5YR 6/4 light reddish brown, 5YR 7/3 pink interior & 7/4 pink exterior surfaces; few large & many small incl

Pl. 3.2   Hellenistic Jars Type A   (cont.)

Pl	Str	Fld, Ar, Bkt	No.	Locus Description	Ware description
	IIIA	VII.1.41	796	sub IIIA Floor 1203	5YR 6/1 gray, 7/3 pink interior and 7/4 pink exterior surfaces; many small inclusions
	IIIA	VII.3.60	1626	removal IIIA Drain 1015-1016	5YR 6/2 pinkish gray, 7/2 pinkish gray interior and 7/3 pink exterior surfaces; few medium inclusions
	IIIA	VII.3.106	1796	on IIIB Hardpack 1017-1019	5YR 5/1 gray, 7/4 pink exterior surfaces; many medium and small inclusions
11	IIIA	VII.4.44	1842	sub IIIA Floor 1227-1511	7.5YR N6/ gray, 7/4 pink surfaces; small organic inclusions
	IIIA	VII.5.85	3978	removal IIIA Wall 1408	5YR 6/1 gray, 7/4 pink exterior surface; many medium and small inclusions
12	IIIA	VII.6.74	1955	sub IIIA Cobbling 1306 and 1307	5YR 6/4 light reddish brown, 7/3 pink interior & 10YR 8/4 very pale brown exterior surface; small limestone incl
	IIIA	VII.7.25	2254	sub IIIA Floor 1801	5YR 7/2 pinkish gray, 7/3 pink interior and 10YR 7/3 very pale brown exterior; few large and many small incl
	IIIA	VII.7.77	4024	removal IIIA Wall 1805N	5YR 5/1 gray, 7/6 reddish yellow interior and 6/4 light reddish brown exterior surfaces; few medium & some small inclusions
	IIIA	VII.9.44	3217	removal IIIA 1707-1705-1701-1601	10YR 5/2 grayish brown, 5YR 5/3 reddish brown interior and 6/4 light reddish brown exterior surfaces; few very large and many small inclusions
	IIIA	VII.9.44	3222	removal IIIA 1707-1705-1701-1601	2.5YR 6/4 light reddish brown, 5YR 7/4 pink exterior surface; few medium and many small inclusions
13	III	57 I.7b.55	318	above Lower Burn 204	10YR 6/1 gray, 7/2 light gray interior & 7/4 very pale brown exterior surf; organic & few large limestone incl
	III	57 I.7b.55	321	above Lower Burn 204	5YR 4/4 light reddish brown, 5/1 gray core, 10YR 7/1 light gray interior and 5YR 7/4 pink exterior surfaces; some small inclusions
14	III	56 I.1	11	L. 3 on Pavement	5YR 7/6 reddish yellow, 7/4 pink interior and 7/3 pink exterior surfaces; many small inclusions
	III	56 I.1	23	L. 3 on Pavement	5YR 6/2 pinkish gray, 7/2 pinkish gray interior & 10YR 7/3 very pale brown exterior surfaces; some small incl
	III	56 I.1	30	L. 3 on Pavement	10YR 7/3 very pale brown, 8/4 very pale brown interior and 2.5YR 7/2 light gray exterior surfaces; many large and small inclusions
15	III/II	III.4.15C	2116	pit between walls B & 606	reconstructed storage jar
16	II	II.1.15	158	Hellenistic House black earth layer Room 1	5YR 6/4 light reddish brown, 7/4 pink exterior & 10YR 7/2 light gray surf, patches 2.5YR 5/6 red on ext; many ceramic & limestone inclusions
17	unstr	III.4.5	247	surface	10YR 7/4 very pale brown, 5YR 7/2 pinkish gray interior and 8/4 pink exterior surface; large limestone and many ceramic inclusions
	unstr	57 I.9.19	181	top of Hellenistic tower	

Pl. 3.3 Hellenistic Jars Type B

Pl	Str	Fld, Ar,Bkt	No.	Locus Description	Ware description
B. Short Neck to rounded Point at Rim, then rounded out and down and into Neck					
3.3:1	IVB	VII.3.145	5648	Fill 1029A below IV installations	7.5YR 7/2 pinkish gray, 8/2 pinkish white surface; some limestone and organic inclusions
	IVB	VII.3.145	6307	Fill 1029A below IV installations	2.5YR 6/6 light red, 5YR 6/1 gray core, 2.5YR 6/4 light reddish brown interior and 5YR 8/4 pink exterior surfaces; some large and many small inclusions
2	IVB	VII.6.123	2170	Probe 1311 in brick debris	7.5YR 3/2 dark brown, 8/6 reddish yellow thick dark core; organic inclusions
	IVB	VII.7.145	6870	Fill 1836-1841 below IV strata	7.5YR 6/4 light brown, 10YR 7/3 very pale brown int and 8/4 very pale brown ext surfaces; few small inclusions
	IVB	VII.9.57	4078	Fill 1609-10,1612-15 in brick debris	5YR 5/2 gray, 6/1 gray int and 7/4 pink ext surfaces; many medium and few large inclusions
3	IVB	IX.3.47	80	occupational Debris 9517C	5YR 6/1 gray, 7/2 pinkish gray interior & 7/3 pink ext surfaces; ceramic & large limestone inclusions
	IVB	IX.3.76	218	IVB Fill 9523	2.5YR 5/0 gray, 5YR 6/1 gray interior and 2/5YR 6/6 light red ext surfaces; some small & few large & medium incl
4	IVA	VII.3.140	5633	removal IVA Wall 1025-1308	5YR 5/1 gray, 6/4 light reddish brown int & 7/3 pink ext surf; many ceramic, few limestone & large organic incl
	IVA	VII.4.111	5557	removal IV Press 1525	5YR 5/1 gray, 6/2 pinkish gray interior & 10YR 7/3 very pale brown exterior surfaces; some large & few small incl
5	IVA	VII.21.89	709	sub IVA or IVB Floor 21.012	10YR 6/1 gray, 7/2 light gray int & 2.5YR 6/8 light red exterior surfaces; ceramic & large limestone inclusions
6	IVA	IX.2.28	38	silty Soil 9262	2.5YR 5/0 gray, 6/6 light red interior & 5YR 7/4 pink ext surfaces; ceramic and few large limestone & organic incl
	IVA	IX.3.40	51	probable Surface 9517B	5YR 6/1 light gray, 7/6 reddish yellow int and 2/5YR 6/6 light red exterior surfaces; some large and medium inc
	IVA	IX.3.52	85	probable Surface 9517B	7.5YR 6/4 light brown, 10YR 7/3 very pale brown interior and 7/4 very pale brown exterior surfaces; many small and few medium inclusions
	cf IV	VII.3.105	1516	Stonefall 1042 in balk	10YR 6/1 gray, 7/4 pink interior and 10YR 8/4 very pale brown exterior surfaces; few large and many small incl
	cf IV	VII.3.141	5637	cleaning IV Drain 1028-1116	2.5YR 6/0 gray, 6/6 light red exterior surface; some large and many small inclusions
7	cf IV	VII.21.106	869	Pit 21.036 dug in III or II	5YR 6/6 reddish yellow, 10YR 6/1 gray core, 10 YR 8/3 very pale brown ext surf; many small-medium ceramic, few medium limestone & evidence of tiny organic incl
	cf IV	VII.23.50	473	above IV Floor 23.005	5YR 6/1 gray7/4 pink interior & 10YR 8/4 very pale brown exterior surfaces; few large and many small inclusions
	cf IV	VII.23.51	476	around IV Column Base 23.004	2.5YR 6/0 gray, 5YR 6/1 gray interior and 7/3 pink ext surfaces; some medium and many very small inclusions

(continued on p. 232)

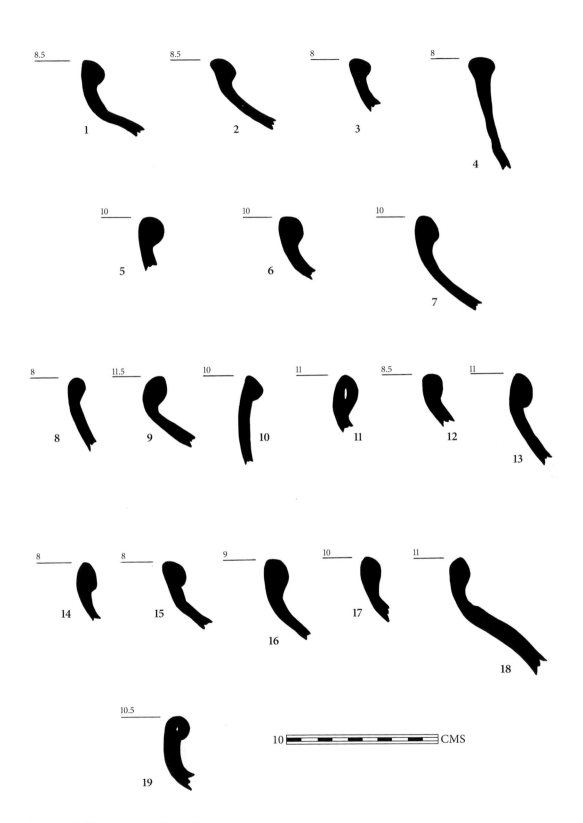

Pl. 3.3 Hellenistic Jars Type B.

Pl. 3.3   Hellenistic Jars Type B   (cont.)

Pl	Str	Fld, Ar,Bkt	No.	Locus Description	Ware description
	IV/III	57 I.5.11	84	layers against Wall B	5YR 7/4 pink, 8/4 pink exterior & 2.5YR 6/6 light red int surfaces; few small ceramic & organic inclusions
3.3:8	IIIB	VII.1.46	832	beneath IIIB Floor 1214	7.5YR 7/6 reddish yellow, 10YR 7/3 very pale brown surfaces; thick gray core
	IIIB	VII.1.61	5293	Fill 1216,1217,1220-1224,1226	5YR 5/0 gray, 7/4 pink exterior surface; several medium and many small inclusions
	IIIB	VII.1.63	930	Fill 1216,1217,1220-1224,1226	10YR 7/1 light gray, 7/2 light gray interior & 7/3 very pale brown exterior surfaces; many very small inclusions
	IIIB	VII.1.63	931	Fill 1216,1217,1220-1224,1226	10YR 6/1 gray, 5YR 8/4 pink exterior surface; few large and many medium and small inclusions
9	IIIB	VII.1.64 VII.1.61	947/ /5296	Fill 1216,1217,1220-1224,1226 Fill 1216,1217,1220-1224,1226	5YR 6/6 reddish yellow, 7.5YR 8/4 pink surfaces; many large limestone inclusions
	IIIB	VII.1.66	966	Fill 1216,1217,1220-1224,1226	5YR 5/1 gray, 5/2 reddish gray core; 7/2 pinkish gray int and 7/3 pink exterior surfaces; few large & many small incl
	IIIB	VII.1.66	967	Fill 1216,1217,1220-1224,1226	5YR 7/6 reddish yellow, 10YR 7/2 light gray int and 8/4 very pale brown exterior surfaces; some large and many very small inclusions
	IIIB	VII.2.49	1006	sub unrelated IIIB Surface 1106	10YR 7/2 light gray, 8/2 white exterior surface; few large and many very small inclusions
	IIIB	VII.3.107	1803	sub IIIB Hardpack 1017-1019	5YR 6/1 gray, 7.5YR 6/4 light brown interior & 7/2 pinkish gray exterior surfaces; few large and some medium incl
10	IIIB	VII.4.76	4958	removal III Wall 1506	10YR 5/1 gray, 7.5YR 7/4 pink surfaces; small limestone inclusions
11	IIIB	VII.4.78	4963	removal III Wall 1506	10YR 7/3 very pale brown, 8/3 very pale brown surfaces; limestone inclusions
12	IIIB	VII.8.54	3862	beneath IIIB Cobbling 1715	7.5YR 6/8 reddish yellow, 7/4 pink surfaces; small organic inclusions
13	IIIB	VII.8.77	4584	sub IIIB Cobbling 1719	10YR 6/4 light yellowish brown, 8/3 very pale brown surfaces; large ceramic inclusions
	cf IIIB	VII.3.93	1765	above IV Surface 1021-1023	10YR 6/1 gray, 5YR 5/2 pinkish gray interior & 10YR 7/2 light gray exterior; some large and many small inclusions
	cf IIIB	VII.7.139	6839	sub IIIB Surface 1808-1507 level	10YR 6/1 gray, 5YR 7/2 pinkish gray interior and 7/3 pink exterior surfaces; few large and some small inclusions
	cf IIIB	VII.22.48	457	sub possible IIIB Floor 22.002	2.5YR 6/0 gray, 10YR gray interior and 6/3 pale brown exterior some large and medium and many small incl
	cf IIIB	VII.22.52	344	sub possible IIIB Floor 22.002	5YR 7/2 pinkish gray, 10YR 8/3 very pale brown exterior surface; few large, some medium, & many very small incl
	IIIA	VII.1.48	842	removal IIIA Walls 1206-1210	5YR 7/1 light gray, 7/2 pinkish gray exterior surface; few large and many small inclusions
	IIIA	VII.1.111	5246	removal IIIA Walls 1206-1210	5YR 7/2 pinkish gray, 7/3 pink exterior surface; few large and many small inclusions

Pl. 3.3   Hellenistic Jars Type B   (cont.)

Pl	Str	Fld, Ar,Bkt	No.	Locus Description	Ware description
3.3:14	IIIA	VII.3.60	1629	removal IIIA Drain 1015-1016	5YR 7/4 pink, 8/1 white surface; some limestone & few medium organic inclusions
	IIIA	VII.3.60	1630	removal IIIA Drain 1015-1016	5YR 7/1 light gray, 7/3 pink interior & 8/4 pink exterior surfaces; few inclusions
15	IIIA	VII.3.63a	1648	removal IIIA Wall 1008-21.007	5YR 5/1 gray, 7/3 pink ext & 10YR 6/2 light brownish gray int surf; few limestone & many small ceramic incl
	IIIA	VII.4.62	3829	removal IIIA Walls 1505-1510	5YR 7/2 pinkish gray, 8/2 pinkish white exterior surface; many small and some larger inclusions
	IIIA	VII.6.77	1965	sub IIIA Cobbling 1306 and 1307	5YR 6/1 gray, 7/4 pink interior and 7/6 reddish yellow exterior surfaces; some medium inclusions
	IIIA	VII.7.57	3124	sub IIIA Floor 1802-1508	5YR 6/1 gray, 10YR 7/2 light gray int & 5YR 7/3 pink exterior surfaces; some large and many small inclusions
	IIIA	VII.7.82	4646	removal IIIA Wall 1805N	5YR 5/1 gray, 7.5YR 7/2 pinkish gray interior & 5YR 7/3 pink exterior surfaces; many medium and small incl
	IIIA	VII.8.41	2799	removal IIIA 1707-1705-1701-1601	10YR 6/1 gray, 8/2 white exterior surface; few large and some small inclusions
16	IIIA	VII.9.44	3216	removal IIIA 1707-1705-1701-1601	10YR 6/3 pale brown, 7/4 very pale brown surfaces; small limestone and organic inclusions
	IIIA	VII.9.45	3231	removal IIIA 1707-1705-1701-1601	5YR 5/1 gray, 6/4 light reddish brown exterior surface; some large and some small inclusions
17	III	57 I.6.12	32	burn above Floor 203	10YR 7/2 light gray, 7/3 very pale brown exterior surface; few ceramic & limestone inclusions
	III	56 I.1	8	L. 3 on Pavement	5YR 7/3 pink, 84/ pink exterior surface; many very small inclusions
	III	56 I.1	65	L. 3 on Pavement	5YR 5/1 gray, 2.5YR 6/6 light red interior and 6/4 light reddish brown exterior surfaces; some small inclusions
	III	56 I.1	82	L. 3 on Pavement	5YR 7/3 pink, 10YR 8/4 very pale brown exterior surface; many small inclusions
18	cf III	57 I.6.84	814	pit in Wall B	2.5YR 6/6 light red, 5YR 8/4 pink interior & 7/3 pink ext surfaces; very small ceramic & limestone inclusions
	II	VII.2.54	1028	removal II Wall 1103	10YR 7/1 light gray, 8/3 very pale brown interior and 8/2 white exterior surfaces; many small and few large incl
	II	VII.2.53	1040	removal II Wall 1103	10YR 5/1 gray, 5YR 8/3 pink interior & 8/2 pinkish white exterior surfaces; few small inclusions
19	I	II.1.117	1086	Hellenistic House Room 1 occupation	10YR 6/1 gray, 5YR 7/3 pink exterior surface; organic & few large limestone inclusions

Pl. 3.4 Hellenistic Jars Type C

Pl	Str	Fld, Ar,Bkt	No.	Locus Description	Ware description

C. Rim curves out, down, and into Neck at lower Point or Angle

Pl	Str	Fld, Ar,Bkt	No.	Locus Description	Ware description
3.4:1	IVA	VII.3.134b	5610/ /5611/	removal IVA Oven 1024A	2.5YR 6/6 light red, 5/2 weak red interior & 10YR 7/4 very pale brown exterior surfaces;
	cf IV	VII.3.96a	/1773	hard-pack 1021-1023 in which Oven 1024 appeared	5YR 6/1 gray, 6/3 light reddish brown interior & 7/4 pink exterior; many limestone & ceramic inclusions
2	IVA	VII.3.140	5631	removal IVA Wall 1025-1308	10YR 5/1 gray, 7.5YR 8/4 pink surface; some organic inclusions
3	IVA	VII.21.82	607	sub IVA Floor 21.011	10YR 71 light gray, 7/2 light gray surface; few organic and limestone inclusions
	IVA	VII.21.89	713	sub IVA or IVB Floor 21.012	10YR 6/1 gray, 7/3 very pale brown interior and 7/2 light gray exterior surfaces; many large and small inclusions
	IVA	VII.23.57	481	sub IVA Floor 23.008	5YR 7/3 pink, 8/4 pink exterior surf; many small & medium incl
	IVA	VII.23.64	497	above IVB floor 23.009	5YR 7/4 pink, 7.5YR 7/6 reddish yellow exterior surface; few medium and some small inclusions
4	IVA	XI.1.39	91	L. 9019 compact gray, sub 9018	2.5YR 5/8 red, 7.5YR 8/4 pink surface, 7.5 YR N7/ light gray core in rim; some medium limestone inclusions
	IV	56 I.1	4	L. 4 fill below Pavement	5YR 5/3 reddish brown, 10Yr 7/2 light gray interior and 7/1 light gray exterior surfaces; few medium inclusions
	IV	56 I.1	119	L. 4 below Hellenistic Tower	10YR 7/2 light gray, 7/1 gray exterior surface; very few large and some small inclusions
	IIIB	VII.1.45	826	beneath IIIB Floor 1214	10YR 7/2 light gray, 8/4 very pale brown interior and 8/3 very pale brown exterior surfaces; some small inclusions
	IIIB	VII.1.45	829	beneath IIIB Floor 1214	5YR 7/5 reddish yellow, 7/4 pink interior and 7/3 pink exterior surfaces; some small inclusions
	IIIB	VII.1.46	833	beneath IIIB Floor 1214	5YR 8/2 pinkish white, 7.5YR 8/2 pinkish white exterior surface; very small inclusions
5	IIIB	VII.1.54	873	beneath IIIB Floor 1214	10YR 7/3 pale brown, 8/4 very pale brown surfaces; small incl
	IIIB	VII.1.54	874	beneath IIIB Floor 1214	10YR 7/3 very pale brown, 8/4 very pale brown int and 8/3 very pale brown ext surfaces; few medium & some small incl
6	IIIB	VII.1.55	881	beneath IIIB Floor 1214	5YR 7/4 pink, 10YR 8/3 very pale brown surfaces; small limestone incl
	IIIB	VII.1.57	891	Fill 1216,1217,1220-1224,1226	10YR 7/2 light gray, 8/4 very pale brown exterior surface; few large and some small inclusions
	IIIB	VII.1.61	5316	Fill 1216,1217,1220-1224,1226	10YR 7/4 very pale brown, 8/3 very pale brown exterior surface; many very small inclusions
	IIIB	VII.1.61	5318	Fill 1216,1217,1220-1224,1226	10YR 7/3 very pale brown, 8/4 very pale brown interior 8/2 white exterior surfaces; many small inclusions
	IIIB	VII.1.63	933	Fill 1216,1217,1220-1224,1226	5YR 7/3 pink, 8/3 pink exterior surface; few very small incl
7	IIIB	VII.1.64	949	Fill 1216,1217,1220-1224,1226	10YR 7/4 very pale brown, 2/5YR 8/2 white surfaces; small organic incl
	IIIB	VII.1.64	950	Fill 1216,1217,1220-1224,1226	5YR 6/1 gray, 7.5YR 7/2 pinkish gray; few large & some small incl
8	IIIB	VII.1.64	953	Fill 1216,1217,1220-1224,1226	10YR 7/4 very pale brown, similar surfaces; small incl
9	IIIB	VII.1.65	955	Fill 1216,1217,1220-1224,1226	10YR 6/3 pale brown, 8/3 very pale brown surfaces; small organic incl
10	IIIB	VII.1.65	959A	Fill 1216,1217,1220-1224,1226	10YR 7/4 very pale brown, 8/2 white surfaces; small organic incl

(continued on p. 236)

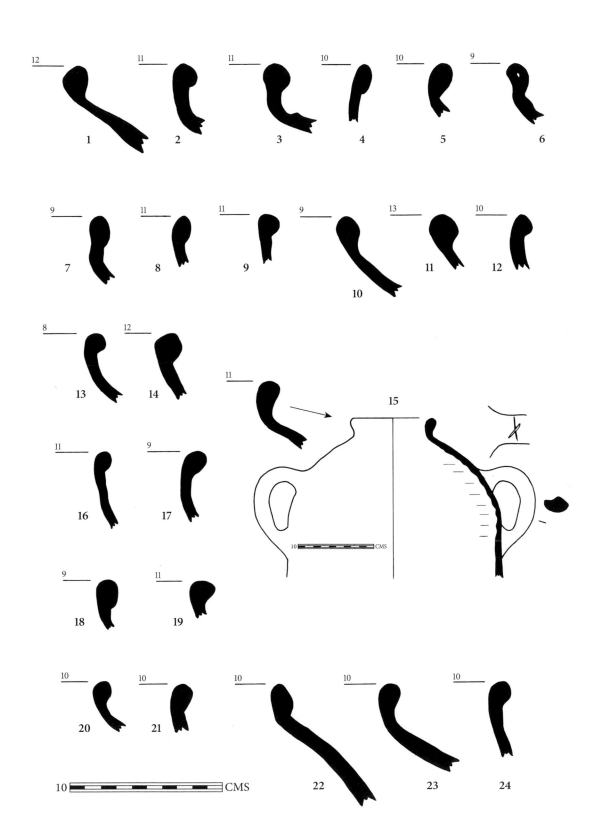

Pl. 3.4 Hellenistic Jars Type C.

Pl. 3.4   Hellenistic Jars Type C   (cont.)

PL	STR	FLD, AR,BKT	No.	LOCUS DESCRIPTION	WARE DESCRIPTION
	IIIB	VII.1.77	2876	Fill 1216,1217,1220-1224,1226	2.5YR 6/4 light reddish brown, 10YR 8/3 very pale brown exterior surface; many small inclusions
	IIIB	VII.3.62	1646	sub IIIB hardpack 1017-1019	5YR /1 light gray, 7/3 pink exterior surf; some large & small incl
	IIIB	VII.4.80	4972	removal IIIB Wall 1513	5YR 8/2 pinkish white, 10YR 8/3 very pale brown exterior surface; some large and small inclusions
	IIIB	VII.8.55	3865	beneath IIIB Cobbling 1715	10YR 7/2 light gray, 8/3 very pale brown exterior surface; some large and small inclusions
	IIIB	VII.8.56	3870	beneath IIIB Cobbling 1715	7.5YR 8/2 pinkish white, 10YR 8/2 white exterior surface; many small and medium inclusions
	IIIB	VII.8.56	3871	beneath IIIB Cobbling 1715	5YR 7/6 reddish yellow, 8/4 pink exterior surface; few large and some small inclusions
	IIIB	VII.8.47	3501	sub IIIB Cobbling 1719	5YR 6/1 light gray, 6/4 light reddish brown interior and 7/4 pink exterior surfaces; few medium inclusions
	IIIB	VII.8.80	4598	sub IIIB Cobbling 1719	10YR 7/3 very pale brown, 8/3 very pale brown exterior surface; many large and small inclusions
	IIIB	VII.8.80	4599	sub IIIB Cobbling 1719	5YR 7/4 pink, 7/3 pink exterior surface; many large incl
3.4:11	IIIB	VII.8.84	4612	sub IIIB Cobbling 1719	7.5YR 8/6 reddish yellow, 10YR 8/4 very pale brown surfaces; light gray core; limestone inclusions
	IIIB	VII.8.90	4634	sub IIIB Cobbling 1719	10YR 0/1 gray, 7/3 very pale brown exterior surface; few medium and many small inclusions
12	IIIB	VII.8.90	4636	sub IIIB Cobbling 1719	10YR 6/3 pale brown, 2.5Y 8/2 white surfaces, light gray core; large limestone inclusions
	IIIB	VII.8.93	5108	sub IIIB Cobbling 1719	5YR 6/4 light reddish brown, 10YR 8/3 very pale brown exterior surface; many small inclusions
	IIIA	VII.1.40	773	sub IIIA Floor 1203	5YR 7/1 light gray, 8/4 pink interior and 7/4 pink exterior surfaces; many medium and small inclusions
	IIIA	VII.1.41	791	sub IIIA Floor 1203	not accessible
	IIIA	VII.1.50	850	sub IIIA Floor 1203	7.5YR 8/2 pinkish white, 10YR 8/3 very pale brown interior & 8/2 white exterior surfaces; many small & large incl
	IIIA	VII.1.89	2911	on IIIB Floor 1214 sub Floor 1203	5YR 7/2 pinkish gray, 7.5YR 7/4 pink interior and 5YR 7/3 pink exterior surfaces; some large & many small incl
	IIIA	VII.2.56	1045	removal IIIA Buttress 1110-1211	10YR 7/5 very pale brown, 7/3 very pale brown interior and 8/2 white exterior surfaces; many small & large incl
	IIIA	VII.2.70	1124	removal IIIA Walls 1107-1109	not accessible
	IIIA	VII.2.70	1127	removal IIIA Walls 1107-1109	5YR 6/1 gray, 7/4 pink interior and 7/3 pink exterior surfaces; some large and many small inclusions
	IIIA	VII.3.60	1624	removal IIIA Drain 1015-1016	5YR 7/2 pinkish gray, 7/3 pink interior and 7/2 pinkish gray exterior surfaces; many small and few large incl
13	IIIA	VII.3.60	1625	removal IIIA Drain 1015-1016	5YR 7/4 pink, 10YR 8/3 very pale brown interior & 8/2 white exterior surfaces; limestone & many small ceramic incl
	IIIA	VII.3.106	1800	on IIIB Hardpack 1017-1019	5YR 7/4 pink, 2.5YR 6/6 light red exterior surf; many small incl
	IIIA	VII.3.117	3800	removal IIIA Wall 1010	5Yr 7/3 pink, 7/2 pink interior and 8/2 pinkish white exterior surfaces; many small and few large inclusions
	IIIA	VII.3.118	3803	removal IIIA Wall 1010	5YR 6/4 light reddish brown, 6/1 gray core, 7/3 pink exterior surface; many small inclusions

Pl. 3.4 Hellenistic Jars Type C (cont.)

Pl	Str	Fld, Ar,Bkt	No.	Locus Description	Ware description
	IIIA	VII.4.62	3877	removal IIIA Walls 1505-1510	5YR 8/4 pink, 7/3 pink interior and 7/2 pinkish gray exterior surfaces; few large inclusions
	IIIA	VII.4.37	1830	cleaning IIIB Tannur 1509	5YR 6/2 pinkish gray, 7/3 pink interior and 7/4 pink exterior surfaces; some large and small inclusions
	IIIA	VII.6.78	1972	sub IIIA Cobbling 1306 and 1307	10YR 6/2 light brownish gray, 5YR 8/4 pink int, 10YR 8/4 very pale brown ext surfaces; some large and some small incl
	IIIA	VII.7.73	3139	removal IIIA Wall 1811 facing	5YR 6/2 pinkish gray, 8/3 pink ext surf; some large & small incl
	IIIA	VII.7.82	4645	removal IIIA Wall 1805N	5YR 6/1 gray, 8/3 pink exterior surf; few large & many small incl
	IIIA	VII.7.82	4649	removal IIIA Wall 1805N	10YR 8/2 white, /2 light gray int surf; some large & many small incl
	IIIA	VII.8.44	3483	sub IIIA Cobbling 1703-1602	10YR 8/2 white, 7/3 very pale brown exterior surface; few large and some small inclusions
	IIIA	VII.9.42b	3205	removal IIIA Cobbling 1604	7.5YR 7/6 reddish yellow, 5YR 8/3 pink interior and 7/4 pink exterior surfaces; some medium and small incl
3.4:14	IIIA	VII.8.50	3512	removal IIIA 1707-1705-1701-1601	7.5YR 7/4 pink, 10YR 8/4 very pale brown surfaces, thin gray core; some inclusions
	IIIA	VII.9.43	3213	removal IIIA 1707-1705-1701-1601	10YR 7/2 light gray, 8/3 very pale brown ext surf; several small incl
15	cf IIIA	62 VII.1.51	541	pit top courses of Wall 1531	not accessible
	cf IIIA	VII.2.44	991	on unrelated IIIB Surface 1106	5YR 6/3 light reddish brown, 6/1 gray core, 5YR 7/3 pink int and 7/5YR 8/2 pinkish white ext surfaces; many large & some small incl
	cf IIIA	VII.4.84	4989	Pit 1514	10YR 7/1 light gray, 7/2 light gray interior and 2.5YR 8/2 white exterior surfaces; many small & medium incl
16	III	57 I.6.10	15	burn above Floor 203	5YR 7/6 reddish yellow, 7/4 pink interior, 8/4 pink exterior surfaces; ceramic and few small limestone incl
17	III	57 I.6.10	34	burn above Floor 203	2.5YR 6/6 light red, 5YR 7/6 reddish yellow exterior surface; very small limestone & ceramic inclusions
18	III	57 I.6.12	16	burn above Floor 203	10YR 7/3 very pale brown, 7/2 light gray exterior surf; few small organic and very few limestone inclusions
19	III	57 I.6.15	41	Floor 203	2.5YR 5/0 gray, 6/4 light reddish brown exterior surface; ceramic and few very small limestone inclusions
	III	56 I.1	13	L. 3 on Pavement	5YR 7/3 pink, 7/2 pinkish gray interior and 8/4 pink exterior surfaces; many large and small inclusions
	III	56 I.1	76	L. 3 on Pavement	5YR 6/2 pinkish gray, 7/2 pinkish gray exterior surface; some large and many small inclusions
20	cf III	57 I.6.55	453	pit in Wall B	5YR 5/1 gray, 6/3 light reddish brown int & 10YR 7/4 very pale brown ext surfaces; many ceramic & few limestone incl
21	cf III	57 I.6.55	457	pit in Wall B	10YR 8/3 very pale brown, 8/2 white exterior surface; many small ceramic & few limestone inclusions
22	cf III	57 I.6.72	637	pit in Wall B	2.5YR 5/0 gray, 6/4 light reddish brown exterior surface; many small ceramic & few limestone inclusions
23	cf III	57 I.6.82	765	pit in Wall B	5YR 8/3 pink, 10Yr 8/3 very pale brown exterior surface; small limestone and ceramic inclusions
24	IIIA/II	II.1.98	932	140-160 cm. below Wall 7013	10YR 7/3 very pale brown, 5YR 8/4 pink interior, 6/4 light reddish brown exterior surfaces; ceramic & small organic incl

Pl. 3.5   Hellenistic Jars Type C

Pl	Str	Fld, Ar, Bkt	No.	Locus Description	Ware description
3.5:1 fig. 3.2 (p. 42)	III/II	III.4.9B	2123	pit between walls B & 606	reconstructed storage jar - with potter's mark
2 fig. 3.1 (p. 42)	III/II	III.4.9C	2117	pit between walls B & 606	reconstructed storage jar
3	II	VII.1.28	117	II occupation Pit 1205-1207	5YR 7/4 pink, 10YR 7 8/4 very pale brown surfaces; limestone & organic inclusions
	II	VII.1.29	735	on IIIA Surface 1203	5YR 8/2 pinkish white, 7/4 pink exterior surface; many very small inclusions
	II	VII.1.29	736	on IIIA Surface 1203	2.5YR 6/6 light red, 6/8 light red interior and 5YR 7/4 pink exterior surfaces; many small inclusions
	II	VII.1.29	744	on IIIA Surface 1203	5YR 7/2 pinkish gray, 2.5YR 8/2 white exterior surface; many very small inclusions
	II	VII.1.87	2895	on IIIA Surface 1203	5YR 8/4 pink, 7/6 reddish yellow exterior surface; many very small and some large inclusions
	II	VII.2.41	988	above IIIA Floor 1227 in Room E	5YR 7/3 pink, 8/4 pink interior and 8/3 pink exterior surfaces; many very small inclusions
4	II	VII.2.53	1041	removal II Wall 1103	10YR 7/2 light gray, 2.5Y 7/2 light gray surfaces; small organic & limestone inclusions
	II	VII.7.22	2222	above IIIA Floor 1802-1508	5YR 5/1 gray, 8/4 pink interior and 7/3 pink exterior surfaces; few large and small inclusions
	II	VII.8.37	2745	above IIIA Cobbling 1703	5YR 7/2 pinkish gray, 8/3 pink exterior surface; few large and small inclusions
5	II	II.1.14	154	Hellenistic House black earth layer Room 1	10YR 6/3 pale brown, 8/3 very pale brown exterior surface; limestone & few small ceramic inclusions

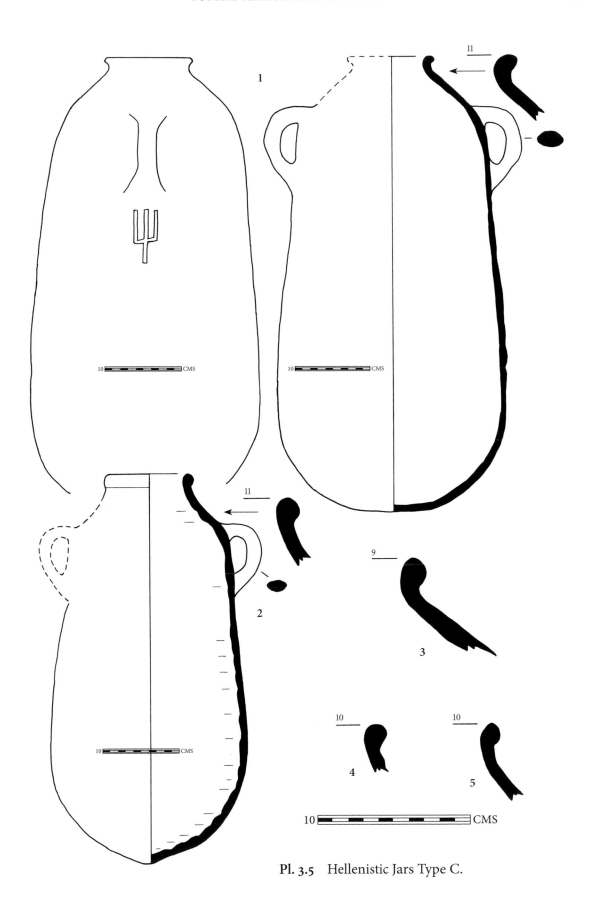

Pl. 3.5 Hellenistic Jars Type C.

Pl. 3.6   Hellenistic Jars Type C

Pl	Str	Fld, Ar,Bkt	No.	Locus Description	Ware description
3.6:1	II	II.1.48	396	black earth layer North Balk	2.5YR 6/4 light reddish brown, 6/6 light red interior & 5YR 8/4 pink exterior surfaces; limestone and small ceramic inclusions
2	unstr	57 I.7b.31	174	surface to west	5YR 7/3 pink, 8/4 pink exterior surface; many limestone & few ceramic inclusions
3	unstr	57 I.9.19	178	top of Hellenistic tower	5YR 6/4 light reddish brown, 10YR 7/3 very pale brown interior & 7/2 light gray exterior surfaces; limestone & many ceramic inclusions
4	unstr	II.1.45b	393	Storage Bin 7106	5YR 5/1 gray, 6/6 reddish yellow surfaces; limestone and few ceramic inclusions
5	unstr	II.1.70	2120	unstratified	reconstructed storage jar

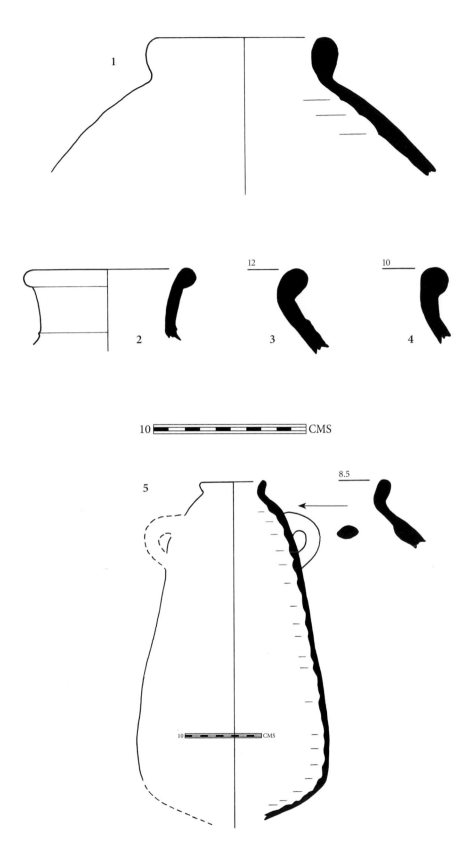

Pl. 3.6   Hellenistic Jars Type C.

Pl. 3.7 Hellenistic Jars Type C

PL	STR	FLD, AR,BKT	NO.	LOCUS DESCRIPTION	WARE DESCRIPTION

Cv as C, rounded Rim, but little Thickening and smooth to Shoulder with no Point or Angle; early (IV) Rims have upper, inner Point, later tend to turn out

PL	STR	FLD, AR,BKT	NO.	LOCUS DESCRIPTION	WARE DESCRIPTION
3.7:1	IVB	IX.3.48	82	occupational Debris 9517C	7.5YR N6/ gray, 7/4 pink rim & interior surface, 8/2 pinkish white exterior surface; some large limestone & evidence of many organic inclusions
2	IVA	VII.3.134b	5608	removal IVA Oven 1024A	5YR 8/4 pink, 8/3 pink surface; many organic inclusions
3	IVA	VII.4.110	5541	removal IVA Floor 1527	10YR 5/1 gray, 7/4 very pale brown surfaces; small straw inclusions
	IVA	VII.5.148	6547	sub IVA Wall 1419	2.5YR 6/4 light reddish brown, 5YR 8/3 pink surfaces; some medium inclusions
4	IVA	VII.5.150	6559	sub IVA Wall 1419	5YR 7/6 reddish yellow exterior surface, N6/ gray core, 10YR 8/3 very pale brown interior surface; some medium limestone & evidence of some medium limestone incl
5	IV	57 I.7b.56	333	in lower IV Floor 205	10YR 6/4 light yellowish brown, 5/1 gray core, 7/2 light gray interior & 8/3 very pale brown exterior surfaces; ceramic and limestone inclusions
	IV	56 I.1	124	L. 4 below Hellenistic Tower	5YR 4/1 dark gray, 7/4 pink exterior surface; many large inclusions
6	IIIB	VII.1.44	812	beneath IIIB Floor 1214	5YR 6/8 reddish yellow, 7.5YR 7/4 pink surfaces, thick gray core; small inclusions
7	IIIB	VII.1.46	834	beneath IIIB Floor 1214	5YR 7/6 reddish yellow, 7.5YR 8/6 reddish yellow surfaces; small organic inclusions
8	IIIB	VII.1.55 VII.1.56	878/ /884	beneath IIIB Floor 1214	7.5YR 6/4 light brown, 2.5YR 8/2 white surfaces; small organic & limestone inclusions
9	IIIB	VII.1.92	2929	beneath IIIB Floor 1214	7.5YR 7/4 pink, 10YR 8/3 very pale brown surface; many limestone, sand, and organic inclusions
	IIIB	VII.1.61	5306	Fill 1216,1217,1220-1224,1226	7.5YR 7/2 pinkish gray; few large and many medium inclusions
	IIIB	VII.1.65	959	Fill 1216,1217,1220-1224,1226	10YR 7/3 very pale brown, 8/2 white exterior surface; few medium and many very small inclusions
	IIIB	VII.8.47	3504	sub IIIB Cobbling 1719	5YR 5/1 gray, 7/4 pink exterior surface; many large inclusions
	IIIB	VII.8.90	4632	sub IIIB Cobbling 1719	5YR 5/1 gray, 7/2 pinkish gray exterior surface; few inclusions
	IIIB	VII.8.91	5100	sub IIIB Cobbling 1719	5YR 6/1 gray, 7/6 reddish yellow exterior surface; few large and medium inclusions
10	IIIA	VII.1.43	1839	sub IIIA Floor 1227-1511	7.5YR 6/8 reddish yellow; evidence of few organic inclusions
11	cf II	II.2.73	2112	black earth layer Area 2	reconstructed storage jar

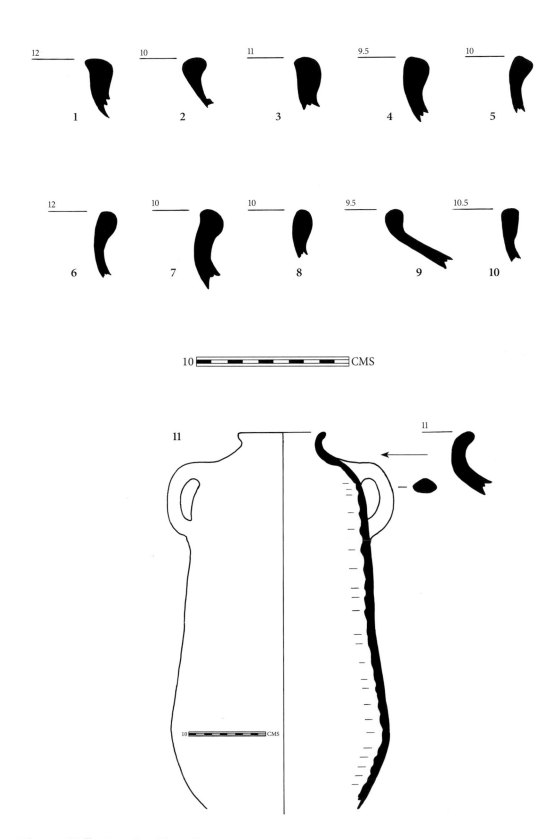

Pl. 3.7 Hellenistic Jars Type C.

Pl. 3.8 Hellenistic Jars Type D

Pl	Str	Fld, Ar,Bkt	No.	Locus Description	Ware description

D. Collar rim

D-1. Everted Rim to Point, lengthened and rounded to lower Point or Angle where Rim meets Neck

Pl	Str	Fld, Ar,Bkt	No.	Locus Description	Ware description
3.8:1	IV/III	57 I.7.23	138	lower H Floors 205 & 206	10YR 7/4 very pale brown, 8/3 very pale brown surfaces; few limestone & few small ceramic inclusions
2	IV/III	57 I.7.23	140	lower H floors 205 & 206	2.5YR 6/6 light red, 5YR 8/4 pink exterior surface; ceramic very small limestone inclusions
	IIIB	VII.1.91	2925	beneath IIIB Floor 1214	7.5YR 7/6 reddish yellow, 10YR 8/3 very pale brown surfaces; small organic inclusions
	IIIA	VII.1.88	2907	sub IIIA Floor 1203	2.5YR 6/6 light red, 5YR 7/4 pink exterior surf; small incl
3	IIIA	VII.1.89	2912	on IIIB Floor 1214 sub Floor 1203	5YR 7/6 reddish yellow, similar surf; large & small incl
4	IIIA	VII.4.44	1840	sub IIIA Floor 1227-1511	5YR 7/6 reddish yellow, similar surfaces; small sand incl
	IIIA	VII.6.78	1971	sub IIIA Cobbling 1306 and 1307	7.5YR 7/4 pink; few medium limestone inclusions
5	IIIA	VII.7.25	2252	sub IIIA Floor 1801	7.5YR 5/8 strong brown, 7/6 reddish yellow surface; very many limestone & some organic inclusions
	IIIA	VII.7.30	2286	sub IIIA Floor 1802-1508	5YR 7/2 pinkish gray, 10YR very pale brown interior & 8/3 very pale brown exterior surfaces; small inclusions
	cf IIIA	VII.4.101	5385	Pit 1514	10YR 7/2 light gray, 8/3 very pale brown interior & 8/2 white exterior surfaces; some small inclusions
6	III	57 I.6.11	66	burn above Floor 203	5YR 6/4 light reddish brown 8/3 pink interior & 8/4 pink exterior surfaces; organic, limestone, & ceramic incl
	III	57 I.6.15	38	floor 203	cf. 66 (same vessel?)
	cf III	57 I.9.9	125	striated makeup over wall A	5YR 7/6 reddish yellow; many small inclusions
7	II	VII.1.29	737	on IIIA Surface 1203	7.5YR 6/4 light brown, 5YR 8/4 pink exterior surface; some very small inclusions
	II	VII.1.29	743	on IIIA Surface 1203	5YR 6/3 light reddish brown, 7/3 pink exterior surface; many very small inclusions
8	II	II.1.25	263	Hellenistic House black earth layer Room 1	2.5YR 6/6 light red, 5YR 7/4 pink interior & 7.5YR 7/4 pink exterior surfaces
9	II	III.3.15	235	foundation of plastered bin	5YR 6/2 pinkish gray, 6/4 light reddish brown core, 7/3 pink interior & 8/3 very pale brown exterior surfaces; few organic and limestone inclusions
	cf II	57 II.2.65	11249	Fill 7080 sub IA Surface 7098	10YR 7/3 very pale brown, 8/3 very pale brown exterior surface; many small inclusions
	I	II.1.124	1195	Hellenistic House deeper in Room 1	10YR 8/3 very pale brown, 8/4 very pale brown interior & 8/2 white exterior surfaces; very small inclusions
10	I	II.1.124	1196	Hellenistic House deeper in Room 1	5YR 7/3 pink, 10YR 8/2 white exterior surface; small ceramic and few limestone inclusions
11	cf I	II.1.35	387	Hellenistic House higher in Room 1	5YR 6/4 light reddish brown, 10YR 8/3 surfaces; limestone and few small organic inclusions
	unstr	VII.1.100	3741	surface fill	2.5YR 6/6 light red, 5YR 7/3 pink interior and 7/4 pink exterior surfaces; some small inclusions

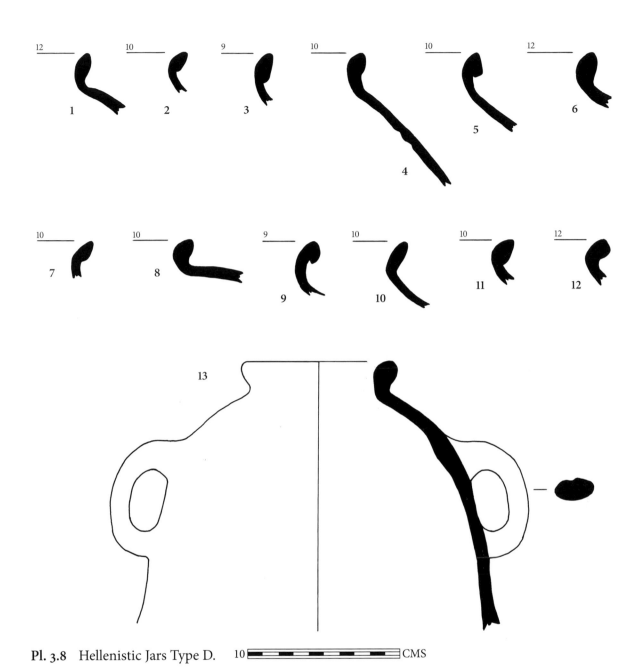

Pl. 3.8 Hellenistic Jars Type D.   10 ▭▭▭▭▭ CMS

Pl. 3.8 Hellenistic Jars Type D   (cont.)

Pl	Str	Fld, Ar,Bkt	No.	Locus Description	Ware description
	unstr	VII.4.56	2952	surface fill	5YR 6/1 gray, 7/4 pink interior and 7/3 pink exterior surfaces; many small inclusions
	unstr	VII.7.54	3179	surface fill	10YR 8/2 white, 8/3 very pale brown ext surf; some small incl
3.8:12	unstr	57 I.11b.5a	888	huwwar to small stones	5YR 8.3 pink, 10YR 8/3 very pale brown exterior surface; small ceramic and few organic & limestone inclusions
13	unstr	III.4.1	237/=	surface	10YR 7/4 very pale brown, 8/3 very pale brown surfaces;
		III.3/4	/427	surface	many small limestone & ceramic inclusions

Pl. 3.9   Hellenistic Jars Type D

PL	STR	FLD, AR,BKT	No.	LOCUS DESCRIPTION	WARE DESCRIPTION
D-2. as D-1, but rounded Rim is flattened					
3.9:1	IIIB	VII.1.43	809	beneath IIIB Floor 1214 Hellenistic House deeper in Room 1	limestone & few small ceramic & organic inclusions
2	IIIB	VII.1.71	2861	Fill 1216,1217,1220-1224,1226	5YR 6/4 light reddish brown, 2.5Y 8/4 pale yellow surfaces; small organic inclusions
	IIIA	VII.1.88	2908	sub IIIA Floor 1203	5YR 7/6 reddish yellow, 7.5YR 7/5 pink exterior surface; very small and few large inclusions
3	IIIA	VII.1.52	861	on IIIB Floor 1214 sub Floor 1203	5YR 8/3 pink, 2.5Y 7/2 light gray surfaces; some small incl
4	IIIA	VII.1.89	2917	on IIIB Floor 1214 sub Floor 1203	5YR 6/6 reddish yellow, 6/1 gray core, 10YR 8/3 very pale interior surf; some small crystal, few medium ceramic incl
	IIIA	VII.2.120	5506	removal IIIA Walls 1107-1109	7.5YR 8/4 pink, 10YR 7/2 light gray ext surf; many very small incl
	IIIA	VII.7.25	2256	sub IIIA Floor 1801	5YR 6/4 light reddish brown, 7/2 pinkish gray interior and 7.5YR 6/4 light brown exterior; very small inclusions
	IIIA	VII.7.25	2260	sub IIIA Floor 1801	10YR 6/2 light brownish gray, 8/4 very pale brown exterior surface; many very small inclusions
	IIIA	VII.7.25	2261	sub IIIA Floor 1801	7.5YR 6/4 light brown; many very small inclusions
	cf IIIA	VII.4.88	5003	Pit 1514	10YR 7/2 light gray, 8/3 very pale brown interior and 8/2 white exterior surfaces; several small inclusions
5	III	57 I.7b.41	207	above Lower Burn 204	10YR 7/3 very pale brown, 8/3 very pale brown exterior; few limestone & many very small ceramic inclusions
6	cf III	57 I.7.14	108	between Floors 202 and 206	10YR 7/4 very pale brown, 8/3 very pale brown exterior surface; small ceramic & many limestone inclusions
7 figs. 1.6, 3.3 (pp. 6, 43)	cf III	56 I.1	#15	near Pavement	found with lamp #16 inside; not accessible
8	IIIA/II	II.1.98	931	140-160 cm. below Wall 7013	10YR 7/1 light gray, 5YR 8/3 pink interior, 8/4 pink ext surfaces; many very small ceramic & few limestone incl
	II	VII.1.29	732	on IIIA Surface 1203	10YR 8/2 white, 8/3 very pale brown exterior surface; some small inclusions
	II	VII.1.29	734	on IIIA Surface 1203	5YR 7/4 pink 8/3 pink interior and 10YR 8/4 very pale brown exterior surfaces; many very small inclusions
	II	VII.4.27	1822	above IIIA Floor 1227 in Room E	5YR 5/3 reddish brown, 6/4 light reddish brown interior & 7/6 reddish yellow exterior surfaces; few small inclusions
9	II	VII.7.22	2217	above IIIA floor 1802-1508	5YR 7/4 pink, 7/3 pink exterior surface; many very small limestone inclusions
fig. 3:4 (p. 43)	cf II	68 II.2.77a	11393	in ash on II Floor fragment 7099	5YR 6/1 gray, 7/6 reddish yellow interior and 7/5YR 7/4 pink exterior surfaces; few medium and many small incl
	cf II	II.2.63	11221	Fill 7080 sub IA Surface 7098	10YR 7/4 very pale brown, 7/3 very pale brown int & 8/3 very pale brown ext surfaces; few large and many small incl
10	I	II.1.109	1051/=	Hellenistic House Room 1 occupation	5YR 8/3 pink, 7/4 pink interior & 8/4 pink exterior
	I	II.1.110	/1049	Hellenistic House Room 1 occupation	surfaces; limestone & few ceramic inclusions
11	I	II.1.111	1057	Hellenistic House Room 1 occupation	5YR 8/4 pink, 7/4 pink interior & 10YR 8/4 very pale brown exterior surfaces; few ceramic & limestone incl

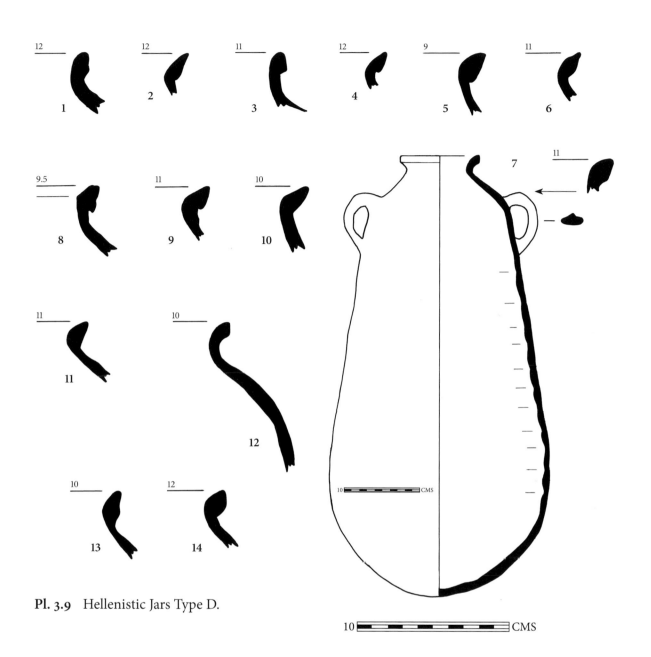

Pl. 3.9 Hellenistic Jars Type D.

Pl. **3.9** Hellenistic Jars Type D (cont.)

Pl	Str	Fld, Ar,Bkt	No.	Locus Description	Ware description
	I	II.1.111	1058	Hellenistic House Room 1 occupation	2.5YR 6/6 light red, 5YR 7/4 pink ext surf; very small incl
3.9:12	I	II.1.116	1071	Hellenistic House Room 1 occupation	2.5YR 6/5 red, 5YR 5/1 gray core, 7/6 reddish yellow int & 10YR 7/4 very pale brown ext surf; many small incl
	I	68 II.1.23	10430	in Fill 7039 above Flagstone 7048	5YR 7/1 light gray, 7/6 reddish yellow interior and 7/5YR 7/4 pink exterior surfaces; few large and some small incl
13	cf I	II.1.33	287	Hellenistic House higher in Room 1	5YR 7/4 pink, 8/4 pink exterior surface; very small limestone and few small ceramic inclusions
14	cf I	II.1.35	376	Hellenistic House higher in Room 1	2.5YR 5/6 light red, 6/6 light red interior & 5YR 7/4 pink exterior surfaces; many very small limestone inclusions

Pl. 3.10   Hellenistic Jars Type D

Pl	Str	Fld, Ar, Bkt	No.	Locus Description	Ware description
D-3. Depressed Collar					
	IIIA	VIII.1.51	855	sub IIIA Floor 1203	10YR 7/1 light gray, 6/2 light brownish gray interior and 7/2 light gray exterior; many small inclusions
3.10:1	IIIA	VII.1.88	2906	sub IIIA Floor 1203	10YR 6/3 pale brown, 7/3 very pale brown surfaces; small ceramic inclusions
2	IIIA	VII.4.37	1828	cleaning IIIB Tannur 1509	5YR 7/8 reddish yellow, 10YR 7/6 reddish yellow surf; large and small inclusions
3	IIIA	VII.7.30	2289/90/ 2291	sub IIIA Floor 1802-1508	10YR 7/4 very pale brown, small organic inclusions
4	IIIA	VII.7.57	3120	sub IIIA Floor 1802-1508	10YR 7/4 very pale brown, 8/4 very pale brown surfaces; small organic inclusions
5	cf III	57 I.6.93	771	pit in Wall B	2.5YR 5/6 red, 5YR 6/4 light reddish brown core, 7/4 pink pink interior and 10YR 7/2 light gray exterior surfaces; ceramic & few large limestone inclusions
6	II	VII.1.18	83	on IIIA Surface 1203	10YR 7/3 very pale brown, similar surface; few small organic inclusions
7	II	VII.4.32a	2453	above IIIA Floor 1227 in Room E	7.5YR 8/4 pink, 8/4 interior and 10YR 7/3 very brown exterior surfaces; small inclusions
	II	VII.4.59	3824	above IIIA Floor 1227 in Room E	10YR 8/2 white, 8/3 very pale brown exterior surface; medium inclusions
	II	VII.4.115	7370	above IIIA Floor 1227 in Room E	5YR 7/4 pink, 7/3 pink interior & 10YR 8/4 very pale brown exterior surfaces; small and medium inclusions
8	II	VII.7.58	3127	above IIIA floor 1802-1508	5YR 7/4 pink, 10YR 7/4 very pale brown surfaces; some limestone inclusions
	II	VII.7.22	2225	above IIIA floor 1802-1508	10YR 7/4 very pale brown, 5YR 7/4 pink int & 8/3 very pale brown ext surfaces; many small & medium incl
9	II	II.1.109	1048	Hellenistic House Room 1 occupation	5YR 5/2 reddish brown, 7/3 pink exterior surface; few large ceramic and many very small limestone inclusions
10	cf II	II.2.68	11284/	Debris 7089 over II Floor 7099	10YR 7/4 very pale brown, 8/4 pink interior & 5YR 8/3
	cf II	II.2.68	/11285/	Debris 7089 over II Floor 7099	very pale brown exterior surfaces; many small ceramic,
	cf II	II.2.77	/11386/	in ash on II Floor fragment 7099	limestone, and few organic inclusions
	cf II	II.2.77	/11391/	in ash on II Floor fragment 7099	
	cf II	II.2.77	/11392	in ash on II Floor fragment 7099	
fig. 3.4 (p. 43)					
11	I	II.1.120	1186	Hellenistic House deeper in Room 1	5YR 6/6 reddish yellow, 8/4 pink exterior & 2.5YR 6/6 light red interior surfaces; many limestone inclusions
12	I	II.1.120	1188	Hellenistic House deeper in Room 1	5YR 6/6 reddish yellow, 8/4 pink exterior & 2.5YR 6/6 light red interior surfaces; few organic & limestone incl
13	cf I	II.1.35	385	Hellenistic House higher in Room 1	5YR 6/3 light reddish brown, 10YR 7/2 light gray int and 7/1 light gray ext surfaces; limestone & few ceramic incl
14	unstr	VII.23.92	763	around VII Wall (?) 23.012	not accessible

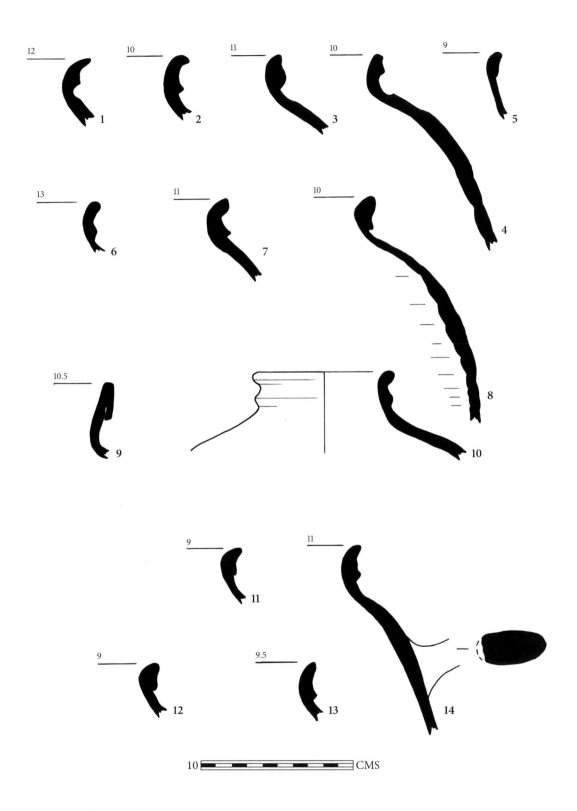

Pl. 3.10 Hellenistic Jars Type D.

Pl. 3.11   Hellenistic Jars Type D

Pl	Str	Fld, Ar,Bkt	No.	Locus Description	Ware description
				Dv. Squared: inner and outer upper Points, usually lower outer Point	
	IIIB	VII.1.55	879	beneath IIIB Floor 1214	5YR 7/4 pink, 10YR 7/3 very light brown exterior surface; many large and some small inclusions
3.11:1	IIIB	VII.1.58	910	fill 1216,1217,1220-1224,1226	7.5YR 7/6 reddish yellow, 10YR 7/3 very pale brown; small ceramic inclusions
2	IIIB	VII.7.75	4018	removal III Wall 1803-1807, 1813	10YR 6/3 pale brown, 7/4 very pale brown surfaces; ceramic & limestone inclusions
3	IIIB	VII.8.79	4593	sub IIIB Cobbling 1719	7.5YR 6/4 light brown, 10YR 7/4 very pale brown surf; thick gray core; organic inclusions
	IIIA	VII.3.116	3797	removal IIIA Wall 1010	10YR 6/1 gray, 7.5YR 6/4 light brown int & 10YR 8/4 very pale brown ext surfaces; many small & few large incl
4	III	57 I.6.12	22	burn above Floor 203	10YR 5/6 yellow, 8/4 very pale brown exterior surfaces; few organic and many smaller ceramic inclusions
5	III	57 I.6.18	101	below Floor 203	5YR 6/4 light reddish brown, 6/2 light brownish gray int and 7/2 light gray ext surfaces; few small ceramic incl
6	cf III	57 I.6.72	641A	pit in Wall B	10YR 6/4 light yellowish brown, 7/4 very pale brown ext and 5 YR 7/4 pink int surfaces; ceramic and large limestone inclusions
7	cf III	57 I.6.82	764	pit in Wall B	5YR 6/4 light reddish brown, 7/4 pink interior & 10YR 8/3 very pale brown exterior surfaces; few organic & large limestone inclusions
8	cf III	57 I.7.8	104	between Floors 202 and 206	2.5YR 6/6 light red, 5YR 7/4 pink int and 10YR 7/2 light gray ext surfaces; ceramic & many small limestone incl
9	II	VII.1.21	98	II occupation Pit 1205-1207	7.5YR 7/5 pink, 10YR 8/4 very pale brown surface; small sand and limestone inclusions
10	cf II	II.2.72	2121	black earth layer West balk	reconstructed storage jar - top 2/3
	I	II.1.120	1183	Hellenistic House deeper in Room 1	5YR 7/3 pink, 8/4 pink int & 10YR 8/3 very pale brown ext surfaces; very small ceramic, few organic and few very small limestone inclusions
	cf I	II.1.32	279	Hellenistic House higher in Room 1	2.5YR 6/8 light red, 7/6 reddish yellow interior & 8/3 pink exterior surfaces; small limestone, few organic, and few large limestone inclusions
11	unstr	57 I.9.19	176/	top of H tower	2.5YR 6/4 light reddish brown, 6/8 light red ext surface;
	unstr	57 I.9.19	/179	top of H tower	very small limestone inclusions
12	unstr	57 I.9.19	175/	top of H tower	10YR 7/4 very pale brown, 8/3 very pale brown ext and
	unstr	57 I.9.7	/46	surface	5YR 8/4 pink int surfaces; ceramic and some large limestone inclusions
13	unstr	III.3.4	425	debris over bin	reconstructed storage jar

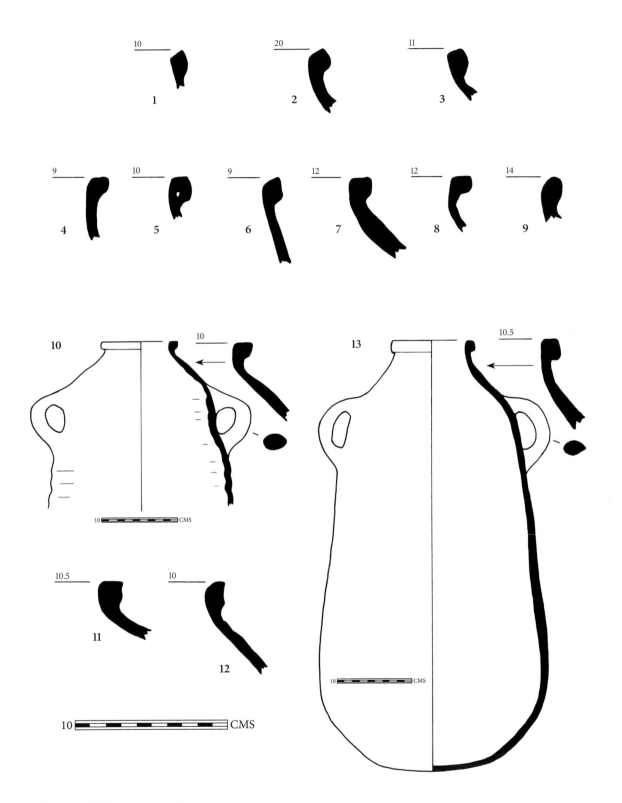

Pl. 3.11 Hellenistic Jars Type D.

Pl. 3.12 Hellenistic Jar Handles

Pl	Str	Fld, Ar,Bkt	No.	Locus Description	Ware description
1 - Rounded to oval Sections					
3.12:1	IVB	VII.6.123	2175	Probe 1311 in brick debris	10YR 7/2 very pale brown, 5YR 6/8 reddish yellow surf; many large & medium limestone & some small organic & ceramic inclusions
	IVB	VII.6.124	2956	Probe 1311 in brick debris	5YR 5/6 yellowish red, 7.5YR N5/ gray core, 5YR 8/4 pink surface; many medium limestone, few small ceramic & crystal, & evidence of tiny organic inclusions
	IVA	VII.3.134b	5612	removal IVA Oven 1024A	2.5YR 6/6 light red, 10YR 7/4 very pale brown exterior surface; many small to large limestone & ceramic incl
2	IVA	VII.3.140	5629	removal IVA Wall 1025-1308	2.5YR 4/0 dark gray, 10YR 6/2 light brownish gray interior & 5YR 7/4 pink exterior surfaces; organic, few large limestone, & many large ceramic inclusions
	IVA	VII.5.135	6395	removal IVA Cobbling 1421 & hardpack north	7.5YR 7/6 reddish yellow, 5YR 6/1 gray core; some medium limestone, organic, & ceramic inclusions
3 fig. 3.5 (p. 44)	IV/III	57 I.5.11	82	layers against Wall B	10YR 8/3 very pale brown, 5YR 8/3 pink interior; large limestone & many ceramic inclusions
	IIIB	VII.1.44	819	beneath IIIB Floor 1214	5YR 8/4 pink, 10YR 8/1 white surface; many small limestone, organic, & ceramic inclusions (greenish ware)
	IIIB	VII.1.45	822	beneath IIIB Floor 1214	2.5YR 6/6 light red, 10YR 6/4 light yellowish brown core, 5YR 8/4 pink surface; few medium limestone, ceramic, & organic inclusions
4	IIIB	VII.1.58	907	Fill 1216,1217,1220-1224,1226	5YR 5/3 reddish brown, 5/1 gray core, 10YR 8/3 very pale brown surface; some large & many small limestone incl
5	IIIB	VII.I.60	964	Fill 1216,1217,1220-1224,1226	2.5YR 6/4 light reddish brown, 10YR 7/2 light gray ext surface; few larger limestone & ceramic inclusions
	IIIB	VII.1.61	5298	Fill 1216,1217,1220-1224,1226	5YR 5/1 gray, 10YR 6/2 light brownish gray interior & 8/4 very pale brown exterior surf; limestone & ceramic incl
	IIIB	VII.1.63	942	Fill 1216,1217,1220-1224,1226	5YR 7/4 pink, 10YR 8/4 very pale brown exterior surface; large limestone & few organic inclusions
	IIIB	VII.3.62	1641	sub IIIB Hardpack 1017-1019	7.5YR 6/4 light brown, 2.5Y N6/ gray, 7.5YR 8/2 pinkish white surface; few medium ceramic & some medium limestone incl
6	IIIB	VII.8.77	4583	sub IIIB Cobbling 1719	10YR 6/1 gray, 5YR 7/4 pink exterior surface; organic & few limestone inclusions
	IIIB	VII.8.78	4588	sub IIIB Cobbling 1719	5YR 5/1 gray, 10YR 7/1 light gray interior and 5YR 7/4 pink exterior surfaces; many small inclusions
	IIIB	VII.8.79	4595	sub IIIB Cobbling 1719	10YR 8/3 very pale brown; ceramic and few limestone incl
	IIIA	VII.3.106	1797	on IIIB Hardpack 1017-1019	5YR 7/3 pink, 7/3 pink exterior surf; very few large & some incl
7	IIIA	VII.4.37	1831	cleaning IIIB Tannur 1509	2.5YR 6/6 light red, 6/4 light reddish brown interior & 10YR 7/2 light gray ext surfaces; ceramic, few organic, & many small limestone inclusions
	IIIA	VII.9.43	3208	removal IIIA 1707-1705-1701-1601	5YR 7/4 pink, 7.5YR 8/2 pinkish white ext surface; few large and many small inclusions

(continued on p. 254)

Pl. 3.12 Hellenistic Jar Handles.

10 ▭▭▭▭ CMS

Pl. 3.12   Hellenistic Jar Handles   (cont.)

Pl	Str	Fld, Ar,Bkt	No.	Locus Description	Ware description
	cf IIIA	VII.1.49	847	removal Mortar 1204 of IIIA occupation	5YR 6/6 reddish yellow, 6/1 gray core; limestone & ceramic inclusions
3.12:8 fig. 3.5 (p. 44)	cf III	57 I.6.84	815	pit in Wall B	7.5YR 6/4 light brown, 10YR 7/4 very pale brown int & 8/4 very pale brown ext surfaces; some large and many small incl
	II	II.1.6	148	Hellenistic House black earth layer Room 1	2.5YR 6/6 light red, 10YR 6/3 pale brown core, 7/3 very pale brown interior, 8/4 very pale brown exterior; limestone and few large limestone, & few ceramic inclusions
	II	VII.2.25	41	above IIIA Floor 1227 in Room E	5YR 6/4 light reddish brown, 7.5YR 6/4 light brown ext surface; small limestone & many small ceramic incl
	II	VII.2.54	1019	removal II Wall 1103	10YR 6/4 light yellowish brown, 8/2 white surface; some small & medium limestone & ceramic inclusions
	I	II.1.117	1084	Room 1 occupation	5YR 6/4 light reddish brown, 7/4 pink interior and 8/4 pink exterior surfaces; some medium inclusions
	unstr	VII.3.25	178	surface fill	5YR 6/4 light reddish brown, 10YR 5/1 gray core, 7/2 light gray surface; many medium & large limestone inclusions
	unstr	57 I.11b.5a	885	huwwar to small stones	10YR 6/1 gray, 8/3 very pale brown ext surface; ceramic & few large limestone inclusions

2 - One End pointed (from Construction)

Pl	Str	Fld, Ar,Bkt	No.	Locus Description	Ware description
9	IVB	VII.5.154	6575	removal IVB Wall 1426	5YR 6/1 gray, 7/6 reddish yellow exterior surface; very few ceramic & limestone inclusions
	IVB	VII.6.123	2171	Probe 1311 in brick debris	7.5YR 6/4 light brown, 10YR 8/4 very pale brown interior & 5YR 7/6 reddish yellow exterior surfaces; many small incl
	IIIB	VII.1.43	806	beneath IIIB Floor 1214	5YR 6/2 pinkish gray, 10Y 7/4 very pale brown exterior surface; ceramic and many limestone inclusions
10	IIIB	VII.1.53	868	beneath IIIB Floor 1214	7.5YR 7/6 reddish yellow, 10YR 8/2 white surface; many small ceramic inclusions
	IIIB	VII.1.56	882	beneath IIIB Floor 1214	5YR 6/4 light reddish brown, 6/1 gray core, 8/3 surf; many medium limestone & evidence of many medium organic incl
11	IIIA	VII.1.52	864	on IIIB Floor 1214 sub Floor 1203	10YR 7/4 very pale brown, 8/2 white surface; sand, few small organic & ceramic, & few medium limestone incl
	unstr	VII.3.19	156	surface fill	5YR 6/6 reddish yellow, 10YR 6/1 gray core, 8/2 white surface; few crystalline, ceramic & limestone inclusions
	unstr	I.11b.5a	890	huwwar to small stones	10YR 7/3 very pale brown, 8/2 white exterior surf; many ceramic & few large limestone inclusions

3 - Central Ridge

Pl	Str	Fld, Ar,Bkt	No.	Locus Description	Ware description
12	IVA	VII.7.110	5840A	removal IVA Cobbling 1824	5YR 8/4 pink, 7/5YR N5/ gray core, 10YR 8/2 white surf; many small limestone & few small ceramic & evidence of few tiny organic inclusions
13	IV/III	I.7.23	136	lower H Floors 205 & 206	5YR 7/4 pink, 6/1 gray core, 8/4 pink interior & 10YR 8/4 very pale brown ext surfaces; organic & very small limestone incl
14	IIIB	VII.4.106	5523	cleaning IV Press 1525	10YR 7/4 very pale brown, 8/2 white surface; few medium limestone & evidence of many tiny organic inclusions

Pl. 3.12   Hellenistic Jar Handles   (cont.)

Pl	Str	Fld, Ar,Bkt	No.	Locus Description	Ware description
	IIIB	VII.8.93	5109	sub IIIB Cobbling 1719	2.5YR 6/8 light red, 10YR 8/1 white surface; some small limestone, organic & sand & evidence of tiny organic incl
	IIIA	VII.1.41	794	sub IIIA Floor 1203	2.5YR 6/6 light red, 7/5YR 8/2 pinkish white surf; many small limestone & sand inclusions
	IIIA	VII.4.39	1834	sub IIIA Floor 1227-1511	2.5YR 6/6 light red, 6/4 light reddish brown exterior; many very small inclusions
3.12:15	IIIA	VII.7.30	2287	sub IIIA Floor 1802-1508	5YR 5/1 gray, 10YR 7/1 light gray surfaces with patches of 2.5YR 6/4 light reddish brown, 6/6 light red int and 5YR 6/4 light reddish brown ext surfaces; few organic & many small limestone incl
16	IIIA	VII.7.66	3995	removal IIIA Wall 1806	5YR 8/4 pink; organic & few limestone & ceramic incl
	I	II.1.109	1046	Hellenistic House Room 1 occupation	10YR 7/3 very pale brown, 7/4 very pale brown interior and 8/3 very pale brown exterior surfaces; some small incl
17	I	II.1.116	1072	Hellenistic House Room 1 occupation	5YR 6/4 light reddish brown, 7/6 reddish yellow int and 8/4 pink ext surfaces; few limestone & ceramic incl
	I	II.1.124	1192	Hellenistic House deeper in Room 1	5YR 6/6 reddish yellow, 10YR 7/3 very pale brown interior and 5YR 8/4 pink exterior surfaces; many small inclusions
	unstr	VII.7.53	3176	surface fill	10YR 7/4 very pale brown & 2/5YR 6/6 light red, 5YR 8/4 pink surface; some small crystalline & ceramic & many small limestone inclusions

4 - Carelessly made

Pl	Str	Fld, Ar,Bkt	No.	Locus Description	Ware description
	IIIB	VII.1.44	817	beneath IIIB Floor 1214	not accessible
	IIIB	VII.1.59	922	Fill 1216,1217,1220-1224,1226	7.5YR 6/4 light brown, 10YR 6/1 gray core, 10YR 8/3 very pale brown surface; many small/medium limestone incl
	IIIA	VII.1.41	797	sub IIIA Floor 1203	not accessible
18	II	VII.2.54	1022	removal II Wall 1103	10YR 7/4 very pale brown, 8/2 white surface; few medium limestone & some sand, organic, & ceramic inclusions
19	II	VII.4.27	1821	above IIIA Floor 1227 in Room E	10YR 7/4 very pale brown, 8/2 white surface; some small medium limestone & few small ceramic & crystalline incl
	II	VII.1.30	748	above IIIA Floor 1227 in Room E	10YR 7/2 light gray, 5YR 8/4 pink interior and 7/2 pinkish gray exterior surfaces; many small inclusions
20 fig. 3.5 (p. 44)	II	II.1.37	293	black earth layer North Balk	5YR 6/3 light reddish brown, 8/4 pink interior & 7.5YR 7/4 pink exterior; many organic & few ceramic inclusions
21 fig. 3.5	II	II.1.37	294	black earth layer North Balk	5YR 8/4 pink, 10YR 8/4 very pale brown exterior surface; very small ceramic inclusions
	I	II.1.120	1184	Hellenistic House deeper in Room 1	7.5YR 6/4 light brown, 6/4 light brown interior & 10YR 8/4 very pale brown exterior surfaces; few medium and some small inclusions
	unstr	I.7b.31	172	surface to west	7.5YR 6/4 light brown, 10YR 8/2 white ext surface, with patches of 7/4 very pale brown; few ceramic & organic incl

Pl. 3.13   Hellenistic Jar Bases

Pl	Str	Fld, Ar,Bkt	No.	Locus Description	Ware description
Rounded spiral Base					
	IVB	VII.7.103	5251	around V Tannur 1828	5YR 6/8 reddish yellow, 7/1 light gray core; small limestone inclusions
3.13:1	IIIB	VII.8.80	4597	sub IIIB Cobbling 1719	5YR 7/6 reddish yellow; small limestone inclusions
2	IIIA	VII.1.41	799	sub IIIA floor 1203	10YR 7/4 very pale brown, 8/2 white surface; few small limestone & evidence of few small organic inclusions
3	cf IIIA	VII.3.51	1583	L. 1009 around IIIA Drain 1015-16	7.5YR 5/4 brown, large gray core, 8/2 pinkish white surface; few very small crystal & limestone inclusions
	cf IIIA	VII.4.84	4986	Pit 1514	10YR 7/2 light gray, 8/3 very pale brown exterior surface; many small inclusions
4	cf III	57 I.6.82	2103	pit in Wall B	not accessible
5	III/II	III.4.9A	2122	pit between walls B & 606	reconstructed; and body
6	III/II	III.4.9G	2113	pit between walls B & 606	reconstructed
7	III/II	III.4.9H	2128	pit between walls B & 606	reconstructed
8	III/II	III.4.12	2127	pit between walls B & 606	reconstructed; and body
9	II	VII.7.55	3117A	Pit 1820 of IIIA Floor 1801 with jar	reconstructed; and body
10	II	II.1.50	1747	black earth layer North Balk	5YR 6/8 reddish yellow; limestone & ceramic inclusions
11	II	II.1.50	1748	black earth layer North Balk	7.5YR 7/4 pink; many ceramic & limestone inclusions
12	cf II	68 II.2.77	11,368=	in ash on II Floor fragment 7099	7.5YR 6/4 light brown; many ceramic, limestone, &
	cf II	68 II.2.68	11,291	Debris 7089 over II Floor 7099	organic inclusions
	unstr	VII.3.19	151	surface fill	7.5YR 8/6 reddish yellow, 8/4 pink surface; some very small limestone inclusions

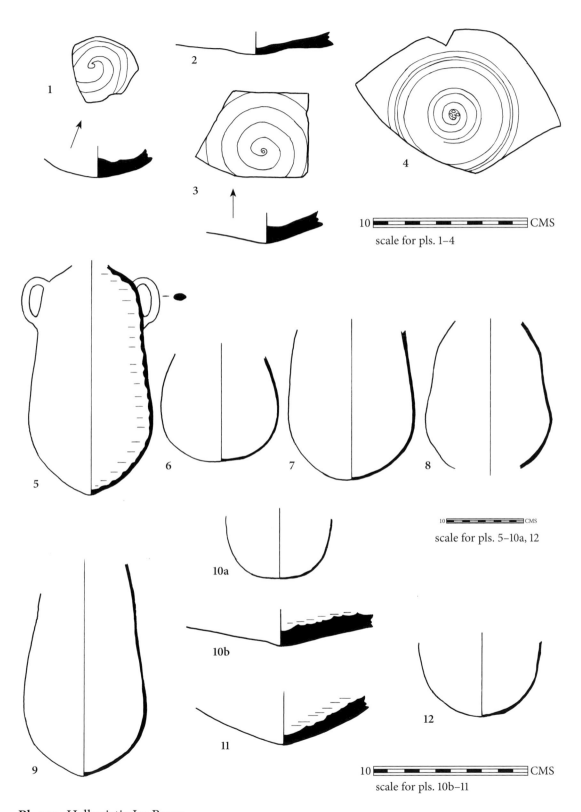

Pl. 3.13 Hellenistic Jar Bases.

Pl. 3.14 Hellenistic Jars: Rhodian Fragments

Pl	Str	Fld, Ar,Bkt	No.	Locus Description	Ware description
3.14:1	IIIB	VII.1.92	2927	beneath IIIB Floor 1214	2.5YR 5/8 red, 7.5YR 7/6 reddish yellow surface; evidence of few tiny organic inclusions
2	IIIB	VII.8.85	4614	sub IIIB cobbling 1719	2.5YR 4/6 red, 5YR 7/4 pink surface; some medium limestone & evidence of some tiny organic inclusions
3	cf II	VII.2.27b	294	around & on II Wall 1103	not accessible
4 fig. 3.6 (p. 46)	cf II	II.2.69	1222	black earth layer Area 2	5YR 76 reddish yellow, 7.5YR 8/2 pinkish white surface; perhaps evidence of few tiny organic inclusions
5 fig. 3.6	cf II	II.2.41	198 #167	black earth layer Area 2	inscribed; to Department of Antiquities
6	I	II.1.111	1059	Hellenistic House Room 1 occupation	5YR 7/6 reddish yellow, 7/4 pink surface; perhaps evidence of tiny organic inclusions
7	unstr	62 VII.1.77	898	balk cleaning	5YR 7/6 reddish yellow, 7/4 pink surface
8	unstr	VII.21.10	75	surface	5YR 7/6 reddish yellow, 7/4 pink surface
9 fig. 3.6	unstr	68 II.2	#1	balk cleaning	not accessible; see Richardson 1957:4
fig. 3.6		64 I.11.231	#513		illegible inscription; to Department of Antiquities

Pl. 3.14 Hellenistic Jars: Rhodian Fragments.

Pl. 3.15   Hellenistic Jugs Types a and b

Pl	Str	Fld, Ar, Bkt	No.	Locus Description	Ware description
a. Plain Rim, narrow-necked					
3.15:1	IVB	VII.2.130	6904	removal IVB Wall 1415-1117	10YR 5/1 gray, 10YR 8/2 white surface; many organic and sand and few limestone inclusions
2	IVB	IX.1.48	97	grayish rubbly Fill 9024	10YR 5/1 gray, 5YR 8/3 pink surf; many limestone & organic incl
	IVA	IX.3.52	84	probable Surface 9517B	7.5YR 6/8 reddish yellow, gray core, 7.5YR 8/4 pink surface; many limestone inclusions
	IIIB	VII.1.43	810	beneath IIIB Floor 1214	5YR 6/6 reddish yellow, 7.5YR 8/4 pink surf; limestone incl
3	IIIB	VII.8.81	4601	sub IIIB Cobbling 1719	2.5YR 6/8 light red, 5YR 8/4 pink surface; very few limestone & organic inclusions
4	cf III	I.6.55	458	pit in Wall B	5YR 7/5 reddish yellow, 7/4 pink surfaces; many small limestone & ceramic inclusions
b. Rounded Rim with Undercut					
5	IVB	62 VII.1.29	263	on IVB metalled Surface 1530-1232	large fragment; not accessible
6	IVB	VII.7.114	5850	removal stones for IVB Jar Stand 1818	5YR 7/1 light gray, 7.5YR 8/2 pinkish white surface; few limestone and organic inclusions
7	IVB	VII.9.48	4040	Fill 1609-10,1612-15 in brick debris	10YR 6/1 gray, 10YR 7/1 light gray surface; many limestone and organic inclusions
8	IVB	VII.9.67	4106	Fill 1609-10,1612-15 in brick debris	7.5YR 7/4 pink, 8/4 pink surface; sand inclusions
9	IVA	62 VII.21.82	608	sub IVA Floor 21.011	5YR 7/8 reddish yellow inner core, 10YR 6/1 gray outer core, 5YR 8/2 pinkish white surface; many organic incl
10	IVA	62 VII.23.56	482	sub IVA Floor 23.008	7.5YR 7/4 pink, 10YR 8/2 white surface; some limestone and organic inclusions
11	IVA	IX.1.35	67	soil Layer 9018, sub L. 9016	5YR 7/6 reddish yellow, 5YR 8/4 pink surface; very many limestone & many organic inclusions
	IVA	IX.1.39	89	L. 9019 compact gray, sub 9018	10YR 8/6 yellow, 8/2 white surface; limestone inclusions
	IV	I.7b.56	341	in lower IV Floor 205	5YR 6/2 pinkish gray, 7/1 light gray surfaces; many organic, sand, & limestone inclusions
12	IIIB	VII.1.44	821	beneath IIIB Floor 1214	2.5YR 6/8 light red, 5YR 8/4 pink; very few organic incl
	IIIB	VII.1.45	827	beneath IIIB Floor 1214	5YR 7/6 reddish yellow; ceramic & limestone inclusions
	IIIB	VII.1.57	892	Fill 1216,1217,1220-1224,1226	10YR 7/4 very pale brown, 7/6 reddish yellow surface; limestone & sand inclusions
13	IIIB	VII.8.86	4619	sub IIIB Cobbling 1719	10YR 6/2 light brownish gray, 8/2 white surfaces; small ceramic incl
14	cf IIIB	62 VII.22.40	235	sub possible IIIB Floor 22.002	7.5YR 8/2 pinkish white, 7.5YR 8/2 pinkish white surface
	cf IIIB	62 VII.22.42	342	sub possible IIIB Floor 22.002	5YR 7/4 pink, 10YR 8/4 very pale brown surface; sand, ceramic & limestone inclusions
	IIIA	VII.1.35	764	removal IIIA Buttress 1110-1211	7/5YR 8/6 reddish yellow, gray core, 7/5YR 8/2 pinkish white surface; limestone & sand inclusions
	IIIA	VII.3.63a	1649	removal IIIA Wall 1008-21.007	7.5 YR 7/2 pinkish gray, large gray core, 7.5YR 8/2 pinkish white surface; limestone & sand inclusions

(continued on p. 263)

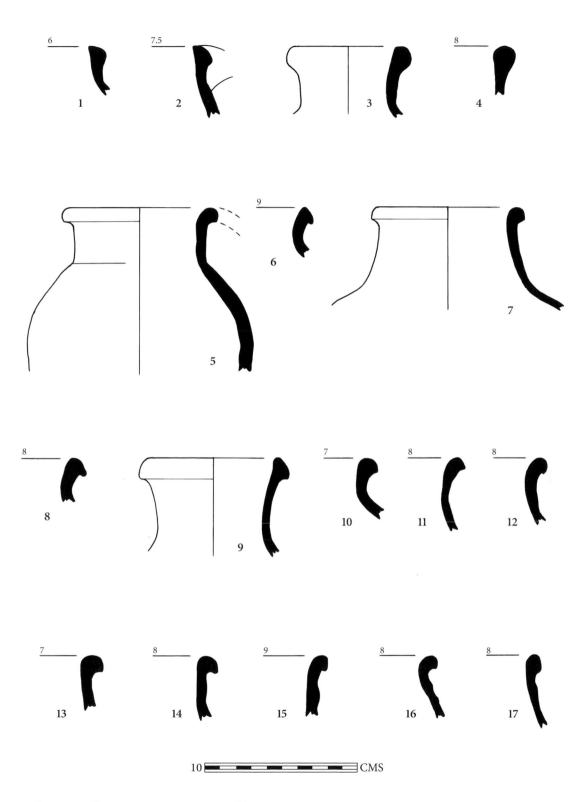

Pl. 3.15 Hellenistic Jugs Types a and b.

Pl. 3.15   Hellenistic Jugs Types a and b   (cont.)

Pl	Str	Fld, Ar,Bkt	No.	Locus Description	Ware description
15	IIIA	VII.6.72	1949	sub IIIA Cobbling 1306 and 1307	5YR 7/8 reddish yellow, 7.5YR 8/4 pink surface; very few limestone inclusions
16	IIIA	VII.7.60	3135	sub IIIA Floor 1802-1508	5YR 7/6 reddish yellow, 5YR 8/3 pink surf; very few sand incl
	cf IIIA	VII.4.100	5377	Pit 1514	10YR 7/3 very pale brown, 10YR 8/2 white surface; limestone & sand inclusions
	cf III	I.9.9	126	striated makeup over Wall A	5YR 7/6 reddish yellow, 7/8 reddish yellow int surf; many large limestone & few large ceramic incl & organic incl
	IIIA/II	II.1.105	925	below 160 cm. in Room 2	5YR 6/1 light gray, 7/1 light gray interior, 7/4 pink exterior; many ceramic & organic inclusions
17	II	VII.2.27a	291	above IIIA Floor 1227 in Room E	7.5YR 8/2 pinkish white, 10YR 8/2 white surface; very few organic inclusions
	II	VII.2.53	1038	removal II Wall 1103	10YR 7/4 very pale brown, 8/3 very pale brown surface; limestone & sand inclusions

Pl. 3.16 Hellenistic Jugs Type c

Pl	Str	Fld, Ar,Bkt	No.	Locus Description	Ware description
c. Rounded Rim					
3.16:1	IVA	IX.1.35	66	soil Layer 9018, sub L. 9016	10YR 7/2 light gray, 10YR 8/2 white surf; some organic incl
2	cf IV	62 VII.23.50	474	above IV Floor 23.005	10YR 8/6 yellow, 10YR 8/4 very pale brown surface; few organic & limestone inclusions
3	IV/III	I.5.10	83	layers against Wall B	5YR 7/3 pink, 8/4 pink ext. surface, 7/1 light gray int. surface; few ceramic & limestone inclusions
	IIIB	VII.1.60	971	Fill 1216,1217,1220-1224,1226	7.5YR 7/4 pink; sand inclusions
	cf IIIB	62 VII.22.42	325	sub possible IIIB Floor 22.002	5YR 6/6 reddish yellow, large gray core, 5YR 8/4 pink surface; sand & limestone inclusions
4	cf IIIB	62 VII.22.45	333	sub possible IIIB Floor 22.002	10YR 7/4 very pale brown, large gray core, 10YR 8/4 pink surface; sand & limestone inclusions
5	IIIA	VII.3.63b	1652	removal IIIA Wall 1007	7.5 YR 6/4 light brown, 5YR 7/4 pink surface; very few organic inclusions
6	IIIA	VII.4.62	3828	removal IIIA Walls 1505-1510	7.5YR 7/4 pink, 10YR 8/3 very pale brown surface; very few organic inclusions
7	IIIA	VII.5.86	3980	removal IIIA Wall 1408	7.5YR 5/4 brown, 10YR 7/4 very pale brown; many limestone & organic inclusions
8	IIIA	VII.5.88	5229	removal IIIA Wall 1408	10YR 7/4 very pale brown, 10YR 7/3 very pale brown surface; many limestone and organic inclusions
9	IIIA	VII.7.57	3126	sub IIIA Floor 1802-1508	7.5YR 7/2 pinkish gray, 7.5YR 7/2 pinkish gray surface; ceramic inclusions
10	IIIA	62 VII.21.64	506	Debris 21.035 sub IIIA walls & Floor 21.031	7.5YR 7/7 light gray, 8/4 pink surface; some large limestone inclusions
11	cf IIIA	VII.1.22	95	removal Mortar 1204 of IIIA occupation	7.5 YR 7/4 pink, 10YR 8/2 white surface; many organic inclusions
12	cf IIIA	VII.3.29	191	L. 1009 around IIIA Drain 1015-16	10YR 5/1 gray, 10YR 7/3 very pale brown surface; some limestone & organic inclusions
	cf IIIA	VII.3.43	1542	L. 1009 around IIIA Drain 1015-16	7.5YR 6/4 light brown, 8/4 pink surf; limestone & sand incl
	cf IIIA	VII.3.46	1551	L. 1009 around IIIA Drain 1015-16	10YR 7/4 very pale brown, 10YR 7/2 light gray surface; sand inclusions
	cf IIIA	62 VII.5.57	687	Pit 1477	10YR 8/2 white; some organic, ceramic, & limestone incl
	III	I.7b.55	323	above Lower Burn 204	5YR 5/1 gray, 6/6/ reddish yellow surfaces; many large limestone & few large organic inclusions
13	cf III	I.6.93	772	pit in Wall B	5YR 7/4 pink, 7/2 pinkish gray surfaces; few limestone and organic inclusions
14	II	II.1.56	593	black earth layer North Balk	5YR 7/6 reddish yellow, 7/3 pink interior and 8/3 pink exterior surfaces; many large ceramic and organic and few large limestone inclusions
15	cf II	VII.2.26	286	around & on II Wall 1103	10YR 7/2 light gray, 2.5Y 8/2 white surface; many limestone & organic inclusions

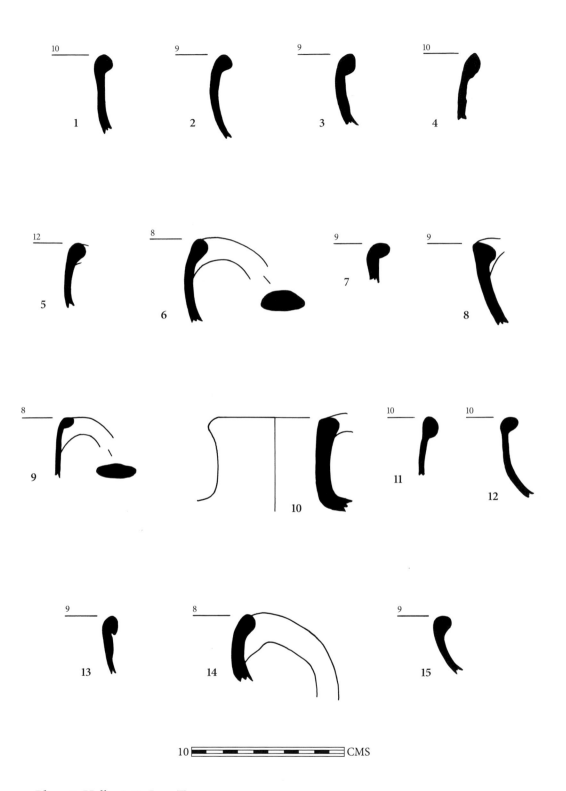

Pl. 3.16 Hellenistic Jugs Type c.

Pl. 3.17   Hellenistic Jugs Types d and e

PL	STR	FLD, AR,BKT	No.	LOCUS DESCRIPTION	WARE DESCRIPTION
d. Out-turned Rim, usually to outer Point					
	IIIB	VII.4.86	4997	on IV Floor 1523	7.5YR 7/4 pink, 8/4 pink surface; limestone inclusions
3.17:1	IIIB	VII.7.79	4028	removal III Wall 1803-1807, 1813	10YR 8/3 very pale brown, similar surface; very few organic inclusions
2	IIIA	VII.1.40	775	sub IIIA Floor 1203	7.5YR 7/6 reddish yellow, 10YR 8/4 very pale brown surface; many organic & limestone inclusions
3	IIIA	VII.1.52	862	on IIIB Floor 1214 sub Floor 1203	10YR 7/2 light gray, 10YR 8/4 very pale brown surface; very few organic inclusions
4	IIIA	VII.5.86	3981	removal IIIA Wall 1408	5YR 7/8 reddish yellow, 5YR 8/3 pink surface; few organic inclusions
5	IIIA	VII.5.88	5228	removal IIIA Wall 1408	7.5 YR 8/2 pinkish white, 10YR 8/3 very pale brown surface; very few organic inclusions
6	IIIA	VII.7.25	2244/47/	sub IIIA Floor 1801	5YR 7/4 pink, 7.5YR 8/2 pinkish white surf; some incl
	IIIA	VII.7.26	2244/47/	sub IIIA Floor 1802	5YR 7/4 pink, 7.5YR 8/2 pinkish white surf; some incl
	IIIA	62 VII.21.44	313	removal IIIA Wall 21.006	10YR 7/3 very pale brown, 8/2 white surface; with few limestone inclusions
	cf III	I.6.59	464	pit in Wall B	5YR 6/6 reddish yellow, 6/1 gray interior & 6/4 pink ext; organic, many small limestone, few sand & ceramic incl
7	cf III	I.6.84	817	pit in Wall B	10YR 8/3 very plate brown, 8/2 white ext. surface, 7/2 light gray int. surface; few large limestone inclusions
	IIIA /II	68 II.1.18	10376	in Foundation Trench 7036	5YR 7/6 reddish yellow, 7/4 pink surfaces; few small ceramic inclusions
8	II	VII.1.30	753	above IIIA Floor 1227 in Room E	5YR 7/4 pink, 5YR 8/4 pink surface; very few sand and organic inclusions
9	II	VII.1.81	2888	II occupation Pit 1205-1207	5YR 7/2 pinkish gray, 7.5YR 8/4 pink surface; very few organic and limestone inclusions
	II	VII.1.87	2896	on IIIA Surface 1203	7.5YR 6/4 light brown, 7/5 pink surface; limestone incl
10	II	VII.7.58	3131	above IIIA Floor 1802-1508	7.5YR 7/4 pink, 5YR 7/6 reddish yellow surface; sand incl
11	II	II.1.56	595	black earth layer North Balk	5YR 6/4 light reddish brown, 7/4 pink int & 2.5YR 5/6 light red interior surfaces; organic & small limestone incl
	II	68 II.2.78	11405	Make-up 7100 for II Floor 7099	5YR 6/6 reddish yellow, 7/4 pink interior, 7/6 reddish yellow ext surfaces; many large & small limestone incl
12	cf I	II.1.34	372	Hellenistic House higher in Room 1	5YR 6/2 pinkish gray, 6/3 light reddish brown int & 7/2 pinkish gray exterior surfaces; few large limestone incl
13	unstr	62 VII.22.57	520	unstratified	large fragment; not accessible
e. Ridged Neck					
3.17:14	IIIB	VII.1.43	805	beneath IIIB Floor 1214	7.5YR 8/2 pinkish white, 10YR 8/2 white surface; some organic inclusions
15	IIIB	VII.1.91	2926	beneath IIIB Floor 1214	10YR 8/4 very pale brown, 7.5YR 8/2 pinkish white surface; few sand & limestone inclusions

(continued on p. 269)

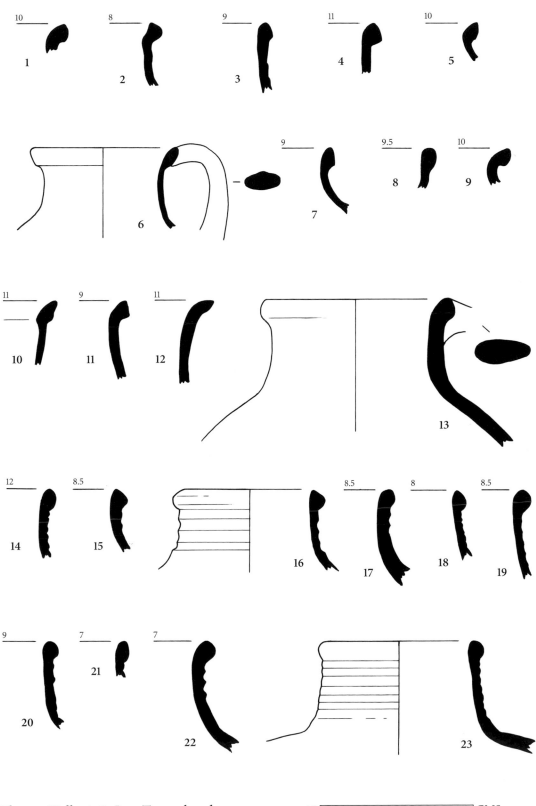

Pl. 3.17 Hellenistic Jugs Types d and e.

10 CMS

Pl. 3.17 Hellenistic Jugs Types d and e (cont.)

Pl	Str	Fld, Ar,Bkt	No.	Locus Description	Ware description
3.17:16 fig. 3.7 (p. 48)	IIIB	VII.4.106	5521	cleaning IV Press 1525	5YR 7/6 reddish yellow, 10YR 8/2 white surface; few sand & limestone inclusions
17	cf IIIB	62 VII.4.132	1529	unsealed in Pit 1522	5YR 7/6 reddish yellow, 7.5YR 8/4 pink surface; many inclusions
18	IIIA	VII.1.89	2915	on IIIB Floor 1214 sub Floor 1203	10YR 8/4 very pale brown, 10YR 8/3 very pale brown surface
	cf IIIA	VII.2.44	992	on unrelated IIIB Surface 1106	5YR 6/6 reddish yellow, 6/3 light reddish interior & 8/2 pinkish white exterior surfaces; small limestone & very many small organic inclusions
19	cf IIIA	VII.4.101	5383	Pit 1514	10YR 8/3 very pale brown, 10YR 8/3 very pale surface; few sand & organic inclusions
20	II	VII.1.32	755	II occupation Pit 1205-1207	10YR 8/2 white, 10YR 8/3 very pale brown surface; few sand & organic inclusions
21	II	VII.1.101	3748	above IIIA Floor 1227 in Room E	7.5YR 7/2 pinkish gray, 7.5YR 8/2 pinkish white surface
22 fig. 3.7	II	II.1.15	157	Hellenistic House black earth layer Room 1	5YR 7/1 pink, 7/3 pink exterior surface; few small ceramic inclusions
	I	II.1.124	1198	deeper in Room 1	5YR 7/6 reddish yellow, 8/4 pink interior & 8/3 pink exterior surfaces; many small limestone inclusions
23 fig. 3.7	unstr	VII.7.149 VII.7.151	7377/ /7381	probe trench unstratified	10YR 7/3 very pale brown, 8/2 white surface; sand incl 10YR 7/3 very pale brown, 8/3 very pale brown surface; limestone & sand inclusions
	unstr	VII.23.87	753	unstratified	5YR 7/6 reddish yellow, 8/4 pink surface; limestone incl

Pl. 3.18   Hellenistic Jugs Type f

Pl	Str	Fld, Ar,Bkt	No.	Locus Description	Ware description
f. Squared Rim					
3.18:1	IIIB	VII.1.57	897	Fill 1216,1217,1220-1224,1226	5YR 8/4 pink, 7.5YR 8/2 pinkish white surface; very few organic inclusions
	IIIB	VII.4.86	4996	on IV Floor 1523	5YR 7/6 reddish yellow, 8/4 pink surface; sand & limestone inclusions
2	IIIA	VII.1.51	853	sub IIIA Floor 1203	10YR 7/4 very pale brown, 10YR 8/3 very pale brown surface; very few organic & limestone inclusions
3	IIIA	VII.3.61a	1632	removal IIIA Wall 1007	10YR 6/2 light brownish gray, 5YR 8/4 pink surface; some limestone inclusions
4	IIIA	VII.7.25	2253	sub IIIA Floor 1801	7.5YR 8/6 reddish yellow, 7.5YR 7/4 pink surface; some sand inclusions
5	IIIA	VII.7.30	2288	sub IIIA Floor 1802-1508	10YR 8/6 yellow, 10YR 8/2 white surface; very few sand inclusions
6	cf IIIA	VII.1.22	94	removal Mortar 1204 of IIIA occupation	5YR 7/6 reddish yellow, 7.5YR 8/4 pink; very few organic inclusions
7	cf IIIA	VII.4.100	5378	Pit 1514	10YR 8/4 very pale brown, 7.5YR 8/4 pink surface; few organic inclusions
8	III	I.6.11	62	burn above Floor 203	5YR 6/6/ reddish yellow, 8/3 pink ext. surface, 7/4 pink int. surface; 7/2 pinkish gray int. handle; many small limestone & organic inclusions
9	II	VII.1.21	106	II occupation Pit 1205-1207	7.5 YR 7/6 reddish yellow, 5 YR 8/4 pink surface; very few organic inclusions
10	cf II	VII.4.49	2937	above & on Hardpack 1500-1400-1300	5YR 7/6 reddish yellow, 5YR 7/4 pink surface; many organic & limestone inclusions
	I	II.1.116	1073	Hellenistic House Room 1 occupation	5YR 6/4 light reddish brown, 7/6 reddish yellow surfaces; many small limestone & few organic inclusions
11	unstr	62 VII.23.91	757	unstratified	large fragment; not accessible

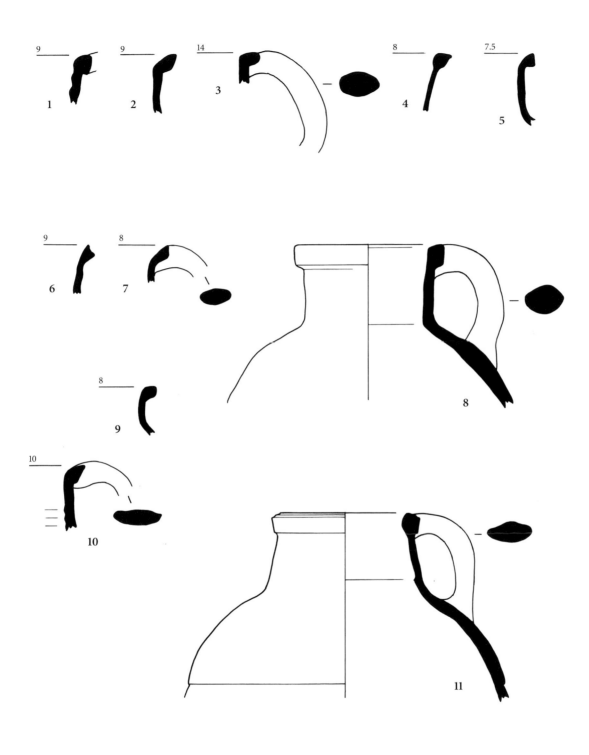

Pl. 3.18 Hellenistic Jugs Type f.

 CMS

Pl. 3.19   Hellenistic Jugs Type g

Pl	Str	Fld, Ar,Bkt	No.	Locus Description	Ware description
	IVA	VII.7.112	5846	removal IVA Floor 1826	5YR 8/4 pink, 7.5YR 8/6 reddish yellow surface; few organic & very few crystalline inclusions
3.19:1	IIIA	VII.1.89	2913	on IIIB Floor 1214 sub Floor 1203	10YR 7/4 very pale brown, 10YR 8/2 white surface; very few organic & limestone inclusions
2	IIIA	VII.7.30	2292	sub IIIA Floor 1802-1508	10YR 7/3 very pale brown, 10 YR 4/2 dark grayish brown surface; few sand, limestone, & organic incl
	cf IIIA	VII.4.85	4992	Pit 1514	7.5YR 8/6 reddish yellow, 8/4 pink surface
3 fig. 3.8 (p. 49)	cf IIIA	62 VII.23.93	883	Pit 23.017 near column base	5YR 8/3 pink, 8/3 pink surfaces; few large organic and limestone inclusions
	IIIA /II	II.1.98	933	140–160 cm below Wall 7013	5YR 7/3 pink, 8/3 pink exterior surface; few large limestone and organic inclusions
4	II	VII.7.46	3165	above IIIA Floor 1802-1508	10YR 7/4 very pale brown, 10YR 7/3 very pale brown surface; very few organic & limestone inclusions
	II	II.1.15	156	Hellenistic House black earth layer Room 1	5YR 7/2 pinkish gray, 8/3 pink interior & 7/3 pink exterior surfaces; many limestone inclusions
	cf II	68 II.2.68	11290	Debris 7089 over II Floor 7099	5YR 7/6 reddish yellow, 7/6 reddish surfaces; many small limestone inclusions
	cf II	68 II.2.68	11289/ 11293	Debris 7089 over II Floor 7099	5YR 5/4 reddish brown, 6/4 light reddish brown surfaces; many small limestone inclusions
5	cf II	II.2.73	1229	black earth Area 2	5YR 6/1 gray, 8/2 pinkish white surfaces; many small limestone & few organic inclusions
6	I	II.1.111 II.1.112	1060= 1061	Hellenistic House Room 1 occupation Hellenistic House Room 1 occupation	5YR 5/4 reddish brown, 8/3 pink interior & 7/4 pink exterior surfaces; many limestone & organic inclusions
	I	68 II.1.12	10297	in Fill 7025 for str. I surface	5YR 7/4 pink, 7/3 pink interior surface; few small limestone inclusions
7	unstr	III.3.10	232	surface	2.5YR 5/0 gray to 6/6 light red closer to neck, 5YR 7/4 pink interior & 7/3 pink exterior surfaces; few large organic, few very small ceramic, and many very small limestone inclusions; complete rim

g. Rim Ledge for Lid

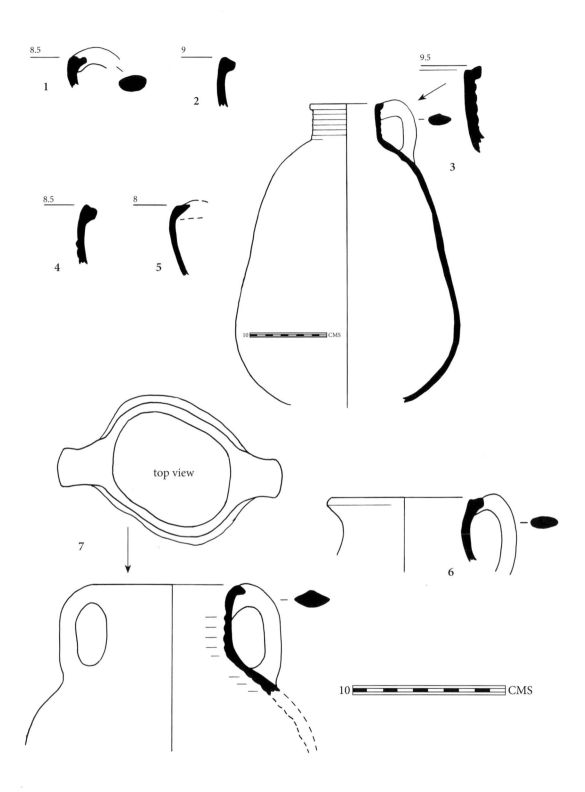

Pl. 3.19 Hellenistic Jugs Type g.

Pl. 3.20   Hellenistic Jug Bases

Pl	Str	Fld, Ar,Bkt	No.	Locus Description	Ware description
Concave Base					
3.20:1	IVA	VII.3.136	5615	removal IVA Oven 1024A	7.5YR 7/2 pinkish gray, 7.5YR 8/2 pinkish white surface; few large organic & limestone inclusions
2 fig. 3.9 (p. 50)	IIIB	VII.1.66	961	Fill 1216,1217,1220-1224,1226	10YR 8/2 white, 10YR 8/2 white surface; some limestone & organic inclusions
3	IIIB	VII.4.78	4964	removal III Wall 1506	2.5YR 6/4 light reddish brown, 7.5YR 8/2 pinkish white surface; very few limestone inclusions
4	IIIA	VII.8.41	2800	removal IIIA 1707-1705-1701-1601	2.5YR 4/8 red, 2.5YR 6/6 light red; many limestone inclusions
5 fig. 3.9	cf IIIA	VII.1.49	844	removal Mortar 1204 of IIIA occupation	5YR 8/1 white, 7.5YR 8/2 pinkish white surface
6	cf IIIA	VII.4.100,101	5379/ /5382	Pit 1514	5YR 7/6 reddish yellow, 5YR 8/4 pink surface; some limestone & organic inclusions
7	cf IIIA	62 VII.23.93	1068	Pit 23.017 near column base	not accessible
8	II	VII.1.87	2892	on IIIA floor 1203	2.5YR 6/6 light red, 5YR 8/4 pink surface; some organic inclusions
	unstr	VII.1.109	5240	surface fill	7.5YR 8/6 reddish yellow, 5YR 8/4 pink surface; sand inclusions
9	unstr	VII.7.149	7374	probe trench	5YR 7/6 reddish yellow; sand inclusions
Angular concave Base					
10	IIIA	VII.1.51	856	sub IIIA Floor 1203	10YR 7/4 very pale brown, 7.5YR 8/4 pink surface; very few organic inclusions
11	II	VII.1.29	746	on IIIA Surface 1203	5YR 7/6 reddish yellow, 5YR 8/4 pink surface; few organic inclusions
12 fig. 3.9	II	VII.1.23	110	above IIIA Floor 1227 in Room E	7.5YR 8/6 reddish yellow, 7.5YR 8/2 pinkish white surface; few organic inclusions
13	I	II.1.111	1054	Hellenistic House Room 1 occupation	5YR 6/6 reddish yellow, 8/4 pink interior & 8/4 pink exterior; few large limestone & few small ceramic incl.
14	I	II.1.117	1083	Hellenistic House Room 1 occupation	5YR 6/1 gray core, 6/6 reddish yellow interior and 7/5 pink exterior; few limestone & few small organic incl
Ring Base					
	IVA	IX.3.58	124	pottery from IVA Wall 9514	5YR 6/1 gray, 7.5YR 8/4 pink surface; limestone & sand inclusions
15	IIIB	VII.1.55	875	beneath IIIB Floor 1214	10YR 7/3 very pale brown, 10YR 8/3 very pale brown surface; some limestone & sand inclusions
	IIIB	VII.8.47	3507	sub IIIB Cobbling 1719	not accessible
16	III/II	III.4.15A	2102	pit between walls B & 606	not accessible
	II	VII.7.22	2221	above IIIA Floor 1802-1508	5YR 8/4 pink, 7.5YR 7/4 pink surface; very few organic inclusions

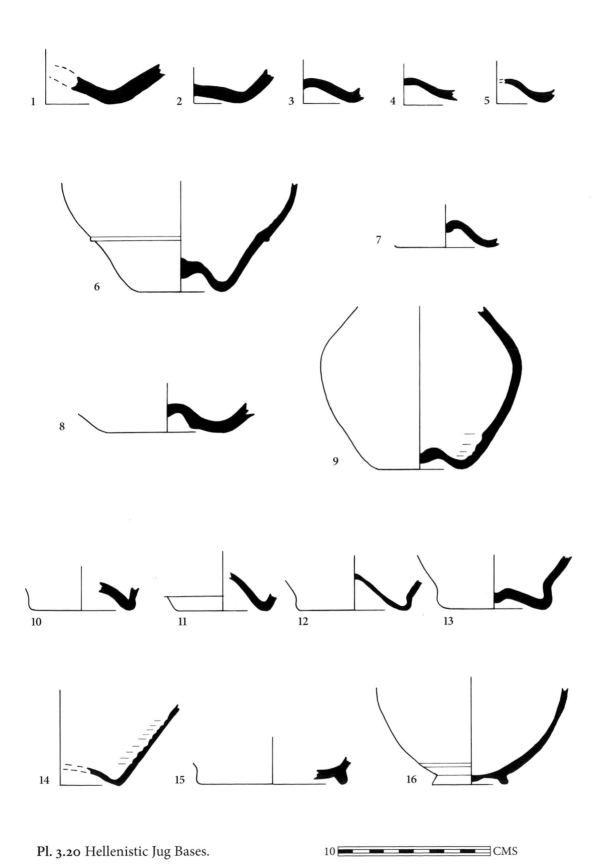

Pl. 3.20 Hellenistic Jug Bases.

10 ▭▭▭▭ CMS

Pl. 3.21   Hellenistic Jugs: Unique

Pl	Str	Fld, Ar,Bkt	No.	Locus Description	Ware description
Unique					
3.21:1	cf IIIA	VII.7.24	2243	sub IIIA Floor 1802-1508-unsealed	10YR 6/3 pale brown, 6/4 pale brown surface; 2.5YR 3/6 dark red paint on top of rim & single band on neck
2	IIIA	VII.7.25	2251/ 46/50/58	sub IIIA Floor 1801	5YR 7/6 reddish yellow, 8/4 pink interior & 8/3 pink exterior surfaces; 2.5YR 6/6 light red painted 7-8 mm wide stripes on exterior; many small limestone and ceramic inclusions
3 fig. 3.10 (p. 50)	II	II.1.52	779	black earth layer North Balk	2.5YR N5/ gray, 5/8 red exterior surface, 5/6 red slip; few medium inclusions
4 fig. 3.10	I	II.1.123	1189 #317	Hellenistic House deeper in Room 1	5YR 4/1 gray, 8/4 pink surfaces; large limestone inclusions
5	unstr	VII.2.51	1013	unstratified	5YR 5/1 gray, 2.5/1 black worn and flaked wash; fairly fine levigation
6	unstr	VII.3.7	97	unstratified	5YR 6/6 reddish yellow, 2.5/1 black worn wash interior and rim exterior; fairly fine levigation
7	unstr	VII.5.9	227	disturbed debris of street	5YR 8/4 pink, 8/4 pink interior & 7/6 reddish yellow exterior surfaces; 7/6 reddish yellow painted exterior rim with 2.5YR 6/6 light red painted strip; many small inclusions
8 fig. 3.11 (p. 50)	unstr	VII.5.69a	3914	unstratified	10YR 5/1yellowish brown, 8/4 very pale brown surface; 2.5YR 6/6 light red painted strip around body; many limestone, sand & organic, & some crystalline incl
	unstr	57 I.6	#29A	unstratified	5YR 6/6 reddish yellow, 2.5/1 black worn and flaked wash; fairly fine levigation

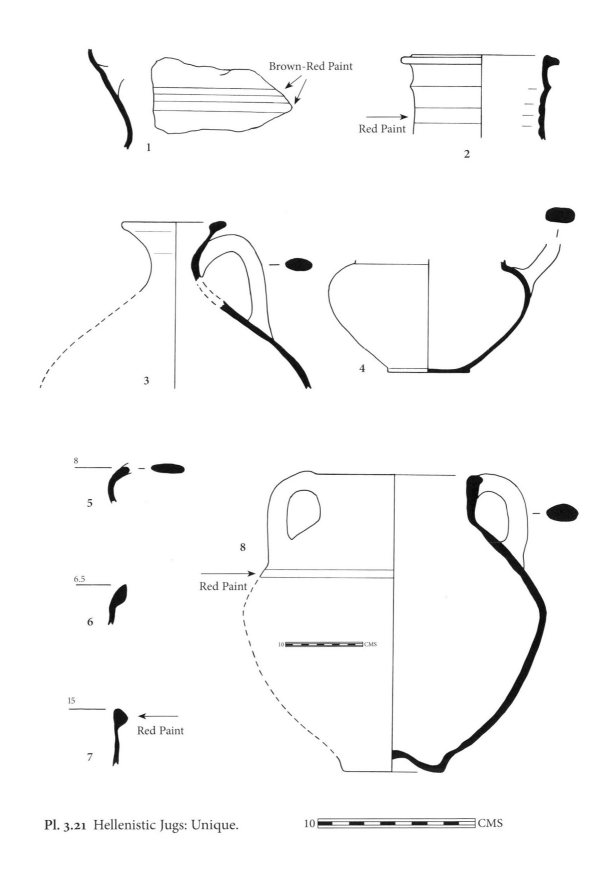

Brown-Red Paint

Red Paint

Red Paint

Red Paint

Pl. 3.21 Hellenistic Jugs: Unique.

10 ▬▬▬▬ CMS

Pl. 3.27   Hellenistic Small Bowls   (cont.)

Pl	Str	Fld, Ar,Bkt	No.	Locus Description	Ware description
3.26:12 fig. 3.18 (p. 56)	I	II.1.109	1045	Hellenistic House Room 1 occupation	5YR 6/6 reddish yellow; limestone inclusions
13	I	II.1.111	1055	Hellenistic House Room 1 occupation	5YR 5/2 yellowish red, 6/1 gray core; limestone incl
14 fig. 3.18	I	II.1.113	1062	Hellenistic House Room 1 occupation	5YR 6/6 reddish yellow to 7/4 pink; ceramic & limestone inclusions
15 fig. 3.18	I	II.1.114	1067 #298	Hellenistic House Room 1 occupation	5YR 6/6 reddish yellow; ceramic & limestone inclusions
16 fig. 3.18	I	II.1.114	1068 #297	Hellenistic House Room 1 occupation	5YR 7/4 pink; ceramic & limestone inclusions
17 fig. 3.18	I	II.1.114	1069	Hellenistic House Room 1 occupation	5YR 5/2 reddish gray to 7/4 pink; ceramic & limestone inclusions
18	I	II.1.114	1070	Hellenistic House Room 1 occupation	5YR 6/8 reddish yellow; few limestone & ceramic incl
19	I	II.1.116	1074	Hellenistic House Room 1 occupation	5YR 6/6 reddish yellow to 7/1 light gray interior surface; few inclusions
20 fig. 3.18	I	II.1.116	1075 #299	Hellenistic House Room 1 occupation	5YR 6/6 reddish yellow; few inclusions
fig. 3.18	I	II.1.117	1076	Hellenistic House Room 1 occupation	5YR 6/6 reddish yellow; few inclusions
21	I	II.1.117	1077	Hellenistic House Room 1 occupation	5YR 6/1 gray; 6/8 reddish yellow to surface; limestone inclusions
22 fig. 3.18	I	II.1.117	1078	Hellenistic House Room 1 occupation	5YR 6/6 reddish yellow; limestone inclusions

Pl. 3.28 Hellenistic Small Bowls

Pl	Str	Fld, Ar, Bkt	No.	Locus Description	Ware description
Incurved Rim (continued)					
3.28:1	I	II.1.117	1079	Hellenistic House Room 1 occupation	5YR 6/6 reddish yellow; limestone inclusions
2 fig. 3.18 (p. 56)	I	II.1.117	1080	Hellenistic House Room 1 occupation	5YR 6/8 reddish yellow with 7/1 light gray core at base; organic, limestone, & ceramic inclusions
3 fig. 3.18	I	II.1.117	1081	Hellenistic House Room 1 occupation	5YR 7/4 pink to 6/6 reddish yellow; ceramic inclusions
4 fig. 3.18	I	II.1.124	1193	Hellenistic House deeper in Room 1	5YR 6/6 reddish yellow; small limestone inclusions
	I	68 II.1.22	10407	in Fill 7039 above Flagstone 7048	5YR 7/6 reddish yellow; small inclusions
	I	68 II.1.22	10409	in Fill 7039 above Flagstone 7048	5YR 7/4 pink; many small inclusions
	I	68 II.1.23	10420	in Fill 7039 above Flagstone 7048	2.5YR 6/8 light red, 5/6 red slip; small incl
	I	68 II.1.23	10421	in Fill 7039 above Flagstone 7048	2.5YR 6/6 light red, N/4 dark gray slip; ceramic incl
	I	68 II.1.23	10431	in Fill 7039 above Flagstone 7048	5YR 7/6 reddish yellow; few inclusions
	I	68 II.1.23	10436	in Fill 7039 above Flagstone 7048	5YR 6/4 light reddish brown; 5/6 red slip; few inclusions
	cf I	II.1.32	283	Hellenistic House higher in Room 1	5YR 7/1 light gray; limestone inclusions
	cf I	II.1.32	285	Hellenistic House higher in Room 1	5YR 6/6 reddish yellow; few inclusions
5	cf I	II.1.33	290	Hellenistic House higher in Room 1	5YR 6/2 pinkish gray, 7/4 pink toward surfaces; limestone inclusions
6	cf I	II.1.33	291 #103	Hellenistic House higher in Room 1	5YR 7/3 pink; limestone inclusions
7	cf I	II.1.35	299 #255	Hellenistic House higher in Room 1	not available; to Department of Antiquities
	cf I	II.1.34	371	Hellenistic House higher in Room 1	5YR 7/4 pink; few inclusions
8	cf I	II.1.35	377	Hellenistic House higher in Room 1	5YR 7/1 light gray; few inclusions
9	cf I	II.1.35	378	Hellenistic House higher in Room 1	5YR 6/2 pinkish gray; ceramic inclusions
	IA	68 II.2.58	11168	I Debris 7074 to Wall 7072	5YR 7/4 pink; ceramic inclusions
	IA	68 II.2.58	11173	I Debris 7074 to Wall 7072	2.5YR N6/ gray; few inclusions
10	unstr	VII.4.89	5008	unstratified	5YR 7/6 reddish yellow, 7/1 light gray core; ceramic inclusions
11	unstr	III.3.10	233	above brick	5YR 6/6 reddish yellow; ceramic inclusions
12	unstr	57 I.10.4	48	surface	5YR 5/6 yellowish red, slight 7/1 light gray core; tiny ceramic inclusions
Incurved Rim flattened					
	IIIA /II	68 II.1.37	10498	beneath flagstone Floor 7048	5YR 6/2 pink; few inclusions
	IIIA /II	68 II.1.53	11005	Fill 7083 in robber trench	2.5YR N5/ gray, 5YR 7/4 pink surface; small to large limestone inclusions
	IIIA /II	68 II.1.54	11008	Fill 7083 in robber trench	5YR 7/2 pinkish gray, 7/4 pink toward interior surface;
13	II	VII.4.59	3825	above IIIA Floor 1227 in Room E	7.5YR 7/8 reddish yellow; few organic incl
	cf II	68 II.2.65	11254	Fill 7080 sub IA Surface 7098	5YR 5/1 gray; few limestone inclusions

(continued on p. 294)

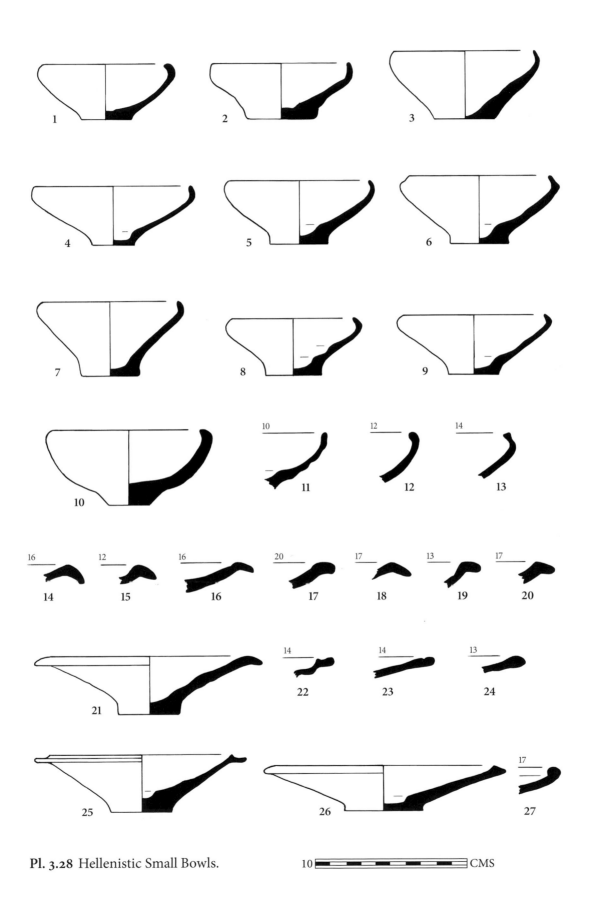

Pl. 3.28 Hellenistic Small Bowls.

10 ▭▭▭▭ CMS

Pl. 3.28 Hellenistic Small Bowls   (cont.)

Pl	Str	Fld, Ar, Bkt	No.	Locus Description	Ware description
Plate with drooping Rim (Fish Plate)					
14	IVB	VII.7.138	6325	Fill 1836-1841 below IV strata	5YR 6/6 reddish yellow, poorly preserved 2.5YR 5/6 red slip over rim & interior; evidence of organic inclusions
	IIIA	VII.1.41	792	sub IIIA Floor 1203	5YR 6/6 reddish yellow, remains of 2.5YR 5/6 red slip; few organic & ceramic incl
15	IIIA	VII.1.89	2916	on IIIB Floor 1214, sub Floor 1203	5YR 7/6 reddish yellow, remains of 2.5YR 5/6 red paint or slip
16	II	III.3.13	236/	foundation of plastered bin	5YR 7/4 pink, 6/1 gray core, 5/6 yellowish red slip interior & over rim .5 cm; few ceramic inclusions
	unstr	III.3.4	/426	debris over bin	
17	II	VII.1.29	741	on IIIA Surface 1203	5YR 7/3 pink, 2.5YR 5/6 red exterior & 5/2 weak red interior slip; small ceramic incl
18	II	VII.1.18	86	on IIIA Surface 1203	5YR 6/6 reddish yellow, remains of 2.5YR 6/6 light red slip; few organic inclusions
19	II	VII.1.21	102	II occupation Pit 1205-1207	5YR 7/6 reddish yellow, poorly preserved 5/6 yellowish red slip on rim; some limestone inclusions
20	II	VII.1.81	2889	II occupation Pit 1205-1207	5YR 4/6 yellowish red; some ceramic incl
	II	VII.1.87	2902	on IIIA Surface 1203	5YR 7/6 reddish yellow; small ceramic incl
	II	VII.7.58	3129	above IIIA Floor 1802-1508	7.5YR 7/6 reddish yellow, remains of 5YR 6/4 light reddish brown slip; small ceramic inclusions
	cf II	II.2.48	601 #210	black earth layer Area 2	5YR 5/3 reddish brown, poor remains of 5/1 gray slip; few inclusions
	cf II	II.2.56	679	black earth layer Area 2	5YR 7/4 pink, remains of 5/2 reddish gray slip; fine levigation
	I	68 II.1.23	10427	in Fill 7039 above Flagstone 7048	2.5YR 6/6 light red, 5/6 red slip; few inclusions [slight overhang]
	cf I	II.1.33	288	Hellenistic House higher in Room 1	5YR 4/8 yellowish red; limestone incl
21	unstr	III.6.1	687	outside wall A	5YR 6/6 reddish yellow; few inclusions
Varied Rims					
	IIIA /II	68 II.1.37	10496	beneath flagstone Floor 7048	5YR 7/4 pink; few inclusions
22	cf IIIA	VII.1.22	92	removal Mortar 1204 of IIIA occupation	7.5YR 7/8 reddish yellow; some organic incl
23	II	VII.1.33	761	above IIIA Floor 1227 in Room E	7.5YR 7/8 reddish yellow; some ceramic incl
24	II	VII.1.21	99	II occupation Pit 1205-1207	5YR 7/6 reddish yellow, 5/4 reddish brown interior
	cf II	68 II.2.77a	11395	in ash on II Floor fragment 7099	5YR 7/4 pink; few inclusions
	cf II	68 II.2.65	11253	Fill 7080 sub IA Surface 7098	5YR 6/2 pinkish gray; few inclusions
25	I	II.1.109	1047	Hellenistic House Room 1 occupation	5YR 6/2 pinkish gray; limestone inclusions
	I	68 II.1.21	10387	in Fill 7039 above Flagstone 7048	2.5YR 6/6 light red; few inclusions
	I	68 II.1.21	10388	in Fill 7039 above Flagstone 7048	2.5YR 6/6 light red; few inclusions

Pl. 3.28 Hellenistic Small Bowls   (cont.)

Pl	Str	Fld, Ar, Bkt	No.	Locus Description	Ware description
	I	68 II.1.23	10418	in Fill 7039 above Flagstone 7048	5YR 7/6 reddish yellow; few inclusions
	I	68 II.1.23	10419	in Fill 7039 above Flagstone 7048	5YR 8/4 pink; few inclusions
	I	68 II.1.39	10503	occupation Debris 7050	5YR 5/6 yellowish red; small inclusions
	IA	68 II.2.56	11134	I Debris 7074 to Wall 7072	5YR 6/6 reddish yellow; ceramic inclusions
26	unstr	VII.5.79	3963A	unstratified	5YR pink; ceramic inclusions

Plate with inverted folded Rim

Pl	Str	Fld, Ar, Bkt	No.	Locus Description	Ware description
	IIIA /II	68 II.1.53	11002	Fill 7083 in robber trench	2.5YR 6/6 light red, N/6 gray core; many small incl
27	II	II.1.48-49	581	black earth layer North Balk	5YR 6/6 reddish yellow; flaky 2.5YR 3/6 dark red slip; few inclusions
	I	68 II.1.13	10295	in Fill 7025 for str. I surface	5YR 7/1 light gray; ceramic inclusions

Pl. 3.29   Hellenistic Small Bowls

PL	STR	FLD, AR,BKT	NO.	LOCUS DESCRIPTION	WARE DESCRIPTION
Ring Bases					
3.29:1	IIIB	VII.1.90	2922	beneath IIIB Floor 1214	2.5YR 5/4 reddish brown, similar reddish brown slip interior; small limestone inclusions
	IIIB	VII.4.80	4969	removal IIIB Wall 1513	5YR 7/6 reddish yellow to 10R 8/1 dark reddish gray interior surface; ceramic inclusions
2	IIIB	VII.7.62	3991	Resurfacing 1816 of IIIB Floor 1816A	5YR 6/4 light reddish brown, 5/8 yellowish red flaked slip interior; ceramic inclusions
	IIIA /II	68 II.1.37	10500	beneath flagstone Floor 7048	2/5YR 6/8 light red, 5/8 red slip interior; few inclusions
	IIIA /II	68 II.1.54	11012	Fill 7083 in robber trench	5YR 7/3 pink, many limestone inclusions
3	II	VII.2.54	1025	removal II Wall 1103	5YR 7/3 pink, remains of 2.5YR N3/ very dark gray slip; few organic inclusions
4	cf II	II.2.50	603	black earth layer Area 2	5YR 8/3 pink, 2.5YR N4/ gray flaked slip; very few inclusions; rouletting interior over base
5	cf II	II.2.51	604	black earth layer Area 2	5YR 8/3 pink, 5/1 gray flaked slip with 5/3 reddish brown slip ext. ring base; very few inclusions
6	cf II	II.2.73	1230	black earth layer Area 2	YR 5/8 yellowish red, 4/1 dark gray slip interior; few tiny limestone inclusions
	I	68 II.1.23	10417	in Fill 7039 above Flagstone 7048	5YR 6/8 reddish yellow, small ceramic inclusions
	IA	68 II.2.58	11171	I Debris 7074 to Wall 7072	5YR 7/6 reddish yellow, badly flaked 5YR yellowish red slip interior; few inclusions
Disk Bases					
	IIIB	VII.1.56	886	beneath IIIB Floor 1214	7.5YR 7/8 reddish yellow; very few small limestone & tiny organic inclusions
7	IIIB	VII.1.68	2850	Fill 1216,1217,1220-1224,1226	7.5YR 7/8 reddish yellow; very few organic inclusions
8	IIIB	VII.7.79	4029	removal III Wall 1803-1807, 1813	5YR 7/2 pinkish gray; few organic inclusions
	IIIB	VII.8.47	3502	sub IIIB Cobbling 1719	7.5YR 7/8 reddish yellow, 10YR 8/3 very pale brown toward surfaces; few small organic inclusions
	IIIA	VII.1.40	777	sub IIIA Floor 1203	5YR 7/3 pink, 7/1 light gray core; few organic inclusions
9	IIIA	VII.1.40	778	sub IIIA Floor 1203	7.5YR 7/8 reddish yellow; organic inclusions
10 fig. 3.19 (p. 56)	IIIA	VII.1.40	787	sub IIIA Floor 1203	5YR 6/6 reddish yellow, 2.5YR 5/6 red poorly preserved slip; few organic inclusions
	IIIA	VII.1.88	2903	sub IIIA Floor 1203	5YR 6/6 reddish yellow, 7/6 reddish yellow toward interior surface; some small limestone & ceramic incl
	IIIA	VII.1.52	866	on IIIB Floor 1214 sub Floor 1203	10YR 8/1 white; few small ceramic inclusions
11	IIIA	VII.1.112	6247	removal IIIA Walls 1206-1210	2.5YR 5/6 red; some ceramic inclusions
12	IIIA	VII.6.74	1957	sub IIIA Cobbling 1306 and 1307	5YR 6/6 reddish yellow; few small limestone inclusions
	IIIA	VII.7.25	2249	sub IIIA Floor 1801	5YR 6/6 reddish yellow; few small crytalline, ceramic, & limestone inclusions
13	IIIA	VII.7.57	3121	sub IIIA Floor 1802-1508	5YR 7/3 pink; many organic inclusions

(continued on p. 298)

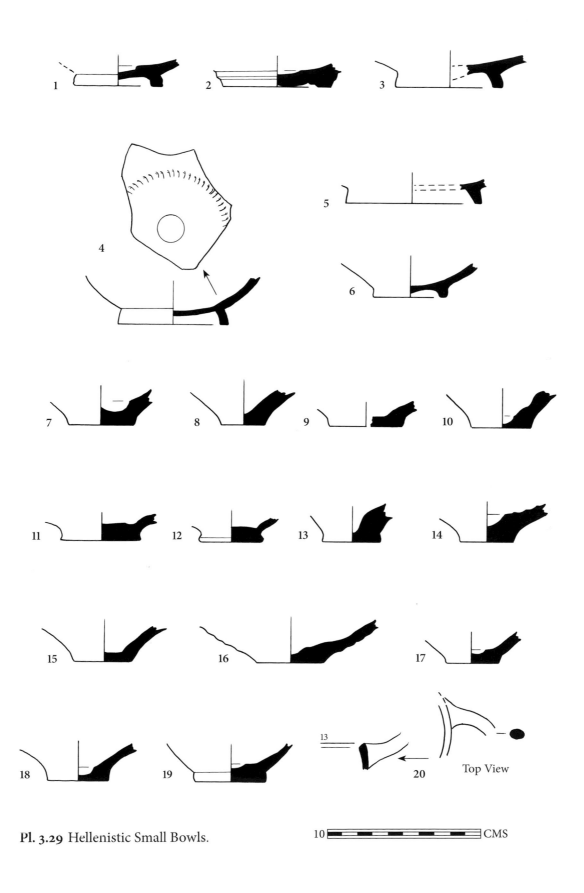

Pl. 3.29 Hellenistic Small Bowls.

10 ▮▭▮▭▮▭▮▭▮ CMS

Pl. 3.29   Hellenistic Small Bowls   (cont.)

Pl	Str	Fld, Ar, Bkt	No.	Locus Description	Ware description
	cf IIIA	VII.3.48	1567	L. 1009 around IIIA Drain 1015-16	5YR 6/4 light reddish brown; ceramic inclusions
3.29:14	III	57 I.7b.41	206	above Lower Burn 204	5YR 7/4 pink; few limestone inclusions
15	II	VII.1.26	115	above IIIA Floor 1227 in Room E	5YR 7/6 reddish yellow, 7/2 pinkish gray core; some limestone inclusions
	II	VII.1.30	749	above IIIA Floor 1227 in Room E	7.5YR 7/8 reddish yellow; small limestone inclusions
	II	VII.4.115	7369	on IIIA room 1227 floor	5YR 7/6 reddish yellow, 5YR 7/1 light gray core; some organic & limestone inclusions
	II	VII.1.29	745	on IIIA Surface 1203	5YR 6/4 light reddish brown, 6/1 gray core; some small limestone & ceramic inclusions
16	II	VII.1.32	758	II occupation Pit 1205-1207	5YR 7/6 reddish yellow; some ceramic & organic incl
17 fig. 3.19 (p. 56)	II	VII.1.87	2890	on IIIA Surface 1203	5YR 7/6 reddish yellow; 7/1 light gray core; some sand inclusions
	II	VII.1.87	2894	on IIIA Surface 1203	5YR 6/6 reddish yellow, 6/1 gray core; few ceramic incl
	II	VII.1.87	2898	on IIIA Surface 1203	5YR 6/6 reddish yellow, 7/2 pinkish gray toward exterior surface; small ceramic inclusions
18 fig. 3.19	II	VII.7.22	2216	above IIIA Floor 1802-1508	5YR 7/8 reddish yellow; few organic inclusions
	II	II.1.10	151	Hellenistic House black earth layer Room 1	5YR 7/6 pink; few limestone inclusions
	cf II	68 II.2.77a	11396	in ash on II Floor fragment 7099	5YR 7/4 pink; tiny inclusions
	cf II	II.2.27	281	black earth layer Area 2	5YR 5/8 yellowish red; many limestone inclusions
	cf II	68 II.2.66	11268	Fill 7080 sub IA Surface 7098	5YR 6/6 reddish yellow; small ceramic inclusions
	cf II	68 II.2.66	11269	Fill 7080 sub IA Surface 7098	5YR 7/3 pink, 7/4 pink toward surface; few inclusions
	I	68 II.1.22	10412	in Fill 7039 above Flagstone 7048	5YR 7/4 pink; few inclusions
	I	68 II.1.22	10413	in Fill 7039 above Flagstone 7048	5YR 7/4 pink; tiny inclusions
	cf I	II.1.32	280	Hellenistic House deeper in Room 1	5YR 8/3 pink, 7/8 reddish yellow toward exterior surface; limestone & gravel inclusions
19	cf I	II.1.32	282	Hellenistic House deeper in Room 1	5YR 7/3 pink, 6/8 reddish yellow surfaces; ceramic inclusions
	cf I	II.1.34	369	Hellenistic House deeper in Room 1	5YR 7/4 pink; few limestone inclusions
	cf I	II.1.35	383	Hellenistic House deeper in Room 1	5YR 7/2 pinkish gray, some places 7/6 reddish yellow toward surface; limestone inclusions
	IA	68 II.2.56	11138	I Debris 7074 to Wall 7072	5YR 6/2 pinkish gray; limestone inclusions
	IA	68 II.2.56	11139	I Debris 7074 to Wall 7072	5YR 7/1 light gray; limestone inclusions
	unstr	57 I.9.12	142	balk	5YR 7/4 pink; few large and some small inclusions

Handles

Pl	Str	Fld, Ar, Bkt	No.	Locus Description	Ware description
20	IIIB	VII.8.78	4590	sub IIIB Cobbling 1719	5YR 5.6 yellowish red, 2.5YR 4/6 red worn slip or wash interior & exterior
	IIIA	VII.7.77	4022	removal IIIA Wall 1805N	5YR 5/8 yellowish red, 2.5YR 5/6 red worn slip
	unstr	62 VII.3.30	217	unstratified	5YR 7/2 pinkish gray, spotty remains of 2.5/1 black slip

Pl. 3.29   Hellenistic Small Bowls   (cont.)

Pl	Str	Fld, Ar,Bkt	No.	Locus Description	Ware description
	unstr	VII.5.129	6162	unstratified	2.5YR 6/6 light red, remains of 5/6 red slip interior & over rim to handle
	unstr	VII.6.85	2001	unstratified	2.5YR N5/gray, 5/6 red toward surface, remains of poor N5/gray wash or slip; few inclusions
	unstr	VII.9.6	2366	surface	2.5YR 6/8 light red, 5/6 red slip interior, remains of 3/6 red to N3/ very dark gray exterior

Pl. 3.30 Hellenistic Imported Bowls

Pl	Str	Fld, Ar,Bkt	No.	Locus Description	Ware description
Attic					
Bowl Rims					
	IIIA /II	68 II.1.64	11095	Fill 7083 in robber trench	5YR 6/6 reddish yellow, 2.5/1 black glaze int & ext
3.30:1	II	VII.7.22	2227	above IIIA Floor 1802-1508	5YR 6/8 reddish yellow, 2.5/1 black glaze int & worn ext
	I	II.1.120	#292	Hellenistic House deeper in Room 1	2.5YR 6/8 light red, N2.5/ black glaze interior & exterior
2	unstr	VII.4.19	267	surface fill	5YR 6/8 reddish yellow, 2.5/1 black glaze int & ext
	unstr	II.1	#145	north balk	5YR 5/8 yellowish red, 2.5/1 black glaze int & ext
bowl bases					
3	cf IIIA	VII.4.103	5268	Pit 1514	5YR 5/3 reddish brown, 7.5YR N2.5/ black slip interior and exterior; stamped palmettes interior over base
	II	II.1.53	592 #186	black earth layer North Balk	not available; to Dept. of Antiq.; rouletting int base
Terra Sigillata					
Incurved Rim rounded off					
4	IIIA	VII.9.44	3219	removal IIIA 1707-1705-1701-1601	5YR 6/6 reddish yellow, 5/1 gray flaked slip exterior to 2.5YR 5/6 red slip over rim & interior; fine levigation
	II	VII.1.32	754	II occupation Pit 1205-1207	2.5YR 6/6 light red, 5/6 red slip interior; fine levigation
5	II	II.1.25	265/ /#63	Hellenistic House black earth layer Room 1	5YR 7/4 pink; 2.5YR 4/6 red slip on surfaces; fine levigation
	unstr	68 II.2.1	10166	Probe Trench 7016	5YR 7/6 reddish yellow, 3/1 very dark gray slip with 2.5YR 5/4 reddish brown slip top rim; fine levigation
Plate with everted/overhang Rim ("Fish Plate")					
6	cf II	II.2.48	599 #210	black earth layer Area 2	5YR 5/6 yellowish red, 2.5/1 black glaze interior and exterior; fine levigation
Plate with inverted Rim					
7	IIIB	VII.1.53	870	beneath IIIB Floor 1214	5YR 7/6 reddish yellow, flaky 2.5YR 4/4 reddish brown slip with a N4/ dark gray 2.5 cm concentric stripe on interior; fine levigation
	IIIA /II	68 II.1.47	10938	embedded in Plaster 7049	5YR 7/4 pink, 5/1 gray slip exterior & rim with line of 2.5YR 5/6 red lower rim; fine levigation
8	II	II.1.51	587	black earth layer North Balk	5YR 6/6 reddish yellow; flaky 4/1 dark gray slip exterior, on rim, and interior; fine levigation
Ring Bases					
9	IIIA /II	68 II.1.54	11011	Fill 7083 in robber trench	2.5YR 6/8 light red, 5YR 3/1 very dark gray slip well bonded interior & exterior; rouletting and palmette interior base; fine levigation
	II	II.1.36	391	black earth layer North Balk	7.5YR 7/4 pink, 2.5YR 4/6 red slip bottom base and badly flaked exterior and interior; fine levigation
10	cf I	II.1.33	316 #107	Hellenistic House higher in Room 1	5YR 8/4 pink, 7/6 reddish yellow toward center, 2.5YR 4/6 red fairly well bonded slip ext. & int.; rouletting interior base; fine levigation
Ware					
	IIIB	VII.1.46	837	beneath IIIB Floor 1214	10R 6/6 light red, 4/6 red surfaces; fine levigation

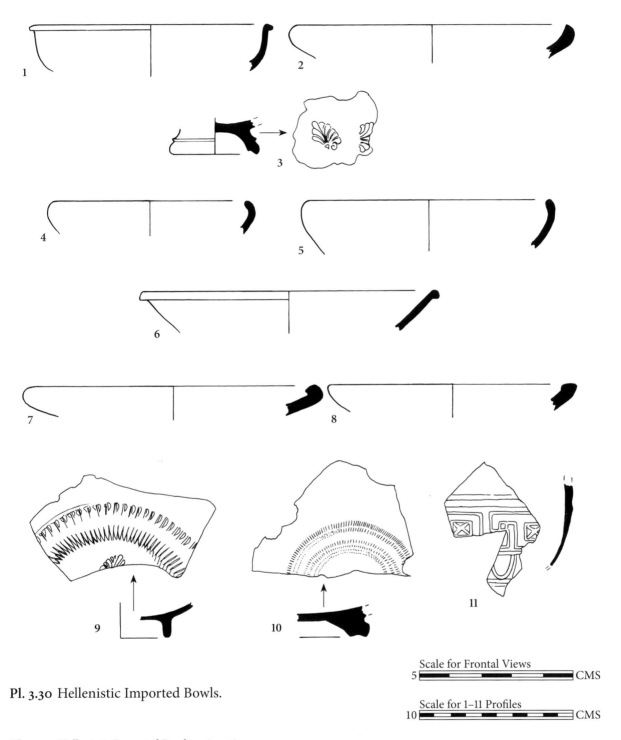

Pl. 3.30 Hellenistic Imported Bowls.

Scale for Frontal Views
5 ▬▬▬▬▬ CMS

Scale for 1–11 Profiles
10 ▬▬▬▬▬ CMS

Pl. 3.30 Hellenistic Imported Bowls (cont.)

Pl	Str	Fld, Ar,Bkt	No.	Locus Description	Ware description
Megarian Bowl Ware					
3.30:11	IIIA	62 VII.1.20	93/	sub IIIA Floor 1227-1511	7.5YR 6/4 light brown, 5YR 3/1 very dark gray
	IIIA	62 VII.4.70	/588	Fill 1530 sub Floor 1227	surface; few inclusions; medium levigation

Pl. 3.31   Hellenistic Medium Bowls

Pl	Str	Fld, Ar, Bkt	No.	Locus Description	Ware description
Rolled Rim					
3.31:1	IVB	VII.2.131 VII.2.135	6908/ /7327	L. 1123A levelling below IV installations	5YR 5/1 gray, 9/4 pink surface; few organic and sand inclusions
2	IVB	62 VII.21.93	714	sub IVB Floor 21.013	5YR 6/4 reddish brown, 10YR 8/4 very pale brown surface; many organic inclusions
3	IVA	62 VII.21.89	711	sub IVA or IVB Floor 21.012	5YR 7/8 reddish yellow, 7/4 pink surface; some limestone inclusions
4	IVA	62 VII.23.56	479	sub IVA Floor 23.008	7.5YR 8/4 pink, 10YR 8/3 very pale brown surface; few organic and some limestone inclusions
	IV	57 I.7b.56	328	in lower IV Floor 205	2.5YR N6/ gray, 6/6 light red surfaces; many limestone and ceramic inclusions
	IV	56 I.1	17	L. 4 fill below Pavement	5YR 8/1 gray, 7/1 light gray surface; ceramic and limestone inclusions
	cf IV	62 VII.21.110	875	Pit 21.036 dug in III or II	10YR 6/2 light brownish gray; medium to large ceramic inclusions
5	IIIB	VII.1.64	944	Fill 1216,1217,1220-1224,1226	5YR 6/4 light reddish brown, 7.5YR 7/4 pink surface; some limestone & sandstone inclusions
6	IIIB	VII.1.77	2874	Fill 1216,1217,1220-1224,1226	5YR 6/6 reddish yellow, 7.5YR 8/2 pinkish white surface; few limestone inclusions
	IIIB	VII.8.78	4589	sub IIIB Cobbling 1719	7.5YR 8/6 reddish yellow, few medium to large limestone and ceramic inclusions
7	IIIA	62 VII.21.67	512	Debris 21.035 sub IIIA walls & Floor 21.031	not accessible
8	cf IIIA	VII.3.28	186	L. 1009 around IIIA Drain 1015-16	5YR 7/3 pink, 7.5YR 8/4 pink surf; some organic incl
9	cf IIIA	VII.3.28	188	L. 1009 around IIIA Drain 1015-16	7.5YR 6/4 light brown, 10YR 8/2 white surface; some limestone and very few organic inclusions
	cf IIIA	VII.4.101	5381	Pit 1514	5YR 6/6 reddish yellow, 6/1 gray core; medium limestone and ceramic inclusions
10	cf IIIA	VII.8.46	3490	over IIIB surface 1719	7.5YR 8/6 reddish yellow, 5YR 8/4 pink surface
11	unstr	II.1.45b	394	Storage Bin 7106	5YR 7/2 pinkish gray, 2.5YR 6/8 light red surfaces; many limestone and ceramic inclusions
	unstr	III.3.11	234	Hellenistic House	5YR 7/2 pinking gray, 6/6 reddish yellow surfaces; ceramic and limestone inclusions
Rolled Rim with slight Grooves					
12	cf IVA	VII.3.141	5636	cleaning IV Drain 1028-1116	5YR N6/ gray, 7/4 pink exterior surface; many small and few large inclusions
13	unstr	VII.4.22	1812	surface fill	2.5YR N6/ gray, 5YR 8/3 pink surfaces; few small, medium, and large inclusions
Medium Bowl Bases					
	IV	56 I.1	128	L. 4 below Hellenistic Tower	5YR 8/3 pink; small limestone & ceramic inclusions
14	IIIB	VII.7.75	4017	removal III Wall 1803-1807, 1813	2.5YR 6/6 light red, N6/ gray core; many limestone incl
15	IIIB	VII.1.60	5282	fill 1216,1217,1220-1224,1226	5YR 7/6 reddish yellow, 7.5YR 7/4 pink surface; many organic inclusions

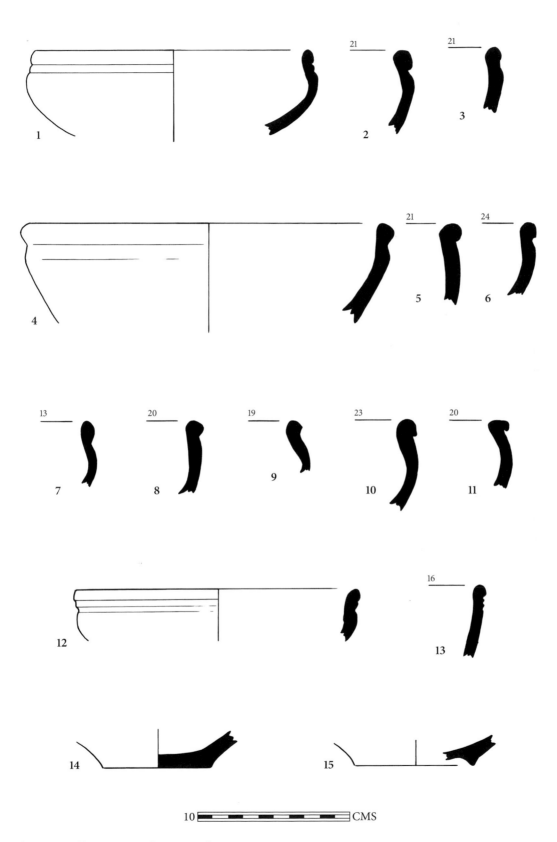

Pl. 3.31 Hellenistic Medium Bowls.

Pl. 3.32 Hellenistic Medium to Large Bowls

Pl	Str	Fld, Ar,Bkt	No.	Locus Description	Ware description
Deep with varied Rims					
3.32:1	IVB	IX.1.68	212	grayish rubbly Soil 9033	10YR 8/6 yellow, 2.5YR 8/4 surface; some organic incl
2	IVA	VII.21.89	710	sub IVA or IVB Floor 21.012	7.5YR 8/4 pink, 2.5YR 6/6 light red surface; many limestone, organic and sand inclusions
3	IVA	IX.2.28	39	silty Soil 9262	10YR 5/1 gray, 7/4 very pale brown surfaces; many limestone and organic, some crystalline inclusions
4	IIIB	VII.1.75	2866	Fill 1216,1217,1220-1224,1226	5YR 7/1 light gray, 8/4 pink exterior surface; many ceramic and few organic inclusions
5	IIIA	VII.3.106	1798	on IIIB Hardpack 1017-1019	2.5YR 5/2 weak red, 8/3 very pale brown surface; many sand, limestone, and organic inclusions
6	IIIA	VII.8.52	3516	on IIIB Cobbling 1715	2.5YR 6/8 light red, 8/4 pink surface; few limestone incl
7	III	57 I.6.15	39	Floor 203	5YR 7/3 pink, 7/4 pink interior & 8/3 pink exterior surf; small organic & limestone and large limestone incl
8	III	57 I.6.22	117	Floor 203	5YR 6/1 gray, 8/4 light reddish brown interior and 7/2 pinkish gray exterior surfaces; large limestone and many small ceramic inclusions
9	I	II.1.113	1063	Hellenistic House Room 1 occupation	5YR 8/4 pink, 7/4 pink exterior surface; many ceramic and organic and few limestone inclusions
	unstr	57 I.7b.31	202	surface to west	5YR 6/6 reddish yellow, 8/4 exterior surface; limestone and few ceramic inclusions
10	unstr	57 I.9.19	182	top of H tower	5YR 7/3 pink, 10YR 8/2 white exterior surface; limestone and many ceramic inclusions
Shallow with unthickened Rim					
11	IVB	VII.5.144	6421	removal IVB Wall 1415-1117	10YR 8/2 white, 8/3 very pale brown surf; some organic incl
12	IVA	VII.4.110	5537	removal IVA Floor 1527	7.5YR N5/ gray, 8/2 pinkish white surf; some organic incl
13	IIIB	VII.8.78	4587	sub IIIB Cobbling 1719	7.5YR 5/4 brown, 8/4 pink surf; some limestone incl
14	IIIB	VII.8.84	4613	sub IIIB Cobbling 1719	10YR 7/2 light gray, 2.5Y 8/2 white surface
15	IIIB	VII.8.90	4635	sub IIIB Cobbling 1719	10YR 8/3 very pale brown, 7.5YR 7/4 pink surface; ceramic inclusions
16	IIIA	VII.21.67	511	Debris 21.035 sub IIIA walls & Floor 21.031	5YR 8/4 pale yellow, 7.5YR 5/4 pink; limestone & ceramic & few small sand and organic inclusions
Shallow with everted and rounded Rim					
17	IV B	IX.2.43	104	Layer 9266 sub 9264	2.5YR 8/4 pale yellow, 8/2 white surface; very few organic and limestone inclusions
18	cf IV	62 VII.22.145	1256	IV Pit 22.010	5YR 6/8 reddish yellow, 7/6 reddish yellow surface; many limestone & some organic inclusions
19	IIIB	VII.8.79	4592	sub IIIB Cobbling 1719	7.5YR 5/2 brown, 10YR 8/2 white surface; very few organic inclusions
	III	56 I.1	88	L. 3 on Pavement	2.5YR 6/4 light reddish brown, 5YR 7/4 pink interior and 7/3 pink exterior surfaces; many inclusions

(continued on p. 307)

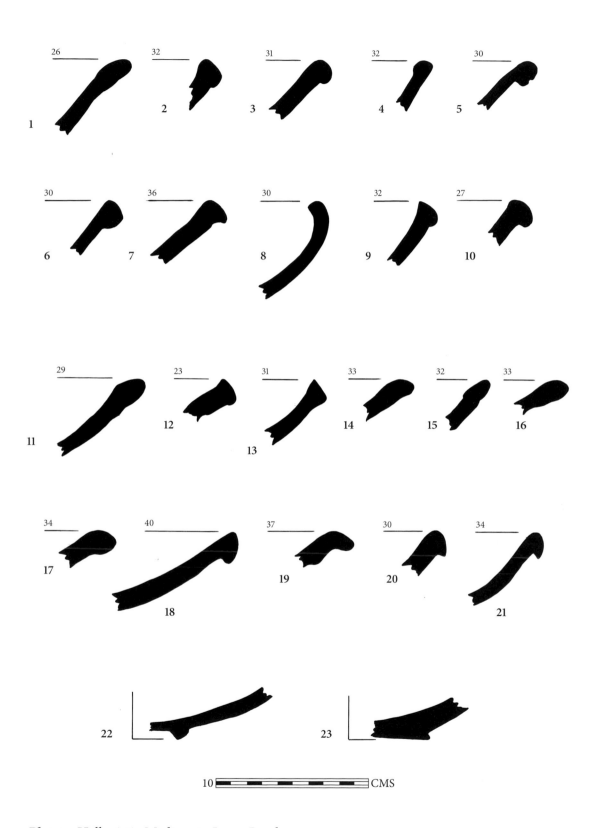

Pl. 3.32 Hellenistic Medium to Large Bowls.

Pl. 3.32 Hellenistic Medium to Large Bowls (cont.)

Pl	Str	Fld, Ar,Bkt	No.	Locus Description	Ware description
3.32:20	cf III	57 I.6.57	459	pit in Wall B	5YR 7/3 pink, 7/2 pinkish gray exterior surface; ceramic & limestone inclusions
21	II	VII.1.101	3744	above IIIA Floor 1227 in Room E	5YR 5/3 reddish brown, 8/3 very pale brown surface; many limestone inclusions
	unstr	57 I.5.3	74	surface	5YR 7/8 reddish yellow, 7/6 reddish yellow interior & 2.5YR 6/6 light red exterior surfaces; many ceramic and large limestone inclusions
	unstr	57 I.9.19	184	top of H tower	5YR 7/3 pink, 7/6 pinkish yellow exterior surface; limestone and few ceramic inclusions

Shallow Bowl Bases

Pl	Str	Fld, Ar,Bkt	No.	Locus Description	Ware description
22	IVB	IX.3.82	284	IVB Fill 9523	10YR 7/2 light gray, 8/4 very pale brown surface; very few organic inclusions
23	IIIB	VII.1.60	5288	Fill 1216,1217,1220-1224,1226	5YR 7/8 reddish yellow, 7.5YR 8/4 pink surface; very many organic and limestone inclusions; rough inside base

Pl. 3.33   Hellenistic Kraters

Pl	Str	Fld, Ar,Bkt	No.	Locus Description	Ware description
Grooved					
	cf V	VII.1.99	1201	in fill below IV metalled Surface 1530-1229-1232-1234	2.5YR 4/8 dark gray, 6/6 light red int & 5YR 7/2 pinkish gray ext surfaces; ceramic, organic, & few limestone incl
	IVB	VII.2.130	6897	removal IVB Wall 1415-1117	5YR 5/1 gray, 7/4 pink interior & 7/3 pink exterior surfaces; ceramic & few large limestone inclusions
3.33:1	IVB	VII.9.46	3232	Fill 1609-10,1612-15 in brick debris	5YR 7/4 pink, 10YR 6/1 large gray core; few organic and limestone inclusions
2	IVA	62 VII.21.87	706	sub IVA Floor 21.011	10YR 7/3 very pale brown, 7.5YR 8/2 pinkish white surfaces; many organic & very few limestone inclusions
3	IVA	IX.1.43	93	L. 9019 compact gray, sub 9018	7.5YR 6/4 brown, 10YR 8/2 white surfaces; organic & very few limestone inclusions
	IV	56 I.1	6	L. 4 fill below Pavement	5YR 56/6 reddish yellow, 7/4 pink exterior surface; few ceramic and many small limestone inclusions
	IV	56 I.1	23	L. 4 fill below Pavement	2.5YR 5/0 gray, 6/6 light red exterior surface; many organic and few ceramic & large limestone inclusions
	IV	56 I.1	30	L. 4 fill below Pavement	5YR 6/1 light gray, 7/3 pink exterior surface; few limestone, ceramic, & very small organic inclusions
4	cf IV	62 VII.22.132	1058/	IV Pit 22.010	5YR 8/2 pinkish white, 7/3 pink interior & 8/4 pink exterior surfaces; limestone, many large ceramic, few organic and large limestone inclusions
fig. 3.20 (p. 61)	cf IIIB	62 VII.22.44	/329	sub possible IIIB floor 22.002	
	IIIB	VII.1.71	2862	Fill 1216,1217,1220-1224,1226	5YR 6/1 gray, 7/3 pink interior & 7/2 pinkish gray exterior surfaces; limestone and few small ceramic inclusions
5	IIIB	VII.8.79	4594	sub IIIB Cobbling 1719	7.5YR 8/4 pink, similar surfaces; very few limestone and many organic inclusions
6	IIIB	VII.8.83	4607	sub IIIB Cobbling 1719	10YR 7/2 light gray, 7.5YR 8/4 pink surfaces; very few limestone inclusions
7	IIIB	VII.8.90	4637	sub IIIB Cobbling 1719	10YR 8/2 white, similar surfaces
	cf IIIB	VII.4.132	1530	unsealed in Pit 1522	5YR 6/4 light reddish brown, 7/3 pink exterior surface; few ceramic and limestone inclusions
	cf IIIB	VII.8.70	4193	unsealed IIIB Fill 1717-20 sub IIIB level	2.5YR 5/0 gray, 5/2 weak red int and 6/4 light reddish brown ext surfaces; few limestone & small ceramic incl
8	cf IIIB	62 VII.22.49	460	sub possible IIIB Floor 22.002	10YR 6/2 light brownish gray, 8/4 very pale brown surfaces; few organic inclusions
	cf IIIB	62 VII.22.50	467	sub possible IIIB Floor 22.002	not accessible
9	IIIA	VII.6.77	1966	sub IIIA Cobbling 1306 and 1307	10YR 7/3 very pale brown, 8/4 very pale brown surface
	IIIA	VII.7.57	3125	sub IIIA Floor 1802-1508	7/5YR 8/2 pinkish white, 10YR 8/2 white surfaces
10	IIIA	VII.8.52	3517	on IIIB Cobbling 1715	5YR 6/4 light reddish brown, 8/3 pink exterior surface; few large limestone & organic inclusions
11	cf IIIA	VII.4.101	5380	Pit 1514	5YR 8/4 pink, 7.5YR 8/2 pinkish white surface; few organic and limestone inclusions
	III	56 I.1	15	L. 3 on Pavement	2.5YR 4/2 weak red, 5/2 weak red exterior surface; limestone and few small organic inclusions

(continued on p. 311)

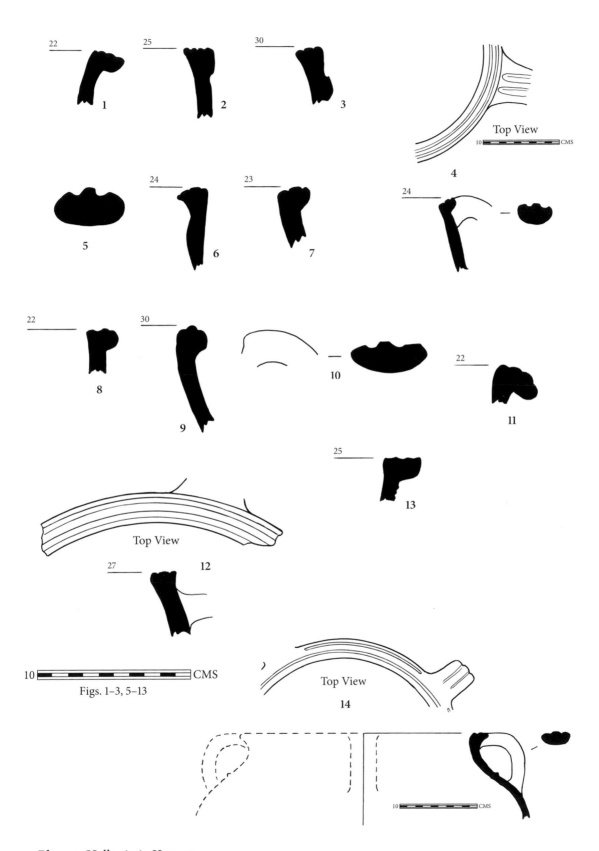

Pl. 3.33 Hellenistic Kraters.

Pl. 3.33   Hellenistic Kraters   (cont.)

Pl	Str	Fld, Ar,Bkt	No.	Locus Description	Ware description
	III	56 I.1	31	L. 3 on Pavement	5YR 5/2 reddish gray, 6/3 light reddish brown int & 7/3 pink exterior surf; few large limestone, ceramic, & organic incl
	III	57 I.6.11	14	burn above Floor 203	5YR 5/1 gray, 7/6 reddish yellow surfaces; limestone and organic inclusions
3.33:12 fig. 3.20 (p. 61)	III	57 I.7b.47	274	above Lower Burn 204	2.5YR 5/0 gray, 5YR 7/4 pink int & 7/2 pinkish gray ext surfaces; organic and few ceramic and limestone incl
13	cf III	57 I.6.76	644	pit in Wall B	5YR 6/1 gray, 7/4 pink exterior surface; organic, many ceramic and few limestone inclusions
14 fig. 3.20	cf III	57 I.9.9 57.1.9.7	123/ /61	striated makeup over Wall A surface	5YR 6/2 pinkish gray, 8/2 pinkish white int and 8/3 pink ext surfaces; large ceramic, few limestone & small organic incl
	cf II	57 II.2.75	1392	black earth layer Area 2	5YR 7/3 pink, 8/4 pink exterior surface; many large and few very small organic inclusions
	unstr	57 I.6.9	7	surface	5YR 5/1 gray, 6/2 pinkish gray interior & 8/4 pink exterior surfaces; few ceramic & large limestone inclusions
	unstr	64 I.17.19	38766	surface	2.5YR 6/0 gray, 6/4 light reddish brown exterior surface; few medium to large ceramic & small limestone incl

Pl. 3.34   Hellenistic Kraters

Pl	Str	Fld, Ar,Bkt	No.	Locus Description	Ware description
Squared					
3.34:1	IVB	VII.9.51 VII.9.51	4057/ /4059	Fill 1609-10,1612-15 in brick debris Fill 1609-10,1612-15 in brick debris	10YR 5/1 gray, 10YR 6/5 pale brown surfaces; many organic inclusions
	IVB	VII.9.67	4102	Fill 1609-10,1612-15 in brick debris	5YR 6/1 light gray, 5/1 light gray interior, 8/3 pink exterior surfaces; many limestone and small organic inclusions
2	IVA	VII.1.62	5319	on IVB plastered Floor 1216	7.5YR 8/2 pinkish white, 10YR 8/2 white surfaces; many limestone & some organic inclusions
	IVA	62 VII.1.64	804	on IVB Surface 1236	5YR 7/3 pink, 5/1 gray core; many ceramic inclusions
	IV	I.7b.56	332	in lower IV Floor 205	5YR 5/3 reddish brown, 6/4 exterior surface; limestone and few large limestone inclusions
3	IIIB	VII.1.59	923	Fill 1216,1217,1220-1224,1226	5YR 7/6 reddish yellow, 7/4 pink surfaces; few organic and very few limestone inclusions
4	IIIB	VII.1.61	5292	Fill 1216,1217,1220-1224,1226	5YR 8/4 pink, 10YR 8/3 very pale brown surfaces; some organic & sand inclusions
5	IIIB	VII.1.74	2865	Fill 1216,1217,1220-1224,1226	7.5YR 8/2 pinkish white, 10YR 8/4 very pale brown surfaces; few organic & limestone inclusions
6	IIIB	VII.8.47	3506	sub IIIB Cobbling 1719	5YR 6/2 pinkish gray, 8/4 pink surfaces; many organic inclusions
7	IIIB	VII.8.104	5863	sub IIIB Cobbling 1719	7.5YR 7/6 reddish yellow, 10YR 8/4 very pale brown surfaces; some organic inclusions
8	IIIA	VII.1.88	2904	sub IIIA Floor 1203	2.5YR 6/8 light red, 5YR 8/2 pinkish white surfaces; very few limestone inclusions
	IIIA	VII.6.75	1963	sub IIIA Cobbling 1306 and 1307	5YR 7/3 pink, 8/2 pinkish white exterior surfaces; few limestone & ceramic inclusions; groove on exterior rim and a groove 3-5 cm. below rim
	IIIA	VII.7.82	4648	removal IIIA Wall 1805N	5YR 6/2 pinkish gray, 7/3 pink exterior surface; many ceramic and few large organic inclusions; groove on exterior rim and a groove 3-5 cm. below rim
9	I	57 II.1.117	1087	Hellenistic House Room 1 occupation	5YR 6/2 pinkish gray, 7/6 reddish yellow exterior surface; limestone and many ceramic and few organic inclusions; groove on exterior rim and a groove 3-5 cm. below rim
Overhang, thickened Exterior					
10	IVB	VII.2.128	6598	removal IVB Wall 1123	5YR 7/4 pink, similar surfaces; very many limestone and some organic inclusions
	IVB	VII.3.158	6305	Fill 1029A below IV installations	2.5YR 5/0 gray, 6/6 light red exterior surface; few limestone, large organic & very small ceramic inclusions
11	IVB	VII.3.172	6640	Probe 1030 beneath IV levels	5YR 4/2 dark reddish gray, 10YR 8/3 very pale brown surfaces; some organic inclusions
	IVB	VII.5.152	6569	removal IVB Wall 1426	5YR 6/6 reddish yellow, 7/4 pink int and 8/4 pink ext surfaces; very small limestone and few organic inclusions

(continued on p. 314)

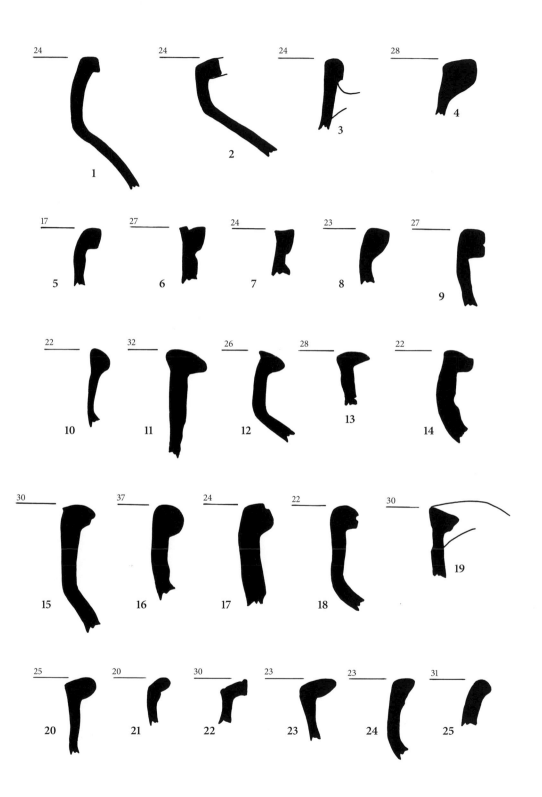

Pl. 3.34 Hellenistic Kraters.

10 CMS

Pl. 3.34   Hellenistic Kraters   (cont.)

Pl	Str	Fld, Ar, Bkt	No.	Locus Description	Ware description
3.34:12	IVA	VII.5.132	6166	removal IVA Wall 1420 of bin	10YR 6/3 pale brown, 7/3 very pale brown surfaces; many large organic and sand inclusions
13	IIIB	VII.1.71	2860	Fill 1216,1217,1220-1224,1226	2.5YR 5/6 red, 5YR 7/3 pink surfaces; few organic and very few limestone inclusions
14	cf IIIB	VII.3.93	1763	above IV Surface 1021-1023	5YR 8/4 pink, 7/4 pink surfaces; many limestone inclusions
15	cf IIIB	62 VII.22.45	332	sub possible IIIB Floor 22.002	10YR 8/2 white, 7/2 light gray surfaces; many organic and limestone inclusions
16	cf IIIB	62 VII.22.47	453	sub possible IIIB Floor 22.002	7.5YR 8/4 pink, similar surfaces; many sand & limestone and few organic inclusions
17	cf IIIB	62 VII.22.50	463	sub possible IIIB Floor 22.002	7.5YR 8/4 pink, 8/2 pinkish white surfaces; very many organic and limestone inclusions; 1 groove on top rim
18	cf IIIB	62 VII.22.50	464	sub possible IIIB Floor 22.002	5YR 7/4 pink, 8/3 pink surfaces; many organic and few limestone inclusions; 1 groove exterior rim
19	cf IIIB	62 VII.22.50	465	sub possible IIIB Floor 22.002	7.5YR 7/4 pink, 8/4 pink surfaces; very many limestone and sand inclusions
	IIIA	VII.1.48	840	removal IIIA Walls 1206-1210	5YR 7/1 gray, 7/3 pink exterior surface; few ceramic and limestone inclusions; faint groove on top rim, 2 grooved lines exterior overhang
20	IIIA	VII.6.75	1961	sub IIIA Cobbling 1306 and 1307	7.5YR 8/4 pink, similar surfaces; few limestone and organic inclusions
	III	56 I.1	89	L. 3 on Pavement	5YR 6/1 light gray, 7/4 pink exterior surface; large to very small limestone and few organic and small ceramic inclusions
21	cf III	57 I.6.72	641	pit in Wall B	2.5YR 6/6 light red, 6/4 light reddish brown interior & 5YR 7/4 pink exterior surfaces; limestone & few organic & ceramic inclusions
	IIIA/II	II.1.105	923	below 160 cm in Room 2	5YR 6/2 pinkish gray; ceramic, few large limestone, & few small organic inclusions
22	II	VII.1.101	3747	above IIIA Floor 1227 in Room E	5YR 6/4 light reddish brown, 7.5YR 8/4 pink surfaces; very many limestone & sand inclusions; 1 faint groove near each edge of top of rim; lighter
23	II	57 II.1.25	264	Hellenistic House black earth layer Room 1	2.5YR 5/0 gray to 5/6 red, 5YR 6/2 pinkish gray interior and 7/4 pink exterior surfaces; small limestone & organic and few small ceramic inclusions

Non-thickened, plain

Pl	Str	Fld, Ar, Bkt	No.	Locus Description	Ware description
24	IVB	VII.1.116	7307	in Probe 1228 below IV installations	2.5YR 5/0 gray core, 5/6 red interior, 4/0 dark gray and 6/6 light red exterior; few organic and ceramic inclusions
	IIIB	VII.8.90	4633	sub IIIB Cobbling 1719	2.5YR 4/0 dark gray, 5YR 7/6 reddish yellow exterior surface; few limestone and organic inclusions

Pl. 3.34 Hellenistic Kraters (cont.)

Pl	Str	Fld, Ar,Bkt	No.	Locus Description	Ware description
	IIIA	VII.6.75	1960	sub IIIA Cobbling 1306 and 1307	5YR 6/2 pinkish gray, 7/4 pink exterior surface; many ceramic inclusions
25	II	VII.2.27A	293	above IIIA Floor 1227 in Room E	7.5YR 7/4 pink, 7/2 pinkish gray surfaces; some limestone and very few inclusions

Pl. 3.35   Hellenistic Mortaria

PL	STR	FLD, AR,BKT	No.	LOCUS DESCRIPTION	WARE DESCRIPTION
3.35:1	IV B	VII.1.115	7301	in Probe 1228 below IV installations	2.5YR 6/6 light red, 6/6 light red surfaces; many limestone and some organic inclusions
2	IVB	IX.1.51	148	grayish rubbly Fill 9024	7.5YR 7/6 reddish yellow, 8/4 pink surfaces; some sand, limestone, and organic inclusions
3	IV B	IX.2.46	106	grayish rubbly Soil 9274	10YR 6/4 light yellowish brown; 8/3 very pale brown surfaces; many sand, few crystalline inclusions
4	IVA	VII.4.110	5540	removal IVA Floor 1527	10YR 8/2 white, similar surface; very few organic incl
5	IVA	VII.23.64	495	above IVB Floor 23.009 sub IV A Floor 23.008	10YR 7/6 yellow; 8/4 very pale brown surfaces; many organic and few sand inclusions
6	IVA	IX.1.40	92	L. 9020 = Layer 9018 removing large stones	5YR 7/8 reddish yellow, 7.5YR 7/6 reddish yellow surfaces; many limestone, sand, and organic incl
	IV	56 I.1	9	L. 4 fill below Pavement	5YR 6/4 light reddish brown, 7/3 pink int & 7/4 pink ext surfaces; few large limestone, ceramic & sand incl
7	IV	56.I.1	102	L. 4 below Hellenistic Tower	5YR 6/3 light reddish brown, 6/4 pink surfaces; limestone and organic inclusions
8	IIIB	VII.1.61	5301	Fill 1216,1217,1220-1224,1226	10YR 8/2 white, 8/3 very pale brown surfaces; few organic incl
9	IIIB	VII.1.63	938	Fill 1216,1217,1220-1224,1226	10YR 6/1 gray, 8/4 very pale brown surfaces; some limestone inclusions
10	IIIB	VII.1.66	968	Fill 1216,1217,1220-1224,1226	7.5YR 8/2 pinkish white, 7/2 pinkish gray surfaces; very few organic inclusions
11	IIIB	VII.4.79	4968	removal IIIB Wall 1516	7.5YR 8/2 pinkish white, 5YR 8/4 pink surfaces; few organic inclusions
12	IIIB	VII.8.77	4585	sub IIIB Cobbling 1719	7.5YR 8/2 pinkish white, 8/4 very pale brown surfaces; very few limestone inclusions
13	IIIB	VII.8.79	4591	sub IIIB Cobbling 1719	7.5YR N6/ gray, 8/4 pink surfaces; many sandstone incl
14	cf IIIB	62 VII.22.42	317	sub possible IIIB Floor 22.002	5YR 6/8 reddish yellow, 7.5YR 8/4 pink surfaces; some organic, limestone, and sand inclusions
15	cf IIIB	62 VII.22.44	322	sub possible IIIB Floor 22.002	5YR 7/8 reddish yellow, 7.5YR 7/6 reddish yellow surf; some organic & many limestone & sand incl
16	cf IIIB	62 VII.22.44	323	sub possible IIIB Floor 22.002	5YR 7/6 reddish yellow, 10YR 8/2 white surfaces; very many organic and limestone inclusions
17	cf IIIB	62 VII.22.50	469	sub possible IIIB Floor 22.002	5YR 6/6 reddish yellow, 10YR 8/4 very pale brown surfaces; some organic and limestone inclusions
18	IIIA	VII.1.48	839	removal IIIA Walls 1206-1210	5YR 7/6 reddish yellow, 7/4 pink surfaces; many limestone and few crystalline inclusions
19	IIIA	VII.7.60	3133	sub IIIA Floor 1802-1508	7.5YR 6/4 light brown, 8/3 very pale brown surfaces; many limestone inclusions
20	IIIA	VII.22.34	228	sub IIIA Floor 22.001 above Floor 22.002	7.5YR 6/6 reddish yellow, 5YR 7/6 reddish yellow surfaces; some organic and limestone inclusions
21	cf IIIA	VII.3.48	1562	L. 1009 around IIIA Drain 1015-16	2.5YR 6/8 light red, 7/5 pink surfaces; few limestone and organic inclusions
22	cf IIIA	VII.22.23	166	on IIIA Floor 22.001	7.5YR 6/4 light brown, 6/2 pinkish gray surfaces; very many limestone and organic inclusions

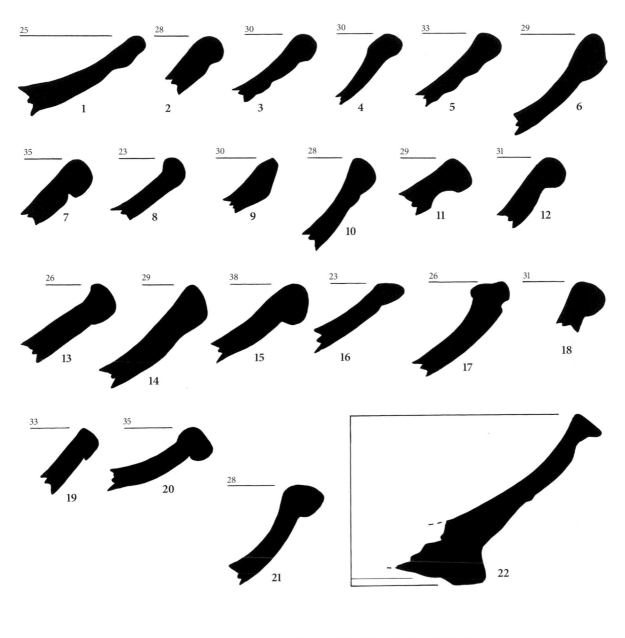

Pl. 3.35 Hellenistic Mortaria.

10 ▰▰▰▰▰▰ CMS

Pl. 3.35 Hellenistic Mortaria (cont.)

Pl	Str	Fld, Ar, Bkt	No.	Locus Description	Ware description
	III	56.I.1	24	L. 3 on Pavement	2.5 YR 5/4 reddish brown, 5YR 6/1 gray core, 5YR 7/6 reddish yellow exterior surface; small limestone and few large ceramic inclusions
	III	56.I.1	64	L. 3 on Pavement	5YR 4/4 light reddish brown, 7/3 pink interior and 7/6 reddish yellow exterior surfaces; ceramic and few smaller limestone inclusions

Pl. 3.36 Hellenistic Mortaria

Pl	Str	Fld, Ar,Bkt	No.	Locus Description	Ware description
3.36:1	III	57 I.6.17	97	below Floor 203	5YR 5/1 gray, 7/3 pink interior and 7/2 pinkish gray exterior surfaces; many organic and few large ceramic inclusions
2	cf III	57 I.6..82	762	pit in Wall B	5YR 7/3 pink, 10YR 7/3 very pale brown exterior surface; many ceramic and organic inclusions
3	II	VII.1.18	85	on IIIA Surface 1203	7.5YR 7/1 light gray, 8/4 pink surfaces; very few limestone incl
4	II	VII.2.31	309	above IIIA Floor 1227 in Room E	7.5YR 7/6 reddish yellow, 8/4 pink surfaces; few limestone incl
5	II	VII.2.53	1033	removal II Wall 1103	10YR 7/2 light gray, similar surfaces
6	II	VII.2.54	1024	removal II Wall 1103	5YR 8/3 pink, 10YR 8/3 very pale brown surfaces; few limestone & organic inclusions
7	unstr	VII.3.27	182	surface fill	5YR 5/1 gray, 7/6 reddish yellow surfaces; many limestone, organic and sand, and few crystalline incl
8	unstr	VII.6.104	2020	unstratified	2.5YR 6/6 light red, 5YR 7/6 reddish yellow surfaces; many sand, organic and limestone inclusions
9	unstr	VII.7.52	3169	surface fill	5YR 7/8 reddish yellow, 8/4 pink surfaces; many organic incl
10	unstr	57 I.6.25	134	top of wall B robber pit	10YR 6/3 pale brown, 8/3 white int and 7/3 very pale brown ext surfaces; many large ceramic & limestone & few organic incl
	unstr	I.7a.34	198	surface	5YR 5/1 gray, 8/4 pink surfaces; large and medium incl
11	unstr	57 I.7b.31	203	surface to west	5YR 7/3 pink, 8/3 pink int and 8/4 pink ext surfaces; many small ceramic & few large limestone & ceramic incl
12	unstr	57 I.7b.38	199	surface	5YR 6/2 pinkish gray, 10YR 7/3 very pale brown int and 7/2 light gray ext surfaces; many ceramic & few organic incl
13	unstr	57 I.9.5	58	surface	10YR 7/3 very pale brown, 7/2 light gray int and 8/3 very pale brown ext surfaces; many large ceramic & limestone incl
	unstr	57 1.9.13	145	balk	5YR 5/3 reddish brown, 8/4 pink interior and 7/3 pink exterior surfaces; few large limestone & ceramic incl
14	unstr	57 I.10.12	161	surface	5YR 6/2 pinkish gray, 6/1 gray core, 7/3 pink int & 7/2 pinkish gray ext surfaces; large limestone & many ceramic incl
15	unstr	57 I.10.12	162	surface	5YR 7/4 pink, 7/3 pink exterior surfaces; many ceramic and very small limestone inclusions
16	unstr	57 I.10.12	163	surface	5YR 6/8 reddish yellow, 8/4 pink exterior surface; ceramic, small organic, and few large limestone incl
	unstr	I.10.15	185	trench along east side of tower	not accessible
17	unstr	III.4	242	surface	10YR 6/2 light brownish gray, 7/1 light gray surfaces with wide patches of 8/3 very pale brown; large and many small ceramic and few limestone inclusions

Ring, concave, and flat Bases

18	IVA	IX.2.28	36	L. 9262 silty soil	5YR 7/3 pale yellow, 10YR 8/3 very pale brown surfaces; ceramic inclusions
19	cf IIIB	VII.3.77	1717	above IV Surface 1021-1023	2.5YR 5/0 gray, 8/2 white surf; many limestone & organic incl
	III	56 I.1	39	L. 3 on Pavement	5 YR 8/4 pink, 6/1 light gray core; many limestone, many large organic, and few smaller ceramic inclusions
20	cf II	VII.2.28	297	around & on II Wall 1103	3YR 8/4 pink, similar surfaces; very few limestone incl

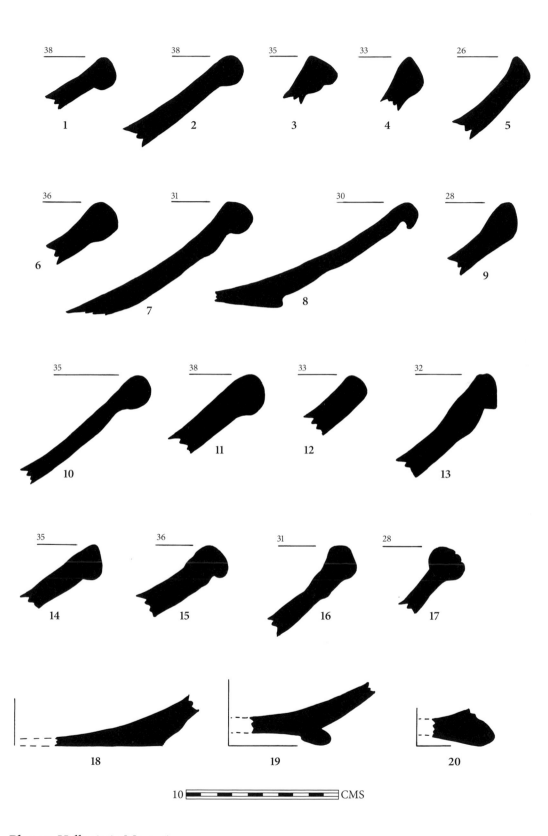

Pl. 3.36 Hellenistic Mortaria.

Pl. 3.37   Hellenistic Cooking Pots

Pl	Str	Fld, Ar,Bkt	No.	Locus Description	Ware description
Rim with Overhang					
3.37:1	IVB fill	VII.1.85	1111	sub IVB Surface 1236 (sub 1216)	2.5YR 4/4 reddish brown, 2/5YR 6/8 light red surface; few organic and sand inclusions
2	IVB fill	VII.3.150	6265	Fill 1029A below IV installations	2.5YR 4/6 red, 2.5YR 6/2 pale red surf; very few sand incl
3	IVB fill	VII.3.175	6804	Probe 1030 beneath IV levels	2.5YR 4/6 red, 2.5YR 6/2 pale red surface; very few sand inclusions
4	IVA	62 VII.21.82	609	sub IVA Floor 21.011	2.5YR 5/8 red, 5YR 6/2 pinkish gray surface; some organic and very few limestone inclusions
5	IVA	62 VII.21.87	707	sub IVA Floor 21.011	2.5YR 4/6 red, 2.5YR 6/8 red surface; some sand and few organic inclusions
6	IVA	IX.1.62	156	occupation Debris 9029	2.5YR 5/6 red, 2.5 YR 6/4 light reddish brown surface; very few organic and limestone inclusions
7	IVA	IX.4.33	87	stony Surface 9760 sub 9759	5YR 5/6 yellowish red, 5YR 6/2 pinkish gray surface
	cf IV	VII.2.84	3769	on & above IV Surface 1124	2.5YR 3/6 dark red, 7.5YR 5/2 brown core, 2.5YR 5/2 weak red and burn on surface; few fine limestone incl
	cf IV	VII.2.108	5194	cleaning IV Drain 1028-1116	10YR 5/8 red, 10R 3/2 dusky red surf; few fine sand incl
	cf IV	62 VII.21.126	1048	Pit 21.036 dug in III or II	10R 2.5/1 reddish black, 3/3 dusky red core, 4/1 dark reddish gray surface; limestone and sand inclusions
8	cf IIIB	62 VII.22.52	343	sub possible IIIB Floor 22.002	2.5YR 3/6 red, 2.5YR 6/4 light reddish brown surface; very few sand inclusions
9	cf IIIB	VII.8.60	3875	unsealed IIIB Fill 1717-20 sub IIIB level	2.5YR 6/6 light red, similar surface; very few organic incl
	IIIA	VII.1.51	852	sub IIIA Floor 1203	2.5YR 5/6 red, 6/4 light reddish brown surface; some fine sand inclusions
10	IIIA	VII.2.120	5507	removal IIIA Walls 1107-1109	2.5YR 4/6 red, 5/6 red core, 5/6 red surface; some sand inclusions
11	IIIA	VII.9.44	3218	removal IIIA 1707-1705-1701-1601	5YR 4/4 reddish brown, 2.5YR 6/4 light reddish brown surface; some organic inclusions
12	II	VII.2.41	989	above IIIA Floor 1227 in Room E	2.5YR 4/4 reddish brown, 10YR 8/2 white surface
13	II	VII.1.81	2887	II occupation Pit 1205-1207	5YR 4/6 yellowish red, 2/5YR 5/6 red surface; few sand inclusions
14	unstr	VII.5.28	424	1485 rockfall or pit	2.5YR 4/6 red, 4/2 weak red surface; few fine quartz and limestone inclusions
15	unstr	57 I.10.8	127	unstratified	2.5YR 6/8 4/4 reddish brown, 2.5/0 black surface (burn?) on rim; few small ceramic inclusions

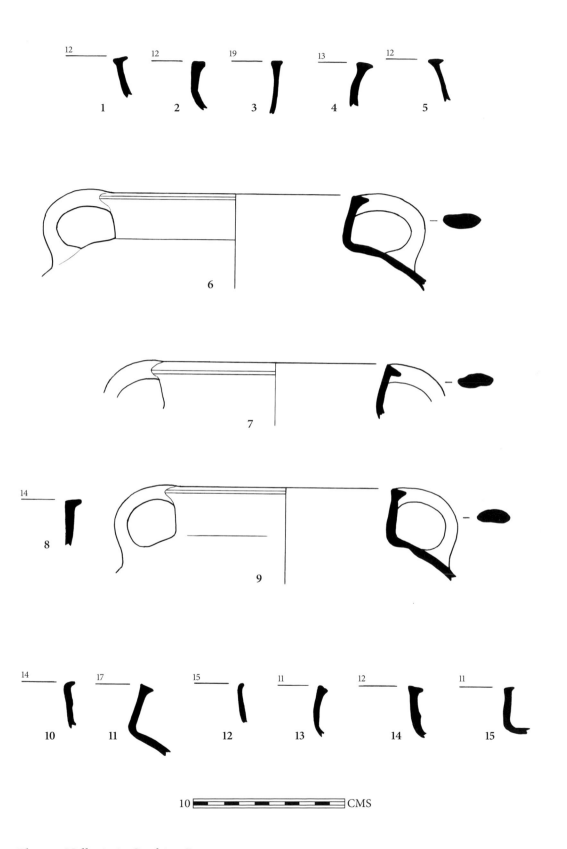

Pl. 3.37 Hellenistic Cooking Pots.

Pl. 3.38   Hellenistic Cooking Pots

Pl	Str	Fld, Ar, Bkt	No.	Locus Description	Ware description
Plain Rim					
3.38:1	IVA	62 VII.21.87	708	sub IVA Floor 21.011	2.5YR 4/2 weak red, 2.5YR 6/4 light reddish brown surface; some crystalline inclusions
2	IVA	62 VII.23.67	502	Fill 23.016 below IV Floor 23.005	5YR 5/4 reddish brown, 5YR 8/2 pinkish white surface; many crystalline and organic inclusions
	IVA	IX.1.45	95	L. 9022 removing upper courses of Wall 9514	2.5YR 4/4 reddish brown, 4/2 exterior surface, burn on handle 3/0 very dark gray; some small limestone incl
3	IVA	IX.3.45	79	probable Surface 9517B	2.5YR 6/8 red, 5YR 6/4 bright reddish brown surface; very few limestone inclusions
4	cf IV	62 VII.3.105	1517	Stonefall 1042 in balk	2.5YR 3/2 dusky red, 5YR 5/2 reddish gray surface; few organic inclusions
5	IIIB	VII.1.44	814	beneath IIIB Floor 1214	2.5YR 6/6 light red, 5/6 red surface, 5/6 red slip; organic inclusions
6	IIIB	VII.1.59	919	Fill 1216,1217,1220-1224,1226	2.5YR 4/4 reddish brown, 2.5YR 6/4 light reddish brown surface; many organic and crystalline inclusions
7	IIIB	VII.1.63	929	Fill 1216,1217,1220-1224,1226	5YR 4/4 reddish brown, 5YR 4/3 reddish brown surface; many limestone inclusions
8	IIIB	VII.3.62	1647	sub IIIB Hardback 1017-1019	5YR 5/3 reddish brown, 5YR 6/3 light reddish brown surface; very many crystalline and some organic incl
9	cf IIIB	62 VII.22.50	466	sub possible IIIB Floor 22.002	2.5YR 4/4 reddish brown, 5YR 6/2 pinkish gray surface; very many crystalline and some organic inclusions
	IIIA	VII.1.40	770	sub IIIA Floor 1203	2.5YR 4/4 reddish brown, 4/2 weak red surface; limestone and some fine sand inclusions
10	IIIA	VII.1.40	772	sub IIIA Floor 1203	5YR 5/8 yellowish red, 5YR 5/4 reddish brown surface; few limestone inclusions
	IIIA	VII.1.40	774	sub IIIA Floor 1203	2.5YR 5/6 red, 2.5YR 6/4 light reddish brown surface; very many limestone inclusions
11	IIIA	VII.1.40	779	sub IIIA Floor 1203	2.5YR 5/6 red, 2.5YR 4/2 weak red surface; few organic and limestone inclusions
	IIIA	VII.1.40	786	sub IIIA Floor 1203	2.5YR 4/6 red, 2.5YR 5/4 dusky red core, 2.5 5/4 reddish brown surface; limestone and quartz inclusions
12	IIIA	VII.1.88	2909	sub IIIA Floor 1203	7.5YR 7/6 reddish yellow, 7.5YR 8/2 pinkish white surface
13	IIIA	VII.7.57	3123	sub IIIA Floor 1802-1508	2.5YR 3/6 dark red, 3/4 dark reddish brown core, 6/6 light red surface; few medium inclusions
14	IIIA	VII.1.35	763	removal IIIA Buttress 1110-1211	2.5YR 4/8 red, 2.5YR 5/4 reddish brown surface
	IIIA	VII.7.82	4647	removal IIIA Wall 1805N	2.5YR 4/4 reddish brown, 5/4 reddish brown surface; limestone and quartz inclusions
	cf IIIA	VII.3.61B	1639	L. 1009 around IIIA Drain 1015-16	2.5YR 5/6 red-brown, 6/6 light red surface; limestone, quartz and sand inclusions
	cf IIIA	VII.4.29	1827	Pit 1514	2.5YR 4/8 red, 2.5YR N5/ gray surface; many fine limestone and some fine sand inclusions

(continued on p. 324)

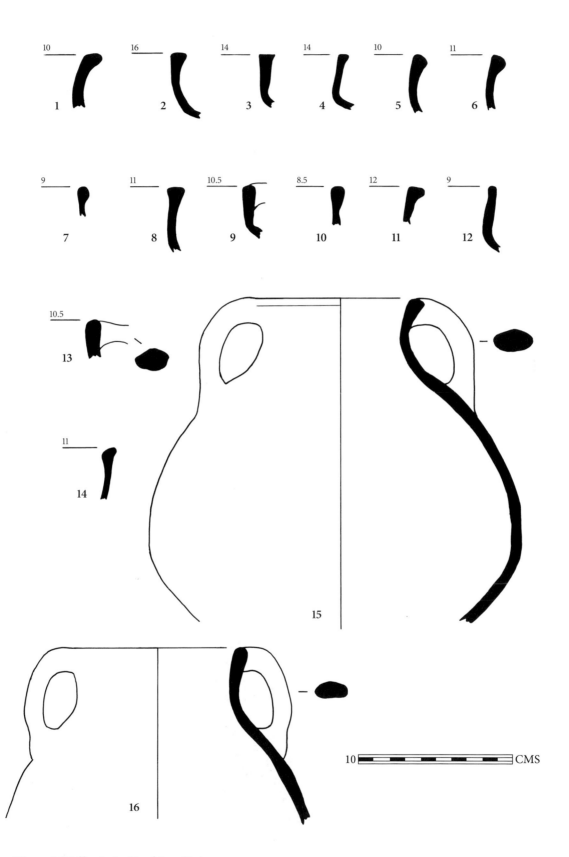

Pl. 3.38 Hellenistic Cooking Pots.

Pl. 3.38 Hellenistic Cooking Pots (cont.)

Pl	Str	Fld, Ar,Bkt	No.	Locus Description	Ware description
	cf IIIA	VII.4.85	4991	Pit 1514	2.5YR 4/8 red, 4/4 reddish brown core, 5/4 reddish brown surface; few medium & fine inclusions
	III	57 I.6.12	21	burn above Floor 203	2.5YR 5/6 red, 5/4 reddish brown interior & 4/4 reddish brown exterior surf; many limestone & few crystal incl
	cf III	57 I.6.55	455	pit in Wall B	2.5YR 4/2 weak red, 3/2 dusky red interior & 4/2 weak red exterior surface; many limestone & few crystal incl
15	cf III	57 I.6.59	463	pit in Wall B	not accessible
	cf III	57 I.6.82	763	pit in Wall B	2.5YR 4/2 weak red, 4/4 reddish brown int & 3/2 dusky red interior surface; large crystal & some limestone & organic incl
16	cf III	57 I.6.91	768	pit in Wall B	2.5YR 4/4 reddish brown, 5/4 reddish brown interior & 4/2 weak red exterior surf; large organic & crystal & few limestone incl

Pl. 3.39　　Hellenistic Cooking Pots

Pl	Str	Fld, Ar,Bkt	No.	Locus Description	Ware description
Plain Rim (continued)					
3.39:1	cf III	57 I.7.14	109	between Floors 202 & 206	2.5YR 6/6 light red int and 6/5 light reddish brown ext surf; 4/0 dark gray core; small organic & limestone incl
2	cf III	57 I.7.14 57 I.7.14	111/ /113	between Floors 202 & 206	2.5YR 5/4 reddish brown, 4/4 reddish brown surfaces; limestone inclusions
3	cf III	57 I.9.9	124	striated makeup over Wall A	2.5YR 5/4 reddish brown, 6/6 light red interior and 6/4 reddish brown exterior surfaces; few limestone, many organic, and many small crystalline inclusions
4	III/II	III.4.15E	2126	pit between Walls B & 606	reconstructed; 6/4 reddish brown, 3/2 dark reddish brown surface; many medium & some large crystalline inclusions
	II	VII.1.24	120	II occupation Pit 1205-1207	2.5YR 3/6 dark red, 5/4 reddish brown core, 3/6 dark red surface; few medium limestone inclusions
5	II	VII.7.55	3118	L. 1820 pit of IIIA Floor 1801 with II storage jar 3117A	10R 4/6 red, 5/6 red surface; sand inclusions
6	cf II	II.2.29	300/301	cp, plain	2.5YR 5/4 reddish brown, 6/4 light reddish brown surfaces; some limestone inclusions
7	cf II	II.2.73	1226	cp, plain	2.5YR 5/8 red, 6/8 light red interior & 4/4 reddish brown exterior surfaces; few limestone inclusions
8	I I	II.1.109 II.1.120	1042/ /1181	Hellenistic House Room 1 occupation	2.5YR N3/0 very dark gray core, 6/4 light reddish brown int, 5/4 reddish brown to 5/6 red ext; few large limestone, many small limestone, & few large organic inclusions
9	I	II.1.111	1053	Hellenistic House Room 1 occupation	10YR 5/2 reddish gray core, 5/4 reddish brown exterior, 5/6 yellowish red interior; many large limestone & organic incl
	I	II.1.117	1082	Hellenistic House Room 1 occupation	2.5YR 5/6 red, 6/4 light reddish brown ext, 5/4 reddish brown int surfaces; few large limestone & organic incl
	I	68 II.1.22	10408	in Fill 7039 above Flagstone 7048	2.5YR 4/4 reddish brown, 5/4 reddish brown exterior surface; few large and many small limestone inclusions
	cf I	II.1.34	370	Hellenistic House higher in Room 1	2.5YR 5/4 reddish brown, N6 gray core; very small limestone and few small organic inclusions

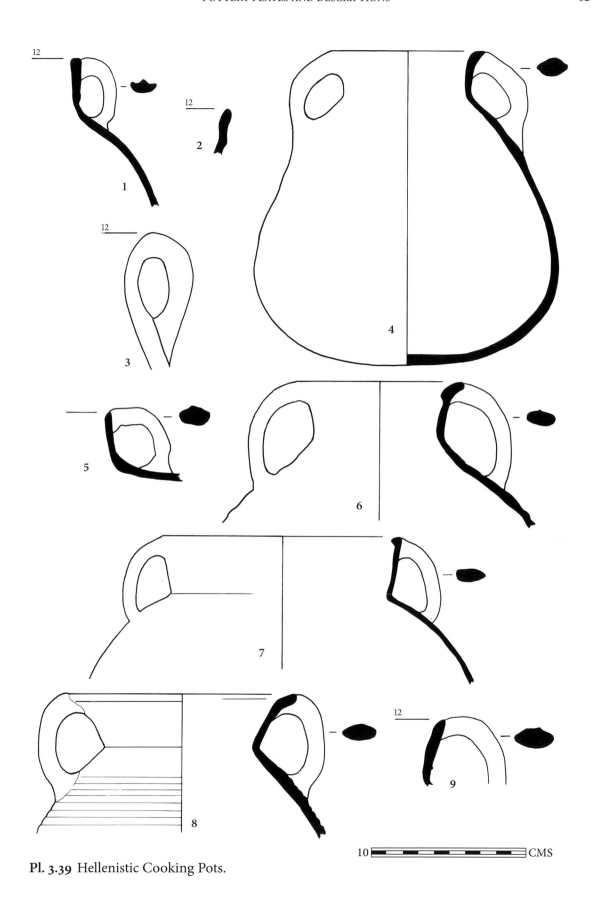

Pl. 3.39 Hellenistic Cooking Pots.

Pl. 3.40   Hellenistic Cooking Pots

Pl	Str	Fld, Ar,Bkt	No.	Locus Description	Ware description
Plain Rim (continued)					
3.40:1	cf I	II.1.34	373	Hellenistic House higher in Room 1	2.5YR 4/2 weak red, 5/4 reddish brown int, 6/6 light red ext; many small limestone and small organic inclusions
2	cf I	II.1.35	382	Hellenistic House higher in Room 1	2.5YR 5/4 reddish brown core, 4/4 reddish brown surfaces; few organic inclusions
3	cf I	II.1.35	428	Hellenistic House higher in Room 1	2.5YR 5/4 reddish brown, 4/4 reddish brown surfaces; few large organic & many very small limestone inclusions
4	unstr	VII.1.99	3736	surface fill	2.5YR 4/4 reddish brown, 2/5YR 6/4 light reddish brown surface; some crystalline inclusions (very thin)
5	cf IIIA	62 VII.23.95	1067	Pit 23.017 near column base	reconstructed top
6	unstr	VII.7.149	7378	probe trench	5YR 5/6 yellowish red, 7.5YR 5/2 brown core, 2.5YR 6/6 light red surf; some fine limestone & few coarse sand incl
7	unstr	III.3.16	356	east balk	2.5YR 5/4 reddish brown, 6/4 light reddish brown surfaces; many very small limestone inclusions
8	unstr	57 I.7.3	12	surface	2.5YR 4/0 dark gray core, 5/4 reddish brown interior, 4/4 reddish brown exterior; small limestone inclusions
9	unstr	57 I.9.4	54	surface	not accessible
10	unstr	III.3.3	132	surface	not accessible
Concave Neck					
11	II	VII.7.46	3162	above IIIA Floor 1802-1508	2.5YR 6/4 light reddish brown, 5YR 5/3 reddish brown surfaces; many limestone inclusions
12	II	VII.7.46	3164	above IIIA Floor 1802-1508	5YR 4/3 reddish brown, 10YR 5/1 gray surface; very few organic inclusions
13	II	VII.1.87	2899	on IIIA Surface 1203	5YR 5/6 yellowish red, 5YR 5/3 reddish brown surface; very few sand inclusions
14	cf II	II.2.73	1103	black earth layer Area 2	2.5YR 5/6 red with 4/10 dark gray core; few large limestone inclusions (very thin)

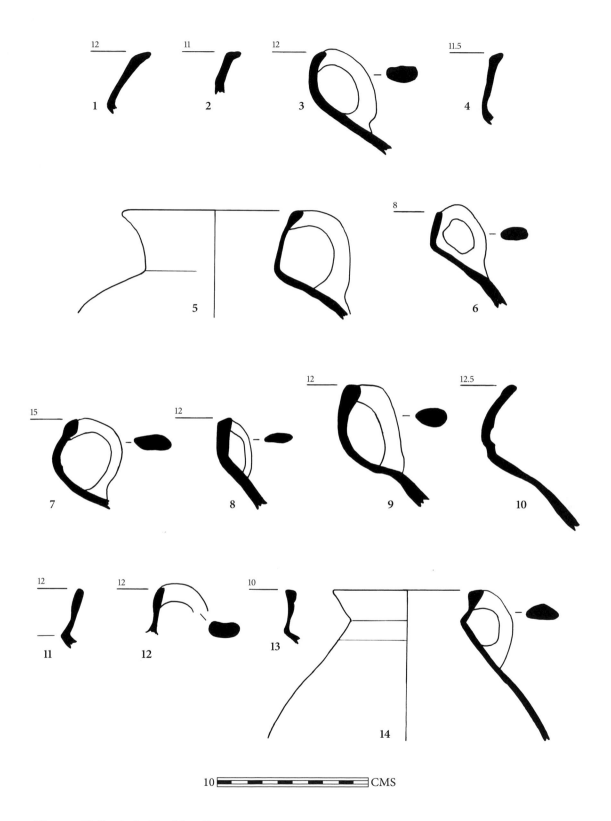

Pl. 3.40 Hellenistic Cooking Pots.

Pl. 3.41   Hellenistic Cooking Pots

Pl	Str	Fld, Ar,Bkt	No.	Locus Description	Ware description
Shallow Pot with Lid Device					
3.41:1	IIIA	VII.1.51	857	sub IIIA Floor 1203	2.5YR 5/6 red, 6/4 light reddish brown surfaces; some limestone inclusions
2	IIIA	VII.7.60	3137	sub IIIA Floor 1802-1508	2.5YR 5/6 reddish brown, N4 dark gray exterior surface (burnt); many large limestone inclusions
3	cf IIIA	VII.1.22	91	removal Mortar 1204 of IIIA occupation	2.5YR 5/4 reddish brown, 6/4 light reddish brown surface; some limestone & very few crystalline inclusions
4	II	VII.1.102	3749	on IIIA Surface 1203	2.5YR 5/4 reddish brown, 6/4 light reddish brown surface; some limestone and organic inclusions
5	II	VII 1.28	119	II occupation Pit 1205-1207	2.5YR 4/6 light red, 4/2 weak red ext and 5/6 red int sufaces
6	II	II.1.50	583	black earth layer North Balk	5YR 7/3 pink, 2.5YR 6/6 light red surf; large limestone and few small organic incl; probably never used as cook pot
7	II	II.1.51	588	black earth layer North Balk	5YR 6/1 gray, 6/4 light reddish brown exterior surface; few limestone and few large crystalline inclusions
8	II	II.1.52	781	black earth layer North Balk	2.5YR 5/2 weak red , 4/4 reddish brown exterior surface; few small limestone inclusions
9	cf II	II.2.40	596	Make-up 7100 for II Floor 7099	2.5YR 5/4 reddish brown, 5/6 red exterior surface; few limestone and organic inclusions
10	cf II	II.2.43	597	Make-up 7100 for II Floor 7099	2.5YR reddish brown, 5/6 red int & 4/4 reddish brown ext surfaces; very small limestone & few organic inclusions
11	cf II	II.2.25	298	black earth layer Area 2	7.5YR 5/4 brown, 5YR 5/8 yellowish red; some large ceramic and limestone inclusions
12	I	II.1.109	1043	Room 1 occupation	2.5YR 3/0 very dark gray core, 5/6 red int, 4/4 reddish brown ext; large limestone & few large crystal inclusions
13 fig. 3.21 (p. 65)	I	II.1.113 II.1.114	1064= 1066	Room 1 occupation Room 1 occupation	2.5YR 3/4 dark reddish brown, 6/4 light reddish brown int & 4/4 reddish brown ext surfaces; large limestone incl
	I	68 II.1.22	10411	in Fill 7039 above Flagstone 7048	2.5YR 3/0 very dark gray core, 5/4 reddish brown interior, 4/2 weak red exterior; few large limestone inclusions
	I	68 II.2.78	11407	Make-up 7100 for II Floor 7099	2.5YR 4/4 reddish brown, 5/4 reddish brown int & 4/2 weak red ext surfaces; few small limestone inclusions
	cf I	II.1.35	379	higher in Room 1	2.5YR 5/4 reddish brown, N4/ dark gray core; large crystalline and few large limestone inclusions
14	cf I	II.1.35	380	higher in Room 1	2.5YR 6/4 reddish brown, 5/4 reddish brown interior and 5/6 red exterior surfaces; small limestone, few large limestone and organic inclusions
15	unstr	III.3.1	131	surface	2.5YR 4/0 dark gray core, 4/4 reddish brown int, 4/2 weak red ext; many small limestone & few small organic incl
	unstr	III.4.1	241	surface	2.5YR 4/4 reddish brown, 4/6 red int & 4/0 dark gray ext surfaces; small limestone & few crystalline inclusions
16	unstr	III.6.1	689	outside Wall A	2.5YR 5/4 reddish brown, 6/4 light reddish brown int & 5/4 reddish brown ext surf; few limestone & few crystal incl
17	unstr	57 I.7.4	11	surface	not accessible

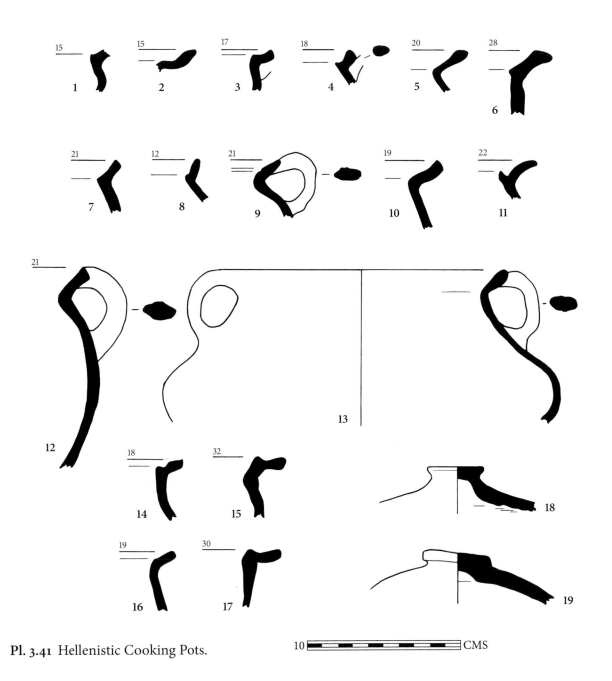

Pl. 3.41 Hellenistic Cooking Pots.

10 CMS

Pl. 3.41 Hellenistic Cooking Pots   (cont.)

Pl	Str	Fld, Ar, Bkt	No.	Locus Description	Ware description
Lids					
18 fig. 3.21 (p. 65)	unstr	II.2.69	1221	north balk	2.5YR 4/8 red, 4/4 reddish brown interior, 5/6 red exterior; many limestone and few organic inclusions
19 fig. 3.21	unstr	57 I.6.8	64	surface	2.5YR 4/4 reddish brown, 5/4 reddish brown surf; small limestone and organic and few small crystalline inclusions

Pl. 3.42   Hellenistic Lamps

Pl	Str	Fld, Ar,Bkt	No.	Locus Description	Ware description
Attic Ware					
3.42:2	IIIB	62 VII.4.142	1542	sealed in Pit 1522	5YR 7/6 reddish yellow, 2.5Y N2.5/0 black glaze
1	cf IIIB	62 VII.4.138	1533	unsealed in Pit 1522	7.5YR 7/6 reddish yellow, 2.5Y N2.5/0 black glaze
3	cf IIIB	VII.3.78	1720	Probe 1018 from III to IV levels	5YR 7/6 reddish yellow, 2.5Y N2.5/0 black glaze
4	II	VII.1.101	3745	above IIIA Floor 1227 in Room E	2.5YR 6/6 light red, 2.5Y N2.5/0 black glaze
	unstr	62 VII.1.32	47	unstratified	5YR 6/6 reddish yellow, 2.5Y N2.5/0 black glaze
5	unstr	VII.2.60	1069/	probe trench	5YR 6/6 reddish yellow, 2.5Y N2.5/0 black glaze
	unstr	VII.2.117	/5221	unstratified	
6	unstr	VII.3.23	172	unstratified	5YR 7/6 reddish yellow, 2.5Y N2.5/0 black glaze
	unstr	57 I.11a&b.1	397 #140	surface	5YR 7.6 reddish yellow, 2.5YR N2.5/0 black glaze exterior and interior; side
Delphiniform					
7	IIIB	VII.1.44	811	beneath IIIB Floor 1214	5YR 7/4 pink, similar surface; very few sand inclusions
8	IIIB	VII.1.90	2923	beneath IIIB Floor 1214	5YR 7/6 reddish yellow, 8/4 pink surf; some organic incl
	IIIB	VII.1.59	927	Fill 1216,1217,1220-1224,1226	5YR 7/4 pink similar surface; very fine sand inclusions
9	IIIB	VII.1.77	2878	Fill 1216,1217,1220-1224,1226	2.5YR 6/4 light reddish brown; very few tiny inclusions
10 fig. 3.22 (p. 67)	IIIB	VII.4.78	3844 #496	removal III Wall 1506	complete: 5YR 7/4 pink, similar surface; very few sand inclusions
	IIIB	62 VII.4.142	1539	sealed in Pit 1522	5YR 6/6 reddish yellow, 7.5YR 6/4 light brown surface; fine sand inclusions
	IIIB	62 VII.4.142	1540	sealed in Pit 1522	5YR 7/6 reddish yellow, 7.5YR 7/4 pink surface; limestone & ceramic inclusions
11	IIIB	VII.8.91	5098	sub IIIB Cobbling 1719	7.5YR 8/4 pink, similar surface; some organic inclusions
12 fig. 3.22	cf IIIB	62 VII.4.134	1532 #425a	to IIIB Installation 1518	to Dept. of Antiquities; complete
	IIIA	VII.1.40	769	sub IIIA Floor 1203	2.5YR 6/6 light red, 5YR reddish yellow surface; worn 10R 3/6 dark red slip; sand inclusions
13	IIIA	VII.4.30	1832	sub IIIA Floor 1227-1511	not accessible
	IIIA	VII.7.58	4001	removal IIIA Wall 1811 facing	10YR 8/4 very pale brown, 8/3 very pale brown surface; sand inclusions
	IIIA	VII.7.25	2257	sub IIIA Floor 1801	7.5YR 7/6 reddish yellow, 8/6 reddish yellow surface; limestone inclusions
14	IIIA	VII.21.71	598	Fill 21.034 below Floor 21.009 (lots of V in this locus)	5YR 6/1 gray, 8/2 pinkish gray exterior surface; medium and large limestone inclusions
15	IIIA	62 VII.22.34	229	sub IIIA Floor 22.001 above Floor 22.002	2.5YR 6/6 light red, similar surface; 10R 5/6 red slip; side knob
16	cf IIIA	VII.3.66	1670	L. 1009 around IIIA Drain 1015-16	5YR 7/4 pink, similar surface; few small ceramic incl
	cf IIIA	VII.4.85	4993	Pit 1514	5YR 6/6 reddish yellow, 7.5YR 7/6 reddish yellow surface; sand inclusions

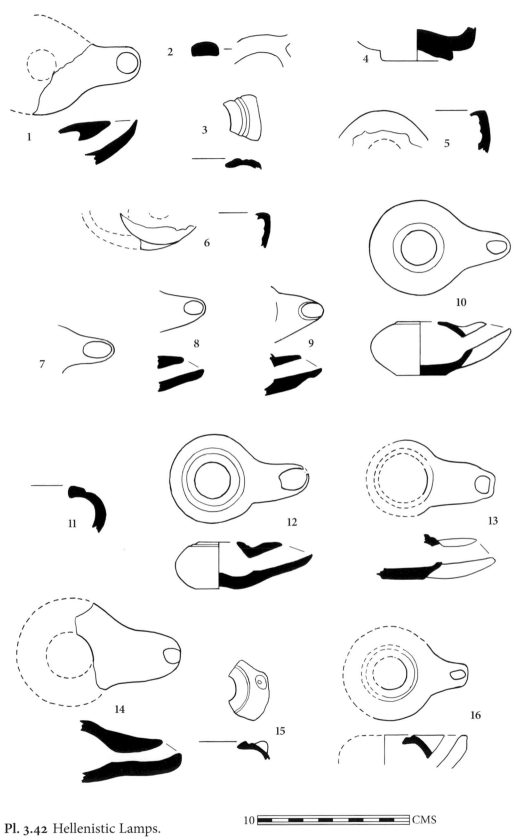

Pl. 3.42 Hellenistic Lamps.

10 ▭▭▭▭▭ CMS

Pl. 3.43 Hellenistic Lamps

Pl	Str	Fld, Ar, Bkt	No.	Locus Description	Ware description
3.43:1	cf III	57 I.6.79	648	pit in Wall B	5YR 7/3 pink, 2.5YR 5/8 red slip interior & exterior; few limestone inclusions; side knob
	cf III	57 I.6.84	820	pit in Wall B	5YR 5/1 gray; few ceramic inclusions
	cf III	57 I.6.91	767	pit in Wall B	5YR 6/6 reddish yellow; few small ceramic inclusions
2	cf III	57 I.6.91	769	pit in Wall B	5YR 6/6 reddish yellow; few limestone inclusions
3	cf III	57 I.6.95	823 #246	pit in Wall B	complete, but broken; 5YR 7/6 reddish yellow, 10YR 8/2 white surface
4 cf. fig. 1.6 (p. 6)	cf III	56.I.1	#16	inside jar # 15 near Pavement	complete; not accessible
5	cf III	57 I.6.72	642	pit in Wall B	5YR 7/4 pink; few limestone inclusions
6	c̄f III	57 I.6.98	822	pit in Wall B	5YR reddish brown, remains of 2.5/1 black slip interior; few limestone inclusions
	IIIA/II	68 II.1.54	11009	File 7083 in robber trench	5YR 7/6 reddish yellow, remains of 2.5YR 4/6 red slip exterior; few limestone inclusions
7	II	VII.1.21	108	II occupation Pit 1205-1207	5YR 7/6 reddish yellow, similar surface
8	II	VII.2.54	1032	removal II Wall 1103	5YR 7/6 reddish yellow, 5YR 5/1 gray slip
	I	68 II.1.22	10415	in Fill 7039 above Flagstone 7048	5YR 6/6 reddish yellow, few ceramic inclusions
	I	68 II.1.32	10468	fill or Foundation Trench 7046	5YR 7/4 pink; ceramic inclusions
	I	68 II.1.32	10474	fill or Foundation Trench 7046	5YR 6/8 reddish yellow; few ceramic inclusions
fig. 3.22 (p. 67)	unstr	VII.8.15	2719 #424	surface fill	complete; to Department of Antiquities
9 fig. 3.22	unstr	VII.1.108	5236 #735	surface fill	complete; 2.5YR 7/5 reddish yellow; 10R 4/6 red slip
10	unstr	I.6.40	289 #115	striated fill over wall	5YR 7/3 pink, 7/6 reddish yellow exterior surface; many very small inclusions
	unstr	64 I.17.5	38605	surface	5YR 6/6 reddish yellow; few limestone inclusions
	unstr	II.1.45	395	Storage Bin 7106	5YR 6/4 light reddish brown; few limestone & ceramic inclusions
	unstr	III.4.1	243	surface	not accessible
11	unstr	III.5.20	802	surface	5YR 7/4 pink; few limestone inclusions
12	unstr	IV.1.10	1541		5YR 8/3 pink, limestone & ceramic inclusions

Molded with Relief Motifs

Pl	Str	Fld, Ar, Bkt	No.	Locus Description	Ware description
13	cf IV	62 VII.21.209	2011	Pit 21.036 dug in III or II	7.5YR N8/0 white, N6/gray surface; sand inclusions; metallic
14	IIIA	VII.7.74	4015	removal IIIA Walls 1810, 1812	5YR 7/6 reddish yellow, 10R 4/8 red slipped surface; sand inclusions
15	IIIA	VII.1.88	2905	sub IIIA Floor 1203	7.5YR N7/0 light gray, 5YR 6/1 gray surface; some organic inclusions; metallic
16	IIIA	VII.1.112	6246	removal IIIA Walls 1206-1210	7.5YR N7/0 light gray, 5YR 6/1 gray surface; some organic inclusions metallic

(continued on p. 337)

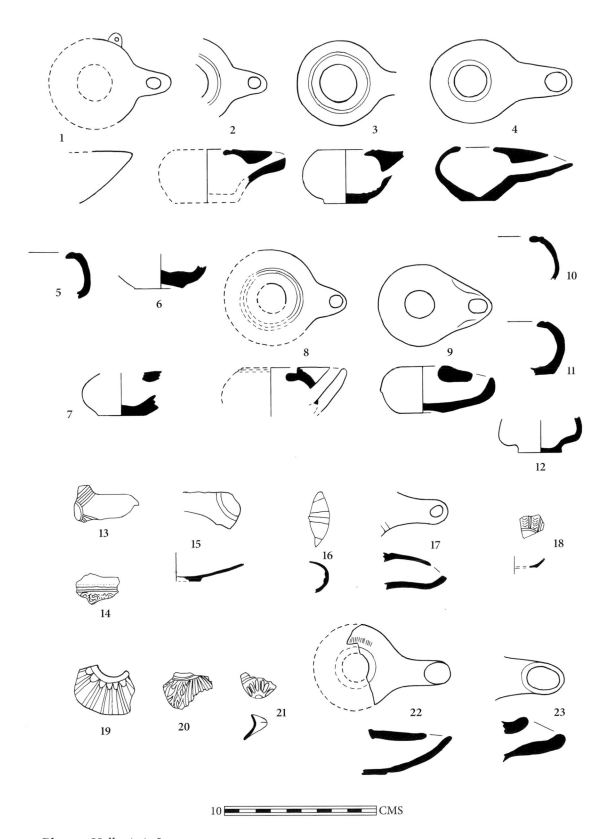

Pl. 3.43 Hellenistic Lamps.